THE IRISH BOUNDARY COMMISSION

THE IRISH BOUNDARY COMMISSION AND ITS ORIGINS

1886–1925

Paul Murray

UNIVERSITY COLLEGE DUBLIN PRESS

PREAS CHOLÁISTE OLLSCOILE BHAILE ÁTHA CLIATH

2011

First published 2011
by University College Dublin Press
Newman House
86 St Stephen's Green
Dublin 2
Ireland
www.ucdpress.ie

ISBN 978-1-906359-24-9 hb
ISBN 978-1-906359-61-4 pb

CIP data available from the British Library

*The right of Paul Murray to be identified as the
author of this work has been asserted by him*

Typeset in Scotland in Adobe Caslon and
Bodoni Oldstyle by Ryan Shiels
Printed in England on acid-free paper by
MPG Books, Bodmin, Cornwall

Contents

—

Acknowledgements

—

This book has its remote origins in my Doctoral dissertation, *Contested Borders and Minority Rights: The Partition of Ireland in Comparative Perspective*, presented at the National University of Ireland, Galway in 2003. I owe a debt of gratitude to my supervisor Dr Niall Ó Dochartaigh of the National University of Ireland, Galway for his help and guidance during the preparation of the dissertation, and to my External Examiner Professor Paul Arthur, University of Ulster, for his advice and encouragement.

I am also grateful to the staffs of the following institutions: The National Library of Ireland; The National Archives of Ireland; The James Hardiman Library, National University of Ireland, Galway; The Public Record Office, London; The Public Record Office of Northern Ireland; House of Lords Record Office; The Bodleian Library, Oxford; The Rhodes House Library, London; The Aidan Heavey Library, Athlone; The Archives Department, University College Dublin and Trinity College Dublin Archives.

The following helped me in various ways: Declan McCormack, Dublin; Dr Conor Molony, Wimbledon; Dr Brian Murphy, Glenstal Abbey, Limerick; Gearóid O'Brien, Chief Executive Librarian, Aidan Heavey Library, Athlone; Pádhraic Folan, Galway; John Donohoe, Athlone; Deirdre Wildy, Special Subject Librarian, Queens University Belfast and Dr Rory McDonnell, University of California, Riverside, USA.

My thanks are also due to The Irish Research Council for the Humanities and Social Sciences (IRCHSS), for its generous funding of my Doctoral research during my period as an Irish Research Council Scholar. I am particularly grateful to the School of Political Science and Sociology, NUI Galway for funding to support the publication of this book. I extend special thanks in this regard to Professor Chris Curtin.

My editor, Noelle Moran, UCD Press, merits particular gratitude. Her expertise, encouragement and valuable advice have greatly benefited this publication.

It has been a great pleasure to work with Barbara Mennell, Executive Editor of UCD Press, who has been supportive throughout.

The County Londonderry Map from Sampson's Statistical Survey (1801) was chosen for the cover because of the strategic importance of Derry City.

On denominational grounds, there was a strong case for the inclusion of Derry City in the Irish Free State. Ultimately, Derry City and Newry were the most extreme examples of the Irish Boundary Commission's failure to meet Nationalist expectations. I am grateful to the National Library of Ireland for permission to reproduce the map.

PAUL MURRAY

Galway, December 2010

Abbreviations

—

AAA	Armagh Archdiocesan Archives
CAB	British Cabinet Papers
DE	Dáil Éireann Papers
EHR	*English Historical Review*
IHS	*Irish Historical Studies*
IPP	Irish Parliamentary Party
IRA	Irish Republican Army
IRB	Irish Republican Brotherhood
IRCHSS	The Irish Research Council for the Humanities and Social Sciences
JP	Justice of the Peace
KC	King's Counsel
NAI	National Archives of Ireland
NLI	National Library of Ireland
PLV	Poor Law Valuation
PP	Parish Priest
PR	Proportional Representation
PRO	Public Record Office (London) (now The National Archives)
PRO CAB	Public Record Office London (Cabinet Papers)
PRONI	Public Record Office of Northern Ireland
PRONI CAB	Public Record Office of Northern Ireland (Cabinet Papers)
PRONI PM	Public Record Office of Northern Ireland (Prime Minister's Papers)
RDC	Rural District Council
RIC	Royal Irish Constabulary
RUC	Royal Ulster Constabulary
TCDA	Trinity College Dublin Archives
TNA	The National Archives (formally the Public Record Office)
UCDA	University College Dublin Archive
UDC	Urban District Council
UPP	Unionist Parliamentary Party
USSR	Union of Soviet Socialist Republics
UVF	Ulster Volunteer Force

Maps

—

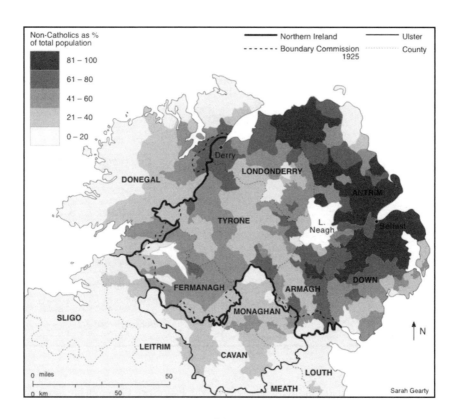

Map 1

Distribution of Catholics and Non-Catholics in Northern Ireland 1925. Figures are based on 1911 Census Returns (Map drawn by Sarah Gearty. A version was previously published in Michael Laffan, 'The emergence of the two Irelands, 1912–25', *History Ireland* (Winter 2004), p. 40.)

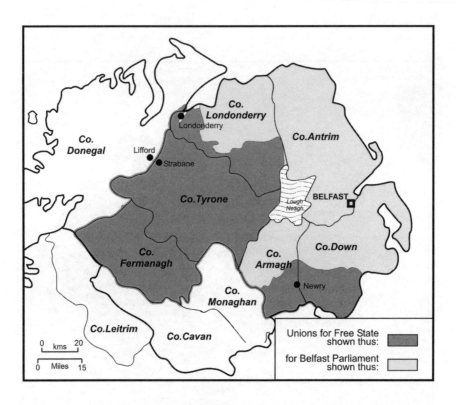

Map 2

Claims to Northern Ireland territory made by the Free State Government based on religious statistics for Poor Law Unions. (Map drawn by Stephen Hannon, based on North-Eastern Boundary Bureau, Handbook of the Ulster Question (Dublin, 1923), p. 52, and previously published in Kevin Matthews, *Fatal Influence: The Impact of Ireland on British Politics 1920–1925* (Dublin, 2004), p. 119.)

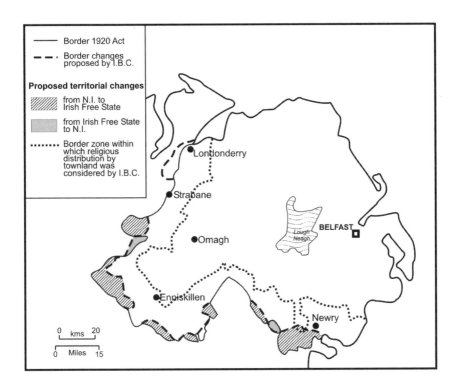

Map 3
Revisions to the border envisaged by the Irish Boundary Commission. (Map drawn by
Stephen Hannon, and previously published in Matthews, *Fatal Influence*, p. 225.)

Introduction

—

This book is the first comprehensive history of the Irish Boundary Commission, from its emergence in the Anglo-Irish Treaty of 6 December 1921 to its outcome at the close of 1925. It is also the first large-scale attempt to consider its significance in the wider international context. The readers I have particularly in mind are students of Irish and British history during the period from 1886 to 1969; political scientists working in the relevant area, and Irish studies academics generally. I have, however, tried to make the work accessible to a wider general readership.

The need for a boundary commission arose from the nature of the 1920 partition of Ireland, which left Northern Ireland with a largely dissatisfied Catholic minority comprising over one-third of its inhabitants. The provision in the Anglo-Irish Treaty for a mechanism to rectify this anomaly was a necessary condition for Nationalist Irish assent to the agreement as a whole: it was, and is, generally accepted on all sides that the Irish negotiators would not have subscribed to the Treaty in the absence of a boundary commission.

Writing a history of the Commission necessarily involves taking account of the remote and proximate circumstances which led to it. These were: the Nationalist demand for Home Rule which divided Irish people into two irrecon-cilable camps, each claiming absolute legitimacy for its own standpoint; British attempts from 1886 on to satisfy this demand; the partition of 1920 as a settlement for most Ulster Unionists but not for six-county Nationalists, or for the Unionists of Cavan, Donegal, Monaghan in particular, and the Free State in general; and the incorporation in the Anglo-Irish Treaty of a boun-dary clause both as a means of addressing northern Nationalist grievances with the 1920 boundary and of facilitating north-south political unity.

The first two chapters of this book, which deal with Home Rule, parti-tion and the Anglo-Irish Treaty, are designed to provide the background necessary to an understanding of the formation, conduct and outcome of the Commission. The third chapter deals with events between the signing of the Treaty and the establishment of the Commission in 1924. In this chapter the implications of this development and of Nationalist vacillation, equivocation, uncertainty and division over the merits of the Boundary Commission are explored. The significance of the general British reluctance to face down the Unionist threat of militant opposition to any finding by the Commission that would involve anything more than a minimal transfer of six-county territory to the Free State are closely analysed.

During this period, both Irish and British statesmen were harbouring significant doubts about the utility of a commission, many of them favouring a negotiated settlement of the boundary by the parties affected. At the same time, members of successive British administrations publicly dissented from Free State interpretations of the boundary clause as giving warrant for substantial transfers of territory from north to south. As the time for the establishment of the Commission approached, there was a developing convergence of view between the British and Northern Ireland authorities that the Commission must not recommend more than minimal rectification of the boundary, against a background of Unionist threats of militant resistance to anything else. This position found theoretical support in the interpretation of the significance of the boundary clause advanced by Ulster Unionists, by those in power in Britain, and ultimately by the Chairman of the Commission, Justice Richard Feetham.

This contentious interpretation goes to the heart of the boundary dispute which Feetham had to resolve. It centred on the view that Northern Ireland, even in the wake of the Treaty, could not be considered a new provisional entity created by the terms of the Treaty. It followed from this that it could not be subject to the large-scale revision demanded by Nationalists. Instead, it must be regarded as a pre-established entity created by the 1920 Government of Ireland Act. It therefore enjoyed prescriptive rights limiting the scope of the Treaty to effect minor territorial adjustments on either side of the 1920 boundary. It must end up, after the Commission had done its work, as substantially the same unit as that described in the 1920 Act.

Much of this book deals with the high politics of the Irish boundary question and its ongoing significance. I have, however, in an analysis of the evidence given to the Commission (Chapter Four) considered the views of people on both sides of the border who might have been affected in their everyday lives by the outcome of its deliberations. This evidence is a valuable record of the texture of daily life in Ulster in the early 1920s. It is also a barometer of the heightened political and religious sentiment generated by partition, and by the Boundary Commission. It throws useful light on the multiple practical inconveniences which the 1920 border and the 1923 Free State customs barrier had brought about, and raises troubling questions about the economic desirability of any border.

Once Feetham had adopted his limited interpretation, the fate of the Nationalist case for substantial boundary revision was sealed. This and Feetham's other views on the import of the boundary clause, and the decisions flowing from these, form the substance of Chapter Five. Another factor working to the advantage of Unionists was the transformation of British politics after the fall of Lloyd George's Liberal-Conservative Coalition Government in November 1922. After that date, the position within the Empire of both parties to the boundary dispute was altered in favour of Unionism. Against the background of increasing Conservative and Unionist hostility to the terms of the Treaty, members of the Coalition Government most closely identified with it – including Birkenhead, Austen Chamberlain, Winston Churchill and Worthington-Evans – were obliged to rebuild their careers by publicly interpreting, or reinterpreting, the boundary clause in a restrictive sense. They also re-emerged as defenders of Ulster Unionism, and protectors of its integrity.

The evolution of the idea of a boundary commission and, above all, the formulation in the Treaty of the task it was to perform gave rise to endless difficulties. The boundary clause – the work of the British negotiators – had no clear, indisputable meaning. It mentioned inhabitants whose wishes were to be consulted without indicating their geographical location. It provided no indication as to how the wishes of these unidentified inhabitants were to be ascertained, leaving it to the imagination and ingenuity of the Commissioners to apply it as they thought best. There was no indication whether large or small units were to be considered for transfer, or whether transfers were to be made in one or both directions. A week after the Treaty was signed, Asquith was at a loss to know whether the Commission was to operate by counties, by any specific areas or merely on an enumeration of population. All that Lloyd George would tell him was that those who framed the boundary clause had avoided giving specific directions of the kind mentioned by Asquith.

How the Irish negotiators could have subscribed to such a clause still remains a mystery, as does the fact that de Valera's Dáil Cabinet, having been afforded an opportunity to scrutinise it, failed to insist on a more sensible, workable provision. Griffith was made aware of the problem by his legal adviser, but failed inexplicably to pursue the matter. It is also surprising that those Irish politicians, including de Valera, who opposed the Treaty, appeared to be unaware of the pitfalls inherent in the boundary clause. In the aftermath of the Treaty, a long succession of British and Irish politicians and publicists displayed the utmost confidence in offering conflicting interpretations of this obscure but vital provision. The only interpretation that mattered in the end was Feetham's. His findings aroused dismay both among northern

Nationalists and Free State Government politicians. A common Nationalist reaction was that he had behaved throughout as a servant of the British Government and that his appointment as Chairman was based on the well-founded belief that his report would reflect the views of those who appointed him. In Chapter Five, which deals with Feetham's judgements, I outline the evidence, never more than circumstantial, tending to reinforce or contradict this view.

In addition, I consider the commonly-expressed view that the appointment of an English-born judge with conservative views as chairman of the Commission was inappropriate, if only because his impartiality was bound to come into question, even more emphatically so after his findings were revealed in a newspaper article before they were suppressed with the agreement of the main participating parties and did not come to public light until 1969. Misgivings about Feetham's appointment were partly inspired by European parallels: post-war commissions were chaired by demonstrably neutral figures having no connection with the parties involved. In this case, it has to be borne in mind that the fixing of the Irish boundary dispute was seen by the British as one between two members of the Empire, and that the Westminster Government in appointing Feetham, a South African by adoption, was acting not as the Government of Britain but as the Imperial Government: a distinction, however, not easy to maintain in practice.

The history of the Irish Boundary Commission is part of a larger European narrative. In Chapter Six, I locate those who participated in its evolution and proceedings in the wider international context. The Irish Commission was only one of many such bodies provided for in post-war treaty settlements with the purpose of fixing the frontiers of wartime belligerents. For this reason, I have thought it useful to go beyond Irish and British contexts to consider how European commission practice relates to the Irish case, and in particular what lessons are to be drawn by looking at Irish departures from European norms in the matter of ascertaining the wishes of the inhabitants of disputed areas. Some of the European parallels, examined in Chapter Six, are instructive: those with Upper Silesia, Klagenfurt, the Aaland Islands and Schleswig, for example. So too are some further afield: the Turk-Kurd conflict in Anatolia, and the French decision to add Muslim-majority territory to the Christian heartland of Mount Lebanon, with the purpose of creating a state large enough to be viable.

In my further study, I analyse the Nationalist and Unionist positions on partition, self-determination, territorial integrity and secession (Chapter Seven) in the light of the considerable existing literature on evolving international norms. My main purpose in this chapter is to suggest that both positions have much to recommend them, and to indicate the difficulty of reconciling them, at any rate in their purest form. Through this close examination I come to the conclusion that neither the Unionist nor Nationalist case on partition can command unqualified assent.

The Irish Boundary Commission, despite the considerable effort expended on all sides on research, propaganda, meetings, intensive lobbying and the preparation of large volumes of evidence, effected no change whatever in the boundary established in 1920. It might therefore be deemed a futile, wasteful exercise, scarcely worthy of serious investigation. It has, nevertheless, significant claims on our attention. Its incorporation in the Anglo-Irish Treaty made it possible for the Irish negotiators to sign the document, an act which soon plunged Nationalist Ireland into civil war, and engendered a sense of betrayal among Unionists. Controversy over its implications dominated British and Irish political discourse for long periods from early 1922 to late 1925, and occupied much parliamentary time in both countries. The seeming threat it represented to the integrity of Northern Ireland greatly strengthened the Ulster Unionist Party, as it adopted the role of aggressive defender of the territorial status quo, uniting all shades of Protestant opinion behind it on the single agenda of maintaining intact the 1920 boundary. Six-county Nationalists, and their political representatives, derived no ultimate benefit from the incorporation of a boundary clause in the Treaty. Encouraged by their leaders and southern politicians to expect considerable transfers of northern territory to the Free State, the generality of border Nationalists kept aloof from the political institutions of Northern Ireland to their ultimate detriment, allowing Unionists to assume long-term control of the great majority of public bodies, many of these traditionally Nationalist, and to shape these in their own long-term interests. The failure of the Commission to meet Nationalist expectations undermined the credibility of the Free State and enhanced that of its southern political opponents. One of the significant consequences of the Commission debacle was the emergence of Fianna Fáil in 1926 and the resulting transformation of southern Irish politics.

The published material on Home Rule, the Ulster question, partition and the Anglo-Irish Treaty is vast. I build on this throughout my first three chapters. I have also drawn on a wide range of British and Irish archival materials: British and Irish parliamentary records; local and national newspaper reports; contemporary pamphlets and other primary sources.

I take existing scholarly positions forward in a number of areas. Hitherto, discussion of the Irish boundary question has been predominantly in terms of its British and Irish contexts. I use extensive material on post-Versailles European and other boundary settlements to draw instructive parallels with the contemporary Irish one, and explore, in depth, the implications of these for discussion of the latter. My analysis of the submissions to the Commission and of the principles underlying Feetham's judgement, the anomalies and apparent double standards involved in this, breaks new ground. Among these anomalies are Feetham's willingness to override the wishes and interests of Mourne Catholics but not of Poyntzpass Protestants.

The significance of Francis Bourdillon's role as Secretary to the Boundary Commission has not hitherto been given the attention it deserves. In the year before his appointment, as Kevin Matthews has briefly noted, Bourdillon, who had worked on the Silesian Boundary Commission, submitted an advisory document to Lionel Curtis at the British Colonial Office on how the Irish boundary clause might be applied in the light of European experience. Bourdillon anticipated the fundamentals of Feetham's approach to Irish boundary determination, particularly in its restrictive view of the territorial implications of the boundary clause. Bourdillon's anticipation of Feetham, not hitherto analysed in the scholarly material, raises questions about the integrity of the Irish Commission, which I explore in this study. In this respect, the Bourdillon material is not unique. In early 1922, Feetham's fellow-Commissioner, the Unionist representative J. R. Fisher, had advised Craig to seek the exclusion of the most troublesome part of Northern Ireland (South Armagh) and the inclusion of Donegal (at the expense of Fermanagh) and North Monaghan. Three years later, Feetham recommended two of these three areas for transfer, along with East Donegal.

Bourdillon's submission throws considerable light on European commission practice, specifically with regard to plebiscites, which he, in contrast to the British authorities, considered essential to boundary determination, advancing compelling reasons for this point of view. Bourdillon's well-documented evidence in support of plebiscites in advance of boundary change reinforces the lessons I draw upon in Chapter Six from my analysis of the cases of Klagenfurt, Allenstein, Marienwerder, Upper Silesia and Schleswig.

In Chapter Six, I also draw attention to the fact that the absence from the Anglo-Irish Treaty of formal guidelines to the interpretation of Article 12 made the Irish Boundary Commission an oddity among bodies of its kind. Another significant departure from Continental practice was that Article 12 conferred on the British Government, a contending party to the dispute, the right to appoint the Chairman of the Boundary Commission. European commissions, in contrast, were presided over by persons from countries with no vested interest in the disposition of disputed territory. In relation to this latter concern, I address the British point of view, which I find not entirely convincing, that the Irish dispute was between two members of the British Empire, the Irish Free State and Northern Ireland, and not between sovereign states, as was the case in Europe, and that it was therefore appropriate that the Chairman should be drawn from the Empire.

There was the further British argument that in appointing a South African judge as Chairman, the Westminster Government was acting, not as the Government of Great Britain but as the Imperial Government. I point out that since the personnel of both these Governments was the same, this argument can scarcely carry conviction. On the Irish Nationalist side, it was commonly felt that Feetham's British birth and conservative political views predisposed him to favour retaining the 1920 settlement virtually intact, a course which his final report recommended. No such argument could have been made had a demonstrably impartial figure, aloof from British or Irish interests, been appointed Chairman.

It may be arguable whether justice was done by the Commission, or whether Feetham tried to act impartially, but my analysis makes clear that, given all the circumstances, justice was not, indeed could not, be seen to be done.

ONE

THE PARTITION OF IRELAND

THE FORCES AT PLAY

—

I HOME RULE: THE IMPERIAL DIMENSION

The formal implementation of partition in 1920 is best understood as the ultimate outcome of the Irish Nationalist demand for Home Rule, and of the attempts of successive British administration to satisfy this demand. For long periods between the British General Election of 1885 and the Tripartite Agreement between the British, Free State and Northern Ireland Governments in 1925, the Home Rule question became the predominant theme of English political debate, undermining governments, splitting the Liberal Party, unleashing furious passions, hatreds and prejudices, generating fears and insecurities among Irish Unionists for their future political, economic and religious prospects, and among Conservatives and Imperialists in general for the future of the British Empire. The Home Rule agitation threatened the conventions upon which the British Constitutional system depended. It saw British Privy Councillors inciting rebellion, and retired law officers of the Crown recommending armed resistance to an Act of the British Parliament, while Army officers prepared to resign their commissions rather than be obliged to move against such resistance. It also saw the leader of the Conservative opposition condoning violent action, if that were found necessary, to prevent Home Rule. The extended history of the Home Rule crisis illustrates the truth of Martin Gilbert's comment that the cause of Ireland poisoned British politics. 'The Conservatives,' he observes, 'remained convinced that Liberalism would betray Ulster,' while the Liberals were confirmed in their view that the Conservatives would use the claims of Ulster as an excuse to disrupt an Irish settlement, and as an opportunity to kill Liberalism.[1]

British Conservative politicians feared that the implementation of Home Rule, under a single Irish Parliament, inevitably dominated by Nationalists, would ultimately lead to the political separation of Ireland as a whole from the

---

1   M. S. Gilbert, *Winston S. Churchill* vol. 3 (London, 1976), p. 30.

British Empire. Since 1800 the Act of Union had politically united Ireland to the rest of the United Kingdom. Preservation of the Union, and the political integrity of the British Isles and by extension of the Empire, was so fundamental to British Conservatives that they adopted the alternative name of Unionists as a token of this. As Lord Hugh Cecil put it to Bonar Law: 'We are the Unionist Party: that is, we exist to oppose Home Rule.'[2] Lord Salisbury, the Conservative Prime Minister from June 1885 to February 1886, and again from July 1886, objected to the First Home Rule Bill on the ground that Irish people as a collective, 'like the Hindus and the Hottentots, were inherently incapable of self-government'.[3] He was certain that the concession of Home Rule to Ireland would lead to the disintegration 'not only of the polity of the United Kingdom, but also, as a result, to the disintegration of Britain's Imperial position.'[4] Democracy, Salisbury believed, 'works admirably when it is confined to people of the Teutonic race.'[5] Lord Randolph Churchill put it more starkly when he claimed that Home Rule would 'plunge the knife in the heart of the British Empire.'[6]

In September 1912, the backbench Conservative peer Lord Willoughby de Broke assured a Loyalist attendance at Dromore, County Down, that English Unionists would rally to the cause of their Ulster brethren if Home Rule were forced upon them by Asquith's 'radical government'. He promised that such a government would find that it faced the opposition of more than Orangemen: 'every white man in the British Empire would be giving support, either moral or active, to one of the most loyal populations who ever fought under the Union Jack.'[7] Over a decade later, the threat that a boundary commission might represent to the integrity of Northern Ireland and by extension to that of the Empire, inspired one English Imperialist, W. Comyns Beaumont, to declare that 'like many others I regard Ulster as the key question of the Empire's maintenance – once weaken there and we are done.' 'For one,' Beaumont promised, 'I am ready at any time to fight for Ulster if she should be

2   Cited by John O. Stubbs, 'The Unionists and Ireland, 1914–18', *Historical Journal* Vol. 33, No. 4 (1990), pp. 867– 93. The term 'Unionist' rather than 'Conservative' can also be taken to refer to the residual presence of the Liberal Unionists, although the latter were increasingly absorbed into the Conservative Party, merging formally with it in 1911.

3   *The Times* (London), 17 May 1886.

4   Paul Johnson, *A History of the English People* (London, 1985), p. 355; Nicholas Mansergh, *Nationalism and Independence: Selected Irish Papers* (Cork, 1997), p. 198.

5   Cited in Jules Abels, *The Parnell Tragedy* (London, 1966), p. 243.

6   Cited in Niall Ferguson, *Empire: How Britain made the Modern World* (London, 2003), p. 25.

7   *Belfast News Letter*, 27 Sept. 1912. Willoughby de Broke's statement that the Ulster Unionists would be supported by 'every white man' in the Empire has the curious implication that Catholic Nationalists and their descendants/sympathisers elsewhere in the Empire could not be classified as white.

compelled to resist the vile intrigues employed against her.'[8] F. E. Smith, the first Earl of Birkenhead, believed that Ireland could not be given even the limited measure of Home Rule envisaged by the Liberals without undermining, by contagion, British India and the worldwide Empire, and furthermore that Ireland occupied too important a strategic position on Britain's Atlantic flank for Britain to permit an arrangement that might lead to secession. Like many contemporary British Conservative and Irish Unionist statesmen, Birkenhead found the Irish demand for Home Rule not only impossible, but also incomprehensible, not being able to understand how anybody could desire to cease being British. He had modified these views by the time he signed the Anglo-Irish Treaty, but neither he nor the other British negotiators was prepared to concede a degree of Irish freedom that might have made the British mainland less secure than it had been under the Union.[9]

In 1885, it was clear that disagreement over Home Rule and concern over its implications for Ulster and southern Irish Unionists had a decisive part to play in domestic British politics, and could be exploited to the detriment of its Liberal Party advocates. The British Conservatives had good reason to be concerned for the southern Unionist landlord class who feared that Home Rule under a Nationalist administration in Dublin would result in their own expropriation. Some leading British Conservatives were also Irish landlords, among them Lords Hugh and Robert Cecil, Halsbury, Selbourne and Walter Long. The southern Irish Ascendancy had close links with the governing landed class in England, which possessed overwhelming influence in the Conservative Party. The use for British Conservative Party advantage of Ulster Unionism, the most committed and effective part of the resistance to Home Rule, was most egregiously exemplified in the activities of Lord Randolph Churchill.

In November 1885, Churchill wrote to Salisbury that the Conservatives had always been damaged by the monstrous alliance with 'these foul Ulster Tories'. When, however, in 1886, Gladstone's Liberal Party took up the cause of Irish Home Rule, Churchill became an instant champion of Ulster Unionist resistance to the measure, and, with other leading Conservatives, he incited Ulster Orangemen to revolt against it. In February 1886, he told a colleague that if Gladstone 'went for Home Rule, the Orange Card would be the one to play', something he did in Belfast during the same month. His violent rhetoric excited a vast crowd to frenzy, leading to 'savage, repeated and prolonged' disturbances.[10] He urged Ulstermen to fight against Home Rule in

8   W. Comyns Beaumont to Viscount Templeton, PRONI PM 4/11/2, 17 May 1924.
9   See John Campbell, *F. E. Smith: First Earl of Birkenhead* (London, 1983), pp. 549–50.
10 W. S. Churchill, *Lord Randolph Churchill* vol. 2 (London, 1906), p. 450.

the knowledge that men of 'position and influence in England' were willing to share their fortune. The tradition of militant Unionist opposition to Home Rule with British encouragement was perpetuated by a later generation of leading Conservatives, among them Joseph Chamberlain, Balfour and the Marquess of Hartington, who frequently visited Belfast to encourage Unionists to oppose Home Rule by violence if necessary. The British Imperialists were not dedicating themselves to the support of Ulster Unionists against Nationalists. The task they set themselves was to employ northern Unionism, particularly at times of political stress, as a barrier against the self-deter-mination demanded by Irish nationalism, with all the dangers this would represent to the integrity of the Imperial heartland. A belief common among Conservatives, and many Ulster Unionists, was that if Ulster resistance made Home Rule impossible in the North, the measure would not, or could not, be imposed on Ireland as a whole or even in southern or western Ireland. Thus, encouragement of Ulster resistance could be seen as part of the Conservative fight for the integrity of the British Empire. The Conservative and Unionist case that an independent Ireland was a potential strategic danger to Great Britain was not unreasonable. Free State statesmen were determined that the Irish Army would be so equipped as to render it capable of 'full and complete coordination with the forces of the British Government in the defence of Saorstát territory whether against actual hostilities or against violation of neutrality on the part of a common enemy.'[11] A key element of de Valera's foreign policy post-1932 was that 'despite the continuing injustice of partition, the State would never allow itself to become a base against Britain.'[12]

The Liberals shared the Conservative assumption that on economic grounds alone, to concede to the Ulster demand for separate treatment, such as county option (the right of any county to opt out of a Home Rule parlia-ment) or the right to be excluded as a unit from Home Rule, would mean abandoning the measure entirely. This assumption was based on the view that southern Ireland could not survive as an entity without the industrial strength of the North East. As a consequence of this shared analysis, the Liberals tended to ignore Ulster's case for separate treatment, while during the early phase of the Home Rule controversy the Conservative strategy had twin elements: to support the Ulster case for exclusion on its own merits, and to foster the expectation that the success of this case would kill Home Rule. The Great War and the formation of a series of coalition governments in which the two parties shared power inevitably altered the Conservative approach, as Liberals as well as Conservatives came to accept Ulster exclusion. During the

11   Eunan O'Halpin, *Defending Ireland: The Free State and its Enemies since 1922* (Oxford, 1999), pp. 91–135.
12   Ibid.

Home Rule debates, the Liberals showed occasional signs of willingness to compromise on Ulster. However, their reluctance to consider any specific compromise in depth was inspired by the fear that the Unionists might exploit any proposed compromise as a basis for demanding further concessions.

Conservative Ulster policy in the period leading to the introduction of the third Home Rule Bill by Asquith's Liberal Government was often condemned by opponents as discreditable, opportunist and subversive. The militant resistance to Home Rule led by Bonar Law between 1912 and 1914 threatened to undermine fatally the British tradition of political compromise at times when the welfare of the nation and the Empire were at stake. Conservative policy at this stage, however, was in part dictated by the circumstances in which the party found itself, and by its perception of itself as the natural party of government. By the time Asquith introduced his Home Rule measure in 1912, the Conservatives had been in opposition for six years; the last Conservative administration, under A. J. Balfour, had been replaced in December 1905 by a Liberal one, under Campbell-Bannerman. The Home Rule issue seemed to present an opportunity for Conservatives to reassume their rightful role. In one sense, they had never fully relinquished this, even in opposition. Their control of the House of Lords gave them a permanent veto over legislation. This veto had been exercised in 1893 when the Lords rejected Gladstone's second Home Rule Bill after it had been passed by the Commons. This situation, intolerable to Liberals and to large sections of public opinion, was partly remedied by the Parliament Act of August 1911, when the veto was limited to two years. The Conservative attitude to democratic governance was neatly described by Winston Churchill in 1911 when he complained to the King of 'their claim to govern the country whether in office or in opposition and to resort to disorder because they cannot have their way'. In 1912, when Bonar Law asserted that he could imagine no limit to the resistance Ulster Unionists might mount against Home Rule in which he would not be prepared to support them, Churchill again made the appropriate comment: 'the veto of violence has replaced the veto of privilege.'[13]

II THE THREAT TO UNIONIST ASCENDANCY

To dwell on the use of the Ulster question by Conservative Party strategists is not to say that considerations of party political advantage represented the sole basis for the support offered by that Party, and other people in Britain of like mind, to the Ulster Unionists. A large section of British opinion represented

---

13   Donald Read, 'History: political and diplomatic' in C. B. Cox and A. E. Dyson (eds), *The Twentieth Century Mind 1900–1918* (London, 1972), p. 36.

by the Conservatives was broadly sympathetic to the predicament of Ulster Protestants living under the threat of Home Rule, an ostentatiously loyal people facing the prospect of being cast out of the United Kingdom against their will and being governed by a Catholic Nationalist administration they could only abhor. As Boyce points out, these Ulster Protestants were supported, not only by the Conservative Party, 'but by important sections of British conservative opinion, by administrators such as Lord Milner, soldiers like Lord Roberts, and even constitutional historians like A. V. Dicey.' [14] On the other hand, Boyce also argues that as far as British Conservative opinion was concerned, the fate of Ulster, or of any part of Ulster, was always secondary to what were regarded as the interests of England and of the British Empire.[15] This is exemplified in the attitude of Milner, who supported a federalist settlement of the Irish question before 1914 if this facilitated an accommodation between Nationalists and Unionists, and stabilised the Empire. For Milner, however, such an arrangement would have to be hedged with the proviso that this would be a final settlement and not lead to Irish political separation from Britain and the Empire. Conservative Party views on Ulster resistance to Home Rule underwent considerable modification between 1886 and 1921 in response to changing political circumstances at home and abroad. In 1886, the Conservative Party supported Loyalist resistance to Home Rule in the interests of British and Imperial solidarity. By the time the Anglo-Irish Treaty was being negotiated in 1921, however, Imperial unity seemed to demand a settlement between northern Loyalists and Sinn Féin involving some form of Irish unity as the likeliest means of keeping Ireland within the British Imperial system.

It would be a mistake to assume that in their struggle against Home Rule, the Ulster Unionists were preoccupied first and foremost with the welfare of the United Kingdom and of the Empire. The primary aim of all their efforts was the retention of their traditional privileges as part of a Protestant ascendancy, a position that had been inherited by them from their seventeenth-century ancestors. To maintain these privileges along with their British birthright and citizenship, they were prepared to resort to extra-legal measures if necessary. Self-interest, even self-preservation, seemed to demand no less. In 1924, Craig's Government prepared some briefing notes on the boundary question in which the British Government was reminded that 'the people of Ulster,' by which was meant the Protestants of the six counties, 'have always

---

14   D. G. Boyce, 'British Conservative opinion, the Ulster question and the partition of Ireland, 1912–21', *Irish Historical Studies* (hereafter *IHS*) 17 (1970), p. 90.

15   Ibid., p. 89.

been very tenacious of their rights as citizens of the United Kingdom and hold fast by the Union Jack and other symbols of loyalty to the Crown and to British traditions.'[16] The Union was seen as conferring important privileges on Protestant Loyalists, as the Constitutional form best designed to protect Irish Protestants from subjugation to a Catholic majority. Thus, 'by defining their nationality as British rather than Irish, the Union incorporated them within a broader Protestant majority'[17] and enabled them to contribute significantly to the common development of the British Isles and the British Empire.[18] The danger to Ulster Protestantism, threatened by Home Rule, united the two main strands of northern Unionism: the Presbyterian-Liberal element and the Protestant Ascendancy element. Leading Ulster Liberals and the great majority of their followers received Gladstone's announcement of his support for Home Rule with consternation, 'assuming that he had changed his mind for narrow party advantage in order to retain power, which he was able to do after joining with the Nationalists to defeat Lord Salisbury's Government on 27 January 1886.'[19] The Home Rule threat contributed to the heavy defeat of the Liberal candidate in the mid-Armagh by-election on 1 February 1886. The anti-Home Rule Liberals, henceforth known as Liberal Unionists, collaborated with their erstwhile opponents in a united front against the Home Rule Bill. The depth of Ulster Liberal resentment at the news of Gladstone's 'betrayal' of the interests of Ulster Unionism is conveyed in Thomas MacKnight's account of his breaking the news to Sir Edward Cowan, the leading Ulster Liberal. When MacKnight informed Cowan that Gladstone had 'gone over to the Home Rulers', Cowan could only reply: 'It means to us utter ruin.'[20] MacKnight's memoir is a lengthy defence of the claim that it was Gladstone who betrayed Ulster Liberalism rather than vice versa.

Ulster Unionists were fortunate in the quality of their leadership at this point in their history. Two remarkable men led their campaign against Home Rule. The first was Sir Edward Carson, a southern Unionist born in Dublin, a brilliantly successful barrister and a Unionist MP for Dublin University from 1892 to 1918, who was elected leader of the Irish Unionist Party in 1910. His total opposition to Home Rule prompted him to take up the cause of northern Unionists, the grouping most likely to be adversely affected by its implementation. The other influential Unionist leader was Sir James Craig, who fought

16   PRONI PM 4/11/2.

17   David Fitzpatrick, *The Two Irelands 1912–1939* (Oxford, 1998), p. 24.

18   Patrick Buckland, in Peter Collins (ed.), *Nationalism and Unionism: Conflict in Ireland* (Belfast, 1994), p. 80.

19   Jonathan Bardon, *A History of Ulster* (Belfast, 2005), pp. 275–6.

20   Thomas MacKnight, *Ulster As It Is* vol. 2 (London, 1896), p. 127.

against the Boers in South Africa and exercised a leadership role in the Orange Order and the Ulster Unionist Council. His most celebrated political remark was to be: 'Ours is a Protestant Government and I am an Orangeman.'

The rhetoric of Carson and Craig is characterised by persistent references to the devotion of their followers to the Empire, as contrasted with the disloyalty of other Irish people. Such rhetoric served Unionists well in winning the sympathy of British statesmen for their cause. It is a matter for debate whether the loyalty of Ulster Unionists to the Empire was ever more than conditional, and contingent upon having their own wishes and self-interest gratified. Craig was particularly skilled at presenting Unionist opposition to Home Rule as a necessary defence of an Imperial birthright. In 1912, he argued that there were certain rights and privileges that might be filched away from his followers in the event of Home Rule. Above all, there was 'a hereditary stake in the Empire which did not belong to them, which was not theirs to part with, which they never intended to surrender.'[21] At the twelfth of July demonstration in 1914, Craig placed Unionist Ulstermen at the heart of the historical defence of the Empire. They were the men, he declared, 'who helped to raise the tottering standard of their Empire into safety under the deadly Boer fire, and they had mourned and not forgotten their Ulster comrades who fell on South African soil, their deaths cheered by treacherous Irish voices.' The treacherous Irish who supported the Boers against the Empire were the very men 'who now demanded of a British Government the lives and liberties of loyal and free Ulstermen as purchase money for their false friendship.'[22] Ulster Unionists also liked to remind the British that the part played by their ancestors in the Siege of Derry had saved the Empire in the seventeenth century from the Roman Catholic threat, newly posed in the twentieth century by Home Rule, against which Unionists would be obliged to make another stand.[23] Here we may observe the Unionist deployment of history to strengthen the emotional and historical links between Great Britain and the Protestants of Ulster, in an attempt to give Unionists what Ian MacBride calls 'a central place in the myth of the unfolding British connection.'[24] The weight of modern academic commentary is on the side of Alvin Jackson when he argues that Ulster Unionists had little interest in the

---

21   *Northern Whig*, 16 Jan. 1912, cited in T. P. Daly, 'James Craig: Chamberlainite imperialist, 1903–14', *IHS* 36 (2008), p. 198.

22   *Northern Whig*, 14 July 1914.

23   T. P. Daly, 'James Craig', *IHS* 36 (2008), p. 198.

24   Ian MacBride, *The Siege of Derry in Ulster Protestant Mythology* (Dublin, 1997), pp. 59–60. Cited in Daly, 'James Craig', *IHS* 36 (2008), p. 198.

Empire except as a resource to advance their own aims, an instrument to be used for dealing with the problems posed for them locally by Home Rule.[25]

R. J. Smith, in a well-argued personal submission to the Irish Boundary Commission, found evidence of Ulster Unionist indifference to the welfare of the Empire in the resistance of its leaders to any reasonable concession to democratic claims by the rest of Ireland for the amendment of the 1920 Government of Ireland Act. Great Britain, Smith remarked, 'may be embarrassed and endangered, the Free State may be smashed up and driven to civil war in which the British must become involved. Nevertheless Unionist Ulster will not budge an inch.' 'Does that attitude,' Smith asked, 'indicate a sincere and self-sacrificing devotion to the interests of the Empire to which they have been given so much lip service and not more help in the war than the Redmondite volunteers gave?'[26] John Redmond's Home Rule Volunteers, it might be argued on the basis of actions as well as words, were, along with their leader, at least as loyal to the welfare of the Empire as Ulster Unionists were. It is reasonable to suggest that Craig's Imperialism was based on his view of the British Empire and the British culture it embodied as a fundamentally Protestant phenomenon, with the result that his Imperialism was essentially religious, a function of his Protestantism, and, hence, narrowly focused, as exemplified in his frequent emphasis of the part played by Ulster Protestants in its extension and defence.

The generality of Irish Unionists, whether in Ulster or elsewhere, could see no good reason for the imposition of a radical new political settlement, given their satisfaction with the status quo, and given that they were the main beneficiaries of the fruits of the Act of Union, although Carson would also argue that the people as a whole, and not merely the Protestant ascendancy, had prospered as a consequence of being part of the United Kingdom. The benefits listed by Carson included local self-government, an educational system created out of Imperial taxation, University education and generous land purchase schemes.[27] For Carson, Home Rule would involve the degradation of Ireland into a province. He regarded the struggle for the preservation of the Union as an assertion and defence of British standards: honour, decency, integrity in public life, justice and the civilising force of Empire,

---

25 See, for example, Alvin Jackson, 'Irish Unionists and the Empire, 1880–1920: classes and masses', in Keith Jefferey (ed.), *An Irish Empire? Aspects of Ireland and the British Empire* (Manchester, 1966); Alvin Jackson, *The Ulster Party: Irish Unionists in the House of Commons, 1884–1911* (Oxford, 1995); Daly, 'James Craig', *IHS* 36 (2008), p. 198.

26 Evidence given to the Irish Boundary Commission, CAB 61/132.

27 Ian Colvin and Edward Marjoribanks, *The Life of Lord Carson* (London, 1934), p. 16.

along with English valour and common sense.[28] The attribution of such admirable qualities to those who subscribed to the British way of life, especially Ulster Unionists, who were characterised by Carson as exhibiting the virtues of honesty, plainness, suffering and a sense of duty, implied that enemies of the Union, in this case English Liberals and Irish Catholics, were characterised by 'their deviousness, deceit in pursuit of self-interest, cowardice, and a Roman style of ornate ambiguity.'[29]

Viewed in the larger historical context, the Home Rule issue was the culminating phase in the struggle for the supremacy between the two communities in Ireland. Throughout the nineteenth century, Irish Protestants had been obliged to accept repeated major concessions to the Catholic majority: Catholic Emancipation, the disestablishment of the Church of Ireland, land reform, and the abolition of the Grand Jury system. This was against the background of the growing assertiveness of the Catholic Church. With the continuous prospect of Home Rule, what remained of the traditional predominance of Protestants, particularly in Ulster, was threatened. Their response to a policy that would establish a Catholic ascendancy in place of their own is well described by Beckett: 'They refused to acquiesce any longer. Irish Protestants of the 1660s had declared that they would not suffer the lands they had won by their swords to be filched from them by Ayes and Noes: their successors of the early 1900s were equally contemptuous of parliamentary procedure in a matter that, as they believed, affected not their property only, but their lives and religion, and they made ready to receive a Home Rule Act, if one should be passed, with rifles and machine-guns.'[30]

The Ulster Unionist leadership could not accept the prospect of a new parliament, based in Dublin, and dominated by Catholic Nationalists. They and their followers were convinced, having experienced Catholic Nationalism in action, that Nationalist politicians were constitutionally incapable of governing the country fairly and completely, or of bringing stability and peace. Carson deplored the role of Home Rule MPs in inciting Irishmen to murder landlords and their agents, and in promoting violence and intimidation. Foreseeing that a Home Rule dispensation would greatly extend the political influence of the Catholic Church, Unionists could only see in this outcome a threat to their Protestant values. The traditional Protestant view of Catholicism as the religion of materially and intellectually backward people also coloured Unionist attitudes to its feared dominance. If Ireland had to endure political separation from Great Britain under Home Rule, the most progressive and

28 Andrew Gailey, 'King Carson: an essay on the invention of leadership', *IHS* 30 (1996), p. 69.
29 Ibid., p. 72.
30 J. C. Beckett, *The Making of Modern Ireland 1603–1923* (London, 1966), p. 418.

intelligent elements in Irish life, the descendants of the British planters, would no longer be able to exert their influence in favour of high culture and progressive ideas. One of Carson's southern associates foresaw under Home Rule 'a desert of dead uniformity, where the poor will have no one to appeal to except the priest or the local shopkeeper . . . where lofty ideals, whether of social or Imperial interest, will be smothered in an atmosphere of superstition, greed and chicanery.'[31] The only realistic accommodation with Nationalism that Carson could envisage was outlined by him in early 1921. No one, he explained, would be more pleased to see 'an absolute unity in Ireland' than he would, but this would have to involve all Irish people together 'within the Empire, doing our best for ourselves and the United Kingdom and for His Majesty's Dominions.'[32]

Ulster Unionists successfully and understandably employed the argument that Home Rule under a Dublin Parliament would have ruinous consequences for the Ulster economy, above all for Protestant businessmen, who dominated economic life in the area. One index of this dominance was that in 1893, when the second Home Rule Bill was being debated, 97 per cent of the membership of the Belfast Chamber of Commerce was Protestant.[33] In that year, the Chamber voted unanimously for a resolution rejecting any dilution of the Union through Home Rule. In an address to Gladstone, the members pointed out that all economic progress in Ulster had been made under the Union. At the end of the eighteenth century Belfast had been a small, disaffected, insignificant town hostile to the British Empire; since the Act of Union it had made unprecedented economic advances. They could not accept the proposition that they should be driven by force to abandon the political arrangement which had facilitated that success.[34] In August 1886, Thomas MacKnight, a disillusioned Ulster Liberal, asked the Chairman of Harland and Wolff, William Pirrie, whether it were true that in the event of Home Rule his firm would withdraw their great shipbuilding works from Belfast and take them to the Clyde, Pirrie answered that it certainly would. Other leading Belfast businessmen told MacKnight that under a Dublin Home Rule Parliament there would be no security for life or property, no fair play for Loyalists, and an absence of commercial confidence. Belfast would not continue to prosper, and its great industrial enterprises would have to seek a home on the other side of the Irish Sea.[35]

---

31   Patrick Buckland, *Irish Unionism 1885–1923: A Documentary History* (Belfast, 1973), p. 49.

32   *Irish Times*, 31 Jan. 1921.

33   D. G. Boyce, *Nationalism in Ireland* (London, 1991), p. 203.

34   Buckland, *Irish Unionism*, p. xxx.

35   MacKnight, *Ulster As It Is*, pp. 152–3.

Ulster Unionist determination to engage in acts which amounted to open defiance of the authority of the Westminster Parliament exposed a paradox at the heart of Ulster loyalism. On the one hand, no other grouping on the island was as ardent in its profession of loyalty to British governance or as determined to persist in the benefits flowing from it. On the other hand, these same Loyalists were ready to offer armed resistance to an Act of parliament and to the Constitution under which they sought to be governed as subjects of the King. Ulster Unionists, however, had their distinctive way of reconciling these apparently contradictory positions. A significant element in Unionist thinking, traceable to the controversies over the disestablishment in 1869 of the Church of Ireland during Gladstone's premiership, was that the position of Irish Protestants within the United Kingdom was an essential part of the British Constitution, and was not subject to alteration by any Parliament.[36] This was one of the arguments taken up by Lord Randolph Churchill in the course of his inspirational address to Unionists in the Ulster Hall in 1886, when he was inciting opposition to Gladstone's first Home Rule Bill. Churchill refused to accept that so 'gigantic' an innovation as Home Rule 'could be accompanied by the mere passing of a law' by the British Parliament.[37]

Ulster Unionists saw a clear distinction between loyalty to the Crown and loyalty to the government of the day. Their political thinking on this matter belonged less to the nineteenth or twentieth centuries than to the seventeenth, when contractarian theories of government had been in vogue. These theories were founded on an imagined agreement between a ruler and his people. They formed the ideological basis for the 'Glorious Revolution' of 1688, honoured ever since by Ulster Unionists as the wellspring of their civil and religious liberties. As seventeenth-century Whigs understood it, the English Constitution was founded on an original contract, somewhat vague in origin, between prince and people. Between 1685 and 1688 the Catholic James II had attempted to subvert the Constitution, and thereby to break the contract, by violating existing corporate rights in extending toleration to Catholics and nonconformists by unconstitutional means. William of Orange restored the Constitution, and Protestant pre-eminence was one of the foundations of the Williamite settlement. Loyalists assembled at the great Ulster Unionist Convention of June 1892 were told by the Liberal Unionist Thomas Sinclair that all those opposed to Home Rule were 'children of the revolution of 1688', who would have nothing to do with a Dublin parliament.[38]

36   Patrick O'Farrell, *England's Irish Question: Anglo-Irish Relations 1534–1970* (London, 1971); Ged Martin, in Malcolm Anderson and Eberhard Bort (eds), *The Irish Border: History, Politics and Culture* (Liverpool, 1999), pp. 249–50; p. 58.

37   R. F. Foster, *Lord Randolph Churchill: A Political Life* (Oxford, 1988), p. 134.

38   *Belfast News Letter*, 18 June 1892.

The Gladstonian impulse towards Home Rule was seen by Unionists as another attempt to undermine the British Constitution, whose twin pillars – the Williamite settlement and the Act of Union – loyal Ulstermen were determined to defend, even when the threat to the privileges they enjoyed under it came from the Government of the United Kingdom. The most fundamental and most cherished of these privileges was the right to their British citizenship: no majority in Parliament could legitimately deprive them of this. At their 1912 Convention, the Presbyterians, the majority Protestant denomination in Ulster, invoked a historically-based justification, with potent moral overtones, for their plea to the British Government to save them from 'the overwhelming calamity of Home Rule'. They argued that the Government had a contractual obligation to Presbyterians to act in this way for reasons with deep roots in seventeenth-century history. Presbyterians were now in Ireland because three centuries ago, their forefathers were planted in Ulster by the English Government in order that, by their loyalty and industry, they might secure the peace and prosperity of Ulster for the mutual welfare of both countries. They and their forefathers had done their best to fulfil the trust committed to them; in return, the Government should protect their heritage as fellow citizens of the United Kingdom, of equal status with their English and Scottish co-religionists.[39]

The Ulster Covenant signed by over 200,000 men on 23 September 1912, while affirming allegiance to the King, had a declaratory preamble confirming steps taken for the establishment of an Ulster provisional government. Miller observes that Ulster Protestants had thereby 'embarked upon a course which, in ordinary commonsense terms, was plainly illegal.'[40] Miller also points to a moral justification for this course of action, emphasised in the conviction of the perpetrators that Home Rule would undermine their 'civil and religious freedom' and be destructive of their citizenship. Upon these assertions rested the Loyalist argument that 'although loyal citizens are bound to obey all ordinary laws, Home Rule would be no ordinary law for it would in itself negate their citizenship.'[41] A. V. Dicey, Vinerian Professor of English Law at Oxford, a determined opponent of Home Rule, in a parallel argument, invoked the old Whig doctrine that oppression, and especially resistance to the will of the people, 'might justify what was technically conspiracy or rebellion'.[42]

Ulster Unionists had little or no time for modern Nationalist theories of identification with the state or automatic loyalty to it. As Buckland remarks,

39 Buckland, *Irish Unionism*, p. 79.

40 David W. Miller, *Queen's Rebels: Ulster Loyalists in Historical Perspective* (Dublin, 2007), pp. 97–8.

41 Ibid., p. 98.

42 D. G. Boyce, in Sabine Wichert, *From the United Irishmen to 20th Century Unionism* (Dublin, 2004), pp. 97–110.

they regarded allegiance to the government as conditional, and considered rebellion justifiable if they deemed that the government was failing in its duty to its citizens.[43] If a Liberal administration with the parliamentary support of Irish Home Rulers enacted legislation which deprived Ulster Loyalists of what they saw as their prescriptive right to be governed from Westminster, and subjected them to a Dublin parliament, they would be disloyal to the Crown if they failed to rebel against such an abrogation of their democratic preference. Carson expressed this point well when he told Asquith how he would have addressed a court had he been indicted for rebellion in Ulster. He would have pleaded guilty, but would, at the same time, have made a virtue of his guilt: 'I was born under the British flag, a loyal subject of His Majesty the King. So much do I value this birthright that I was even prepared to rebel in order to defend it. If to fight, so as to remain, like yourselves, a loyal subject of His majesty, be a crime . . . I plead guilty.'[44] Ulster Unionists could also argue that what might in other circumstances be regarded as treasonable activity was being pursued in a constitutional vacuum. This was because, at the time of Asquith's Home Rule Bill, the British Constitution was in suspense as a result of the 1911 Parliament Act, which radically altered the traditional balance of power between the Houses of Parliament to the detriment of the House of Lords, at the same time removing the strongest bulwark Unionists had against the imposition of Home Rule. In such circumstances, Unionists considered themselves 'absolved from Home Rule'.[45]

III THE RELIGIOUS ASPECT

Throughout the entire course of the Home Rule controversy, denominational religion assumed a central importance. It served as a convenient indicator of political allegiance. It also formed a significant part of Unionist discourse on the perils for Protestants of Home Rule. The religious dimension of Ulster's resistance to Home Rule emerges forcibly in Rudyard Kipling's propagandist poem 'Ulster 1912'. This presents the opposition to the measure as a spirited response to the threat of Catholic dominance over Protestants, to which Home Rule would lead:

43   Patrick Buckland, 'Irish Unionism and the New Ireland', in Boyce (ed.), *The Revolution in Ireland, 1879–1923* (Dublin, 1988), p. 90.

44   H. Montgomery Hyde, *The Life of Sir Edward Carson: Lord Carson of Duncairn* (London, 1953), p. 359.

45   Patrick Buckland 'Carson, Craig and the partition of Ireland', in Peter Collins (ed.), *Nationalism and Unionism: Conflict in Ireland, 1885–1921* (Belfast, 1994), p. 84.

We know the war prepared, on every peaceful home,
We know the hells declared, for such as serve not Rome

One Unionist apologist after another tended to equiparate Irish Catholicism with Irish Nationalism, the former often exercising controlling influence over the political outlook and activities of the latter. In 1911, James Craig described Ireland as 'probably the most priest- ridden country in the World.'[46] During the Commons debate on the first Home Rule Bill in 1886, William Johnston, Unionist MP for Belfast South, declared that what Ulster Protestants dreaded was that if Home Rule were enacted, 'the Protestants of Ulster would be dominated and tyrannized over by the [Catholic] majority.' As evidence for this, Johnston observed that 'the Church of Rome in Ireland at the present moment did not hesitate to proclaim that she looked for coming triumph and victory for her cause to an Irish Parliament.'[47] Johnston's observations were not without substance. The identification of leading Home Rulers with members of the Irish Hierarchy and clergy was a matter of public knowledge. Church leaders successfully enlisted the aid of members of the Irish Parliamentary Party in the Commons in furthering the interests of Catholic education.[48]

At an organisational level, Catholic clergy wielded considerable influence on the Irish Party, attending county conventions in large numbers, and presiding over party meetings. Soon after the Parnell split, Archbishop Logue of Armagh reminded Archbishop Walsh of Dublin how much the Parliamentary Party owed to the Catholic clergy. They had 'climbed to their present influential positions on the shoulders of Irish priests and Irish bishops'; the priests had 'worked up the electoral registers for them, fought the elections and contributed to the sinews of war.'[49] In his history of the Party written in 1910, Frank Hugh O'Donnell, a former Home Rule MP and Council member of the Home Rule League of Ireland, provided overwhelming evidence, mainly derived from contemporary journals, of the extent of reliance of the Party on Catholic clergymen of every rank. Among one of his many examples of 'the dependence of Mr John Dillon MP on the clergy', O'Donnell found it instructive to cite the names of his leading nominators: all four were Parish Priests. O'Donnell's characterisation of the political role of Bishop Patrick O'Donnell of Raphoe would have made welcome propagandist material for such Unionist opponents of Home Rule as the Belfast Quaker John Pim, who

46 St John Ervine, *Craigavon: Ulsterman* (London, 1949), pp. 193–4.
47 *Hansard*, House of Commons, Vol. 304, Cols 1227–30, 9 Apr. 1886.
48 F. S. L. Lyons, *Parnell* (Dublin, 1963), p. 14.
49 Ibid., p. 471.

feared that it would 'surrender Irish society to the invisible and visible tyranny of the Romish clergy.'[50] It was 'no exaggeration to say,' O'Donnell wrote of his namesake the Bishop, 'that his nod can make 20 members of Parliament and can influence the chances of 20 others . . . no financial trustee more influential could protect the pecuniary interests of the Parliamentary Party.'[51]

An interesting effect of the Home Rule agitation on the Loyalist side was its unifying influence on the various Protestant churches, whose former rivalries were set aside as they made common cause against a common danger: the encroachment of papal power through the imposition of Home Rule, a measure designed to suppress the Protestant faith. At the Annual Conference of the Church of Ireland in Belfast in 1893, when controversy over the second Home Rule Bill raged, G. T. Stokes, Professor of Ecclesiastical History at Trinity College Dublin, emphasised the shared faith of all Irish Protestants as a protection against 'foreign sway and jurisdiction as embodied in Papal claims and domination', his assumption being that this threat would be made manifest through the agency of a Home Rule parliament in Dublin. They in the Church of Ireland, Stokes proclaimed, 'recognise every orthodox Presbyterian, every sound Wesleyan, Congregationalist, and even Plymouth Brethren.'[52] Anglicans, Methodists and Presbyterians, in pamphlets, manifestos and speeches, all focused on the single dominant reason for their opposition to Home Rule: that it would usher in a period of Catholic political ascendancy. In 1893, the Reverend W. Nicholas, in a pamphlet explaining why Methodists were opposed to the measure, argued that it was evident that Roman Catholic influence must be predominant in an Irish parliament and that the dominant power in Nationalist ranks was the Church of Rome. He invoked the recent testimony of Henry Mathews, the British Home Secretary and a Roman Catholic, that the Protestants of Ireland would have reason to fear 'for their property, their liberties, and their faith' if the power of government and legislation were handed over to their hereditary enemies.[53] A parallel manifesto issued by the Presbyterian authorities about the same time suggested that their religious liberties would be imperilled under a Nationalist Home Rule parliament, 'the majority in which would be elected on the nomination of Roman Catholic priests.' This Parliament would claim and exercise the right to tax Protestants for the maintenance of Catholic religious institutions, would 'legalise the desecration of the Lord's Day', and would ultimately 'establish and endow the Roman Catholic Religion in Ireland'. The

---

50   Desmond Bowen, *History and the Shaping of Irish Protestantism* (New York, 1995), p. 370.

51   F. H. O'Donnell, *A History of the Irish Parliamentary Party* vol. 2 (London, 1910), pp. 381–3.

52   Cited in Bowen, *History and the Shaping*, p. 369.

53   Buckland, *Irish Unionism*, p. 76.

interesting feature of this argument is that what its Presbyterian proponents feared was that one religious ascendancy, that of the Church of Ireland disestablished in 1869, would be replaced by another, the Catholic Church, which would tax Protestants for the benefit of Catholics, just as the Church of Ireland, when established, taxed Catholics, through a system of tithes, for the benefit of its own institutions, educational as well as ecclesiastical.[54]

Fear of Catholic dominance under Home Rule was not limited to the clergy of the Protestant Churches; it was shared by members of their congregations. Protestants in the three Ulster counties, Cavan, Monaghan and Donegal, whose exclusion from Home Rule remained problematic, were increasingly alarmed when six-county exclusion began to be mentioned, even by George V, as the realistic form of partition. Members of the Monaghan branch of the Ulster Women's Unionist Council were alerted to the threat posed by the inclusion of Monaghan in an Irish Home Rule state. A militant opponent of such an arrangement, Miss Murray-Ker, told the Loyalist women of Monaghan that the prospect before them was that of 'being placed under a Dublin Roman Catholic parliament which would be under priestly influence and dominated – and this I fear most – by Mr Devlin's anti-Protestant Ancient Order of Hibernians.'[55] As a token of her resistance, Miss Murray-Ker offered her house as a UVF hospital in the event of a civil war in Ulster.

At its convention in Belfast in 1912, the Presbyterian Church devoted much of its agenda to protests against Home Rule. A new threat to the protection of the Protestant minority in Ireland and its long-term survival under Home Rule had emerged in 1908, when the Vatican issued the *Ne Temere* decree. For Catholics, this meant that Catholic canon law on marriage took precedence over common law: the decree meant that a mixed marriage performed according to law in a Protestant church, although legally valid, was declared by the Catholic Church to be no marriage, and the wife was considered to be living in concumbinage. It also meant that if marriage were performed before a priest in a Catholic church, a declaration had to be signed by both parties undertaking to bring their children up in the Catholic faith. Protestants of all denominations believed that marriage law under Home Rule would be framed in the spirit of *Ne Temere*, and that non-Catholics, undertaking marriage to Catholics, would be absorbed into the Catholic Church.

Ne Temere was merely one manifestation of a growing tendency in Catholicism to affirm with renewed vigour its claim to be the one true Christian Church, thereby widening the gulf between it and non-Catholic Churches. In 1894, persuaded by Cardinal Vaughan, Pope Leo XIII issued an

54 Desmond Bowen, *The Protestant Crusade in Ireland* (Dublin, 1978), pp. 157–77.

55 Cited in Jonathan Bardon, *A History of Ulster* (Belfast, 2001), p. 446.

encyclical letter *Ad Anglos* inviting the non-Catholic English population to make their submission to the Catholic Church. In the following year, he declared Anglican ordination 'utterly null and void' in his Bull *Apostolicae Curae*, thereby suggesting that Anglican bishops and clergy, as well as those in the Church of Ireland, were to be regarded as laymen. If there was to be union between the Catholic Church and those in the Anglican Communion, this, in the Catholic view, must involve the total submission of Anglicans to Papal authority. The impression made on Irish Protestants by *Apostolicae Curae and Ne Temere* only served to deepen their suspicion that a Home Rule parliament operating under Catholic auspices would be unlikely to respect or even tolerate, their religious convictions. It is a matter for ironic contemplation that Cardinal Cullen, in the initial stages of the Home Rule controversy in 1886, could be posthumously represented as having been strongly opposed to Home Rule for reasons quite contrary to those advanced by Loyalists. Far from believing that a Home Rule parliament would legislate in the interests of the Catholic religion, he had suggested that it would pass laws to weaken and ultimately destroy the influence of the Catholic Church.[56]

In 1885, Lord Randolph Churchill, in a letter published by Winston Churchill in his *Life* of his father, seemed to feel as Cullen did. He declared that he looked to the Irish Catholic bishops, 'who didn't give a snap for Home Rule,' having safely acquired control of education, 'to mitigate or to postpone the Home Rule onset.' Conservative Party policy, Churchill believed, should hinge on obtaining 'the confidence and friendship of the bishops.'[57] The implication of Churchill's observation was that the Catholic hierarchy could achieve their aims under the Westminster Parliament without the need for a Dublin one. The views of Cardinal Cullen and Lord Randolph Churchill should alert us to the fact that it would be misleading to assume a seamless unity of purpose between Home Rulers and their Sinn Féin successors in the leadership of Nationalism on the one hand and the Catholic Church leadership on the other. In fact, there was a strongly entrenched tradition of Irish Episcopal support for the British connection in the late eighteenth century and for the Union in the nineteenth. Violent threats to the continuance of the Union such as that of the Fenians in the 1860s were met with the sternest Episcopal strictures. The strongest champions of monarchy could be found in the ranks of eighteenth-century Irish Catholic bishops. Troy, the Archbishop of Dublin, was a notable example. In 1793, in his exposition of Church teaching on the relationship between Irish Catholic subjects and their

56   *The Tablet*, 27 Mar. 1886. Cullen died in 1878.

57   Churchill's comments were reproduced as anti-clerical Republican propaganda in *Sinn Féin*, 13 Oct. 1923.

Protestant King, Troy 'dismissed accusations of Catholic disloyalty by showing the very nature of the Catholic faith as Royalist.'[58] In 1798 the Irish Catholic bishops devoted a bilingual pastoral letter to outlining the duties of 'fealty and allegiance' owed by Catholics to King George III, the strict observance of which, they claimed 'has, for centuries back, marked the behaviour of Irish Catholics.' The law of God, they affirmed, clearly prescribed allegiance to King George as an indispensable duty, and should deter Catholics from having their royalist principles 'poisoned by the infectious influence' of those 'evil agents' promoting the Rebellion of 1798.[59] Many of the latter were northern Presbyterians. In some Fenian and post-Treaty Republican discourse, the Catholic Church establishment was characterised as an inveterate enemy of Irish independence. The Fenian John O'Leary claimed that the Catholic clergy expressed their opposition to Fenianism by deeming it a mortal sin 'even to wish that Ireland should be free', and by 'doing the work of the [British] enemy'.[60]

Leading Civil War Republican diehards, heirs to the Fenian tradition, saw the political role of the Catholic Church leadership much as O'Leary did. In 1922, Liam Mellows held that the members of the Irish Hierarchy were 'invariably wrong' in their political outlook, from the time they took sides with the British Government 'against the people': Adrian's Bull, Edward Bruce's War, the Union, the Fenian Rising, the Plan of Campaign, the Irish Volunteers, 1916 and the declared Republic.[61] Some of the older members of the Hierarchy had little sympathy with the independence movement and even less with the aspiration to establish a republic. A few, such as the conservative monarchist Bishop Kelly of Ross, would probably have been happier with the maintenance of British rule. Cardinal Logue declared the 1916 Rising 'foolish and pernicious'.[62] Like Cardinal Cullen before him, Logue expressed fears that Home Rule would be inimical to the interests of the Catholic Church. In 1911, as a measure of Home Rule seemed imminent, the parliamentary leaders of Nationalism, anxious to placate Unionists, were emphasising that a Home Rule parliament would be secular in character and deny any claims the Pope might make to interfere in Irish politics. This caused Logue to fear further that if Home Rule were granted, 'it would mean freedom for Irish Protestants

---

58 Marianne Elliott, *Wolfe Tone: Prophet of Irish Independence* (London, 1989), p. 204.

59 Quotations are from the Pastoral of Bishop Edward Ffrench of Elphin, 1 Apr. 1798, in B. Ó Cúiv (ed.), *Eigse* XI (n.d.), pp. 57–62.

60 John O'Leary, *Recollections of Fenians and Fenianism* (London, 1896), p. 199.

61 For Mellows see Seán Cronin (ed.), *The McGarrity Papers: Revelations of the Irish Revolutionary Movement in Ireland and America 1900–1940* (Tralee, 1972), p. 122.

62 D. W. Miller, *Church, State and Nation in Ireland, 1898–1921* (Dublin, 1973), pp. 11–12.

and forge shackles for Irish Catholics.'[63] Thus, in 1910, he made a pronouncement suggesting that Ireland should be given the same degree of freedom as
Canada had. As a consequence of the freedoms Canadians enjoyed, 'no people
were more devoted to the interests of the Empire than they were. Given
similar freedom, Irish people 'would be just as loyal in this country, if they
were not so already.'[64]

There is further evidence of the lack of support of the Catholic Church for
Home Rule. In 1915, Bishop Brownrigg of Ossory sent a letter to a local
recruiting meeting 'heartily endorsing the Allied cause and appealing in the
name of fallen and captured Kilkennymen for more Kilkenny recruits.'[65]
Bishop Browne of Cloyne maintained the friendliest contact with British
forces in Cobh both before and after the Anglo-Irish Treaty.[66] In 1917, Bishop
Morrisroe of Achonry, responding to the 1916 Rising, had no doubt that the
British administration in Ireland held authority from God, and condemned
those who argued that the people of Ireland 'owe no allegiance to the powers
that rule us in the country because the Union was effected by fraud.' His
answer was that 'the seal of our subjection is stamped on the current coin,' and
that existing rulers, the only lawful defenders of 'our persons and property,'
must be obeyed.[67] In 1915, Bishop Foley of Kildare and Leighlin, a strong
advocate, like many Catholic clergy, of the recruitment of Irishmen for British
regiments during the Great War, wrote to a meeting of the Red Cross in
Carlow of the need to ignore 'the handful of extremists' opposed to this. He
would, he declared, 'regard it as treason to the best interests of our country to
be led astray from the clear path of duty in this crisis of the fortunes of our
country and of the great world wide Empire, to which, in common with all
other constituents, we are proud to belong, and around which, in her day of
trial, we are expected, as loyal and devoted citizens, to rally as one man.'[68] In
1914, the Bishop of Derry, Charles McHugh, declared that 'the Irish people,
one and all, were with the arms of England.'[69]

It is one of the paradoxes of Irish political discourse that Catholic
Republicans often demonstrated an extreme attachment to the egalitarian
spirit which long distinguished low- church Protestantism, while Protestant

63 John Privilege, *Michael Logue and the Catholic Church in Ireland, 1879–1925* (Manchester, 2009),
    p. 91.
64 Ibid.
65 Ibid., p. 312.
66 Information from Canon Séamus Corkery, Charleville, Co. Cork.
67 *Roscommon Herald*, 24 Feb. 1917.
68 *Freeman's Journal*, 6 Jan. 1915.
69 Privilege, *Michael Logue*, p. 98.

Loyalists have been equally extreme in their devotion to a central element of Catholic ecclesiastical tradition, its monarchical character. During the Anglo-Irish Treaty debates in the Dáil, Piaras Beaslaí, a pro-Treaty Deputy, observed that the doctrinaire Republicans who opposed it had little or no historical warrant for their position. He suggested that Republicanism was an ideology alien to the sensibilities of Gaelic Ireland, whose instincts were firmly on the side of monarchy. Drawing on his knowledge of Gaelic literature and tradition, Beaslaí pointed out that 'all the old Gaelic poets sang of the going of the foreign hosts [the British] out of Ireland as an unreal dream of far off happiness.' They did not, he added, 'sing of a Republic. They sang of a Gaelic Monarch as a symbol of association between the three Kingdoms.'[70]

IV THE EMERGENCE OF PARTITION: HOME RULE
AS THE CATALYST

To trace the landmarks on the road to partition is to identify the stages of a long process, beginning in 1886 in the course of which Home Rule, and Ulster exclusion from this, gradually became inevitable. Definitions of the key terms of the Nationalist-Unionist dispute are uncontroversial. A useful definition of Home Rule is that provided in a Liberal Unionist handbook in 1887: 'Any scheme or policy which involves the establishment of a Parliament in Ireland, together with an Executive Government responsible to that Parliament.'[71] The other key term, Ulster exclusion – in effect partition – is less straightforward, and is subject to a number of differing interpretations based on how the various parties involved understood the meaning of 'Ulster,' and on what kind of exclusion they had in mind. The fundamental issue here was the extent of the geographical area to be excluded. At various times during the exclusion debate this was understood to mean the four Ulster counties with Unionist majorities: Antrim, Armagh, Londonderry and Down. At other stages, it was considered preferable to exclude all nine counties of the province of Ulster, until it eventually became clear that Ulster Loyalist interests would be best served by the exclusion of all of Ulster with the exception of Cavan, Monaghan and Donegal. Ulster exclusion from Home Rule was not simply a matter of deciding on a specific geographical area. An issue much in contention between the parties was whether exclusion should be temporary or permanent: Nationalists favouring the former, Unionists the latter. Then there was the matter of the governance of the excluded area. Would

---

70 *Dáil Debates*, Official Report, 3 Jan. 1922, p. 178.
71 Cited in Alan O'Day, *Irish Home Rule 1867–1921* (Manchester, 1998), p. 122.

jurisdiction over this be retained by the Westminster Parliament or would a separate Ulster legislature be created, resulting in two Irish Parliaments, one in Dublin and one in Belfast?

On 17 December 1885, Gladstone's son Herbert announced that his father had been converted to the cause of Irish Home Rule. On 1 February 1886, Gladstone was appointed Prime Minister, his Liberal administration having the support of a disciplined, effective Irish party with 86 Westminster MPs led by Parnell. On 8 April 1886, Gladstone introduced the first of his two Home Rule Bills, officially designated The Government of Ireland Bill, in the House of Commons. He had gradually, and painstakingly, reached the conclusion on moral, Christian and political grounds, that Ireland must be given Home Rule and that the Irish people were fitted for self government. He had, in addition, been deeply impressed by 'the strength and tenacity of the Irish demand' and 'the political genius of Parnell'.[72] During the Commons debate on the Bill, Parnell indicated the nature of the demand when, in a tribute to Gladstone, he declared that 'whatever may be the fate of this measure, the cause of Irish autonomy will have gained enormously in a way it could never otherwise have gained, by the genius of the Right Honourable gentleman.'[73] The Nationalist demand had been more emphatically expressed at a Home Rule conference in November 1873, when the first two resolutions declared that it was 'essentially necessary for the peace and prosperity of Ireland that the right of domestic legislation on all Irish affairs should be restored to our country,' and that the time had come for 'solemnly reassuring the inalienable right of the Irish people to self-government.'[74] Gladstone's Bill provided for the establishment of an Irish parliament in Dublin with an Irish executive responsible to it for the management of Irish domestic affairs. Large Imperial matters, including the Crown, foreign relations, peace and war, and armed forces, were reserved to the Parliament at Westminster. Ireland's share of the Imperial Contribution was set at one-fifteenth.[75] The terms of the 1886 measure were a significant advance on those offered under Grattan's Parliament in 1782. Under its Constitution, the Irish Executive under British control; under the terms of Gladstone's Bill, the Executive would be answerable to an Irish Parliament, although subject to the ultimate supremacy of the Imperial Parliament.[76]

72   Lyons, *Parnell*, p. 17.

73   *Hansard*, House of Commons, Vol. 304, Cols 1124–34, 8 Apr. 1886.

74   Edmund Curtis and R. B. Mc Dowell (eds), *Irish Historical Documents 1172–1922* (London, 1943), p. 276.

75   Details of the measure are in O'Day, *Irish Home Rule*, pp. 319–20.

76   See Lyons, *Parnell*, p. 348.

Gladstone's 1886 attempt to implement Home Rule was frustrated by a split in his own Liberal Party. Led by Lord Hartington, the Whig section, composed of right-wing Liberals who believed that an extension of a proposed measure of *local* government to Ireland would be going far enough in the circumstances, withheld support. The Radicals, led by Joseph Chamberlain, whose opposition to Home Rule led to his resignation from Gladstone's Cabinet in March 1886, convened a meeting on 31 May of over 50 Liberal MPs who decided to vote against the Bill on its second reading. This signalled the death of Home Rule for the immediate future: the Bill was defeated in the Commons by 341 votes to 311 on 8 June 1886. Whatever might have been the fate of the measure in the Commons, even if it had passed by a substantial majority there, it would certainly have been rejected in the House of Lords. Gladstone's well-meaning attempt to do what he thought best for Ireland exposed the fragility of the Liberal Party and the opportunism of the Conservatives, who were less interested in the fate of Ireland, or indeed of Ulster, than in turning Liberal advocacy of Home Rule to their own political advantage. Gladstone proved incapable of convincing either the majority of the House of Commons or public opinion of the merits of Home Rule. The opposition came from four principal quarters: Conservatives, two groups of dissident Liberals, Irish Unionists and British nonconformists.

There was no special provision for Ulster exclusion or for partition in Gladstone's Home Rule Bill of 1886, nor was there in either his 1893 measure or Asquith's 1914 Act. During the Commons debate on the 1886 Bill, it was clear that a major objection of opponents was the Government's failure to give special treatment to Ulster or the predominantly Protestant part of it. The Ulster dimension of the Home Rule agenda was a primary influence on Joseph Chamberlain's withdrawal of support from Gladstone and on his conversion from Radicalism to aggressive British patriotism and, more particularly, support for a separate Belfast administration.[77] All the main participants in the Home Rule debate recognised that the most troublesome issue was the future position within any settlement of the Loyalist Protestant minority in Ireland as a whole. During the Commons debate on the Bill, Gladstone rejected the idea that 'the Protestant minority in Ulster or elsewhere is to rule the question at large for Ireland.' He went on to conclude that the Protestant minority 'should have its wishes considered to the utmost practicable extent in any form which they may assume.' In calling for 'an unprejudiced discussion of Ulster's options,' he hinted at the possibility that Ulster, 'or perhaps with more appearance of reason, a portion of Ulster, should be excluded,' but insisted

---

77   See James Loughlin, 'Joseph Chamberlain, English Nationalism and the Ulster Question', *History* 77 (1992), p. 219.

that such concession should be made 'only after the principle of Home Rule had been agreed.' The exclusion of Ulster from Home Rule had thus, by 1886, crossed Gladstone's mind as a possibility and Joseph Chamberlain's as the preferred consequence of a Home Rule Act.[78]

A similar possibility had occurred to Thomas Babington Macaulay in 1833 during a debate in the Britain House of Commons on Daniel O'Connell's motion to repeal the Act of Union, the consequence of which would have been the establishment of a separate domestic legislature in Ireland. Macaulay maintained that the clearest ground which could be guessed at as the basis of O'Connell's repeal scheme 'would apply *a fortiori* to a separation of the legislatures of the North and South of Ireland.' Macaulay's key argument was that the same circumstances that might be invoked in favour of a separate parliament of Ireland could equally be invoked in favour of the exclusion of Ulster from the jurisdiction of that parliament. 'If a rooted difference of religion,' he declared, 'and the existence of the worst consequences of that difference, would justify the separation of the English and Irish legislatures, the same difference, and still more, the same baleful consequences, would warrant the separation of Protestant Ulster from Catholic Munster.' O'Connell's reasoning, Macaulay suggested, 'that only a domestic legislature would remedy a domestic grievance, would in a tenfold degree apply in favour of one domestic legislature in Dublin, and another in Derry, or some other large town in the North of Ireland.' Macaulay anticipated a twentieth-century Unionist argument against Home Rule when he described the project for the repeal of the Union as 'mere delusion,' but if it were practicable, 'there was no part of the Empire to which it would be so fatally ruinous as to Ireland itself.'[79]

O'Day identifies four propositions on which those who demanded Ulster exclusion based their arguments: 'its different history, the existence of a local Protestant plurality, the wishes of people there and the region's greater economic vitality and integration into the British and Atlantic markets.' O'Day, however, points out that the principal advocates of Ulster exclusion were British, not Irish, Unionists.[80] Some influential Ulster Unionist leaders and the generality of southern Unionists, while opposed to Home Rule, at the same time rejected Ulster exclusion. Colonel Edward Saunderson, MP for North Armagh and Chairman of the Ulster Unionist Party, declared in the course of the Home Rule debate that Ulster Unionists could not isolate themselves from their Unionist brethren in the south in the common battle

78   *Hansard*, House of Commons, Vol. 304, Cols 1053–4, 8 Apr. 1886; See J. L. Hammond, *Gladstone and the Irish Nation* (London, 1938), pp. 516–7.

79   *Hansard*, House of Commons, series 3, Vol. 1, Cols 258–9, 6 Feb. 1833.

80   O'Day, *Irish Home Rule*, pp. 113–14.

against Home Rule: he and his Ulster colleagues were 'prepared and determined to stand and fall, for weal or woe, with every loyal man who lives in Ireland.'[81] A Protestant-Nationalist MP, the Methodist William Abraham who represented County Limerick, suggested that the pan-Unionist alliance favoured by Colonel Saunderson would prevent either of the two main religious groupings in Ireland 'from being tyrannical or illiberal,' and that Ulster exclusion, and the attendant loss of Ulster Protestants to a truncated Home Rule Ireland would disturb the present religious equilibrium in the country as a whole.[82] William O'Brien, Nationalist MP for South Tyrone and ultimately a strong proponent of reconciliation with Unionists, saw in Gladstone's Home Rule proposal, 'a most marvellous plan' for recreating Irish society out of its ruins, as well as offering considerable benefit to Protestants, who would be the national minority under the proposal. As O'Brien put it, somewhat indelicately, it would be 'giving to a caste that is fallen and helpless such a chance as it has never had before, and never could have anticipated, and I must say as it scarcely deserves.'[83] The Protestants O'Brien had in mind were mainly those of the south and west of Ireland, described by John Redmond as being 'in such a miserable minority'.[84]

In 1893, Gladstonian Liberals and Irish Home Rulers had a majority of 40 in the House of Commons: 350 to 310. This gave Gladstone the confidence to introduce a second Home Rule Bill in that year. The Ulster case against all-Ireland Home Rule was pursued with much greater vigour than in 1886. Again, as in 1886, the absence of special arrangements for Ulster from Gladstone's latest Bill were deplored. At the recent General Election, a majority of the MPs elected for the province were opposed to Home Rule. T. W. Russell, an Ulster Unionist MP, outlined what the measure, if it became law, would mean for Ulster Protestants: 'the degradation of their civil rights, the loss of their religious freedom, and the commerce of their province placed at the mercy of people who had laid waste great tracts of the country.'[85] Addressing a rally at the Ulster Hall, during the Easter Parliamentary recess of 1893, Arthur Balfour, who exerted powerful influence in the British Conservative Party, encouraged Ulster opposition to Home Rule by implying that his Party would support Ulster Protestants in their refusal to recognise a Dublin parliament.[86] The introduction of the Bill prompted Ulster Unionists to organise widespread

---

81   *Hansard*, House of Commons, Vol. 304, Cols 1335–6, 12 Apr. 1886.

82   Ibid., Vol 304, Col. 1247, 9 Apr. 1886.

83   Ibid., Vol. 305, Col. 631, 10 May 1886.

84   Ibid., Vol. 305, Col. 970, 13 May 1886.

85   Ibid., series 4, Vol. 7, Col. 253, 9 Aug. 1892.

86   O'Day, *Irish Home Rule*, p. 162.

resistance. Two hundred Unionist clubs were formed, and the Ulster Defence Union was founded. At this time, as Edward Carson was to recall in 1911, there were extensive discussions among leading British and Irish Unionists on the Ulster Question, with Joseph Chamberlain 'particularly keen to pursue the case for Ulster exclusion, but the concerns for an all-Ireland Unionism prevailed.'[87] On 3 September 1893, however, Gladstone's second Home Rule Bill was passed by the House of Commons by 307 votes to 276. However, it was soon rejected by the House of Lords by 419 votes to 41. This defeat, and Gladstone's resignation from office and from the leadership of the Liberal Party, marked the suspension of his Party's engagement with Home Rule.

H. H. Asquith, a Gladstonian Home Ruler, became Prime Minister in 1908. Asquith won the support of the Irish Parliamentary Party for his abolition of the absolute veto of the House of Lords: the Parliament Act of 1911 removed from the Upper House the right to strike down a Bill outright, leaving it with the power to veto a Bill for up to two years only. This change removed a major obstacle to Home Rule, since there had been no prospect that the Lords would permit its enactment. Redmond supported Asquith on the Lords issue after the latter had committed the Liberal Party to Home Rule at the Royal Albert Hall prior to the General Election of 1910. The atmosphere of British politics underwent a radical transformation between 1909 and 1911. The Conservative-Irish Unionist alliance felt betrayed by three interlocked developments: the socially-progressive 'people's budget' of 1909–10, which was rejected by the House of Lords; the consequent diminution of the power of the Lords, and the Liberal alliance with the Irish Home Rulers, considered by Conservatives as 'a corrupt bargain'. The Liberal Government was accused by its opponents of having created a double constitutional crisis. By removing the Lords' veto on legislation passed by the Commons, Asquith and his ministers were accused of breaching the Constitution, giving England a unicameral parliament determined to implement a second major change, in the form of Irish Home Rule, which would lead to the dismemberment of the United Kingdom, without consulting the electorate.[88]

V ULSTER EXCLUSION: THE GROWING DEMAND

With Home Rule becoming increasingly likely under Asquith's Premiership, influential Unionist intellectuals with close associations with the British Conservative Party began to canvass the possibility of Ulster exclusion. Two of

---

87   Carson Memorandum, 18 Nov. 1911. Cited by Alvin Jackson, *Home Rule: An Irish History, 1800–2000* (London, 2003), p. 120.

88   D. G. Boyce, in Peter Collins (ed.), *Nationalism and Unionism*, p. 92.

these, J. L. Garvin, Editor of *The Observer*, and John St Loe Strachey, Editor of *The Spectator*, have a special importance in the history of partition. By 1910, Garvin had come to believe that if northern Unionists did not wish to participate in an all-Ireland assembly based in Dublin, it would not be desirable to coerce them into joining such a body. As a solution, which he offered tentatively with regret, he suggested that 'a distinct Belfast Assembly for the great northern Conclave' might be necessary. He did not advocate what he called the 'permanent vivisection' of Ireland. Instead, he visualised an Irish Upper House or National Council for the whole of Ireland, 'elected under conditions ensuring the predominance of moderate opinion,' to deal with matters of common concern, such as railways and marketing, relating to all parts of Ireland. Ulster might be given the opportunity to decide whether to 'throw in its lot completely with the common Irish system.' If the Dublin Parliament desired this outcome, 'it would have to subordinate everything to the goal of winning Ulster over,' and promote 'the definite reconciliation of sects and classes North and South.'[89] Later, in 1914, Garvin was to suggest the establishment of two parliaments in Ireland.[90] Garvin's scheme anticipated important features of the Government of Ireland Act of 1920, with its two legislatures and its provision for unity, and the Anglo-Irish Treaty of 1921, with its similar provisions.

St Loe Strachey, another pioneer of partition, began lobbying senior Unionists on the possibility of Ulster county option and exclusion in 1910–11. At the end of October 1910, on the day before Garvin's article appeared in *The Observer*, Strachey wrote to the Unionist lawyer William Moore setting out a detailed plan of exclusion whereby individual Irish counties could vote themselves out of the Home Rule scheme, and then be treated for administrative purposes as English counties. If this proved impossible to attain, Unionists should insist that Home Rule be granted for both the north and the south of Ireland. The political separation of the two underlying Strachey's plan was based on the assumption that Ireland consisted of two nations, an Irish and a British, and that political separation represented a just and logical way of confronting that fact.[91] A year later in November 1911, Strachey wrote to Bonar Law that there were 'two nations in Ireland, and therefore two national units.'[92] Strachey's thoughts on the Irish question are expounded at length in

---

89   *The Observer*, 30 Oct. 1910.

90   Ibid., 1 Nov. 1914. For Garvin's contribution to the exclusion debate, see G. K. Peatling, *British Opinion and Irish Self Government 1865–1925: From Unionism to Liberal Commonwealth* (Dublin, 2001), p. 129.

91   For a good treatment of Strachey's ideas, see Jackson, *Home Rule*, pp. 121–2. Jackson asserts that Strachey believed in the merits of partition from the start, and that his proposal for Ulster exclusion was not merely a device to expose the folly of the Home Rule project.

92   Ibid., p. 122.

his undated autobiography, published in the aftermath of the Treaty. He believed that when Home Rule became almost inevitable after 1918, the partition of Ireland was the only means of avoiding civil war. He would have preferred to see the six-county area 'become one or two English counties,' but this being unrealistic, 'the setting up of the Northern Legislature and the Northern State became the inevitable compromise.'

His ideas for dealing with the rest of Ireland following Ulster exclusion are interesting. He would not force the southern Irish 'Protestants and Roman Catholic Loyalists to forfeit their citizenship of the British Empire,' but allow them instead 'to come away from the South with full compensation for their disturbance' if they so desired. As for the remainder in southern Ireland, he would have preferred to see the 26 counties 'detached from the Empire,' having himself no desire to be 'a fellow-citizen with Mr de Valera or any other Sinn Féiner, Regular or Irregular, or again, with the Hierarchy of the Roman Catholic Church in Ireland', since these had 'evidently different views on the crime of murder than those of the rest of the British race.' The British people must, he believed, give up any attempt to teach an incorrigible Ireland better. Since Nationalist Ireland had failed to grasp the truth 'that to be included in the British Empire is one of the highest and greatest privileges obtainable by any community', Strachey was not going down on his knees 'to beg an unwilling southern Ireland to enjoy this privilege.'[93] On 26 August 1911, Augustine Birrell, Chief Secretary for Ireland, made a significant intervention in the Home Rule debate when, in a letter to Winston Churchill, he raised the possibility of Ulster exclusion; each of the nine counties in the province might decide individually whether to join or remain aloof from an Irish parliament for a period of time. This was the county option formula, which was to feature prominently in discussions of Home Rule between 1911 and 1916. Birrell believed that the procedure he suggested would probably mean that all nine Ulster counties, with the exception of Antrim and Down, would offer majority support for Home Rule.[94]

Effective Unionist resistance to Home Rule got under way in 1911, the year before Asquith brought the third Liberal Home Rule Bill before the House of Commons. The campaign of resistance organised by the leadership of Ulster Unionism was enthusiastically supported by influential British Conservatives, including Bonar Law and F. E. Smith, later Lord Birkenhead. Conservative and Unionist opposition to Home Rule was based on the argument that it

93   St Loe Strachey, *The Adventures of Living: A Subjective Autobiography* (London, n.d.), pp. 293–4.
94   Birrell's suggestion is discussed in Patricia Jalland, *The Liberals and Ireland: The Ulster Question in British Politics to 1914* (Brighton, 1980), p. 59.

would deprive Ulster Protestants of their 'birthright'.[95] Irish Unionist MPs responded to the challenge of Home Rule by persuading Edward Carson to assume the leadership of their Party in February 1910. Carson and Captain James Craig, spokesman for the Ulster Unionist MPs since 1906, became leaders of the Irish Unionist Campaign against Home Rule. Craig organised a massive protest demonstration at his home at Craigavon with two aims in mind: to indicate the strength of Loyalist opposition to Home Rule, and to introduce Carson to his northern supporters. The demonstration, on 23 September 1911, was a striking success. Carson told over 50,000 men from Orange Lodges and Unionist clubs that he was ready to enter into a compact with them to defeat what he called 'the most nefarious conspiracy that has ever been hatched against a free people.' He proposed a plan of campaign against the imposition of Home Rule. Should the measure pass, Unionists would ignore it, and take responsibility 'for the government of the Protestant province of Ulster.'[96] Carson's proposal for the self exclusion of Ulster from any measure of Home Rule was at least partly motivated by his conviction that the Irish Nationalist leadership would not accept Home Rule with Ulster excluded. If, therefore, Carson believed, Ulster Loyalists could show that they would fight rather than submit to Home Rule, then the British Government, in the absence of any Irish support for the measure, would be obliged to abandon it.[97]

The Ulster Unionist Council followed Carson's startling incitement to unconstitutional action by setting up a commission to draft a constitution for Loyalist Ulster and to prepare the way for taking over the civil administration. Just before Asquith introduced his Home Rule Bill on 11 April 1912, a modest measure of self government proposing a separate parliament for Ireland as a whole with jurisdiction over internal affairs, Ulster Unionists organised a mass demonstration at Balmoral, a suburb of Belfast, on Easter Tuesday, 9 April 1912. By the beginning of 1912, however, the strength of Unionist feeling against the proposed measure had already prompted leading Liberals to reconsider the imposition of unconditional Home Rule on Ulster. In February 1912, the possibility of Ulster exclusion again came to the fore when Lloyd George and Winston Churchill urged county option for Ulster in Cabinet. On 7 February 1912, Asquith wrote to King George V, who was soon to become an advocate for the rights of Ulster Loyalists, that public opinion might demand special treatment for Ulster.[98] Bonar Law, Conservative Party

---

95 F. S. L. Lyons, *Ireland since the Famine* (London, 1974), pp. 301–3.

96 See A. T. Q. Stewart, *Edward Carson* (Dublin, 1981), pp. 72–3; Beckett, *The Making of Modern Ireland*, p. 425.

97 See Beckett, *The Making of Modern Ireland*. p. 425.

98 O'Day, *Irish Home Rule*, pp. 246–7.

Leader since 1911, accompanied by 70 English, Scottish and Welsh MPs, addressed the crowds at Balmoral, and 100,000 mean marched past the platform. This event, as Stewart puts it, 'solemnised the wedding of Protestant Ulster and the Conservative and Unionist Party', and made it evident that Unionist opposition to Home Rule was going to assume the character of a religious crusade.[99] The solemn proceedings at Balmoral opened with prayers by the Church of Ireland Primate John Baptist Crozier, and the Moderator of the Presbyterian Church led in the singing of the 90th Psalm. Caught up in the passion of the event was Charles Frederick D'Arcy, Bishop of Down, Connor and Dromore, who addressed the men and dedicated the colours of various detachments of the Protestant Ulster Volunteers.[100] The climax of Bonar Law's public advocacy of the cause of Ulster was the great rally held on 29 July 1912, at Blenheim Palace, the seat of the Duke of Marlborough. This was a Conservative Party demonstration also attended by Edward Carson, together with 120 Unionist MPs and some 40 Peers, including the Duke of Norfolk, the leading Catholic layman in England. The presence of the latter aroused fury among Irish Nationalists.

Bonar Law's contribution to the proceedings achieved notoriety for its extreme militancy. Now absorbed heart and soul in the Ulster cause, Law, the son of a Presbyterian Minister from Coleraine,[101] described Asquith's Government as 'a revolutionary committee which has seized upon domestic power by fraud.' He doubted whether the Government would dare to force Ulster Protestants to submit to the rule of a Dublin parliament, and then made the declaration which in effect was 'to break the conventions on which Parliamentary democracy is based'.[102] If an attempt were made, he declared, to deprive Ulster men of their birthright, 'they would be justified in resisting such an attempt by all means in their power, including force.'[103] The contribution of Bonar Law to the cause of Ulster exclusion from Home Rule can scarcely be overestimated, as his biographer, Robert Blake has pointed out. Blake observes that the survival of the six counties as an autonomous province of the United Kingdom is in no small measure the achievement of Bonar Law. Blake argues that 'without his much criticised decision to pledge the whole of the English Conservative Party to the Ulster cause, it is unlikely that Ulster

99   Stewart, *Edward Carson*, p. 77.
100 For an account of the Balmoral demonstration, see Robert Blake, *The Unknown Prime Minister: The Life and Times of Andrew Bonar Law 1858–1923* (London, 1955), p. 129.
101 Bowen, *History and Shaping*, p. 373.
102 Blake, *Unknown Prime Minister*, p. 130.
103 Ibid., p. 130.

would stand where she does to-day.'[104] During 1913, Bonar Law was contemplating a mass Unionist withdrawal from Parliament as a means of frustrating the passage of the Home Rule Bill, and as an alternative, 'provoking such disorders as to bring the proceedings to a standstill.'[105]

On 28 September 1912, designated 'Ulster Day,' the Old Testament religious dimension of Ulster opposition to Home Rule was affirmed when 237,386 Ulster men signed 'Ulster's Solemn League and Covenant', and 234,046 women signed a parallel declaration.[106] Those who subscribed their names to the covenant affirmed that they were 'loyal subjects of His Gracious Majesty King George V, humbly relying on God whom our fathers in days of stress and trial confidently trusted.' They also declared themselves convinced that Home Rule would be 'disastrous to the well being of Ulster as well as the whole of Ireland,' in addition to being subversive of their civil and religious freedom, destructive of their citizenship, and 'perilous to the unity of the Empire'. More tellingly, they threatened that in the event of a Home Rule parliament being forced upon them, they pledged themselves 'to refuse to recognise its authority.'[107] The extraterrestrial aspect of the Covenant was later recognised by *The Times* of London, which saw it as 'a mystical affirmation' through which 'Ulster seemed to enter into an offensive and defensive alliance with the Deity.'[108] At a more mundane level, Ulster resistance to Home Rule was more menacingly expressed in the creation of the paramilitary Ulster Volunteer Force, which, by 1913, with over 90,000 part-time volunteers, had virtually created a state within a state, and by 1914 had the added bargaining power of 25,000 rifles and three million rounds of ammunition.

In 1914, the British and Imperial dimensions of the Ulster question were made strongly manifest, first through the contribution of the Ulster Union Defence League, whose object was 'the rescue of the white settler colony of Ulster from submersion in a sea of inferior Celts.'[109] The leadership of this primarily British Unionist organisation included Walter Long, who was to be chief architect of the 1920 Government of Ireland Act, and Lord Milner. The latter, who was to be Colonial Secretary from 1919 to 1921, sought and received large sums of money from prominent Imperialist financiers, publicists and landed millionaires, among them Rudyard Kipling, Lord Rothschild, The

---

104 Ibid., p. 531. See also Kevin Matthews, *Fatal Influence: The Impact of Ireland on British Politics 1920–1925* (Dublin, 2004), pp. 109–10, for a similar assessment.

105 Roy Jenkins, *Asquith, Portrait of a Man and an Era* (New York, 1964), p. 282.

106 Stewart, *Edward Carson*, p. 77. See Jackson, *Home Rule*, pp. 159–60.

107 The Covenant is reproduced in facsimile in Buckland, *Irish Unionism*, p. 224.

108 *The Times*, 6 May 1913.

109 Paul Johnson, *A History of the English People* (London, 1985), p. 350.

Earl of Iveagh, Lord Astor and the Duke of Bedford. The money was to be used for the purchase of arms and ammunition for the Ulster Volunteer Force, helping to fund the Larne gun running enterprise of April 1914. In the same year, another wave of Imperialist support for Ulster came with the publication in March of the British Covenant, modelled on the 1912 Ulster Solemn League and Covenant. The first signatories of the British version included Kipling, Sir Edward Elgar the composer of 'Pomp and Circumstance' and Earl Roberts of Kandahar, the most popular living British soldier, who recommended the appointment of General Sir George Richardson of the Indian Army as Generalissimo of the UVF.[110]

The first specific formal parliamentary proposal in the period for the partition of Ireland dates to 11 June 1912, when two Liberals, Agar-Robartes and Neil Primrose, moved an amendment to Asquith's Home Rule Bill which could have made acceptance of the proposed Home Rule Parliament conditional upon the exclusion of the counties of Antrim, Armagh, Down and Derry[111] from its jurisdiction. Agar Robartes, a young Liberal of strongly Protestant views, proposed the amendment, which was seconded by Primrose, whose father, Lord Rosebery, had been Prime Minister and leader of the Liberal Unionists who broke with Gladstone when the latter made Home Rule for Ireland part of the programme of the Liberal Party. It must be noted that Agar-Robartes and Primrose were not opposed to the principle of Home Rule for Ireland. Nevertheless they felt that their compromise amendment permitting the exclusion from its provisions of the four Ulster counties in which Protestants could claim to be in a majority would meet Unionist fears of coercion and of being governed from Dublin. The House of Commons debate on the Agar-Robartes amendment gave Carson an opportunity to explain the Unionist attitude to Home Rule and to partition in the summer of 1912. Carson declared that he would vote for the amendment because it would make the Home Rule Bill unworkable, but that he could never accept a settlement which excluded Tyrone and Fermanagh from a Unionist-controlled enclave. More significantly, he made it clear that he was less concerned with areas to be excluded from the operation of the Bill than with the absolute rejection of Home Rule for any part of Ireland.[112]

The amendment attracted no support from any of the British parties. But Walter Long, who was to play a vital role in the partition of Ireland as Chairman of the Cabinet Committee on the Irish Question in 1919, suggested that 'local powers to a suitable historical and geographical area might be given

---

110 Jackson, *Home Rule*, p. 120.

111 Mansergh, *Nationalism and Independence*, p. 13.

112 *Hansard*, House of Commons Debates, Vol. 46, Col. 1076, 13 June 1912.

subject to central government.'[113] Towards the close of 1912, three Ulster MPs, including Carson, advanced the exclusion debate when, on 28 December they sponsored an amendment to Asquith's Home Rule Bill to exclude the nine Ulster counties. The amendment, debated on 1 January 1913, represented an implied concession by British and Irish Unionists of Home Rule for Ireland minus Ulster, a solution not welcome to southern Unionists. To reassure the latter, Carson, while arguing for Ulster exclusion, purported to be urging support for his amendment as a means of defeating Asquith's entire measure.[114] Jalland[115] sees the Agar-Robartes Amendment of 11 June 1912 as the point when most British Unionists tacitly recognised the inevitability of Home Rule for the south, with Ulster excluded.

The momentum for Ulster exclusion was maintained throughout 1913, as the Ulster Unionist campaign won the sympathy of the King, the Army and the British public. Through the spring and summer of 1913, the King received numerous constitutional complaints and much advice on how to deal with Ulster from Unionist leaders, elder statesmen and anonymous sympathisers with the Ulster cause. He sought the views of opposition leaders, including Bonar Law and Lord Lansdowne. In an audience with Asquith on 11 August 1913, he conveyed his fears about the effect of the Ulster situation upon the Crown; he was especially concerned that Home Rule would 'certainly alienate Ulster Protestants' from him.[116] A letter to Asquith on 22 September indicated that the King was profoundly influenced by Conservative arguments against Home Rule per se. The purpose of his letter was to dissuade Asquith from proceeding with Home Rule until after a General Election. The generality of Irish people, the King argued, were no longer enthusiastic for it. What would happen if 'tumult and riot' occurred when Home Rule was forced on Ulster? The possible use of the Army as the agent of such enforcement was of vital concern to George V. By 'birth, religion and environment' soldiers might have 'strong feelings on the Irish question', in this context, favourable to the Loyalist cause. Would it then be fair, the King asked rhetorically, to expect the Sovereign 'as head of the Army to subject the discipline, and indeed the loyalty of his troops, to such a strain?' The King made the interesting claim, not entirely without substance, that 'the hierarchy of the Church of Rome is indifferent, and probably at heart would be glad not to come under the power of an Irish Parliament.'[117] This latter point of view had earlier been expressed by Cardinal

---

113   Notes on Ulster, Desmond FitzGerald Papers, UCDA P80/363 (5).

114   *Hansard*, House of Commons, Vol. 46, Cols 377–91, 1 Jan. 1913.

115   Jalland, *The Liberals and Ireland*, p. 94.

116   Jenkins, *Asquith*, pp. 282–3.

117   Ibid., p. 285.

Cullen, as already mentioned in this chapter, who, in a statement first made public during the 1886 Home Rule controversy, feared that a Home Rule parliament, whose strength, he thought, would come from revolutionary sources, would pass laws 'to weaken and destroy' the influence of the Catholic Church, and restrain the Catholic bishops 'in the performance of their undoubted duty'.[118]

On 22 January 1914, Asquith's Cabinet decided to propose another veto on any act of a Dublin parliament which might affect adversely the Protestant counties. The King told Asquith that this was not enough to satisfy Loyalists: 'I have always given you as my opinion,' he reminded Asquith, almost as if he were a Unionist spokesman, 'that Ulster will never agree to send representatives to an Irish Parliament in Dublin, no matter what safeguards or guarantees you may provide', and went on to hint at further concessions for Loyalists.[119] In April 1914, the King made Asquith aware of the nature of the concerns he had in mind. He wanted the six counties to be allowed to contract out without a plebiscite and for an indefinite period in the interests of a peaceful solution, and in view of the 'terrible position in which he, the King, would be placed if that solution was not found'.[120] The King's assessment of the dangers which would attend the enforcement of Home Rule on an unwilling Ulster was in accord with that of Bonar Law. On 26 January 1914, the latter warned Lord Stamfordham, the King's secretary, that Asquith's Government had only two courses open to it: submit the Home Rule Bill to the judgement of the people in an election or prepare to face the consequences of civil war.[121] The King's concerns about putting the loyalty of the Army to the test were justified on 20 March 1914, when a group of Army officers at the Curragh Camp signified their intention to resign their commissions rather than use force against Ulster resistance to Home Rule. This affair made it evident that the Army could not safely be employed to impose Home Rule on Ulster. The landing of 35,000 rifles at Larne, County Antrim between 24 and 25 April 1914 was a further confirmation of the power of Ulster Unionists to prevent Home Rule. The decision to import these armaments was taken by Carson in January 1914, with the possible knowledge and approval of the Conservative leadership, one member of which, Walter Long, who had strong southern Unionist connections, helped to fund the enterprise.[122]

---

118 Cullen's comments, originally published in *The Tablet*, an English Catholic weekly, on 27 Mar. 1886, were used as anti-Home Rule propaganda by the Irish Loyal and Patriotic Union, a southern Unionist organisation.

119 Jenkins, *Asquith*, p. 300.

120 Ibid., p. 316.

121 Blake, *The Unknown Prime Minister*, p. 169.

122 Jackson, *Home Rule*, p. 133.

Between the autumn of 1913 and the spring of 1914, events moved towards narrowing the ground on the Ulster problem. Lloyd George influenced Cabinet policy 'intermittently but powerfully' in the direction of an Ulster exclusion compromise, enthusiastically supported by Winston Churchill.[123] In September 1913, Winston Churchill told Bonar Law, who in turn told Carson, that he had long thought 'it might be well to leave Ulster as she is', as part of Great Britain, and 'to have some form of Home Rule for the rest of Ireland'. Having thus conceded the principles of Ulster exclusion and of Home Rule for what remained of Ireland, Churchill, worried about the residual problem: 'The whole question as to the exclusion of Ulster turns on this, whether or not it would be regarded as betrayal by the solid body of Unionists in the South and West.'[124] With characteristic acuity, Churchill here anticipated the difficulty Carson would have to contend with from 1919 to 1920. Carson concurred in Churchill's exclusion of Ulster, sensing that 'things are shaping towards a desire to settle on terms of leaving Ulster out.' However, he had difficulty in defining the excluded Ulster. His own view was that 'the whole of Ulster should be excluded, but the minimum would be the plantation counties and for that a good case could be made.'[125] Having had secret talks with Bonar Law in October and on 6 November 1913, Asquith arrived at an exclusion plan for Ulster. This envisaged the temporary exclusion of an undetermined portion of the province, but did not involve giving this Ulster area a parliament and executive of its own: legislation should remain with the Imperial Parliament, since Ulstermen, if they were not to sacrifice their root principle, could not recognise any other parliament.[126]

Equally significantly for Ulster exclusion, John Redmond, on 2 March 1914, agreed with Asquith's proposal, formulated by Lloyd George, that counties had the right to decline Home Rule where this course was favoured by a simple majority in a plebiscite. Under pressure, Redmond agreed to a six-year exclusion period with automatic inclusion after that. Carson, while acknowledging that the acceptance by Asquith and Redmond of the principle of exclusion was an advance, nevertheless adopted the position that he was to maintain to the end, and that was ultimately to prevail in 1925. 'Ulster,' he told the Commons, 'wants this question settled now and for ever. We do not want sentence of death and a stay of execution for six years.'[127] On 23 May 1914, the

---

123　Jalland, *The Liberals and Ireland*, p. 143.

124　Blake, *The Unknown Prime Minister*, p. 156.

125　Jalland, *The Liberals and Ireland*, p. 147. By the 'six plantation counties' Carson meant Ulster without Cavan, Donegal and Monaghan. The original six plantation counties were Donegal, Cavan, Coleraine (later Londonderry), Tyrone, Fermanagh and Armagh.

126　Jenkins, *Asquith*, p. 291.

127　Parliamentary Reports, House of Commons, Vol. 15, Cols 933–4, 9 Mar. 1914.

Government introduced an Amending Bill in the House of Lords to receive the Royal assent simultaneously with Home Rule. The new Bill would provide for counties to exclude themselves from the provisions of the Home Rule measure for six years. The third reading of the new Bill passed in the House of Commons on 25 May, but on 2 July the Lords substituted permanent exclusion of nine counties without a plebiscite, going even further than the King had suggested in April. Since this amending Bill was unlikely to pass in the Commons, stalemate was reached. During the first half of July 1914, Asquith, anxious for a compromise, used a variety of intermediaries: Lloyd George interviewed Redmond and Dillon together; Lord Murray, the former Liberal Chief Whip, saw Carson. The aim of these discussions was a sensible one: to try and limit the differences between the sides to the single question of geography.[128] Geography, however, given the complexity of the demographic patterns in the counties at stake, gave rise to an intractable problem: what to do about Tyrone. On this, there was no agreement between the parties. Nor is it easy to see how there could have been, given that both Carson and Redmond wanted Tyrone in its entirety for his own side. The problem here was that the majority of the inhabitants of east, west and north Tyrone were Catholic, while the majority of inhabitants in both south Tyrone and north Fermanagh were Protestant.

The final pre-war attempt at a settlement was the Buckingham Palace Conference, convened at the suggestion of George V between 21 and 24 July 1914. Asquith and Lloyd George represented the Government, Bonar Law the Conservative opposition, John Redmond and John Dillon MP the Irish Parliamentary Party, and Sir Edward Carson and Sir James Craig the Ulster Unionists. Lord Lansdowne, a Kerry landlord who was Conservative Leader in the House of Lords, and a former British Secretary of State for War, thus wielding considerable political influence, represented the southern Unionists. Lansdowne's interest was in trying to preserve the Union as a whole, and not in salvaging the North East for loyalism. Carson's position was similar to that taken by the King and the House of Lords: he was, as Rankin remarks, 'nurturing his own idea of a 'clean cut' without recourse to time limits and plebiscites.'[129] Redmond's position, as recorded in his own memorandum of the Conference, and published by Gwynn, was that the time limit for Ulster exclusion would be contingent on the area to be excluded.[130] In a memorandum he circulated to the Conference, Redmond provided statistical evidence

---

128 Michael Brock and Eleanor, Brock (eds), *H. H. Asquith: Letters to Venetia Stanley* (Oxford, 1982), p. 105.

129 K. J. Rankin, 'The search for statutory Ulster', *History Ireland* (May/June 2009), p. 30.

130 Denis Gwynn, *The History of Partition, 1912–1935* (Dublin, 1950), p. 119.

based on the most recent census, that of 1911, to show that Catholics formed the same proportional majorities in Fermanagh and Tyrone as Protestants did in counties Derry and Armagh, where the combined Catholic minority was actually greater than the combined Protestant minority in Fermanagh and Tyrone by 5,258.[131] As was the case with the previous attempt to reach consensus, Tyrone proved the fundamental obstacle. Redmond could not agree to Carson's opposition to allowing any part of Tyrone to be included in Home Rule, pointing out that in three of the four Parliamentary divisions in the county, Catholics were 54.7, 54.8 and 62.6 per cent of the population, while in the other division, the south, Protestants had a small majority: 51.3 per cent as against 48.7.[132]

To avert a breakdown of the Conference, the Speaker of the House of Commons, James Lowther, who presided, suggested that Tyrone should be excluded from Home Rule at the beginning, but that following a plebiscite, the county should be able to come into the Irish Parliament after a short period. Carson observed that this proposal had the defect that Tyrone would be excluded only for a short period, after this it would 'certainly be included under the Home Rule Bill.'[133] In this way Carson acknowledged that if given the choice of a plebiscite, the majority in Tyrone would vote for Home Rule, an issue which was to be dramatically revived during the proceedings of the Boundary Commission in 1924/5. Asquith, much frustrated by the contention about Tyrone, described the county as 'the most damnable creation of the perverted ingenuity of man.' He identified as the most extraordinary feature of the discussion, the complete agreement (in principle) of Redmond and Carson: each said 'I must have the whole of Tyrone or die, but I quite understand why you say the same.'[134] The most significant aspect of the Buckingham Palace Conference was the agreement reached by all parties on the central issue: that all or part of Ulster had to be excluded from Home Rule, whether this meant six counties, as Bonar Law thought it should, the nine-county arrangement which Carson suggested, and thought Redmond should be willing to accept as facilitating the earliest possible unity of Ireland, or a smaller unit than the six-county one that Redmond had in mind. Partition was now the agreed basis for discussion, whatever the area on which it was to be based.[135] All that remained was for the parties to determine the nature and extent of this partition. European events soon made all discussion impossible for the immediate

131 Rankin, 'The search for statutory Ulster', p. 30, for statistics supplied by Redmond.

132 Gwynn, *The History of Partition*, p. 125.

133 Ibid., p. 129.

134 Cited by Rankin, 'The search for statutory Ulster,' p. 31.

135 See Gwynn, *History of Partition*, pp. 121–3.

future. On 4 August 1914, Britain was at war with Germany, and all the parties suspended consideration of the Irish boundary to concentrate on the War effort. This was supported, at least initially, by a large majority of Irish people.

VI ULSTER EXCLUSION: THE FINAL PHASE – WARTIME EFFORTS AT SETTLEMENT

The Home Rule Act, officially the Government of Ireland Act, 1914, was placed upon the Statute Book in October 1914. This was by no means a grant of unqualified Home Rule to Ireland. There were two major qualifications on this. A Suspensory Act (1914), associated with the Home Rule Act, deferred the operation of the latter until after the conclusion of the Great War. Of much greater significance was the understanding that the British Parliament would have the opportunity, at the end of the War, to pass a measure amending the 1914 Home Rule Act and exempting Ulster, or part of it, from its effect. The outbreak of the Great War had a profound effect on the fortunes of traditional Irish nationalism. With the progress of the conflict, the political influence of the Irish Parliamentary Party at Westminster diminished, particularly when the two major British parties united in common cause against the Central Powers, Germany and the Austro-Hungarian Empire. In May 1917, the British War Cabinet included Carson as Attorney General, while Craig was to retain minor ministerial posts in the Government until 1920. Their allies Bonar Law and Arthur Balfour also served in wartime cabinets, the former joining Lloyd George's War Cabinet in December 1916 as Chancellor of the Exchequer, the latter joining Asquith's 1915 Cabinet as First Lord of the Admiralty. Unionists predominated in Lloyd George's Coalition Government of December 1916, which helped to restore Ulster Loyalist belief in the British Government's capacity to maintain the United Kingdom against the disruptive forces of an emerging militant republican nationalism.

The second major event which was to radicalise Irish Nationalist politics was the Rising in Dublin in April 1916, and the British Government's ruthless and ill-judged response to it. Within three years, the heirs to the 1916 Rising generated a much more radical demand than the measure of Home Rule involving some form of Ulster exclusion in which the Irish Parliamentary Party had come to acquiesce. The new demand was for an all-Ireland Republic independent of the United Kingdom. This demand was endorsed by the southern Irish electorate in the General Election of December 1918, which returned 78 Sinn Féin candidates, and virtually eliminated the Irish Parliamentary Party, which returned only 6. When the elected representatives of Sinn Féin used their mandate to establish Dáil Éireann as the national parliament, and declined to attend the Imperial Parliament, the Republican demand was formally affirmed in January 1919. It seems not unreasonable to say, as D. G. Boyce remarks, 'that the partition of Ireland, unthinkable in the Home Rule episodes of 1886 and 1893, but emerging, painfully, as the possible base of some from of compromise in 1913–14 was, after the Easter Rising, hard to avoid.'[136] J. L. Garvin, who had followed Irish affairs all his life, writing during the Irish War of Independence in March 1921, was conscious that 'the triumph of Sinn Féin extremists,' fighting in the spirit of 1916, would make 'irreparable the breach between Ulster and the rest' and by extension, mean Ulster exclusion.[137] Patricia Jalland contemplates the possibility that the Irish problem would have been solved between 1911 and 1914 if Asquith had provided special terms for Ulster in the 1912 Home Rule Bill. Such a settlement, she argues, 'would at least have provided a starting point and offered better prospects for the evolution of a more stable, non-violent relationship between the North and the South of Ireland and Great Britain. This might gradually have developed into Dominion status and ultimate independence for the South, without the tragedy of 1916 and the bloody events of 1919–21.' At the end of this vista, Jalland even glimpses a United Ireland.[138]

The impact of the Rising on popular Irish Nationalism was not immediate. It was, however, quickly followed by British Government action to deal with the Home Rule question. The Rising, and the manner in which it was suppressed, enlarged the international dimension of the Nationalist case for Home Rule, the implementation of which was increasingly seen on all sides as essential to good Anglo-American wartime relations. In August and September 1914, Nationalist leaders, among them Redmond and T. P. O'Connor, had warned British ministers that Irish-American opinion would be active against Britain if Home Rule continued to be postponed. Unionists were being warned by their American sources that 'incredible harm' would be done to the British cause if the Irish question remained an active political issue. The Liberal and Conservative Parties were acutely aware of the significance of the Home Rule question in determining the American attitude to the War.[139] American pressure on Britain for an Irish settlement intensified as American entry into the war appeared more and more likely. Shortly before declaring

136   D. G. Boyce, 'The Ulster crisis: prelude to 1916', in Gabriel Doherty and Dermot Keogh (eds), *1916: The Long Revolution* (Cork, 2007), p. 60.

137   Cited in Peatling, *British Opinion*, p. 155.

138   Jalland, *Liberals and Ireland*, p. 262.

139   Patricia Jalland and John Stubbs, 'The Irish Question after the outbreak of war in 1914: some unfinished party business', *English Historical Review* (*EHR*) Vol. 96, No. 377 (1981), p. 786.

war in April 1917, President Wilson asked his Ambassador in London to impress upon Lloyd George that British failure to find a satisfactory system of self government for Ireland was the only circumstance standing in the way of cordial cooperation with Britain by practically all Americans.[140] The British Ambassador in Washington, Sir Cecil Spring-Rice, urged his own Government in 1917, just after the American declaration of war, to remove the obstacle to American confidence raised by British treatment of Nationalist Ireland's demands. Spring-Rice observed that as long as they were not satisfied, Americans cited this as proof that the British were not waging war totally for the freedom of small nations.[141]

At the same time, Imperial pressures were also being exerted on the British Government, most notably by W. M. Hughes, Prime Minister of Australia, who was unable to attend a meeting of the proposed Imperial War Cabinet because of domestic repercussions over the lack of an Irish settlement. Hughes argued that a disaffected Ireland 'not only makes the ideal of Imperial Unity impossible, but greatly imperils existing Imperial relations and prevents the Empire putting forth maximum manpower and strength.'[142] The point made by Hughes about wartime manpower and strength was a telling one. With the need for Irish conscription becoming a pressing issue as the war reached a critical phase and the toll of casualties mounted, it would scarcely be feasible to try to impose conscription on Ireland without first implementing Home Rule.

Towards the end of May 1916, Lloyd George undertook a new initiative when he outlined proposals for an Ulster settlement to representatives of northern Unionists. A series of settlement proposals formulated in May and June 1916 would, if accepted by representatives of Irish opinion north and south, have meant that the Government of Ireland Act, 1914, would have been brought into operation as soon as possible after the passing of a measure incorporating these proposals. The Act would not apply to the six-county area, which would remain intact during the continuance of the war and for 12 months thereafter, to allow Parliament to make permanent provision for the government of Ireland. It was to be understood that an Imperial conference would consider the permanent settlement of Ireland after the war.[143] Carson accepted the proposal to exclude six Ulster counties for the duration of the war, while Redmond conceded that these six counties should be treated as a

140 John Stubbs, 'The Unionists and Ireland, 1914–18, *Historical Journal* Vol. 33, No. 4 (1990), p. 885.

141 Cited in Frank Gallagher, *The Indivisible Island: The History of the Partition of Ireland* (London, 1959), p. 126. For a general study of the American dimension of Home Rule, see F. M. Carroll, *American Opinion and the Irish Question, 1910–1923* (Dublin, 1978).

142 D. G. Boyce, 'British Opinion, Ireland and the War, 1916–18', *Historical Journal*, 17 Mar. 1974, p. 584.

143 Details of the Lloyd George Proposals are in F. S. L. Lyons, *John Dillon: A Biography* (London, 1968), pp. 484–5.

unit. Relatively small differences now separated the two main disputants, and an agreement might have been concluded between them, but as Jackson observes, Lloyd George's proposals 'were ripped apart, not by either Carson or Redmond, but by critics outside the negotiations with other interests to defend.'[144] In June 1916, Carson won agreement for the exclusion plan for Cavan, Monaghan and Donegal Unionists not covered by it, while a decided majority of Ulster Nationalists also approved. There remained, however, two critical difficulties. One was that the 200,000 or so southern Unionists outside Cavan, Donegal and Monaghan had not been given a voice in the formulation of the proposals. The other was that Nationalists had understood from Lloyd George that Ulster exclusion would be temporary, while Carson seemed to understand that it would be permanent unless Parliament deemed otherwise.

Lloyd George's scheme thus collapsed because of the degree of concentrated opposition to its implementation. Throughout the negotiations, Carson consistently put the cause of Ulster ahead of the larger interests of Unionism in the rest of Ireland and Britain. Walter Long influenced his Unionist Cabinet colleagues to believe that in his endeavour to reach an Irish settlement, Lloyd George had behaved improperly by failing to secure a basis for agreement among all Irish Unionists, not merely those in the province of Ulster. Led by Viscount Midleton and Lord Lansdowne, southern Unionists formed alliances with Conservative malcontents. Many Nationalists outside East Ulster, who would have been deprived of self government by the scheme, feared the dominance of a triumphant loyalism, an issue that would again come to the fore after the 1920 Government of Ireland Act. The bulk of Conservative members, particularly Peers with southern Irish connections, saw the speedy implementation of Home Rule as a surrender to the treachery of the 1916 Rising.[145]

As a token of this, 80 Conservative Unionist MPs publicly expressed opposition to immediate Home Rule. Walter Long undermined Carson's influence by representing to some of his followers that they had assented to Lloyd George's proposals under false pretences.[146] The collapse of these proposals finally came on 19 July 1916 when British Cabinet Ministers were persuaded by Lansdowne and Long to emphasise the permanence of exclusion, thus causing Redmond to reject the Lloyd George initiative.[147] At the Cabinet meeting of 27 July 1916, arrangements were made for burying this

144 Jackson, *Home Rule*, p. 159.

145 Jenkins, *Asquith*, p. 399.

146 John Kendle, *Walter Long: Ireland and the Union, 1905–20* (Dublin, 1992), p. 115.

147 See Jackson, *Home Rule*, pp. 157–68, for an authoritative account of the Lloyd George proposals, details of which were published in the *The Times* (London), 12 June 1916. Redmond's account of the negotiations on these proposals can be studied in Parliamentary Debates, House of Commons, Vol. 84, Cols 1427–34, 24 July 1916.

agreement.[148] On that date, the Cabinet agreed that for the immediate future, 'the simplest and least disagreeable plan would be to revert for the time being to the old system of a Lord Lieutenant and a Chief Secretary.'[149]

The Irish Parliamentary Party was profoundly demoralised and damaged by the collapse of the Lloyd George initiative. During the period that followed, Redmond and his followers were relatively quiescent while the Sinn Féin programme of radical separatism acquired credibility with much of the electorate. On 5 May 1917, Lloyd George tried another initiative, offering Redmond a choice between immediate Home Rule for the 26 counties and a National convention as a forum for debate on the wider issue of self government for Ireland.[150] On 25 July 1917, the Irish Convention assembled, attended by 95 representatives from a wide range of bodies and political interests. Its sole practical function, as Fitzpatrick remarks, was to suggest that 'the attempt to resolve Ireland's constitutional future had not been completely abandoned.'[151] Two disabling features were the absence of Sinn Féin from the proceedings and the intransigence of the Ulster Unionist delegates, who refused to consider any kind of all-Ireland settlement. The Nationalist Home Rulers were frustrated in their hope of using the Convention, which did not issue its report until 5 April, 1918, for the purpose for which it was set up: an agreed settlement. Meanwhile, Sinn Féin was steadily filling the political vacuum, its democratic strength bound to be augmented by the extension of the franchise for the 1918 General Election. The Irish Convention exposed a divergence of approach between Ulster and southern Unionists. The latter, represented by Viscount Midleton's Irish Unionist Alliance, were willing to compromise with Constitutional Nationalists, and to accept an Irish Parliament with wide powers, which would at the same time offer safeguards to both Unionist and Imperial interests. When Midleton's position was rejected by the hardline rank-and-file of the Irish Unionist Alliance, he and his supporters formed the Irish Unionist Anti-Partition League. Although the hardliners were in the majority, most of the experienced and politically influential southern Unionists sided with Midleton, and the Anti-Partition League therefore enjoyed much greater influence at Westminster. Midleton, who had been British Secretary of State for War during the Boer War, was later to play a leading part in securing safeguards for the Unionist community in the Irish Free State, including considerable representation in the Free State Senate.[152] The

148 Jenkins, *Asquith*, p. 402.
149 Stubbs, 'The Unionists and Ireland', p. 383.
150 Denis Gwynn, *The Life of John Redmond* (London, 1932), pp. 547–9.
151 David Fitzpatrick, *The Two Irelands*, p. 71.
152 Donal O'Sullivan, *The Irish Free State and its Senate* (London, 1940), pp. 75–82.

Ulster Unionist demand was for exclusion from the jurisdiction of an Irish parliament and the partition of Ireland.

The southern Unionist case against partition was a strong one, particularly from the point of view of non-Ulster loyalism. The exclusion of Ulster would inevitably weaken the influence of southern Loyalists and constitutionalists in a 26-county parliament, which might well be financially straitened by the absence of the wealth and industry of the North East. A strong Unionist minority under an all-Ireland arrangement would act as a corrective to extreme Nationalism, while a United Ireland with safeguards would permit the minority to contribute significantly to the well being of the new Irish State. There was also a fear among southern Unionists that unfavourable treatment of the Catholic minority in a six-county state might bring about retaliation on southern Protestants. Lord Desart, a southern Loyalist and anti-partitionist, one of the advisers to the British Cabinet, declared that the exclusion of Ulster would be 'a betrayal of the loyal men in the South', lead to perpetual bitterness between the two parts of Ireland, and result in the establishment of a Sinn Féin government on the flank of England, 'unchecked by the influence or power of Loyalist elements from the North.' In short, nothing could be more disastrous to both islands than partition.[153]

Southern Unionists were understandably concerned that undue concentration on the Ulster question tended to obscure the opposition to Home Rule among Loyalists, whether Catholic or Protestant, in the rest of Ireland, with the result that the Irish Unionist struggle against Home Rule from 1886 on often appeared in the guise of a conflict between Irish Nationalism and southern Unionism. Irish Nationalists often failed to recognise the necessary divergence between the outlook, ambition and needs of northern and southern Unionists. The former were prepared, and equipped, to resist Home Rule by force of arms if necessary, a course not open to the latter. The great majority of the Nationalist leadership were familiar with Unionism mainly, if not exclusively, in its southern aspect, and understandably thought of northern Unionism as something not essentially different. Lyons reminds us that Parnell underestimated northern Unionists from a southern perspective.[154] There was a tendency among Nationalists, seeing southern Unionists as an obsolescent elite, ultimately bound by their circumstances to seek accommodation with the majority, to assume that northern Unionists could not be radically different. Nationalists were aware of the sacrifices many southern Unionists were prepared to make to ensure any form of stable government that would

153 PRO CAB, 27/69/2/41, 22 Nov. 1919. Public Records Office is now The National Archives (TNA).

154 Lyons, *Parnell* (1978 edn), pp. 350–55.

guarantee their lives and property in the partitioned Ireland which they feared might be controlled by extremists.

In 1918, one Dublin Unionist, A. F. Blood, believed in 'joining hands with our Nationalist fellow-countrymen, who look for Unionist co-operation to strengthen their hands in a bona fide contest with anarchy and lawlessness.'[155] A significant minority of southern Unionists thought like Blood. Anxious for accommodation with moderate Nationalists, they broke away from the Irish Unionist Alliance, which steadfastly rejected any compromise on Home Rule, and formed their own organisation, the Unionist Anti-Partition League, led by Viscount Midleton, and with the objective of taking their place with all Unionists in a united, self-governing Ireland. The people who took the Ulster resistance seriously were the southern Protestants who feared partition, and who, as Walter Long, on the authority of his southern Unionist connections, reminded Lloyd George in May 1916, 'held strongly that they had not been sufficiently represented or protected by the Ulster people.'[156]

VII THE GOVERNMENT OF IRELAND ACT, 1920: A SETTLEMENT FOR SOME UNIONISTS

At the end of the Great War, the British Government would be obliged, by the terms of the Home Rule suspensory measure of 1914, to deal with the Irish question. By way of preparation, the Cabinet established a committee on 11 April 1918, with Walter Long as Chairman, to draw up a Bill which would have three broad aims: to preserve the Union and overall British interests, to protect Ulster and southern Unionists, and to give self government to the Irish Nationalist majority as a means of removing an overwhelming British presence from Irish affairs.[157] Convinced at this stage that trying to get Ulster Unionists, southern Unionists and the two strands of Irish Nationalism to reach agreement was futile, the Government now sought to formulate a measure which would implement Irish self government and, at the same time, be acceptable to the parties making up the unevenly balanced Lloyd George Coalition and not imperil its survival. By the end of June 1918, Long had drafted a federal scheme in which Ireland would be only one component of a wider United Kingdom and Dominion arrangement. As Long put it in a memorandum of 14 April 1918, it was desirable to devise a measure 'which would if necessary be

155 *Irish Times*, 9 Mar. 1918.
156 Kendle, *Walter Long*, p. 101.
157 John Kendle, *Ireland and the Federal Solution: The Debate over the United Kingdom Constitution 1870–1921* (Montreal, 1989), p. 208.

adopted as a basis for Federation of the United Kingdom.'[158] On 25 July 1918, Lloyd George announced that his Government would not be implementing Home Rule in the foreseeable future, and Long's Committee was without a purpose.

On 7 October 1919, the Government took a decisive step when it appointed a Cabinet sub-Committee, composed of leading members of the two Coalition parties, to advise on Irish policy and to formulate draft legislation which would be the basis of an Irish settlement. This Committee, like the 1918 one, was chaired by Walter Long. It was given the task of drafting a Bill along federalist lines, and of reporting on the likely effect on opinion in Britain and abroad on possible solutions to the Irish problem. The Long Committee issued a report on 4 November 1919. This ruled out county option and an all-Ireland Parliament. Instead, it suggested a federal arrangement involving two Irish parliaments and an overarching Council of Ireland with 20 members from each parliament which would deal with matters of common interest and concern.

Long, who had more influence with Unionist backbenchers than any other member of the Unionist hierarchy,[159] and whose influence on the proceedings and decisions of the Cabinet sub-Committee was decisive, was the ideal choice for the role he was given: to devise a settlement that would deal with the Ulster question on terms acceptable to Ulster Unionists, without losing sight of the concerns of southern Unionists. He had close links to both groups. He had been at the heart of the Ulster resistance to Home Rule, had been deeply implicated in the importation of UVF arms in April 1914 and had contributed to the financing of the operation.[160] He was Carson's predecessor as Ulster Unionist Leader, and had equally close ties with southern Unionists and with southern Irish landowners. Long had been Chief Secretary of the Irish office from March to December 1905, was Chairman of the Irish Unionist Party in the House of Commons from 1906 to 1910, and remained its Vice-Chairman until May 1921. In the course of his work on the 1919 Cabinet sub-Committee, Long was extremely reluctant to sanction a settlement that would make partition permanent. In this he was influenced by his concern for southern Unionists, whose interests would not be served by partition, and by his overriding commitment, shared with other Imperial federalists, to the stability and unity of the British Empire. His strategy was to work for a federalist solution to the Irish problem as a whole, within a British Isles and Imperial framework. Having tried to devise a federalist solution, he then

158 O'Day, *Irish Home Rule*, p. 291.
159 Kendle, *Walter Long*, p. 180.
160 Jackson, *Home Rule*, p. 133.

favoured the creation of a nine-county Ulster rather than a six-county one, a choice based on the argument advanced by Carson to Redmond at the Buckingham Palace Conference in 1916: that a nine-county Ulster held out a greater promise of ultimate unity and would be less likely to be final.

It must be noted, however, that this Irish settlement about to be shaped by the Long Committee was arrived at in circumstances distinctly unfavourable to the political interests of northern Nationalists. The British General Election of 1918 had resulted in the overwhelming triumph in Irish constituencies of Sinn Féin candidates pledged to abstain from the Westminster Parliament. The Irish MPs who did attend Parliament comprised seven Nationalists and 26 Ulster Unionists. The 73 Sinn Féiners, having abandoned Westminster, and, thus, having forgone any opportunity to influence the proceedings of Long's Committee, which was to have a permanent influence on the course of Irish politics for generations to come, set up Dáil Éireann as an alternative parliament. This meant a change in the balance of power at Westminster from Nationalism to Unionism. It was left to the seven Nationalist members of the Irish Parliamentary Party to represent the interests of Ulster Nationalism at Westminster in the face of a formidable alliance of Ulster Unionists and Conservatives. As Fitzpatrick remarks, 'the absence of effective Nationalist representation at Westminster enhanced the influence of the Ulster Unionists in shaping a settlement.'[161] The British Cabinet included such active supporters of Ulster Unionism as Bonar Law, Walter Long and the Earl of Birkenhead. Ulster Unionist views were, inevitably, effectively represented to Long's Committee. In such circumstances, there was little possibility that any settlement of the Home Rule question, or of the Ulster question associated with it, would satisfy the political interests of Ulster Nationalists. The latter could only observe with deep unease the nature of the unanimity displayed by Liberals and Conservatives on the Ulster question, exemplified in the joint manifesto issued in November 1918, outlining the future policy of the Liberal-Conservative Coalition. Lloyd George and Bonar Law, Party leaders in that Coalition, agreed to rule out 'the forcible submission of the six counties of north-east Ulster to a Home Rule Parliament against their will.'[162] This was merely the latest in a series of assurances, real or assumed, given to Ulster Unionists by British political leaders over a long period of time.

161 Fitzpatrick, *The Two Irelands*, p. 77.
162 Thomas Jones, in Keith Middlemas (ed.), *Whitehall Diary* vol. 3 (London, 1971), pp. 7–8.

VIII THE CHOICE OF UNIT: A DILEMMA FOR UNIONISTS

Aside from that of partition, the principal question before Long's Irish Committee, and the one with the greatest long-term implications, was whether the nine-county historic province of Ulster should be the unit excluded from the provisions of Home Rule and given a separate parliament, or whether exclusion should apply to only six counties.[163] Here, the Ulster Unionists had long faced a difficult decision. Lloyd George's pledge of a permanent exclusion of six counties was no doubt reassuring, but it represented a retreat from established Unionist positions. If exclusion were limited to six counties, this would involve the abandonment of the 70,510 Unionists in the border counties of Cavan, Donegal and Monaghan, on the aggregate of which well over 20 per cent of the population was Protestant. The Unionists of these three counties formed an integral part of the 1912 Covenant, and many men from their Ulster Volunteer Force Units were in France with the 36th Ulster Division in 1916 when Carson presented Lloyd George's six-county exclusion proposals to the Ulster Unionist Council on 12 June. Carson felt obliged to balance the wishes of his supporters in the three border counties against the larger interests of Ulster Unionism. He argued that the best service that the Unionists of Cavan, Donegal and Monaghan could give to the general body of Irish Unionists would be to facilitate the creation of the strongest possible Unionist stronghold in a six-county Ulster, which would include far fewer Nationalists than would a nine-county unit, and thus facilitate the formation of a state in which Unionist dominance would be a permanent feature.[164] Alison Phillips offers a more benign interpretation of the northern sacrifice of southern Unionists. 'The Ulster argument,' he suggests, 'was that they were keeping the Covenant in the spirit, if not in the letter, because a separate Ulster Government, with a Catholic minority under it, would be a better guarantee for the just treatment of Protestants in Catholic Ireland than if the whole Protestant body were to form a hopeless minority in a Catholic State.'[165] The Unionist leadership issued a statement explaining why its six-county population had been obliged to 'wring the hands of our brethren in Donegal, Cavan and Monaghan in agony and regret, and bid them good bye if we are to save ourselves. . . . Nothing but absolute loyalty to the Empire has made this last, and in some respects greatest, sacrifice possible.'[166] The

---

163 See Eamon Phoenix, *Northern Nationalism, Nationalist Politics, Partition and the Catholic Minority in Northern Ireland, 1890–1940* (Belfast, 1994), p. 72.

164 T. G. Fraser, *Partition in Ireland, India and Palestine: Theory and Practice* (London, 1984), p. 32.

165 W. Alison Philips, *The Revolution in Ireland, 1906–1923* (London, 1923), p. 111.

166 *Belfast Telegraph*, 13 June 1920.

statement did not explain what six-county Unionists were saving themselves from: being part of a polity in which they would have formed 56.3 per cent of the population instead of the six-county one in which their percentage was 65.6 per cent.

In the course of the debate on the Government of Ireland Bill in the Commons in March 1920, Sir James Craig, who like many of his Ulster Unionist colleagues, was less concerned about the fate of the Protestant minority in the south than about the possible effect of exclusion on whatever Ulster area was chosen, was to provide a frank analysis of the reasons for the Unionist preference for the six-county state: if they had a nine-county parliament with 64 members, the Unionist majority would be three or four, but in a six-county parliament it would be about ten. The three other Ulster counties, he explained, 'contain some 70,000 Unionists and 226,000 Sinn Féiners and Nationalists, and the addition of that large block of Sinn Féiners and Nationalists would reduce our majority to such a level that no sane man would undertake to carry on a Parliament with it . . . a couple of Members sick, or two or three Members absent for some accidental reason, might in one evening hand over the entire Ulster Parliament, the entire Ulster position, [to the South]. A dreadful thing to contemplate.'[167] Implicit in these comments is that no Unionist politician wanted a state in which the permanence of Unionist rule would be in jeopardy either in 1920 or in the future. What the comments also imply is that the six-county boundary of 1920 always would be, and should be, the defining issue of Northern Ireland politics, all other issues being distractions. The Unionist nightmare which a nine-county Ulster represented was conjured up in a different context in December 1921, when Captain Charles Craig, brother of Sir James, dealt with the boundary commission provided for in the Anglo-Irish Treaty, which 'may mean that our northern areas will be so cut up that we shall no longer be masters in our own house.'[168] The only kind of state acceptable to Unionists was a six-county entity with a sufficiently large population to ensure viability, and whose demographic balance would guarantee perpetual dominance over the Nationalist minority.

The apparent anomaly of seeking much more territory than was actually Unionist, in electoral or population terms, was of little concern: the overriding issue was how much territory Unionists could safely control. Early in 1920, after Long had visited the north to confer with Ulster Unionist leaders, he

167 Parliamentary Reports, House of Commons, Vol. 127, Col. 991, 29 Mar. 1920.
168 *Irish Boundary, Extracts from Parliamentary Debates, Command Papers, etc, Relevant to Questions arising out of Article XII of the Articles of an Agreement for a Treaty between Great Britain and Ireland, dated 6 December, 1921*, H. M. Stationery Office (London, 1924), p. 33.

reported to Lloyd George on his return that 'the inclusion of Donegal, Cavan and Monaghan would provide such an access of strength to the Roman Catholic party that the supremacy of the Unionists would be seriously threatened,'[169] thus implying that the perpetuation of Unionist supremacy was the *sine qua non* for any northern state that might emerge as a result of British legislation. Long made it clear that he would not press for a settlement that would put the interests of Ulster Unionists at risk. A majority of the members of his Committee, however, was prepared to recommend the nine-county option as more likely to lead to the unification of Ireland, whereas a six-county Ulster with a deliberately tailored Unionist majority would be permanently divisive. The nine-county option remained the choice of the Committee until 14 February 1920, one day before the first reading of the Government of Ireland Bill was scheduled.[170] Despite the conclusions of the Irish Committee, the Cabinet, anxious to have Unionist support for its Government of Ireland Bill, agreed on 24 February 1920, that six of the nine Ulster counties would become a separate political entity, and that this entity, Northern Ireland, would consist of the counties of Antrim, Armagh, Down, Fermanagh, Londonderry and Tyrone and, in addition, the parliamentary boroughs of Belfast and Londonderry.

Long, who was given the task of chairing a small committee to guide the Government of Ireland Bill through its committee stage, was concerned that it might not pass, given the lack of interest being taken in it by the Conservative Party MPs, while Liberal and Labour members absented themselves from the proceedings. The Ulster Unionist MPs, as Long observes 'stood coldly aloof, did not want the Bill and were not inclined to provide the only active support the Bill was likely to get.' Following secret negotiations with Carson and Craig, Long was made aware of the price demanded by the two Unionist leaders in return for their support: if Ulster Unionists and their associates in the House of Commons actively supported the legislation in the House of Commons, the Government would guarantee the sanctity of the boundaries of a six-county Ulster. Long was authorised by the British Cabinet to give the Unionist leaders a definite pledge that if they agreed to accept the Bill and tried to work it when passed, 'it would be on the clear understanding that the Six Counties, as settled after the negotiations, should be theirs for good and all, and there should be no interference with the boundaries or anything else, excepting such slight adjustments as might be necessary to get rid of projecting bits, etc.'[171] Long gave what he called 'countless pledges' that

169 Memorandum by Walter Long, 3 Feb. 1920. Cited in Richard Murphy, 'Walter Long and the making of the Government of Ireland Act 1919–20', *IHS* 25 (1986), p. 86.
170 Kendle, *Walter Long*, p. 185.
171 Ibid.

a six-county Ulster would endure and be maintained by the British Government. These pledges would assume a vital importance following the incorporation in the Anglo-Irish Treaty of December 1921 of a clause making provision for boundary adjustment. In 1924, worried that the Labour Government might unwittingly renege on this guarantee, Long confirmed to Lord Londonderry that 'it was on this distinct pledge that we were able to pass the Government of Ireland Bill with the aid of the Ulstermen.'[172] It was to be on what the Sinn Féin Treaty plenipotentiaries regarded as a contradictory pledge, that the territory under the Belfast Parliament would be significantly reduced by a boundary commission, that the British negotiators were able to get an Anglo-Irish Treaty signed.

Long's Irish Committee considered only two methods of meeting Unionist demands: the six-county model and the nine-county one. The nine-county Ulster, which would have placed the 260,000 Nationalists in Donegal, Cavan and Monaghan, under the northern Parliament, would at the same time have gratified the wishes of 70,510 Unionists in the same counties. The demand for a six-county exclusion was being endorsed not only by Craig and his Ulster Unionist colleagues, but also by Sir James O'Connor, a Catholic Loyalist in the south, a Lord Justice who was thought to reflect the views of the Catholic Hierarchy. O'Connor communicated with Lloyd George and Bonar Law, and his submissions were carefully weighed by the Cabinet and the Long Committee.[173] There were strong objections among influential sections of Unionism to the partition of historic, nine-county Ulster. Those who objected to the exclusion of these counties from the northern Parliament requested a special meeting of the Ulster Unionist Council on 23 April 1919 to reconsider the matter. At the same time a well-argued pamphlet entitled: *Ulster and Home Rule: No Partition of Ulster* was published on behalf of Donegal, Cavan and Monaghan Unionists.[174] The authors of the pamphlet were obliged to address the fundamental objection of six-county Unionists that a nine-county arrangement, incorporating three overwhelmingly Nationalist counties, might eventually undermine Unionist dominance, the principle on which all Unionist thinking and political action was based.[175]

The case made in the pamphlet that in a nine-county state the Unionist majority of 200,000 would still guarantee a substantial parliamentary majority,

172 Murphy, 'Walter Long and the making of the Government of Ireland Act', p. 88.

173 Nicholas Mansergh, *The Unresolved Question: The Anglo–Irish Settlement and its Undoing, 1912–1972* (London, 1991) p. 128.

174 There is a copy of this pamphlet, henceforth cited as *Ulster and Home Rule*, in PRONI, D1545/8.

175 A further threat to Unionist dominance was the increasing support for Labour in working-class Protestant Belfast.

was not wholly convincing for some Unionists seeking a perpetually secure dominance. Other arguments against the partition of Ulster were, however, well made. One in particular suggested that any form of partition, but above all the six-county one, could not be based on a self-consistent, principled approach. The authors of the pamphlet observed that every argument that might be employed to justify their exclusion from an Ulster government might with equal validity be used in favour of excluding Derry City, Tyrone, Fermanagh, south Armagh, south Down and the Falls area of Belfast. There were also the strong economic and geographic arguments that much of the trade of Belfast was with the whole of historic Ulster, that the trade of Donegal was almost entirely with Derry and that Cavan and Monaghan formed 'a natural boundary to the South of Ulster, and Monaghan runs up to a point between Tyrone and Armagh into the very heart of the province.'[176] One line of argument, that a six-county parliament would become parochial and that the Unionist majority would be too large for its own good, had much to recommend it. As Fraser remarks, all of the arguments advanced in the pamphlet 'made perfect sense in the context of the government's aim of accommodating Ulster inside a framework which would encourage Irish unity.'[177] To the great majority of six-county Unionists, at this stage, however, any kind of Irish unity, even if this involved the closest links with Britain, had far less attraction than the creation of a distinctively Unionist state.

IX DEFENDING THE 1920 ACT

In the Commons on December 22, 1919, Lloyd George offered an extremely able and coherent exposition of the main outlines of the Government of Ireland Bill, and of the considerations underlying its provisions. Two fundamental facts had to be taken into account. The majority in Ireland claimed the right to control their own domestic concerns, without interference from Englishmen, Scotsmen and Welshmen. It was also a fact that a considerable section of the people of Ireland were just as opposed to Irish rule as the majority were to British rule. The legislation he was proposing, in its Ulster aspect, had to confront the problem that in the North East there was a solid, homogeneous population, alien in race, sympathy, religion, tradition and outlook from the rest of the population, and that it would be an outrage on the principle of self government to place them under the rule of the rest of the population: to do so would alienate the best elements

176 *Ulster and Home Rule*, p. 1.
177 Fraser, *Partition in Ireland*, p. 35.

of northern Unionism from the machinery of law and order. With his accustomed dexterity, Lloyd George invoked the testimony of two Catholic priests in support of his ethical defence of Ulster exclusion. One was Father O'Flanagan, 'a very able Catholic priest,' who found it objectionable that Nationalists might reject Home Rule rather than agree to the exclusion of the Unionist part of Ulster. The other was Walter MacDonald, a Professor of Theology at Maynooth, who had claimed that were Ireland made an independent Republic, she would be bound to allow Home Rule to the North-East corner, on the principles underlying the Nationalist claim for Home Rule within the United Kingdom. A third fundamental argument underlying the Bill was that 'any arrangement by which Ireland is severed from the United Kingdom, either nominally or in substance and, in fact, would be fatal to the interests of both'.[178] This argument was to persist during the Treaty negotiations.

The Government of Ireland Bill was based on three fundamental realities outlined by Lloyd George. His three main legislative proposals were framed to deal with these realities: Ireland must remain an integral part of the United Kingdom; self government must be conferred upon Ireland in all its domestic concerns; and two parliaments, not one, must be set up in Ireland. The powers to be remitted to these two local parliaments were not extensive: the control of Irish finance, for example, was to remain with the Imperial Parliament at Westminster. However, each Irish Parliament would have control of domestic services such as education, local government, justice and social welfare. The Westminster Parliament would retain control of foreign policy, external trade and the armed services. The Northern Ireland Parliament could not impose or collect customs, excise duties, income tax or taxes on profits or capital. The Imperial Parliament would retain 88 per cent of revenue derived from Northern Ireland, and control 60 per cent of its expenditure. There were few safeguards for the minority in the south and west of Ireland. Irish constituencies would retain some parliamentary representation at Westminster. The Bill, which became the Government of Ireland Act of 1920, had one paradoxical feature. It did not exclude six counties from the jurisdiction of a Dublin parliament, the constant demand of Ulster Unionists, but instead applied Home Rule to Northern Ireland. The 1920 'Partition Act' had profoundly contrasting implications for the two northern communities. Northern Nationalists found partition no less objectionable than Ulster exclusion from Home Rule, and now found themselves 'an embattled minority sidelined by all the major protagonists': for them 'subjection to northern Protestant control was an even less agreeable prospect than perpetuation of direct Home Rule under the Union.'[179]

178 Parliamentary Reports, Vol. 123, Cols 1171–3, 22 Dec. 1919.
179 Fitzpatrick, *The Two Irelands*, p. 101.

A significant difference between the 1919 proposals and the Act of 1914 was that every opportunity would now be afforded to Irish people to establish unity: the Council of Ireland proposed in the Bill would constitute the obvious agency from which the two parliaments would ensure that certain common services, such as railways and canals, which it would be undesirable to divide, could be administered as a single Irish service. The Bill would endow the two Irish legislatures with full constituent powers so that they could, without further reference to the Imperial Parliament, and by identical legislation, create a single Irish legislature. The Irish unity provision in the Bill reflected the British Government position under Lloyd George that the Ulster Unionists should ideally join the Free State. The logic of this preference was that such an outcome would have the consequence of strengthening the Imperialist element in the south, and thereby diminish the likelihood that the Free State would break away from the Empire. The same British preference was evident in the complexion of the Anglo-Irish Treaty, in particular the boundary clause, but also the financial provisions, which, it is plausible to argue, were framed to persuade the northern Government to reunite with the rest of Ireland. This analysis runs counter to a common perception among Nationalist apologists that partition was the work of British politicians anxious to defend the Loyalists of Ulster against the perceived dangers of living under a Dublin parliament. In effect, the ultimate architects of partition were the Ulster Unionists and the southern Nationalists. The former were able to insist on exclusion from an all-Ireland settlement, a course which inevitably meant partition, while the latter were not willing to diminish the degree of sovereignty they had over 26 counties, even if this meant submitting to partition. On this view, both sides can be seen to have preferred sovereignty over their respective areas to the kind of unity favoured by Lloyd George and his Government from 1919 to 1921.

Lloyd George revealed that four different proposals had been discussed by the Cabinet sub-Committee in relation to the area of Ulster to be excluded, outlined the major objections to three of these, and enlarged on the merits of the fourth. The first proposal, that the whole of Ulster should form one unit, was open to the objection that this would leave a large area 'where there is a predominantly Catholic and Celtic population in complete sympathy with the Southern population.' The second suggestion – county option – would be unacceptable because it would have solid communities of Protestants in sympathy with the Unionist state outside it, under a government to which they were hostile. The third suggestion considered was that the six north-eastern counties should form a unit. Here, Lloyd George identified the problem which, because it was made part of the 1920 Bill and not solved by the

Boundary Commission, would only serve to create long-term damage to north-south relationships, intensify bitterness and a sense of grievance among border Nationalists, and, thus, a dysfunctional northern state would result. It is worth noting that Lloyd George, in somewhat ambiguous language, seemed to look at the problem posed by a state incorporating the entire six counties not from the point of view of the potential Catholic victims, but from that of the large Unionist majority. Recognising the presence of 'solid Catholic communities in at least two of these counties conterminous with the Southern population,' it would, he suggested, 'be undesirable from the point of view of the North-Eastern Province to attach them to the Ulster Parliament.'[180] One assumes that by 'the North-Eastern Province' Lloyd George meant a six-county state.

The most significant aspect of Lloyd George's analysis of the four proposals for choosing the appropriate Ulster unit for exclusion was his implicit recommendation of the fourth proposal as a means of avoiding the dangers posed if the third were implemented. The fourth proposal was that a homogeneous north-eastern section should be ascertained, and constituted as a separate, excluded area, 'taking the six counties as a basis, eliminating, where practicable, the Catholic communities, whilst including Protestant communities from the conterminous Catholic counties of Ireland, in order to produce an area as homogeneous as it is possible to achieve under these circumstances.' Had this kind of exercise been performed prior to the passing of the 1920 Act, the history of Northern Ireland and of Ireland as a whole might well have been much different. For one thing, a boundary commission would not have been considered on the Irish side as an essential component of the Anglo-Irish Treaty of 1921.

X OTHER POSSIBILITIES

The British preoccupation with county boundaries meant that the possibility of creating a border much more in accord with the wishes of inhabitants than the six-county one, received little or no consideration. The parliamentary constituency boundaries established by the Redistribution of Seats Act (Ireland), 1917, would have provided a much more refined basis upon which to mark out a partition line. Had those who drafted the 1920 Act based a northern state on those constituencies which had returned Unionist members in 1918, its territorial extent would have been considerably less than the six-county unit that emerged. The constituencies of Derry City, south Down,

180 Parliamentary Reports, Vol. 123, Cols 1175–3, 22 Dec. 1919.

south Armagh, south Fermanagh, north-west and north-east Tyrone would have been assigned to the Free State, while the result would still have made geographical sense. This arrangement would still have given the northern state a Catholic population of 28 per cent. Of six-county Catholics, 148,239 would have been placed south of the border, along with 96,197 Protestants.[181] Partition based on local government rural district boundaries would also have been more equitable than the six-county one, and given a Catholic population of 26 per cent to the northern state.[182] Had a boundary been based not on the results of the elections in the northern constituencies but on the declared religious affiliations of the populations of these constituencies – as recorded in the most recent census of 1911 – the total population of Northern Ireland would have been 939,047, consisting of 690,808 Unionists and 248,239 Nationalists. The Nationalist percentage would have been 26.5. Under this arrangement, 185,922 Catholics would have been on the Free State side of the border, and 129,562 Protestants. The six-county partition arrangement had the advantage of geographical tidiness, achieved, however, at the cost of ethnic homogeneity. An arrangement based on the 1918 constituencies would have been less tidy geographically but much more homogeneous. Another scheme canvassed by Nationalists had the advantage of leaving far fewer dissatisfied Nationalists in a more homogeneous state. This would have involved the exclusion from the northern state of the predominantly Nationalist areas of West Ulster, in practice Tyrone and Fermanagh.

Not all apologists for Unionism thought it wise to insist on a six-county state. In July 1914, Lord Milner told Carson that 'there is no particular virtue in counties that I can see, as long as the excluded area is one solid block.' Milner, however, thought that if the six counties were secured to begin with, 'it might be worthwhile to swap bits of them, south Down and south Armagh, for instance, for bits of Monaghan and Donegal.'[183] The strongly pro-Unionist Editor of *The Spectator*, St Loe Strachey, in a letter to a 'very able Ulster Protestant,' Professor McElderry of University College, Galway, argued that the ideal plan from a Unionist point of view, 'might have been to take Ulster as a whole and then cast out therefrom as many Catholic districts, unions and parishes as could possibly be eliminated, subject to the absolute and impera-tive anti-island rule.' Strachey was anxious to avoid large Catholic enclaves in the northern state. He would 'cut out every district in which there was a

---

181 These figures based on Kevin O'Shiel, *Handbook of the Ulster Question*, published by North-Eastern Boundary Bureau (Dublin, 1923), p. 48.

182 See F. W. Boal and J. N. H. Douglas (eds), *Integration and Division: Geographical Perspectives on the Northern Ireland Problem* (London, 1982), pp. 110–12.

183 Milner to Carson, PRONI D1507/A/6/39, 21 July 1914.

Catholic majority of over say 60 per cent, provided it always was conterminous with some portion of the non-Protestant segment of Ireland.' He looked forward to the decision of some 'enlightened Boundary Commission, which would go through the map, parish by parish, intent upon getting nothing but the maximum homogeneity for the North-East Ulster area.' He would like to see one qualification on the work of such a commission: an automatic rule by which 'parishes within a year of separation could on their mere motion demand to come in or out of the Protestant Ireland,' subject to the rule that islands must never be created.

One of Strachey's ideas, if implemented, might have led to the avoidance of much later trouble. 'As to making the border-line rather like a jig-saw puzzle,' he told McElderry, 'I shouldn't mind if thereby I got more concentration and more homogeneity both for the Roman Catholics and for the Protestants.' He suggested transplantation as a further means of securing homogeneity: the grant of 'a couple of millions to be spent in bringing Protestant farmers and tradesmen from the South up into Ulster and taking Roman Catholics from Protestant Ulster districts and putting them into the South.'[184] Carson, to whom Strachey communicated similar views, replied that the ultimate shape of the northern state was something to be determined by the practical consideration of what would ensure lasting Unionist predominance.[185] The de facto partition of Cyprus in 1974, which sacrificed the then normative principle of territorial integrity to minority self-determination, showed how Strachey's scheme for transferring ethnic minorities from north to south and vice versa might have worked out in practice. It is interesting to note that in April 1923, before the establishment of the Boundary Commission, Wilfred Spender, the Secretary to the northern Cabinet, wrote to a Church of Ireland clergymen in Clones, J. R. Mearn, that Craig was 'most anxious to include in Northern Ireland certain districts in Donegal and Monaghan [later to be recommended for transfer from the Free State by the Boundary Commission] where there is a splendid type of Loyalist population.' Craig was suggesting that if the Free State would agree to let each of its border counties bargain with its opposite number in Northern Ireland regarding the transfer of equal areas and populations, 'there would be a great prospect of an amicable settlement being arrived at which would prove to the advantage of the North and South.'[186]

184 St Loe Strachey to Professor McElderry, Ardgriana, Galway, PRONI D1507/A/33/38, 12 Feb. 1920.
185 Carson Papers, PRONI D1507/A/33/37/1920/9A.
186 Spender to Mearn, cited in Jackson, *Home Rule*, p. 210.

It has often been argued that northern Unionists insisted on retaining six counties intact because a revised boundary involving the loss of substantial territory with Nationalist majorities would leave the entity that remained economically unsustainable. This was a central issue during the Treaty negotiations. On the Irish side, enthusiasm for the Boundary Commission was largely associated with the belief inspired by the suggestions of Lloyd George, that it would recommend handing over to the south areas of such large extent that the northern state must collapse.[187] It is by no means certain, however, that even a much reduced, and more homogeneous, northern state would not have survived. Several commentators have made a reasonable case for the proposition that the separate political survival of northern Unionism did not depend on keeping the entire area of the six counties. The Unionist historian, Tom Wilson, argues that a substantial transfer of six-county territory to the south 'could have left the Unionists with an almost impregnable, if smaller, area which might also have been to the advantage of the remaining minority who would have been living with a more secure and therefore, perhaps, more tolerant majority.' Wilson further suggests that a smaller northern state would have been strengthened, not weakened, economically 'by removing some of the poorer rural areas'.[188] Wilson also argues that it would surely have been wholly beneficial to have got rid of 'the fiercely Republican salient at Crossmaglen in the interests of a more defensible boundary.' At a conference with members of the Free State Government in January 1924, E. M. Stephens, Secretary of the Boundary Bureau, claimed that it would be easier for the northern government to carry on 'if they were relieved of Tyrone and Fermanagh'. This would give 'a more homogeneous population which would be more industrially concentrated, and involve less police work. At the same conference, Kevin O'Higgins was anxious to explore the idea that 'relief from Tyrone and Fermanagh would render the North more financially sound.'[189]

Joseph Johnston and George Ruth, the economic advisers to the Boundary Bureau established on 2 October 1922, with the object of compiling data for the Boundary Commission, obtaining Nationalist opinion and preparing the case for the inclusion of border areas in the Free State,[190] contended that there were 'states in America and Australia and provinces in Canada which, with a population very considerably less than the population to which Northern Ireland would be reduced by the proposed line, nevertheless maintained

187   See Michael Laffan, *The Partition of Ireland, 1911–25* (Dundalk, 1983), pp. 85–7.
188   Tom Wilson, *Ulster: Conflict and Consent* (Oxford, 1989), p. 67.
189   Boundary Conference, National Archives of Ireland (hereafter NAI) S3986, 29 Jan. 1924.
190   Provisional Government minutes, NAI G1/3, 2 Oct. 1922.

provincial governments with powers as great as the Government of Northern Ireland.'[191] J. J. Lee argues that the Protestant heartland, Belfast, north Down, north Armagh, east Derry and south Antrim, 'didn't need the periphery to survive economically. On the contrary, the periphery was probably an economic burden on the prosperity of the primarily Protestant east.'[192] Tom Garvin agrees: 'A smaller, more solidly unionist Northern Ireland as imagined by Collins in 1921 would have been more, rather than less, viable.'[193]

The 1920 exercise in boundary drawing was subject to the working out over time of the same processes governing similar exercises: no matter how 'correctly' territorial frontiers are drawn at a given moment, the momentary match between what Brubaker calls 'the division of territory and the distribution of persons'[194] will not endure. The political period since the imposition of the Irish partition has seen significant demographic change, with possible implications for the future shape of the unit, and with obvious effects on the nature of the political competition within it. The 2001 Census returns showed that the Protestant population, at 53.13 per cent, had fallen by 5 per cent since 1991, while the Catholic population, at 43.76 per cent, had risen by 2 per cent.[195] The 2001 figures for the two ethnic groups are significant in more than one respect. They show that by the end of the twentieth century, the percentage of Protestants in the six counties had fallen to its lowest level in 90 years.[196] Much more telling, in an historical context, is a comparison between the denominational returns for the 1911 Census, the last one taken before partition, and those for 2001. Unionist leaders rejected a nine-county Ulster because its Catholic population, as recorded in 1911, was 690,816, compared to a Protestant population of 890,880, the Catholic percentage being 43.67. This percentage of Catholics was regarded by Unionist leaders in 1919 as being too large to afford them a secure grasp on long-term power, which accounts for their strategic contraction of the original demand for a nine-county unit, in the face of stern opposition from Unionists in the three 'lost' border counties.[197] By 2001, however, the Catholic percentage in the *six* counties had

---

191 Report by Stephens, Johnston and Ruth, Blythe Papers UCDA, P24/171 9 Jan. 1923.

192 J. J. Lee, *Ireland 1912–1985: Politics and Society* (Cambridge, 1989), p. 148.

193 Tom Garvin, *The Birth of Irish Democracy* (Dublin, 1996), p. 184.

194 Roger Brubaker, *Nationalism Reframed: Nationhood and the National Question in the New Europe* (New York, 1996), p. 40.

195 See http://www.nisra.gov.uk/Census/Census2001Output/standard–tables.html

196 For an account and detailed analysis of the 2001 Northern Ireland Census figures, see *Irish Times* 20 Feb. 2002.

197 See David Fitzpatrick, 'The Orange Order and the border', *IHS* 23 (2002), pp. 52 ff.

reached a level (43.76), almost identical to that in the *nine* counties in 1911.[198] If the 1919 Unionist leadership judged correctly when it deemed a nine-county unit inappropriate to the creation and sustenance of a Protestant state, the newest population returns for the six-county unit provide an insecure foundation for the kind of state originally conceived in 1920. The 2001 figures for Belfast show an even more remarkable demographic change. In 1911, when the total population of the city was 386,947, Protestants numbered 293,704 and Catholics 93,243, the latter thus constituting 24 per cent of the total. In 1981, Catholics formed 38 per cent of the total. In 2001, out of a total population of 347,931, there were 158,207 Catholics, or 45.5 per cent of the total.[199]

These statistics illustrate the effects of time and changing circumstances on even the most careful system of boundary drawing. A boundary that seemed, in 1920, to ensure perpetual Unionist political control in Northern Ireland now seems ill designed to promote that end. The minority population has by now attained the critical mass which makes ongoing single party rule impossible to sustain, and makes power-sharing increasingly attractive to Unionists. When the Anglo-Irish Treaty was being negotiated in 1921, such outcomes were far from the minds of either the British and Irish delegations or the leaders of Ulster Unionism.

198 See *Irish Times*, 20 Feb. 2002.
199 Kevin Boyle and Tom Hadden, *Ireland: A Positive Proposal* (London, 1985), p. 34.

TWO

THE ANGLO-IRISH TREATY AND THE ULSTER QUESTION

I PRELIMINARIES

At the end of 1920, at the height of the grimmest and culminating phase of the War of Independence, the Government of Ireland Act was placed on the Statute Book, under which subordinate parliaments were to be set up in Dublin and Belfast, with a reduced Irish representation at Westminster. Unionist Ulster, having little alternative, was prepared to work the Act. Sinn Féin ignored its mechanisms, but made use of its provisions to elect a new Dáil, whose members would decline to take their seats in the southern Parliament envisaged in the Act. As a consequence of this, if the British Government was determined to implement the Act in full, it would be obliged to invoke its reserve provision, and establish Crown Colony Government in the 26 counties. The prospect of having to embark on this unsatisfactory course of action generated a growing desire for a settlement with southern Ireland among key members of the British Government, including Sir Austen Chamberlain, Winston Churchill and Lord Birkenhead. The two Conservative leaders, Chamberlain and Birkenhead, advocated 'the fairest offer combined with the most drastic threats.'[1] British public opinion was influenced in favour of a political settlement with Irish nationalism by widespread unease at the policy of coercion and reprisals in Ireland. An English movement to combat these, the Peace with Ireland Council, established in October 1920 and led by the Imperial historian Basil Williams and Oswald Mosley, was particularly effective. A variety of emissaries visited Dublin in the spring and early summer of 1921 to explore the possibility of direct negotiations between the British Government and Sinn Féin. Among these were Lord Derby, the British diplomat who stayed at the Shelbourne Hotel under the name of Edwards and met de Valera, the South African statesman General Smuts and Alfred (Andy) Cope, Assistant Under-Secretary at Dublin Castle, acting as agent for Lloyd

---

1 Earl of Longford (Frank Pakenham), *Peace by Ordeal: The Negotiation of the Anglo-Irish Treaty, 1921–25* (London, 1972), p. 65.

George. Sir James Craig, soon to become Prime Minster in the new Ulster Government, had a secret meeting with de Valera in May 1921.

The visit of King George V to Belfast to open the first session of the Northern Ireland Parliament is commonly, though mistakenly, regarded as marking a decisive step in preparing the British Government for negotiations.[2] In a conciliatory speech prepared for him by General Smuts, the King appealed to all Irishmen to 'stretch out the hand of forbearance and conciliation'. The King's Private Secretary appealed to Lloyd George to act in the spirit of the King's speech while its effect was still widely felt. It is, however, best regarded as the reflection of a growing disposition in Britain for a peace settlement rather than a pioneering initiative. Lloyd George responded by inviting de Valera to London in company with Sir James Craig to explore the possibility of a settlement of the Irish question. Lloyd George accepted de Valera's insistence that a truce be declared before negotiations began. When Lloyd George told Edward Carson privately that negotiations with representatives of Irish nationalism were being mooted, Carson replied that he hoped he would not involve the Conservative members of the Government, Austen Chamberlain and Lord Birkenhead, 'in the discredit of such a surrender.' He soon learned that the suggestion of talks with Sinn Féin had come from Chamberlain, with Birkenhead's support.[3] The essential impulses behind British willingness to come to terms with Irish nationalism was provided by the Government of Ireland Act of 1920. The two main British political parties, led by Lloyd George and Bonar Law, resolved not to allow the Irish question to involve them in a return to what Fitzpatrick terms 'the stark polarities of 1914' and not to make the election of 1918 a test of strength between them.[4] In their manifesto for the 1918 Election, the leaders jointly endorsed the principle of self government for Ireland. They also concurred that 'there are two paths which are closed – the one leading to a complete severance of Ireland from the British Empire, and the other the forcible submission of the six counties of Ulster to a Home Rule parliament against their will.'[5] The Buckingham Palace Conference of 1916 and the Irish Convention of 1917 had demonstrated the futility of inclusive negotiations involving parties taking irreconcilable positions as a means of reaching an Irish settlement. The Government of Ireland Act removed a major barrier by abstracting the Ulster problem from the Irish equation. The introduction of de facto partition, and the Ulster Unionist secession from all-Ireland Home

2 Roy Foster, *Modern Ireland 1600–1972* (London, 1988), p. 504.
3 A. T. Q. Stewart, *Edward Carson* (Dublin, 1981), p. 123.
4 David Fitzpatrick, *The Two Irelands 1912–1939* (Oxford, 1998), p. 75.
5 Ibid.

Rule, meant that the British state could concentrate on making a treaty with Nationalist Ireland with the assurance that Unionist Ulster had been separately catered for.[6] In this case, Nationalist Ireland meant Sinn Féin, which secured an overwhelming mandate in the 1918 Election.

Although the 1920 Act formalised the preference of the British Government for an Irish state with a single parliament, empowering the two parliaments by mutual agreement to terminate partition by setting up one parliament and one government for the whole of Ireland, this amounted to little more than an empty aspiration. Even before the Act reached the Statute Book at the end of 1920, administrative partition was in place: a separate Belfast administration had been created by dedicated civil servants during 1920. By the time the Anglo-Irish Treaty came to be negotiated, the transfer of services to Belfast had been effected. While the Irish treaty delegates were to claim that they were representing the people of the entire island, the existence of a functioning political and administrative system in the North East deprived this claim of practical significance.

The truce was promulgated on 9 July 1921, and came into force two days later. Among those who accompanied de Valera to London were Arthur Griffith, Robert Barton and Erskine Childers, later to be chosen by him as members of the Treaty delegation, the first two as plenipotentiaries, the third as one of the secretaries. Four meetings between Lloyd George and de Valera [14–21 July] proved extremely discouraging to the Irish side. All that Lloyd George was prepared to offer representatives of a parliament that had unanimously declared an Irish republic at the beginning of 1919 was qualified dominion Home Rule for southern Ireland. The vital qualifications on dominion status included a limitation on the size of any future Irish army, the continuation of voluntary recruiting in Ireland for the British Army, the granting of air and naval facilities to Britain, and payment to Britain of a contribution to the war debt. As for the north, the government and parliament there were to retain 'all their existing powers and privileges which cannot be abrogated without its own consent'. This could only be interpreted as meaning that the 1920 partition would endure as long as Northern Ireland so desired. Craig had refused to participate in the discussions, informing the press that de Valera's claim to speak for Ireland as a whole had no foundation. He had no intention of saying or doing anything to accommodate de Valera: his only interest was to retain what the 1920 Act had given the Unionists of Ulster. 'It now remains,' he declared, 'for Mr De Valera and the British people to come to terms regarding the area outside that of which I am Prime

6   Foster, *Modern Ireland*, pp. 503–4.

Minister.'[7] While taking no part in the talks between Lloyd George and de Valera, Craig met the latter, giving him a piece of advice that, as Lyons suggests, 'he might have done well to heed.'[8] When Craig asked him if he intended to see Lloyd George alone, and de Valera said yes, Craig replied: 'Are you mad? Take a witness. Lloyd George will give any account of the interview that comes to his mind or that suits him.'[9]

The Lloyd George offer of dominion status for the 26 counties was, not surprisingly, rejected by the Dáil Cabinet, whose members, however, were not unanimous on the merits of the proposal, a token of major internal divisions on the Irish side soon to become obvious. Griffith found it encouraging, but Cathal Brugha argued that no Dáil cabinet claiming to be the government of an all-Ireland republic should even consider it. The ensuing correspondence between Lloyd George and de Valera, extending over the period from 20 July to 30 September 1921,[10] exposed the difficulty of reconciling the respective positions of the two leaders. De Valera's side of the correspondence must be understood in the context of the restrictions imposed on him by the formal declaration of an Irish Republic by the Dáil in early 1919. Two members of his Cabinet, Cathal Brugha and Austin Stack, had made it clear that they were irreconcilable Republicans, while the majority, it was also clear, would settle for less than the full Republican demand. De Valera had to avoid an open split on this fundamental issue. With this necessity in mind, he had to ensure that each letter to Lloyd George was couched in terms which, on the one hand, would not antagonise his Cabinet hardliners, and on the other, would not cause a break with the British. Thus, he avoided any positive statement which might offend either: the word 'Republic' was not used, and nothing was said which directly implied a readiness to accept the Crown, which Lloyd George repeatedly tried to get him to recognise as a basis of negotiation.[11] Lloyd George, as he made clear in his proposals for an Irish settlement on 20 July 1921, could not contemplate an Ireland outside the British Empire, and insisted that any settlement must incorporate full recognition of the powers and privileges vested in the Parliament of Northern Ireland under the 1920 Act.[12] De Valera's

7   D. G. Boyce, *Englishmen and the Irish Troubles: British Public Opinion and the Making of Irish Policy 1918–22* (London, 1972), p. 144.

8   F. S. L. Lyons, *Ireland since the Famine* (London, 1974), p. 427.

9   Ibid.

10   Official Correspondence relating to the *Peace Negotiations, June–September, 1921* (Dublin, 1921). Henceforth cited as *Peace Negotiations*.

11   Desmond FitzGerald, 'Mr Pakenham and the Anglo-Irish Treaty', *Studies* Vol. XXIV, No. 95 (Sept. 1935), p. 407.

12   *Peace Negotiations*, pp. 6–8.

response was that the claim of the British Government to interfere in Irish affairs could not be admitted. On the issue of Ulster, the Irish position was that it 'must remain a question for the Irish people themselves to settle'. De Valera rejected the partition imposed in 1920: 'We cannot admit the right of the British Government to mutilate our country, either in its own interest or at the call of any section of our population.'[13]

In reply to this, Lloyd George observed that no British government could compromise on the Irish claim that Britain should acknowledge 'the right of Ireland to secede from her allegiance to the King', since the destinies of the British Isles and Ireland were 'indissolubly linked', and 'great numbers, in all the Irish provinces', were 'profoundly attached to the Throne'. On one point, Lloyd George applauded de Valera for agreeing that 'Northern Ireland cannot be coerced'.[14] On this subject, Lloyd George touched on a matter of fundamental importance; in British eyes, Irish independence, even confined to the 26 counties, would constitute an unwarranted and impermissible secession, which implied that the only political unit to be considered in any negotiations was that which incorporated the British Isles and the whole of Ireland, to which unit all its inhabitants owed allegiance since Great Britain and Ireland formed 'the heart of the Commonwealth' and since their continuing as a single political unit was 'vital to the welfare and safety' of both.[15] Irish arguments to the contrary were met with the warnings that the British people were resolved 'to resist with their full power any attempt at secession by one part of Ireland' [the south] and that it carried with it 'of necessity an equal resolve to resist any effort to coerce another part of Ireland [the north] to abandon its allegiance to the Crown'.[16] In the Dáil, in August 1921, de Valera declared that 'They had not the power, and some of them had not the inclination, to use force in Ulster. . . . Ulster would say that she was as devotedly attached to the Empire as they were to their independence, and that she would fight for the one as much as they would fight for the other . . . In the case of coercion, she would get sympathy and help from her friends all over the world.'[17] Collins had little patience with this kind of argument. During the debate on the Treaty he asked: 'If we didn't agree to coerce Ulster, what was the use of talking of not agreeing to the partition of our country?'[18]

13   Ibid., pp. 10–11.
14   Ibid., p. 11.
15   Ibid., p. 7.
16   Ibid., pp. 11–12.
17   Private Sessions of the second Dáil, 22 Aug. 1921 (Dáil Éireann, 1972), p. 29.
18   Dáil Éireann, Treaty Debates, 19 Dec. 1921, p. 35.

De Valera's rebuttal of this line of argument was, in Longford's words, 'an agreeable academic triumph', perhaps his most effective contribution to the correspondence. He resented Lloyd George's insistence that the principle the Irish people were obliged to accept was that the 'geographical propinquity' of Ireland to Britain 'imposed the condition of the subordination of Ireland's right to Britain's strategic interests as she envisages them'.[19] There are suggestive echoes of this in de Valera's classic reply to Winston Churchill's offensive comments made in May 1945 on Ireland's role in the Second World War, when he accused the southern Government of frolicking with Japanese and German representatives 'to their heart's content'. Churchill's entire argument rested on the postulate, subscribed to by Lloyd George in 1921, that self-defined British interests enjoyed an absolute right of enforcement, no matter what the consequences might be for other nations.[20] De Valera exposed the weakness of Churchill's position, striking with deadly effect where he was most vulnerable, and assuming the role of political moralist more convincingly than his adversary had been able to do. Churchill, de Valera observed, 'makes it clear that in certain circumstances he would have violated our neutrality and that he would have justified his action by Britain's necessity'. He found it strange that Churchill did not see that this, if accepted, 'would mean that Britain's necessity would become a moral code, and that when this necessity became sufficiently great, other people's rights were not to count.'[21]

In his reply to de Valera's invocation of the moral principles which he thought should govern relations between peoples, Lloyd George appealed to brute fact, suggesting that there was no political principle, however clear, that could be applied 'without regard to limitations imposed by physical and historical facts'. These physical and historical facts, as he had already suggested, were such that his Government, in common with its predecessors through the ages, could not dissolve the connection between the two islands, or recognise Ireland as a foreign power. Lloyd George's approach was in conformity with Conservative Imperialist thinking. J. L. Garvin, the editor of *The Observer*, for example, rejected de Valera's claims to 'unqualified self-determination as geographically and historically unreal'. Garvin also found the unity of Ireland and the Republican claim, both of these central to the Irish case, 'utterly and eternally incompatible'.[22] The governing force in this matter was threefold:

---

19 *Peace Negotiations*, 24 Aug. 1921, p. 13.

20 Churchill's speech is reported in *The Times*, London, 14 May 1945.

21 The entire speech is printed in Maurice Moynihan (ed.), *Speaches and Statements of Eamon de Valera 1917–1973* (Dublin, 1980), pp. 474–7.

22 Cited in G. K. Peatling, *British Opinion and Irish Self-Government 1865–1925: From Unionism to Liberal Commonwealth* (Dublin, 2001), p. 158.

'the geographical propinquity of these two islands, and of their long historic association' along with 'their historical interdependence'.[23] These three facts imposed the conditions which Irish negotiators were expected to accept as a preliminary requirement for any negotiations with the British Government. The conditions were sevenfold: the Royal Navy should control the seas around Ireland; Britain should have the right to place a limitation on the size of an Irish territorial force; Ireland must facilitate the Royal Air Force 'for all purposes that it serves', Ireland should be willing to contribute a proportion of her wealth to the maintenance of the British armed forces; Ireland must agree to refrain from imposing protective duties on imports from Great Britain, and Britain must agree to a reciprocal arrangement; the Irish people must agree to assume responsibility for a share of the present debt of the United Kingdom; finally, and most significantly, Irish negotiators must, in effect, recognise that the Act of 1920 had constituted a de facto settlement of the Ulster question, and no material adjustment of this position could be contemplated.

The essence of the British case, far from being simply academic, was that Irish independence would not be tolerable should this threaten Britain's security, if, for example, an independent Irish state permitted its territory, or its territorial waters, to be used by a power hostile to Britain. On this issue, at any rate, de Valera's recorded views were fully in accord with those of Lloyd George. In February 1920, during his lengthy American tour, de Valera, as a means of trying to engage with the British Government, made his celebrated 'Cuban' declaration, which dealt with the suggestion central to the argument advanced by Lloyd George that the interests of British security demanded military control over Ireland. De Valera's declaration was published in *The Westminster Gazette* on 5 February 1920 and in *The New York Globe* on the following day.

The purpose de Valera had in mind was to assure the British Government that the welfare of Great Britain could be safeguarded without any infringement of the right of Ireland to independence, recalling that the United States, by means of the Monroe Doctrine, made provision for its security without depriving the Latin Republics of the south of their independence. He saw the dealings of the USA with Cuba as a model for the dealings of Britain with Ireland. The 1901 Treaty between the USA and Cuba stipulated that 'the Government of Cuba shall never enter into a treaty or other compact with any foreign power or powers which will impair or tend to impair the independence of Cuba'. Under the terms of the Treaty, Cuba was not permitted to grant any foreign power 'to obtain lodgement in control' over any portion of Cuba, for military or naval purposes. De Valera wondered why Britain didn't declare a

---

23   *Peace Negotiations*, 26 Aug. 1921, pp. 13–15.

Monroe doctrine for the British Isles. 'The people of Ireland,' he asserted, 'so far from objecting, would cooperate with their whole soul in a regional understanding of that sort.'[24] Numerous republican commentators in Ireland and the United States responded by accusing de Valera of being ready to accept much less than complete sovereignty for Ireland. An editorial in *The New York Globe* suggested that his Cuban proposal 'represented a withdrawal by the official head of the Irish Republic of the demand that Ireland be set free to decide her own international relations'.[25] Critics failed to recognise that the Cuban proposal was in perfect accord with the realities of British-Irish relations, and demonstrated, as Fanning observes, 'how de Valera conducted foreign policy on the basis of *Realpolitik.*' It was also an impressive illustration of his ability to grasp what none of his contemporaries did: that the Irish revolutionary tendency to enter into alliances with Britain's enemies would run counter to an independent Ireland's national interest.[26] However, as de Valera's American critics, led by John Devoy and Judge Cohalan, saw it, the Cuban analogy was fatally flawed from the Irish point of view, since the guarantees Cuba gave to the US formally allowed the latter to invade Cuba and overthrow its government whenever it felt like doing so. There was the further problem that Cuba was neither independent nor a republic, so that de Valera, claiming to be President of the Republic of Ireland, seemed prepared to accept less than complete sovereignty for Ireland.[27]

At this point, the correspondence was becoming tedious, the two contributors repeating previous arguments with relatively minor variations. In his final substantive contribution, however, de Valera tried to expose the weaknesses of the British case as outlined by Lloyd George. He rightly observed that 'Great Britain acts as though Ireland were bound to her by a contract of union that forbade separation', and that Irish representatives were not being invited to enter into 'a free and willing' partnership with the free nations of the British Commonwealth. He was particularly conscious that the dominant tone of Lloyd George's contribution was that of a superior to an inferior, the frequent use of 'Ireland shall' and 'Ireland must' being a characteristic feature of his

---

24 Patrick Murray, 'Obsessive historian: Eamon de Valera and the policing of his reputation', *Royal Irish Academy* Vol. 101c, No. 2 (Dublin, 2001), p. 54.

25 *New York Globe*, 6 Feb., 1920. The reference to de Valera as head of an Irish republic in 1920 is misapplied. Dáil Éireann had declared a republic in 1919, but this enjoyed no international recognition, either de jure or de facto.

26 Ronan Fanning, 'The evolution of Irish foreign policy', in Michael Kennedy and J. M. Skelly (eds), *Irish Foreign Policy, 1919–66* (Dublin, 2000), pp. 308–26.

27 See Charles Callan Tansill, *America and the Fight for Irish Freedom 1866–1922* (New York, 1957), pp. 359–68.

discourse. On the Ulster question, he pointed out that the conditions Britain now sought to impose on Ireland 'would divide her into two artificial states each destructive of the other's influence in any common Council, and both subject to the military, naval and economic control of the British Government'. Lloyd George had interpreted Anglo-Irish history as dictating union; de Valera read it as dictating separation.[28] Lloyd George's last word was to warn de Valera that the British Government could not accept 'as a basis of practical conference' any interpretation of the principle of government by consent of the governed which might involve the Irish people in setting up a Republic [which the Dáil had declared Ireland to be in January 1919] and repudiating the Crown.'[29] With this, Lloyd George indicated that the correspondence had lasted long enough, and suggested a conference 'to ascertain how the association of Ireland with the community of nations known as the British Empire can be reconciled with Irish national aspirations.' The Irish reply was ambivalent. De Valera was willing to send representatives of the Dáil Government to the conference suggested by Lloyd George, but argued, somewhat dubiously, that 'the Irish nation' had already formally declared its independence and recognised itself as a sovereign state.[30] Lloyd George reaffirmed his Government's position that no British government could accept this self definition, and that Ireland would be obliged to remain within the Empire, of which it was an indispensable part. Anxious to negotiate, however, Lloyd George broke the deadlock by renewing his invitation to a conference and ignoring all previous correspondence. The Dáil Cabinet accepted this offer, and de Valera now felt able to claim he had agreed to a conference without preconditions. This, however, was not the true position, since by agreeing to negotiate, Sinn Féin, ipso facto, was making a fundamental compromise since it was now clear that whatever the outcome of a conference, it was not going to be an Irish republic.

It is curious that after Lloyd George had informed de Valera that a republic could not form part of any peace settlement, he and Cathal Brugha, his most radical lieutenant, argued successfully that he should assume the formal title of President of the Republic, in addition to that of Dáil President.[31] This was a further barrier to a settlement with Britain, as was de Valera's public rejection, while the Treaty negotiations were proceeding in London, of the idea of accepting the Crown.[32] De Valera's actions during this period made the task of the negotiators more difficult than it might otherwise have been. Joseph

28   *Peace Negotiations*, 30 Aug. 1921, p. 17.
29   Ibid., 7 Sept. 1921, p. 17.
30   Ibid., 12 Sept. 1921, p.19.
31   Dáil Éireann, private sessions, 23 Aug. 1921, pp. 54–6.
32   Michael Laffan, *The Resurrection of Ireland: The Sinn Féin Party 1916–1923* (Cambridge, 1999) p. 347.

Connolly, who became a minister in the first Fianna Fáil Government in 1932, told one of de Valera's staunchest allies in America in 1922 that having prepared for a compromise with Lloyd George, he had 'rushed back to the rock of Republicanism' while the plenipotentiaries were still in London, because he had allowed himself to be subjected to the will of the most uncompromising of his ministers, Cathal Brugha and Austin Stack.[33]

II THE TREATY NEGOTIATIONS

The radical differences between what Sinn Féin demanded and what the British Government was prepared to concede, which emerged in the Lloyd George-de Valera exchanges, did not bode well for the prospects of a negotiated settlement, above all of the Ulster question. On the Irish side, Oliver Mac Donagh identifies an extraordinary failure to consider seriously the limits of British concession on Ulster. Two influences were at play here. Firstly, Lloyd George's Coalition Government depended for its continuance on Conservative and Unionist support in the House of Commons and in the country, and Unionists were not disposed to abandon Ulster to majority Nationalist governance. This factor alone ensured that the formal separation of the new six-county Ulster from Britain could never be a realistic prospect in the circumstances prevailing in 1921. Secondly, de Valera and his Cabinet were not fully alive to the new security which the 1920 Act had afforded to Ulster, which now had a constitutional government of its own, along with an operative civil service, rendering it safe in practice, as MacDonagh observes, 'from a unilateral British disposal of its territory'[34] and, moreover, sustained by British Government guarantees, given to Craig in 1920, of the virtually complete inviolability and permanence of its territorial unit. Political effect was given to these guarantees by the creation of an apparatus of state after Lloyd George had agreed to transfer administrative services to Northern Ireland: the relevant Order in Council was made on 9 November 1920, and the process was completed in the first part of 1921. The significance of this as a barrier to Irish political unity seems to have been lost on Sinn Féin which acquiesced without protest.[35] Ulster confidence in the security of its boundaries was rhetorically affirmed by Craig to Lloyd George in the aftermath of the Treaty: 'There is, I believe, no precedent in the history of the British Empire for taking away territory from

33 Joseph Connolly to Joseph McGarrity, 8 July 1922. McGarrity Papers, NLI 17654 (i).

34 Oliver MacDonagh, *Ireland: The Union and its Aftermath* (Dublin, 2003), p. 108.

35 John McColgan, 'Implementing the 1921 Treaty: Lionel Curtis and constitutional procedure', *IHS* Vol. xx, No. 79 (Mar. 1977), p. 69.

an established government without its sanction.'[36] The likely consequences of trying to deprive Ulster of what it achieved as a result of the 1920 Act were also made plain to Lloyd George by Lord Derby during the Treaty negotiations. Derby told the Prime Minister that if he attempted an all-Ireland parliament, 'without the willing assent of Ulster, at all events in this part of the world, there would be a tremendous rally to Ulster's side.'[37] Even de Valera had recognised this reality in August 1921. Louis Walsh, an Ulster nationalist and confidant of Collins, stressed the power and influence of Ulster Unionists in the context of negotiations on their political future or threats to the integrity of their state. 'People will not face the fact,' he wrote to Hugh Kennedy, Cosgrave's Attorney General, in September 1923, 'that there is here in the north a solid population, alien from us in thought and outlook, distrustful of our character and capacity, and with a big empire standing behind them.'[38]

On the Irish side also, there appeared to be little understanding of the difficulties facing British negotiators on the Ulster question. These difficulties were outlined by Lloyd George to Collins, Griffith and Duffy on 14 October 1921, during the first meeting of the Treaty Conference to consider the question of partition. Collins put the point to Lloyd George that the 1920 partition had produced a largely artificial situation which had left the British Government and Northern Ireland responsible for the coercion of one third of the people of the six counties. Lloyd George then reviewed the failed Liberal attempts since 1886 to settle the Irish problem on the basis of Irish autonomy, and each time the Conservative opponents of Home Rule saw that Ulster, armed and ready to fight, was the stumbling block, and they used Ulster resistance to defeat the measure. The Liberals were powerless in the face of this. To ignore these governing circumstances, as the Irish Cabinet and Treaty delegates seemed to want to do, was to ignore reality. Lloyd George suggested that the Irish side wanted him to deal out abstract justice 'without reference to the forces around him'. He then went to the heart of the matter in a memorable statement of the Ulster problem from the British point of view, at the same time justifying the exclusion of the six counties: 'You had to ask the British to use force to put Ulster out of one combination, in which she had been for generations, into another combination, which she professed to abhor, whether for practical or religious reasons. We could not do it. If we tried, the instrument would have broken in our hands. Their case was *Let us remain with you.* Our case was *Out you go or we fight you.* We could not have

36   PRONI CAB 92/3/1, 14 December 1924.

37   Lord Derby to Lloyd George, 18 Nov. 1921. Cited in Shelia Lawlor, *Britain and Ireland 1914–23* (Dublin, 1983), p. 123.

38   Kennedy Papers, UCDA, P4/1092.

done it . . . The first axiom is whatever happened we could not coerce Ulster . . . it would resolve itself into a civil war.'[39]

Churchill, likewise, identified the major British problem: they could not give way on Irish demands in relation to the six counties, since they were not free agents. Ulster autonomy must stand. The British might try to prevail on Craig to include an autonomous Ulster in a larger Irish parliament and to press him to hold autonomy for the six counties from the south instead of from Britain. The British could not extricate themselves from the 'impossible' situation created by Ulster: all they could do was to appeal to Craig to extricate them from it.[40] Craig was not disposed to help in this regard, nor did circumstances oblige him to: he could safely position himself on his Ulster rock while British and southern Irish tried to resolve their differences. In one respect, conditions were now more favourable to a settlement of the southern Irish problem than they had been in 1916 and 1918, when negotiations broke down over differences between Irishmen. Success came in 1920, as O'Day points out, because southern Protestants and northern Catholics were left out of the negotiations between Northern Unionists and the British Government leading to a partition acceptable to the former. In the Treaty negotiations southern Nationalists, although theoretically negotiating on behalf of Ireland as a whole, came to a settlement with Great Britain without the direct involvement of northern Unionists, an arrangement which simplified the problems confronting the British.

Although its members can have been in no doubt that the Ulster question was bound to be central to any negotiations on a treaty, the Dáil Cabinet had not even formulated its Ulster policy when it sent its negotiators. These negotiators went to London without a detailed alternative to the proposals made by Lloyd George on 20 July.[41] Instead, they brought with them a sketchy proposal headed 'Draft Treaty A' which did not confront the Ulster question.[42] Partition, even in de Valera's view, was to be little more than a tactic in the negotiations.[43] This proved to be a significant disadvantage, but there were others. The British negotiating team was the most experienced and talented that could have been assembled, consisting of Prime Minister Lloyd George, the Colonial Secretary, Winston Churchill, the Irish Secretary, Sir Hamar Greenwood, Austin Chamberlain, leader of the House of Commons, the Lord Chancellor, Lord Birkenhead, and the Secretary for War, Sir Laming

39 Thomas Jones, in Keith Middlemas (ed.), *Whitehall Diary* vol. 3 (London, 1971), pp. 129–30.
40 Lawlor, *Britain and Ireland*, p. 125.
41 *Peace Negotiations*, pp. 6–8.
42 For this document, see Dorothy Macardle, *The Irish Republic* (Dublin, 1951), pp. 937–9.
43 Laffan, *Resurrection of Ireland*, p. 232.

Worthington-Evans. Of the Irish plenipotentiaries, only Arthur Griffith, Chairman of the delegation, and Michael Collins, Minister for Finance, made any serious impression.

In general, de Valera's choice of negotiators left much to be desired. He himself was the only member of the Dáil Government fitted by capacity and experience to cope with the skills of the formidable British team, a fact recognised by his cabinet colleagues, who wanted him to lead the delegation. De Valera was instrumental in conferring the responsibility for negotiating a settlement on people he knew were more moderate than he was. This, Robert Barton, one of the plenipotentiaries, remarked, was a disaster, since, as he put it, 'we were not a fighting delegation.'[44] In an extraordinary letter to his American friend Joe McGarrity, de Valera revealed that he had deliberately chosen a divided delegation. He had no doubt that Griffith would accept the Crown and that Collins was contemplating doing the same, and hoped that this would, as he put it, 'simply make them a better bait for Lloyd George – leading him on and on further in our direction.' At the same time he was convinced that he and those who remained with him in Dublin would be able to hold Griffith and Collins 'from crossing the line'. It is not easy to divine the import of this subtlety. Barton was chosen, as a 'retarding force to any pre-cipitate giving away by the delegation, and Erskine Childers, as Secretary, would give Barton, his close relative and friend, added strength'. He had chosen the remaining two plenipotentiaries, Duggan and Duffy, as 'mere legal padding'. His final comment shows clearly what he had in mind: Duggan was certain to be influenced by Michael Collins, but 'Duffy was more likely to be on the Childers-Barton side'.[45] In the event, the negotiators behaved as he thought they would. Collins and Griffith, as Hart observes, ended up feeling like allies with each other against outsiders (especially Childers, Barton and Duffy),[46] not to mention de Valera, Stack and Brugha at home. Foster's not unreasonable verdict is that de Valera's intention was 'to balance the delegation, to a point where its will was almost paralysed'.[47]

There was what Lyons terms an 'inexcusable ambiguity'[48] about the instruc-tions issued by de Valera to the members of the Treaty delegation. During the private sessions of the Dáil before the negotiations began, de Valera defined plenipotentiaries as 'men who are sent over to make peace [who] come back

44   T. Ryle Dwyer, *De Valera: The Man and the Myths* (Dublin, 1991), p. 85.
45   Seán Cronin (ed.), *The McGarrity Papers* (Tralee, 1972), pp. 110–11.
46   Peter Hart, *Mick: The Real Michael Collins* (London, 2005), p. 296.
47   Foster, *Modern Ireland*, p. 505.
48   Lyons, *Ireland since the Famine*, p. 430.

and their actions were (*sic*) ratified or not'.[49] However, if 'envoys plenipo-
tentiary' meant anything, it meant envoys with full powers to sign the Treaty
and to take responsibility for what they had agreed to. Before they left for
London, however, de Valera issued them with explicit instructions to submit
to Dublin the full text of any draft treaty about to be signed, and to await a
reply before taking any further action. This contradiction between the powers
of the plenipotentiaries and the powers of the Dáil Cabinet inevitably caused
confusion, and during the post-Treaty period was the source of bitter debate.
Whatever freedom of action the negotiators believed their formal instructions
gave them, de Valera was bent on being involved, even if at a distance, in the
shaping of the settlement. In practice, Griffith and Collins were the only
members of the delegation who might justifiably have claimed plenipotential
status, since they relegated the others to the margins of the Conference. The
benign explanation for the anomalous arrangements made in Dublin is that in
the absence of de Valera, if the negotiators were to be taken seriously by the
British, they would have to be publicly acknowledged as having the status of
plenipotentiaries. In the end, they acted independently of the Dáil Cabinet in
subscribing their names to the Treaty. Middlemas records the threatening
circumstances in which they felt obliged to do this: 'The ultimate choice
remained: status within the Empire or nothing. Lloyd George refused even to
consider Griffith's plea to refer this to the Dáil . . . If the answer was no, it was
war. The Irish had to sign and disregard whatever their Sinn Féin mandate
said, or, if they believed the Prime Minister, face the accumulated might of
the British forces. . . . The ultimatum of war within three days was matched by
the equally impressive appeal to preserve the peace . . . Strangely, no one, not
even Childers, invoked the Cabinet mandate they had the day before, and no
one thought to use the telegraph to Dublin.'[50]

De Valera's role in the Treaty negotiations has had its apologists, although
it was never quite clear what he stood for, 'or with whom he stood, at least
from December 1920 until June 1922.'[51] Lee, however, accepts that unity on his
own side was his overriding objective, and suggests that his behaviour prior to
and during the negotiations was governed by a desire to maintain harmony
between extreme and moderate elements in Sinn Féin: 'realising that bitter
controversy was likely to arise over the terms of any possible agreement, he
could wean the doctrinaires into accepting "external association" as an
honourable solution.'[52] His own primary explanation for remaining at home

49   Dáil Éireann, private sessions, 26 Aug. 1921, p. 83.
50   Jones, *Whitehall Diary* vol. 3, p. 183.
51   Lawlor, *Britain and Ireland*, p. xi.
52   J. J. Lee, *Ireland 1912–1985: Politics and Society* (Cambridge, 1989), p. 49.

was that by doing so he would provide the negotiators with the tactical excuse that they had to refer proposals to him, thus affording them valuable respite from the pressures of negotiation.[53] De Valera, given, as Lloyd George was, to formulating ingenious compromises to resolve irreconcilable contrarieties, produced a remarkable constitutional formula: external association. This, had the British negotiators been prepared to accept it, would have resulted in an Irish sovereign state within the Empire, externally and voluntarily associated with the dominions of the Empire for matters of common concern such as defence and external relations. De Valera regarded this formula, ultimately unacceptable to the British side but with considerable significance for future relations between Britain and its Commonwealth, as a means of satisfying the minimum Republican demands of his diehards, while not fracturing Nationalist unity. John M. Regan's comment is apt: 'There is no denying the integral beauty of external association in its abstract form. While it fell far short of the fundamental strains of both Irish Republicanism and British Imperialism, its chief attribute was that it held the possibility, arguably the only one available in 1921, of reconciling both forces without recourse to further unwanted bloodshed.'[54] Although external association was imaginative, ingenious and innovative, it was, as Foster observes, ahead of its time, 'since the contemporary constitutional framework could not incorporate it.'[55]

The Irish delegation was riven by animosity, at times even hatred. Relations between Griffith and Duffy had been strained long before they were appointed plenipotentiaries as a consequence of vigorous chastisement visited by the former upon the latter, who still bore deep resentment.[56] Erskine Childers, one of the secretaries to the negotiators, was the most accomplished of those on the Irish side, possessing a keen analytical intelligence as well as being an experienced draftsman. Both Collins and Griffith frequently showed contempt for Childers, rightly suspecting that he was reporting back to de Valera on the progress of the negotiations[57] Griffith disliked him as a man and for being English. Coogan claims that Griffith and Collins both had an interest in common with the British, since both sides wanted to be rid of Childers.[58] De Valera may have engineered a divided delegation, but the behaviour of

---

53   See Earl of Longford and T. P. O'Neill, *Eamon de Valera* (Dublin, 1970), pp. 147–8.

54   John M. Regan, *The Irish Counter-Revolution 1921–1936* (Dublin, 1999), p. 6.

55   Foster, *Modern Ireland*, p. 505.

56   FitzGerald, 'Pakenham and the Anglo-Irish Treaty', p. 407.

57   Dáil Éireann, 2/304/2 NAI. Peter Hart, however, remarks that the 'much-speculated-upon secret letters' from Childers to de Valera 'were actually straightforward reports on the negotiations, with only approving comments about Collins'. Hart, *The Real Michael Collins*, p. 292.

58   T. P. Coogan, *Michael Collins: A Biography* (London, 1990), p. 243.

Griffith and Collins towards their colleagues soon created two cliques. Eventually, Collins and Griffith became a clique of two. They persuaded the British to arrange sub-conferences,[59] with the result that the greater part of the negotiating on the Irish side was done by Griffith and Collins in private sessions with senior British ministers, rendering the other delegates largely superfluous. When the delegation returned with the fruits of their labour to a fraught Cabinet meeting in Dublin on 3 December 1921, Cathal Brugha, who had little respect for either Collins or Griffith, remarked in reference to their activities in London that the British Government had 'selected its men'.[60] The superiority thus affected by Griffith and Collins was not entirely well founded. For the final defence Committee meeting, Collins submitted a document arguing that control of Ireland in a naval war was not indispensable to British interests. Churchill found the document 'very able and considered,' and 'logically sound' on its own terms, while Lloyd George considered it 'formidable'. Such praise was misapplied; Childers, the only person among the Irish delegates with naval experience, was actually the source of the ideas expressed in the document and responsible for their formulation.[61]

In the Dáil, Griffith did not refrain from making his disapproval of Childers, whom he called a 'damned Englishman', a matter of public record, suggesting that he was a British spy. Among the less offensive of his comments was the following: 'I was Chairman of the Delegation of which Childers, not with my approval, was Secretary.'[62] For his part, Childers was severely critical of both Collins and Griffith, who, he recorded in his diary, 'don't understand the meaning of half the points' brought up by skilled English draftsmen. As he observed Collins and Griffith, the latter 'muzzy with whiskey', displaying ignorance and incompetence by his own exacting standards, Childers 'thought of the fate of Ireland being settled hugger-mugger by ignorant Irish negotiators and A. G. [Griffith] in genuine sympathy with many of the English claims.' According to Childers, Collins revealed a strange inability to grasp the meaning of British proposals on income tax for Ulster; M. C. 'did not understand the subject or only imperfectly.' Childers expressed his frustration that he had been left in a waiting room while Collins attended a meeting at the Treasury: another instance of the reluctance of the leadership of the Irish delegation to make appropriate use of his expertise.[63] In assessing

---

59 Jones makes it clear that the real authors of this proposal were Collins and Griffith, not the British. See Jones, *Whitehall Diary* vol. 3, p. 141.

60 Childers Diary TCD, MS 7814, 3 Dec. 1921.

61 Hart, *The Real Michael Collins*, p. 298.

62 Dáil Debate on the Treaty, private sessions, 15 Dec. 1921, p. 172.

63 Childers Diary, TCD, MS 7814, 2 Dec. 1921.

the historical value of the comments of Childers on Griffith and Collins it should be borne in mind that he was a biased witness: perhaps inevitably so, given the wide differences in temperament, background and education between him and his colleagues. His assessment reflected his personal dislike for Griffith, his own sense of intellectual supremacy, his contempt for the imperfect work practices of Collins and Griffith and their general lack of sobriety and high seriousness, in contrast to what he saw as his own dedicated professional approach to the task in hand.

A much-quoted comment on Childers attributed to Collins is of dubious historical value: 'The advice and inspiration of C. [Childers] is like farmland under water: dead . . . Soon he will howl in triumph for what it is worth.' The source of this is Rex Taylor's biography of Collins. Taylor, a limestone-quarry labourer and a poet, quotes it from a letter allegedly written by Collins to a London-Irish businessman John O'Kane from County Galway, at the end of the London talks. The same letter contains the celebrated 'claim' by Collins that in signing the Treaty he had signed his own death warrant. However, as Deirdre McMahon points out, no one of the name O'Kane is listed in the London business or residential directories of the period. Even if O'Kane was a pseudonym, the problem remains that Taylor, the only person who used this material, if it ever existed, is now dead and that the papers he used in the preparation of the biography cannot be located. There is thus no way of knowing whether the London-Irish businessman and the letters to him from Collins were products of Taylor's poetic imagination. McMahon's conclusion is sensible: 'The question marks over this material should, I think, make scholars of the period cautious.'[64]

Hart's verdict is that 'Collins was a mediocre negotiator' and that Griffith and the others were 'not much better'.[65] Lloyd George, whose tactics through-out were masterly, confided to C. P. Scott, Editor of *The Manchester Guardian*, that Collins was 'an uneducated, rather stupid man'. In June 1922, Lloyd George, regretting the fewness and weakness of contemporary Irish leaders, suggested that 'there was only Griffith. Collins was just a wild animal- a mustang.'[66] Regan suggests that Griffith 'played a remarkably maladroit game in London and in the process compromised the entire position of the Irish delegation'.[67] Lionel Curtis, who, as British Secretary to the Treaty Conference was ideally placed to assess Collins, was equally scathing. He described him as

64   Deirdre McMahon, 'Michael Collins – his biographers Piaras Beaslaí and Rex Taylor', in G. Doherty and D. Keogh (eds), *Michael Collins and the Making of the Irish State* (Cork, 1998), pp. 127–33.
65   See Hart, *The Real Michael Collins*, p. 294.
66   Jones, *Whitehall Diary* vol. 3, p. 206.
67   Regan, *Counter-Revolution*, p. 22.

'the corner-boy in excelsis' and remarked that Collins 'could never quite see the picture through his own reflection in the glass'. During a break in the Treaty negotiations in November 1921, Collins met Mark Sturgis, Assistant Under Secretary at Dublin Castle, in the Gresham Hotel, Dublin. Sturgis observed that Collins was 'just like the big, young, pleasant prosperous self-satisfied cattle-dealer in a big way of business, with which Ireland is full'.[68] Collins himself acknowledged his innocence of the complexities of high politics, asserting that he understood things only in 'the plain Irish way' and was 'befogged by constitutional and legal arguments'.[69] At this remove, it is easy to enlarge on the inadequacies of the Irish negotiators. However, even if one were to concede that they were, as a body, ill qualified for the task assigned to them, and that the result of their labours was a disastrous civil war, most of the blame for this situation must be laid at the door of de Valera, who chose them, and then repudiated them. In repudiating them, he was in effect, repudiating his own considered judgement.

The vital importance of Ulster as a factor in the negotiations was never fully grasped by the Irish delegates or their advisers. Formally, they were representing Ireland as a unit, a claim not recognised by Craig. The position of the Northern Ireland Government was that the Ulster state established under the 1920 Act was an entity not liable to alteration; Craig had made it clear that whatever arrangements the British and southern Irish arrived at could have no bearing on the territory or status of Northern Ireland. On the other hand, the southern Treaty delegates were regarded by the Dáil Government as speaking for the whole of Ireland and as negotiating in a 32-county context. As a token of this, the two principal delegates represented Northern Ireland constituencies: Griffith, Tyrone North West, and Collins, Armagh. However, the full record of the preliminaries on the Irish side and of the discussions in London suggests that the real focus was on the future political and constitutional relationship of the 26 counties and the British Government. That this emphasis was shared by the great majority of the membership of Dáil Éireann is clear from the printed record of the public and private sessions of the Dáil when the terms of the Treaty were being debated from December to January 1921–2. The Dáil was opposed to the partition of

---

68 Sturgis Diary, 13 Nov. 1921. Cited by Brian P. Murphy, *John Chartres: Mystery Man of the Treaty* (Dublin, 1995), p. 69.

69 See Hart, *The Real Michael Collins*, p. 296. Those seeking a more benign view of Collins will find this generously conveyed in the following: P. S. O'Hegarty, *The Victory of Sinn Féin* (Dublin, 1924); Piaras Beaslaí, *Michael Collins and the Making of the New Ireland* (Dublin, 1926); T. P. Coogan, *Michael Collins* (London, 1990); T. P. Coogan, *De Valera: Long Fellow, Long Shadow* (London, 1993); T. Ryle Dwyer, *Michael Collins: The Man who Won the War* (Cork, 1990).

Ireland, reflecting widespread nationalist anger when the island was divided by the 1920 Act, while de Valera had told his first New York audience in 1919 that there was no question of Ulster exclusion. On the other hand, de Valera, in common with most other southern Irishmen, had no clearly defined Ulster policy, and no viable plan to deal with the Ulster issue when it emerged, as it inevitably would, in the Treaty negotiations. Being uncertain as to how best to proceed, all he could suggest to the Irish Cabinet was that if other aspects of the settlement offered were unsatisfactory, they should break off the negotiations on Ulster.[70] Thus, Ulster was to be regarded not as the major issue it was, but as a mere tactic, a useful excuse on which to break. This mentality is reflected in the Treaty debates. In the course of these, little was said either about Ulster or partition. Anti-Treaty speakers concentrated on the Crown, the Oath and the Empire. Some of the few references to Northern Ireland concentrated not on the loss of the six counties, but on their possible use in the future as a bridgehead to be used by Britain to re-establish control over the rest of Ireland.[71]

In the course of the public debates on the Treaty, of 338 pages, nine are devoted to the north. Virtually all the deputies who spoke were preoccupied with the degree of independence which the rest of the country was to enjoy, and with largely symbolic matters such as the Crown and the Oath. In the private sessions, speakers for and against the Treaty showed even less interest in Northern Ireland: out of 181 pages, only three are taken up with any aspect of the Ulster question. During these debates, de Valera issued his alternative to the Treaty, Document No. 2, which, on the face of it seemed to embody contradictory thinking on the Ulster question. The document contained a declaration that the Dáil would not recognise the right of any part of Ireland to be excluded 'from the supreme authority of the National Parliament and Government', but went on to incorporate the Ulster clauses of the Treaty, which made provision for just such exclusion. On one interpretation, as Ryle Dwyer observes, de Valera was saying that he would not recognise the right of Northern Ireland to secede but would nevertheless recognise the de facto secession for the sake of peace. Dwyer also argues de Valera was not concerned about the partition issue, citing de Valera's own comment in support: 'As far as we are concerned, [the Ulster Question] is a fight between Ireland and England. I want to eliminate the Ulster Question out of it.'[72]

---

70   Cabinet Minutes, NAI DE 1/3, 13 Nov. 1921.

71   For an analysis of the Treaty debates, see Maureen Wall, in T. D. Williams, *The Irish Struggle 1916–26* (London, 1966), p. 87 ff.

72   Dwyer, *De Valera*, p. 90.

There are three plausible explanations for the paucity of references to Ulster during the Treaty debates. The first is that Dáil deputies probably believed that the operation of the boundary commission, provided for in the Ulster clauses of the Treaty, would leave only a truncated, and unviable Ulster, which would consequently be forced to come within an all- Ireland parliament. The second is related to the first. The 1920 Act had placed severe financial restrictions on Northern Ireland, which could not collect customs, excise duties, income tax or surtax, purchase tax, tax on profits or any general tax or capital. In addition, Westminster retained 85 per cent of revenue derived from Northern Ireland, and controlled 60 per cent of its expenditure.[73] Griffith and Collins were convinced that Craig's administration would find it difficult to operate for long in such straitened circumstances, while Craig himself saw the financial clauses of the 1920 settlement as a greater threat to Northern Ireland than that posed by the boundary commission.[74] Thirdly, the casual nature of Sinn Féin thinking on Northern Ireland reflects a partitionist mentality in the south, a general lack of interest in the north, an unsympathetic attitude to its heritage and political culture, a sense that it was a different, sometimes hostile territory, a virtual *terra incognita*. Not all southerners regarded the prospect of unity with Northern Ireland as desirable. One outspoken Dáil Deputy, J. J. Walsh, Postmaster General in Cosgrave's first administration, thought of northern Unionists as 'three-quarters of a million West British cutthroats that had dominated the country and claimed they owned two-thirds of it'. Walsh was among those who believed that the Irish revolution was a political one only, confined to the south. He argued that acceptance of partition would give the Free State a chance 'to re-establish our own language, games and popular culture, and enable us to bide our time, no matter how long, in removing partition by the removal of the partitionists.' The integration of the north with the south, Walsh feared, would mean that Unionists would again influence national policy, that the Irish language would suffer, and that 'everything we fought for through 800 years would be smashed to atoms and swallowed up in the British Empire'.[75] Many southerners probably shared some or all of these beliefs but were reluctant to express them as frankly as this.

The Sinn Féin Party in the country, its membership in the Dáil, and the Dáil Cabinet, had manifested little interest in the north of Ireland in the years prior to the Treaty. It was only on the eve of the Treaty negotiations, in

73   Alan O'Day, *Irish Home Rule 1867–1921* (Manchester, 1998), p. 297, p. 328.

74   See Kevin Matthews, *Fatal Influence: The Impact of Ireland on British Politics 1920–1925* (Dublin, 2004), p. 63.

75   Jed Martin, *The Irish Border: History, Politics and Culture* (Liverpool, 1999), p. 68.

September 1921, that the Dáil set up a special Ulster Committee to assemble facts and arguments for use during the London talks. Eoin MacNeill, a northerner, was appointed Chairman and Seán Milroy, TD for Cavan, was Secretary. The views of six-county Nationalists were widely canvassed. However, the Dublin authorities rejected the help of resident northern Nationalist advisers. The Belfast Nationalist MP Joseph Devlin, who had experience of negotiating with Lloyd George, was not consulted. Cahir Healy, the veteran Ulster Nationalist MP and a splendid judge of politics and politicians, claimed that the three leaders of southern nationalism, de Valera, Collins and Griffith, did not understand Northern Ireland. He remarked that Griffith, 'the sanest and best informed of them all,' nursed a delusion for years that 'the beginning and the end of the problem lay in London'. Healy also dismissed de Valera's strategy of withholding recognition from the Northern Ireland administration, along with 'the rather jumpy efforts which, with Collins, passed for statecraft' as not calculated to bring Ireland one day nearer peace.[76]

As the parties began the negotiations leading to a treaty, both sides were agreed on the ideal solution: a united Ireland with generous provision for Northern Ireland within that framework. It was clear, nonetheless, that this could not become a reality without the agreement of those whose political destiny was bound to be a central issue for consideration and who were formally excluded from the process: the Ulster Unionists. They were not, however, without a decisive say when the Ulster question came up for consideration: Lloyd George was obliged to consult Craig when Irish unity became a pressing issue in the negotiations, as a condition advanced by the Irish plenipotentiaries for their acceptance of the Crown and Empire.

For both British and Irish negotiators, the talks turned on two major issues: the relationship of Nationalist Ireland to the United Kingdom, and, as the talks progressed, the much more difficult matter of Northern Ireland's relationship with the rest of the island. Lord Longford's comment on the position that was reached prior to full negotiations is worth noting: 'the British government had pledged themselves in no circumstances to allow Ireland to retire from the Empire, while the Irish Government had *not* pledged themselves in no circumstances to come inside.' Longford points out that the settlement would leave Ireland a member of the Empire, and 'a Dominion settlement now became the reasonable, a Republic the unreasonable, course'.[77] For Lloyd George, the fundamental objective was first of all to get the Irish negotiators to accept the minimum British demands on Crown and Empire,

76   Eamon Phoenix, *Northern Nationalism, Nationalist Politics, Partition and the Catholic Minority in Northern Ireland 1890–1940* (Belfast, 1994), p. 315.
77   Longford, *Peace by Ordeal*, p. 79.

and having accomplished this, to try to win Craig's agreement on Irish unity. On the first, the key point at issue was whether, or to what extent, Ireland should recognise the British Crown. This symbolic question had vital significance for both sides. For the British, Irish recognition of the Crown was an essential token of imperial unity and sovereignty, as well as an absolute *sine qua non* of any agreement. For the Irish, the Crown was a symbol of national bondage. Eventually, the British won their point, although the agreed oath prescribed that members of the southern Irish Parliament were to affirm that their primary allegiance was to the Free State, and to promise 'fidelity' to the Crown. This implied a greater degree of independence of the Crown than that prevailing in the British Dominions, where the oath was a simple one of allegiance to the King. The Irish concession on the oath, even in its minimalist form, could be interpreted as representing a useful friendly gesture in the direction of Ulster Unionists, even as the expression of a common link between north and south which might facilitate ultimate unity. In any case, the relatively benign form of the oath finally agreed was the maximum concession to separatist demands consistent with a realistic prospect of Irish unity. Oliver MacDonagh argues that 'some shadow of imperial allegiance, some obeisance to the British Crown, was indispensable if the North East were ever to be joined politically with the remainder of the island'.[78]

From the Irish point of view, willingness to accept the Crown and Empire depended on their being satisfied on Ulster. Once they had got the assurances they wanted on the Crown and Empire and in effect settled the relationship between Nationalist Ireland and the United Kingdom, the British were ready to satisfy the Irish negotiators on Ulster by trying to persuade Craig to meet a fundamental Irish demand: the essential unity of Ireland, which meant that an Irish administration 'should be given legal sovereignty over the whole island'.[79] There was no suggestion of trying to coerce Craig into yielding on this. In 1920, as the price of Ulster Unionist support for the Government of Ireland Bill, the British Government had pledged not to force the newly established Northern entity into any union with the rest of Ireland. 'Secure behind the rampart of her own parliament, Ulster was now going to be more difficult than ever to persuade out of it.'[80] The Irish negotiators, however, were conscious of a serious deficiency in the 1920 Act, which left 450,000 Catholic Nationalists under a Unionist-controlled parliament against the declared wishes of the great majority of their representatives. The British negotiators found this position difficult to justify, as Sir Austen Chamberlain acknowledged. Reporting to his

---

78   MacDonagh, *Ireland: The Union and its Aftermath*, p. 112.

79   Hart, *The Real Michael Collins*, p. 293.

80   John Campbell, *F. E. Smith: The First Earl of Birkenhead* (London, 1983), p. 565.

colleagues on a meeting at which Collins and Griffith had pressed him on why the British would not allow county option, or consider reducing the area of Northern Ireland by holding local plebiscites, he admitted that 'they could not put a more difficult question', while Birkenhead regarded the British position on the six counties 'an impossible one'.[81]

In dealing with Irish demands on the Ulster issue, Lloyd George demonstrated his remarkable diplomatic and negotiating skills, while his Irish counterparts were, by contrast, amateurs in these respects. The dominance of Lloyd George was attested to by Robert Barton, one of the Irish delegates, an expert witness, who had the leisure to observe his activities throughout. In a contribution to the Dáil debate on the Treaty, Barton provided a perceptive and frank account of the Prime Minster's manipulative gift. Barton paid tribute to 'the power of conviction that he alone, of all men I met, can impart by word and gesture – the vehicles by which the mind of one man oppresses and impresses the mind of another'.[82] They allowed Lloyd George to control the proceedings throughout the negotiations on Ulster. When it came to achieving essential unity in the face of opposition from Ulster Unionists and their powerful Conservative allies, the dominant party in the Coalition Government which he led, Lloyd George knew that his task was impossible. Notwithstanding this, he allowed Griffith to believe that essential unity was possible, and as Lee observes, 'Griffith merely reflected the immaturity of nationalist thinking about Ulster in allowing himself to be deluded.'[83]

Before proceeding with the discussion of Ulster with the Irish delegates, Lloyd George decided, by 25 October 1921, that he would try to resolve the Irish question by obtaining assurances from them on the 'vital things', allegiance to the Crown and the Empire, in return for Irish unity. He indicated that he would be willing to discuss the Ulster area, and consider 'any machinery' by which the unity of Ireland 'should be recognised and strengthened'. If the Irish accepted 'all subject to unity', he would be in a position to go to Craig.[84] Griffith and Collins made it clear that 'the only way to reconcile Ireland to the Crown was to secure Irish unity', which did not mean 'a denial of autonomy to Ulster', but on the other hand, 'Ulster and Ireland could not be equal.'[85] Griffith was prepared to accept the 'vital' demands of the British in return for Irish unity. By 30 October 1921, Lloyd George believed that the Irish delegation would settle on the King, the Empire and naval facilities for Great

81 Jones, *Whitehall Diary* vol. 3, p. 146.
82 Debate on the Treaty, 19 Dec. 1921, p. 49.
83 Lee, *Ireland 1912–1985*, pp. 52–3.
84 Jones, *Whitehall Diary* vol. 3, p. 146.
85 Ibid., p. 145.

Britain, 'in return for Tyrone, Fermanagh and customs, with excise and the post office to be controlled by one parliament instead of two, Northern and Southern.' Lloyd George was determined not to continue the Irish war if a settlement were possible on these lines.[86] In an attempt to bring the Ulster question to a head, Lloyd George, on 2 November 1921 secured a letter of assurance from Griffith with which to confront Craig. In the letter, eventually approved by the 'Republicans' Barton, Duffy and Childers, Griffith declared himself satisfied to recommend a free partnership of Ireland with the other states associated with the British Commonwealth, that Ireland should consent to a recognition of the Crown as head of the proposed association of free states, and that the British Navy should be afforded such costal facilities as might be necessary. These assurances were 'conditional on the essential unity of Ireland'.[87] On 7 November Lloyd George saw Craig, who told him that 'under no circumstances could Ulster look at an all-Ireland parliament'.[88] After a Cabinet meeting on 10 November, Lloyd George told his colleagues that he proposed to write to Craig warning him of the fundamental disadvantages of staying out of an all-Ireland parliament. In his letter, Lloyd George told Craig that the settlement towards which he was working would involve Irish allegiance to the Crown, partnership in the Empire, provision of naval securities, retention by Northern Ireland of all the powers conferred by the establishment of an all-Ireland parliament upon which further powers would be devolved.[89]

Craig remained adamant. In his reply, he rejected Lloyd George's settlement proposals, seeing no point in discussing them further. Northern Ireland could not accept an all-Ireland parliament: such a parliament was what Ulster had resisted for many years. He reiterated the traditional Unionist point of view that Northern Ireland had accepted the 1920 Act as 'a final settlement and supreme sacrifice'. He could not countenance his government entering into a conference in which an all-Ireland parliament was open to discussion.[90] Craig was extremely disappointed at the trend of Lloyd George's thinking, deeply uneasy at his attempts to induce the Northern Ireland Government to solve the Anglo-Irish problem by compromising its own status and privileges. He spoke to Lord Curzon, the Foreign Secretary, of being betrayed, and turned out of the British system. He expressed anxiety that Ulster was being abandoned, and in danger of losing two of its six

---

86 Lawlor, *Britain and Ireland*, p. 129.
87 Jones, *Whitehall Diary* vol. 3, pp. 153–4.
88 Ibid., p. 160.
89 Lloyd George to Craig, 10 Nov. 1921, LG F/11/3/19.
90 Craig to Lloyd George, 11 Nov. 1921, LG F/11/3/20.

counties. Bonar Law, the Conservative Party leader and a principled upholder of Northern Unionist interests remarked that the Ulster Parliament, at present enjoying definite powers, prerogatives and functions, with a share in the Imperial Parliament, now saw itself 'degraded to the position of a subordinate assembly from having been almost a Dominion Parliament'.[91] By this time, the British negotiators, faced with Craig's intransigence, were beginning to find their commitment to the integrity of Ulster, as it had been created in 1920, increasingly irksome. As a way out of the impasse, the idea of a boundary commission as an element in the Treaty gained currency among the Irish and British negotiators. Austen Chamberlain found Craig's reply to Lloyd George's request for help in finding a solution to the Ulster problem distasteful, remarking that if the correspondence were published, 'there would be a great revulsion against Ulster',[92] and arguing that if Ulster refused unity, she could not have her 1920 boundaries.

By now, Lloyd George had the support of Bonar Law for a proposal to allow the south to have a dominion parliament, Northern Ireland to remain in the United Kingdom, the establishment of a boundary commission, and the north to have representation at Westminster and to share United Kingdom taxation.[93] By 9 November, Griffith had decided that it did not matter if Craig refused an all-Ireland parliament, because a boundary commission would deal with the Ulster problem, and told Lloyd George that if he made a proposal for a boundary commission, the Irish delegates, while not giving him a pledge, would 'not turn him down on it', although 'it would have to be not for Tyrone and Fermanagh only, but for the Six Counties'.[94] Three days later, the pivotal exchange of the entire conference took place. Lloyd George exacted a secret undertaking from Griffith that he would not refuse to sign a treaty merely because of disagreement on Ulster and that he would not obstruct the boundary commission proposal. Lloyd George convinced Griffith that he would need such an undertaking to prevent a Conservative and Ulster Unionist Party repudiation of the Treaty negotiations at the impending conference of the Conservative Association at Liverpool on 17 November. Although Griffith did not actually pledge to accept a boundary commission, his assurance implicitly conveyed acceptance. Thomas Jones, Principal Assistant Secretary to the British Cabinet, put Griffith's assurance into a short memorandum. Griffith approved its contents in the presence of Jones. As a piece of evidence, this document was to prove of crucial importance at the concluding stage of the

91 Jones, *Whitehall Diary* vol. 3, p. 161.
92 Ibid., p. 163.
93 Ibid.
94 Ibid., p. 157.

negotiations, when Lloyd George was able to invoke it as proof that the Irish delegation had undertaken not to obstruct a settlement, despite the fact that Griffith subscribed to the document without the knowledge of the other Irish plenipotentiaries. By doing so, he had considerably limited the agreed option of breaking on Ulster. On the other hand, Griffith may have been attracted to Lloyd George's boundary commission proposal because he felt that the findings of such a commission were likely to settle the Ulster question permanently. Chamberlain believed that it was the opinion of the Irish negotiators that a vote by constituencies or poor law areas in the six counties, if mandated by a boundary commission, would give the south more than two counties and would leave Northern Ireland 'economically paralysed'.[95] Griffith had already conveyed a similar impression to de Valera, telling him on 9 November that the boundary commission arrangement 'would give most of Tyrone and Fermanagh, and part of Armagh, Londonderry, Down etc'.[96]

Before the boundary commission proposal changed the position previously taken by Griffith and Collins on the Ulster question, the chances of concluding a treaty looked remote. As the situation presented itself to the British delegates in early November, the possibility existed that the Irish, if given an all-Ireland parliament, would accept Crown and Empire, while, on the basis of Irish acceptance of Crown and Empire, Northern Ireland might, however reluctantly, consent to an all-Ireland parliament. Craig, however, was adamant in his refusal to consent to an all-Ireland parliament, while Griffith, without that concession from Craig, was not willing to make concessions on Empire and Crown. Lloyd George's singular achievement was to convince the Irish side that there was an honourable way of escape from this vicious circle.

The boundary commission proposal was the ultimate British tactic in inducing Griffith and the other Irish delegates to sign a treaty. On 5 December, the day before the Treaty was signed, Lloyd George confronted Griffith with the memorandum which signified the latter's assent to a boundary commission as the means by which Irish unity would emerge. MacDonagh remarks that a combination of 'hope, fear, pressure and illusion' caused the Irish delegates to endorse partition in the end.[97] Those who signed, particularly Griffith and Collins, did not necessarily believe that they were subscribing to a permanent partition, or reinforcing the geographical configuration of the 1920 arrangement. What was significant about the proposal for a boundary commission was not its use as a means of satisfying the Irish delegation on the prospect of eventual Irish unity, but the essentially different,

95   Chamberlain to Lloyd George, 11 Nov. 1921, LG F/14/5/53.
96   Griffith to de Valera, 9 Nov. 1921, ED 2/304/8.
97   MacDonagh, *Union and its Aftermath*, p. 113.

even contradictory, forms it took from the time it was first proposed by the British side. On 13 November 1921, Thomas Jones showed Griffith the document he had drawn up outlining the British boundary commission proposals, to which Griffith assented. This document made provision for what would happen if Northern Ireland 'did not see her way to accept immediately the principle of a Parliament of all-Ireland'. In that case, it would be necessary to revise the boundary of Northern Ireland, and a boundary commission 'would be directed to adjust the line both by inclusion and exclusion so as to make the boundary conform as closely as possible to the wishes of the population'.[98] On 16 November 1921, a British draft treaty was submitted to the Irish negotiators. Northern Ireland was, in theory, to start under the jurisdiction of the new Irish state, but could opt out within a year and retain the position it enjoyed under the 1920 Act. If, however, this option was exercised, a boundary commission would be appointed 'to determine in accordance with the wishes of the inhabitants the boundaries between Northern Ireland and the rest of Ireland'. As Longford points out, the wording, or rather the omission of words, in these draft terms of reference for the commission are of exceptional significance. 'Wishes of the inhabitants alone are to decide. There is no mention of the economic and geographic considerations that four years later were to prove decisive in losing the Irish Free State every atom of anticipated benefit.'[99]

A further formulation of the boundary commission proposal was contained in a letter from Lloyd George to Craig as the Treaty negotiations were nearing their end. The letter warned Craig that if the Government of Northern Ireland did not enter the Free State, the British Government would be unable to defend the 1920 boundary, 'which must be subject to revision on one side and another by a boundary commission.'[100] None of these versions anticipated what eventually emerged in the boundary commission provisions included in the Ulster clauses of the Treaty signed on 6 December 1921. The major differences between earlier British versions and the conditions imposed by the Treaty were twofold. The chairman of the three-person commission provided for in the Treaty was to be appointed by the British Government, and the boundary was to be determined not merely in accordance with the wishes of the inhabitants, but such wishes had to be 'compatible with economic and geographic conditions'. Thus a process which originally seemed straight-forward was now rendered open to an unpredictable variety of interpretations, and made to depend in the final analysis on the character and outlook of a

98 Longford, *Peace by Ordeal*, pp. 177–8; Jones, *Whitehall Diary* vol. 3, p. 164.
99 Longford, *Peace by Ordeal*, p. 184.
100 Lloyd George to Craig, 5 Dec. 1921, LGF/11/3/24.

chairman appointed by one of the parties. Almost to the end, the Irish negotiators demanded a statement from Craig on essential Irish unity before signing. Lloyd George, however, had known for weeks that Craig would not concede on this point in any circumstances. If both Craig and the Irish delegation remained adamant, the negotiations would break on Ulster, some-thing Lloyd George wanted to avoid at all costs. Had the Irish side broken on King and Empire, he told his Cabinet, Britons would fight them on such a vital issue, but would not fight for the retention of Tyrone and Fermanagh. Lloyd George's actual words involved a pun on Throne/Tyrone: 'Men will die for Throne and Empire. I do not know who will die for Tyrone and Fermanagh.'[101] The British were extricated from their major problem when Lloyd George dramatically produced the document approved by Griffith in November which effectively promised not to break on Ulster, and implied support for a boundary commission as an alternative to Ulster assent to the principle of the essential unity of Ireland. Lloyd George's views on what such a commission might achieve are still not possible to determine. What is not in dispute is the lack of irrefutable evidence that he provided the Irish side with any assurances, promises or guarantees on the future of the boundary, or on the work of the commission. There is, however, persuasive evidence from many sources, British and Irish, that he encouraged them to believe that the commission would have results highly favourable to the Free State.

When the Treaty came before the Dáil for approval, the negotiators who signed it were subject to strong criticism by anti-Treaty deputies for conceding on the Oath, the Crown and the Empire. At the same time, there was general acquiescence in what they had achieved on Ulster, specifically in relation to a boundary commission. This was reflected in the relatively small emphasis on the Northern Ireland issue during the debates in the private and public sessions. Most modern historians see this emphasis as misguided. If the negotiators deserved praise, it was for what they achieved on the issue of the relationship of nationalist Ireland to the United Kingdom. For example, the Oath pro-vided in the Treaty, which required Dáil deputies to swear true faith and allegiance to the Constitution of the Irish Free State and fidelity to George V, represented, from an Irish point of view, the best and least humiliating form of words possible in the circumstances. On 5 December 1921, Collins had been successful in having the Oath thus modified in accordance with de Valera's recommendation of two days earlier. The amended oath represented a signi-ficant improvement from the Irish point of view, since it provided for 'the establishment of a relationship between the Irish people and the British Crown through their own Constitution to which they gave allegiance: they

101 Quoted in Michael Laffan, *The Partition of Ireland 1911–25* (Dundalk, 1983), p. 78.

agreed to accept the King as head of State by virtue of that agreement.' As John M. Regan remarks, the difference between giving allegiance directly to the King, as in the draft Treaty, and being faithful to the King as part of their Constitution 'was the volition of the Irish people and the semblance of popular sovereignty.'[102] Those who blamed the negotiators for not winning a republic, either independent or externally associated, should have realised that this was a demand which no British government could then have conceded. On the other hand, most impartial historians tend to agree with Oliver MacDonagh's verdict that 'Ulster was handled disastrously by the Irish'.[103] Griffith and Collins seemed all too ready to discern an early prospect of Irish unity as a result of the work, at an unspecified time in the future, of a boundary commission whose remit was left deliberately vague, and whose terms of reference contained a phrase which left the commission, on which the British-appointed chairman was bound to have the decisive voice, free to determine a border 'upon any criterion which they wished to choose'.[104]

The two principal Irish negotiators, who despised Childers for what they saw as his tiresome pedantry, but what was really a meticulous attention to detail and a tendency to scrutinise documents for finer shades of meaning, would have done well to apply his methods to the Ulster clauses of the Treaty. As Hart points out, 'in the end, checking the final print on the final draft of the Treaty and getting it lawyer-proofed would be crucial.'[105] It is difficult to suggest adequate explanations for such catastrophic failure on the part of Griffith and Collins, and also on the part of the members of the Dáil Cabinet, including de Valera, who had time to digest the Ulster clauses on the weekend before the Treaty was signed, but who preferred to concentrate on ultimately less significant areas of conflict: the Crown, the Empire, defence and, above all, the form the oath should take. By way of mitigation, it is right to observe that coming to the end, the Irish delegates were exhausted, which might explain why they failed to challenge Lloyd George on his ultimatum that they must sign because he must let Craig know on the morning of 5 December what had happened, although there was in reality no urgency about this. They also failed to point out that they had demanded Craig's adherence to the terms of the Treaty before signing.[106] It is difficult to avoid the conclusion that

---

102 Regan, *Counter-Revolution*, p. 31.

103 MacDonagh, *Union and its Aftermath*, p. 112.

104 Ibid., p. 113.

105 Hart, *The Real Michael Collins*, p. 296.

106 One of the secretariat at Downing Street, Geoffrey Shakespeare who was to carry Lloyd George's 'urgent' letter to Craig by special train and destroyer, reflecting afterwards on the events on 5 December 1921, wondered why the Irish accepted Lloyd George's ultimatum at face value. He believed

Griffith and Collins talked themselves, and others, into believing that a boundary commission would inevitably transfer extensive Nationalist areas from the jurisdiction of Northern Ireland, and that Lloyd George and other British ministers while not explicitly fostering this belief, did not discourage it.[107] For Lloyd George, the Boundary Commission was a convenient device for postponing a decision on Ulster; it enabled him to keep on giving the most favourable assurances as to its outcome to southern Nationalists and Ulster Unionists at once. Craig, as Campbell observes, 'was given the impression that Ulster had nothing to fear, while Collins, at a private interview with Lloyd George on the morning of 5 December, was given the impression that the Free State had everything to gain.'[108]

Barton was right in claiming that he and the four other Irish negotiators were not a fighting delegation. Much more significantly, Griffith and Collins, alienated from most of their Cabinet colleagues in Dublin and from two of their fellow plenipotentiaries, Gavan Duffy and Barton, had formed sympathetic relationships with Lloyd George, Birkenhead and Churchill, finding them more congenial than most of the people on their own side. Such relationships were not fully compatible with the kind of task they were in London to perform. There is much truth in Campbell's verdict on a fundamental condition of Lloyd George's achievement of a settlement which got the British out of the greater part of Ireland: 'What Lloyd George did, in the tense, historically-charged atmosphere of Downing Street, was to persuade Griffith and Collins to place the obligations of mutual trust built over the previous two months higher than their obligations to the Prime Minster and Cabinet whom they were in London to represent.'[109] In addition, Griffith was disloyal to his fellow plenipotentiaries as well as to the Dáil Cabinet in entering into a secret and personal agreement with Lloyd George on 13 November, not to let him down on Ulster, without taking anybody on the Irish side into his confidence. The British were able to play on the obvious disharmony within

---

that Griffith should have said: 'What is so sacrosanct about Tuesday? We have waited hundreds of years for a settlement. Ask Craig to wait one more week. If you feel you must inform him tomorrow, telephone to Dublin Castle, or direct to Belfast, and explain the delay. Are you really going to break the Truce and plunge Ireland again into war without giving the Irish Cabinet the chance even of discussing your latest proposals?' Shakespeare regretted that the Irish delegation did not counter the ultimatum with logic, but bowed to it and signed. Geoffrey Shakespeare, *Let Candles Be Brought In* (London, 1949), cited in Frank Gallagher, *The Anglo-Irish Treaty*. Edited with an introduction by T. P. O'Neill (London, 1965), p. 167.

107 Martin, *The Irish Border*, p. 67.

108 Campbell, *F. E. Smith*, p. 571.

109 Ibid., p. 573.

the Irish delegation to considerable effect. 'Lloyd George managed to build an alliance between himself and Griffith – and by extension Collins and Duggan – against not only his Conservative allies, but also the other members of the Irish delegation. This would be the foundation on which he would build the final agreement.'[110] It is difficult to argue with Regan's conclusion that 'Griffith played a remarkably maladroit game in London, and in the process compromised the entire position of the Irish delegation'.[111] Like Griffith, Collins acted independently of all the other Irish negotiators and of the Dáil Cabinet during the talks. This arose from his dual allegiance: to the Dáil Cabinet as Minister for Finance, and to the IRB, a secret, self-perpetuating, oath-bound élite, of which he was President and a member of the Supreme Council, and, by the terms of its Constitution, President of the Irish Republic, although he was obliged to relinquish that title after de Valera assumed it on 26 August 1921.

Throughout the negotiations, Collins travelled to Dublin at weekends to keep the IRB Supreme Council membership informed on progress in London, and was prepared to act on IRB recommendations.[112] At a crucial final stage in the negotiations, when the delegates travelled to present the ultimate British draft to the Dáil Cabinet, Collins, during a break in Cabinet discussions, sent a copy of the draft Treaty to the members of the IRB Supreme Council, which was meeting in the Gresham Hotel. The IRB looked favourably on the British proposals, but suggested a change in the oath. The members doubted, however, that the draft Treaty would 'satisfy the fighting men'. Despite his Cabinet commitments, Collins twice met Seán Ó Muirthile, Secretary of the Supreme Council, on 3 December.[113] Collins's limited allegiance to democratic principles and collective Cabinet responsibility is underlined in Regan's observation that 'the apparent endorsement of the Supreme Council opened to him the possibility of circumventing the Cabinet and still achieving a consensual response in the Dáil and the army to a settlement in London'.[114]

The Treaty settlement antagonised two significant groups: Ulster Unionists and Irish Republicans. The former regarded the Treaty as a betrayal of their interests, and blamed the Conservative members of Lloyd George's Coalition Government for reneging on solemn promises made to Ulster that the 1920 Act was to be understood by Unionists as a final, irrevocable settlement. Southern Republicans, including de Valera, Brugh, Stack and a host of non-political militants, blamed the negotiators for betraying the declared, if

110 Hart, *The Real Michael Collins*, p. 302.
111 Regan, *Counter-Revolution*, p. 22.
112 Seán Ó Muirthile Memoir, Mulcahy Papers, P7a/209(2) UCDA.
113 Ibid.
114 Regan, *Counter-Revolution*, p. 30.

internationally unrecognised, Republic to which members of the Dáil had sworn loyalty in January 1919. The most objectionable element of the Treaty for Unionists was the boundary commission promised in Clause 12. Their case was trenchantly argued in the immediate aftermath of the Treaty by Lord Carson, the Marquess of Londonderry, the Marquess of Salisbury in the House of Lords and by Bonar Law, Captain Craig and Sir Robert O'Neill in the Commons. Bonar Law recalled recent British guarantees on the security of the boundaries of Northern Ireland. Lloyd George, he reminded the House, had written to him just before the last election 'that in dealing with Ireland, anything which interferes, not with Ulster, but with the six counties, is impossible'. It had been a great mistake, he believed, that the Government should have put the boundary commission in the Treaty, 'signed, sealed and ratified, without consulting Ulster' failing, however, to remark that Ulster had declined to be consulted. Carson, speaking with the authority conferred by intimate personal involvement, also reminded Lloyd George that the 1920 settlement was made possible only after 'the most solemn assurances' that the 1920 boundaries would be permanent.[115]

The speakers in the debates in both houses hoped that the effect of a boundary commission would not be a major alteration of boundaries and territories. Captain Craig, invoking the interpretation advanced by Michael Collins, that 'large territories were involved in the Commission and not merely a boundary line, as Sir James Craig had been given to understand privately by members of the Government', was assured by Austen Chamberlain, a party to the Treaty negotiations, that Lloyd George never used the words 'large territories'. Winston Churchill, who also helped to negotiate the Treaty, pronounced it an 'absurd supposition' that a boundary commission would 'reduce by way of further reassurance to Unionists, Ulster to its preponderating Orange areas'.[116] The Marquess of Salisbury, however, who considered 'a gentle readjustment of the frontiers, a few acres here and there', acceptable, was not convinced that this would be the outcome of the deliberations of the commission.[117] Lloyd George, like Chamberlain and Churchill, tried to calm the fears of Unionists by assuring them that he had never 'told the Sinn Féiners that in so much as they had a majority in Tyrone and Fermanagh, they would get the whole of those counties'. Indeed, contrary to Nationalist interpretations, he 'could not say beforehand what the result would be,

---

115 *Irish Boundary: Extracts from Parliamentary Debates, Command Papers, etc., relevant to Questions arising out of Article XII of the Articles of an Agreement for a Treaty between Great Britain and Ireland, dated 6th December, 1921.* H. M. Stationery Office (London, 1924), pp. 55–8.

116 Ibid., pp. 63–4.

117 Ibid., p. 60.

whether to add the number of the population of Ulster or to diminish it'. This was a signal to Unionists and their supporters that at no time during the Treaty negotiations did he promise, or even suggest, that the findings of the commission would favour southern Ireland, either in territory or in population. He reinforced this point by sharing with MPs the opinion of an unnamed 'prominent Ulster man' that the commission 'might have an effect which would be favourable to the Ulster area.'[118]

Two days after the Treaty was signed, a Conservative Party diarist noted: 'Ireland squared and nearly everyone happy.'[119] This was to prove to be far from the case. The Irish negotiators had failed to achieve essential aims. Through his boundary commission stratagem, which Griffith, wrongly, and baselessly, concluded would give the Free State those areas in Northern Ireland in which Catholics were in a majority, Lloyd George had prevented the Irish negotiators from breaking on the partition issue. The terms of the Treaty represented only a small advance on those proposed by the British Cabinet in July 1921. The description of the Free State as a 32-county, self-governing dominion within the British Empire was essentially meaningless, since the Ulster clauses undermined this by giving Northern Ireland the right to withdraw from the jurisdiction of this unit. In return for the dubious benefits promised by the ambiguous terms of the boundary commission, the Irish negotiators were forced, under threat of immediate war, to accept 'terms as uncompromising as ever on the Crown and Empire and without any concrete guarantee of essential unity'.[120] The aspirations of Catholics in the borderlands of Northern Ireland were set aside, to be adjudicated upon by an arbitrator appointed by the British Government at an unspecified time in the future, with their fate largely depending on the interplay of British political parties, the outlook of future British governments, and the ability of the Northern Ireland Parliament to delay the constitution of the boundary commission to its own advantage while it consolidated its position. The Irish delegation, in particular its chief negotiator Arthur Griffith, committed to essential unity, eventually agreed to terms which would make this impossible: by accepting Lloyd George's boundary commission proposal, Griffith was acknowledging that there would be a border, and by failing to insist on a set of clear and unambiguous criteria for the operation of the commission and by agreeing to a British-appointed chairman, he, and the other delegates, as well

118 Ibid., p. 57.
119 D. G. Boyce, in Peter Collins (ed.), *Nationalism and Unionism: Conflict in Ireland* (Belfast, 1994), p. 103.
120 Phoenix, *Northern Nationalism*, p. 51.

as the Dáil Cabinet, contributed to rendering the commission a useless instrument for the remedy of Ulster Catholic grievances.

When Thomas Jones asked Collins what he thought of a boundary commission, the latter responded that he 'did not like the suggestion at all, because it sacrificed unity entirely',[121] Collins's first instinct was sound. In theory, the argument subsequently advanced by Griffith and Collins that a boundary commission would lead to essential unity, depended on a most unlikely outcome, which would have proved intolerable to any British administration as well as to Unionists: the reduction of the territory of Northern Ireland to the point of being half a statelet and hence possibly unviable. But even before it was constituted, the boundary commission provided by Clause 12 of the Treaty proved to be a significant obstacle to good relations within Ireland, and between Britain and Nationalist Ireland. Many British Imperialists perceived the boundary fixed in 1920 between Northern Ireland and the south as far from ideal, but would have preferred a settlement of this difficult question by agreement between the northern and southern authorities. Lionel Curtis, Secretary to the Irish Treaty Conference and Colonial Office adviser on Irish Affairs from 1921 to 1924, believed that moderate Irish opinion shared his view that an award of Ulster territory to the Free State through compulsory arbitration would embitter Irish Unionists and 'defer the day of Irish union'.[122]

Other Unionists and intransigent Imperialists were appalled by the implications of the Treaty. Sir Henry Wilson regarded the agreement as a complete surrender, involving a farcical oath of allegiance, a withdrawal of British troops, and their replacement by a rebel army, with the result that the British Empire was doomed.[123] Carson's response to the Treaty, as Gailey remarks, was prompted by the fact that it confronted him with his real failure: 'His beloved Ireland had degenerated into two provincial, illiberal statelets, a process which in truth had been in progress since at least the 1890s, and which his rhetoric had served to disguise, especially from himself.'[124] In the House of Lords in December 1921, Carson denounced the Treaty as a cowardly surrender to terrorism and a humiliation of the British Empire. While Irish Republican opponents of the agreement saw it as the result of British threats of military force, Carson suggested that the British negotiators had submitted to its terms 'with a revolver pointed at your head . . . because you were beaten'.[125]

121 Jones, *Whitehall Diary* vol. 3, p. 156.

122 Cited in Peatling, *British Opinion*, p. 163.

123 Foster, *Modern Ireland*, pp. 507–8.

124 Andrew Gailey, 'King Carson: an essay on the invention of leadership', *IHS* Vol. xxx, No. 117 (1996), pp. 66–87.

125 Campbell, *F. E. Smith*, p. 576.

Carson's condemnatory speech described by Nicholas Mansergh as 'the authentic cry of Irish (as distinct from Ulster) Unionism at the last, with only oblivion before it'.[126] reflected his disappointment at the break up of the Union: by conceding to Nationalist Irish demands, the British Government, some of whose Conservative Party members had once been his friends and political allies in the cause of Ulster and the Empire, had connived at the partition of the United Kingdom, and finally signalled the end of his hopes for a politically united Ireland firmly within the British Empire. Carson reserved his bitterest rebuke for Lord Birkenhead who had once acted as his aide-de-camp in a pre-war UVF parade in the heroic days of Ulster resistance to Home Rule, and was now the principal Government apologist for the Treaty. With Birkenhead evidently in mind, Carson declared that 'of all the men in my experience that I think are the most loathsome, it is those who will sell their friends for the purpose of conciliating their enemies'.[127] He could not value any friendship like Birkenhead's that was not founded on confidence and trust. He now believed that he had been a fool in earnestly espousing the cause of Ulster when his supposed allies were only too eager to betray it. He was only a puppet, 'and so was Ulster, and so was Ireland, in the political game that was to get the Conservative Party into power.'[128] A southern Unionist peer, Lord Farnham, whose proposal to include all nine counties of Ulster in Northern Ireland had been decisively rejected by the Ulster Unionist Council in March 1920 was equally disillusioned. He wondered whether Birkenhead , in the event of an Irish civil war, would land in 'the Sinn Féin saddle as canterer to Michael Collins'.[129]

Carson was on slippery ground when he spoke of betrayal: in 1920 he had been willing to sacrifice 70,000 fellow Unionists in Donegal, Cavan and Monaghan in the pursuit of a six county settlement. Against this, Carson would have argued that this sacrifice was necessary for the Loyalist and Imperial cause. However, the price of a secure Ulster unit was to leave 300,000 southern Unionists, however reluctantly, to their fate, which, as it transpired after the Treaty, was far from being an utterly unhappy one, and certainly less so than that endured by the six-county Nationalist minority following partition. Carson's membership of the House of Lords, after he had accepted judicial office as Lord of Appeal, marked an adjustment in the nature of his political preoccupations. Ulster, as he told Craig in 1921, had always been his

---

126 Cited in Alvin Jackson, *Sir Edward Carson* (Dundalk, 1993), p. 61.

127 Campbell, *F. E. Smith*, p. 577.

128 Hugh Montgomery Hyde, *The Life of Sir Edward Carson, Lord Carson of Duncairn* (London, 1953), p. 405.

129 Campbell, *F. E. Smith*, p. 577.

first love, but he was a southern Unionist and, as Jackson remarks, Ulster was always external, and 'it was to the interests of his own people – the beleaguered loyalists of the South and West, that he turned as a law lord between 1921 and 1929'. His fury at the Treaty was driven by the absence of any protection for southern Unionists, the landowners, civil servants and the Church of Ireland professional classes among whom he had grown up, and to whom he was bound by fundamental ties.[130] During the debate on the Free State Constitution Bill in December 1922, he launched a savage attack on those British statesmen responsible for the desertion of those loyal friends of Britain south of the border. He referred to 'a junta of ministers in Downing Street' who 'made what they called a Treaty on the part of the British Government by which they agreed to surrender to the forces of murder in Ireland'.[131]

Craig, however, although depressed by the terms of the Treaty settlement, was determined to marshal Ulster resistance to any boundary commission that might do more than what Lloyd George had promised him on 9 December 1921. Then, the latter had explained to Craig that 'it was only intended to make a slight readjustment of our boundary line so as to bring into Northern Ireland Loyalists who are now just outside our own area, and to transfer correspondingly an equivalent number of those having Sinn Féin sympathies to the area of the Free State'. Craig now accused the Prime Minister of a complete reversal of his Government's previous policy on Ulster, which was that Northern Ireland should remain out 'until she chose of her own free will to enter an all-Ireland Parliament'. The Treaty now placed Northern Ireland automatically in the Free State until she voted herself out under the penalty of a boundary commission. Like Carson, Craig thus regarded the Treaty as a violation of solemn promises given to Northern Ireland in the recent past as well as a surrender to Sinn Féin. It also provided his Government with a reason for finding Irish political unity a permanent impossibility. This was because Sinn Féin had demanded, and the British Government had accepted, a different oath of allegiance and therefore a different standard of loyalty, than that required of all other parts of the British Empire. This, Craig concluded, 'appears to us to make it impossible for Ulster to enter the Irish Free State'.[132] Less than a year after the signature of the Treaty, the Northern Ireland and Free State Governments would be obliged to deal on the boundary issue not with Lloyd George's Liberal-Conservative Coalition, but with a succession of administrations, Conservative as well as Labour, generally unsympathetic to Irish nationalism, but with the interests of Ulster Unionists as well as British

130　Jackson, *Carson*, p. 62.
131　*Hansard*, House of Lords, Vol. 52, Col. 174, 1 Dec. 1922.
132　Craig to Lloyd George, 14 Dec. 1922. Published in *The Times*, 16 Dec. 1921.

and Imperial interests, at heart. Carson's ideal had been that Northern Ireland would develop into a tolerant society, with a government working impartially in the interests of all its people. Initially, Craig committed himself to similar principles, but failed to establish equitable government and seemed content 'to let Northern Ireland drift with no sense of direction and to let the minority question fester'.[133] More even-handed governance might have made Nationalist dissent a less acute problem than it became, and might have made Ulster Catholics less inclined than they were to rely on a boundary commission as the instrument to liberate them from their perceived servile status.

This was all for the future. In the immediate aftermath of the Treaty, Lloyd George enjoyed the general approval of the British press. His Coalition Government was thought to have been vindicated, and the Irish problem removed them from the sphere of British politics. The Treaty could be seen as an ingenious solution to a converging series of seemingly intractable difficulties. The key to this solution, for Lloyd George, lay in the Ulster clauses, designed by him to provide Ulster Unionists with serious inducements to accept an Irish dominion with a single parliament. These inducements were two fold. If Northern Ireland agreed to be part of a 32-county dominion arrangement, there would be no boundary commission and none of the burdensome financial restrictions which the 1920 Government of Ireland Act would continue to impose on a Northern Ireland which decided to remain outside the single parliament arrangement envisaged in the Treaty.

The consequent penalties would include the retention by the Westminster Parliament of the almost exclusive power of raising revenue. This meant that Northern Ireland would be excluded from its control of such forms of taxation as customs and excise duties, income tax, surtax and taxes on profits. It also meant that 80 per cent of the Belfast Government's revenue would come from London, leaving the former in control of relatively minor tax-raising measures. In this way, as Matthews points out, Lloyd George could say that he had kept his promise to Unionists not to interfere with the 1920 Act, while at the same time 'he could sell the Treaty to Griffith and his colleagues as a contract that made reunification possible'.[134]

133 Patrick Buckland, in Collins (ed.), *Nationalism and Unionism*, pp. 88–9.
134 Matthews, *Fatal Influence*, p. 41.

THREE

ANTICIPATING THE BOUNDARY COMMISSION

—

The terms of Article 12 of the Anglo-Irish Treaty of 6 December 1921 gave the Northern Ireland Parliament the right to sever itself from the 32-county Free State, which was provided for in the first ten articles of the Treaty. The agreement had been framed on the assumption that the northern parliament might elect to come under the jurisdiction of a united Irish state. The Irish Treaty delegates claimed to negotiate not as representatives of the 26 counties but on behalf of Ireland as a whole, and the terms of the Treaty were formulated to recognise this: the 'Irish Free State' described in the Treaty was the 32-county unit. Articles 11 to 14, however, made provision for the dismemberment of this unit if the Northern Ireland Parliament desired that outcome. In keeping with the aspiration towards a 32-county state which informed the Treaty, Article 12 embodied what the great mass of northern Catholics and their southern protectors under the Treaty interpreted as an assertion of the right of large numbers of border Nationalists from Derry to south Down to choose the ultimate jurisdiction under which they would like to live.[1] The terms of Article 12 were regarded on the Irish side as a stark admission of the fundamental defect in the Government of Ireland Act of 1920 from the point of view of the northern Nationalist minority: the imposition by the British Government of a boundary which failed to take account of the interests and aspirations of almost 35 per cent of those affected by it. Had the boundary under the 1920 Act not been arbitrarily drawn, but had instead been in conformity with the wishes of the inhabitants as ascertained by means of a plebiscite, provision of a boundary commission in Article 12 would not have been necessary.[2] The consequence would have been a smaller, but much more ethnically homogeneous, north-eastern state.

1   For the terms of Clauses 11 to 14, see Appendix 1.
2   See Sir Andrew Cope to W. T. Cosgrave, Blythe Papers P24/129 UCDA.

I THE EVOLUTION OF ARTICLE 12: FREE STATE AND
NATIONALIST INTERPRETATIONS

Any impartial examination of the evolution of Article 12, and of the reasons
for its inclusion in the Treaty, should lead to the conclusion that the Irish
delegates were induced to sign the document as a whole because they were led
to believe, or because they judged that the trend of the negotiations compelled them to believe, that the boundary commission clause in Article 12 was
designed to effect a major revision of the 1920 boundary to satisfy the aspirations of northern Nationalists and even to facilitate the ultimate unity of
Ireland.[3] Such an examination will also suggest that Article 12 was presented
by the British side and accepted by the Irish side in the Treaty negotiations as
a major qualification 'upon the right of the six counties to go out of the
jurisdiction of the Irish Free State,' as the Free State Attorney General
subsequently put it.[4]

When the Anglo-Irish Peace Conference met in London from 11 October
until 6 December 1921 to negotiate a settlement of the Irish problem, the
Ulster question was central to the talks. The Irish delegates regarded the
righting of what Nationalist Ireland saw as the wrong done to the northern
Nationalist minority by the imposition of partition in 1920 as an essential part
of any peace settlement. As Gwynn points out, Griffith and his colleagues
'held out resolutely on the principle of national unity, against every ingenious
formula which was suggested as a means of satisfying the Ulster Unionists'.[5]
Action to release large numbers of Nationalists from the control of a hostile
régime seemed especially urgent in the light of widespread mob action against
Catholics in Belfast.[6] One obvious solution to this problem was an all-Ireland
parliament. Well over a month after the negotiations began, Lloyd George
appears to have believed that he could persuade the Ulster Unionists to accept
an all-Ireland arrangement if he could persuade the Irish delegation to accept
dominion status. He also appears to have believed that if he could get the
south to accept dominion status, he could get the Unionists to accept essential
unity. Before dealing with the Unionists, he asked Griffith to give him
assurances. These were provided in a letter dated 2 November 1921. In return

3   T. Ryle Dwyer, 'The Anglo-Irish Treaty and why they signed', *Capuchin Annual* (Dublin, 1971),
p. 333.

4   Geoffrey Hand, *Report of the Irish Boundary Commission* (Shannon, 1969), p. 38.

5   Denis Gwynn, *The History of Partition 1912–1935* (Dublin, 1950), pp. 199–200.

6   Eamon Phoenix, *Northern Nationalism, Nationalist Politics, Partition and the Catholic Minority in
Northern Ireland 1890–1940* (Belfast, 1994), pp. 87ff.

for essential Irish unity, Griffith was prepared to recommend 'a free partnership of Ireland with the other states associated within the British Commonwealth, the formula defining the partnership to be arrived at in a later discussion'. He was also willing to recommend that Ireland should consent 'to a recognition of the Crown as head of the proposed association of free states'.[7] Such proposals were rendered nugatory by Sir James Craig, Northern Prime Minister, who was determined to maintain the six-county area separate and inviolate, and who was fortified by earlier pledges from Lloyd George that the entire entity he, Craig, now presided over, would remain intact.[8]

The promise of a boundary commission was Lloyd George's master stroke in averting the breakdown of the Treaty negotiations, but the most bitterly contested question arising from this promise was whether he left the likely outcome of its proceedings to the imagination of Griffith and Collins or whether he told them directly, or implied, that the purpose of a commission would be a substantial rectification of an obvious anomaly in the 1920 partition which left a large population of unwilling border Catholics in Northern Ireland. Collins met Lloyd George on 5 December 1921, the day before the Treaty was signed, and compiled a record of this meeting on the same day. He appeared convinced, or Lloyd George encouraged him to believe, that if the north rejected Irish unity, the boundary commission would yield the entire counties of Tyrone and Fermanagh, as well as parts of Derry, Armagh and Down to the south, and thus force the remainder of the north to come in, if only through force of economic circumstances.[9] Collins had reached this conclusion when Lloyd George gave him an assurance in writing similar to the one he had already given to Griffith to the effect that if Unionists rejected Irish unity, a boundary commission 'could be directed' to adjust the boundary line so as to make it 'conform as closely as possible to the wishes of the population'.[10] Collins's memorandum of his meeting with Lloyd George makes it clear that the latter had given him to understand that any adjustment of the boundary would be based on the ascertained wishes of the inhabitants, without qualification. Later in the day of his meeting with Collins, however,

7   Dorothy Macardle, *The Irish Republic* (Dublin, 1951), pp. 555–6.

8   Roy Foster, *Modern Ireland 1600–1972* (London, 1988), p. 505.

9   Tim Pat Coogan, *Michael Collin: A Biography* (London, 1990), p. 270. The Collins memorandum cited is in Coogan's possession. See Coogan, p. 442. Lloyd George's ability to induce Irish politicians to construe his calculated ambiguities in a sense favourable to their own negotiating positions was demonstrated in the course of his separate talks with Redmond and Carson in May 1916.

10 Earl of Longford (Frank Pakenham), *Peace by Ordeal: The Negotiation of the Anglo-Irish Treaty, 1921* (London, 1972), pp. 236–7.

Lloyd George was assuring his Cabinet that what he had been encouraging Collins to believe was false, and that the commission would merely readjust the boundaries. He made no mention of the likelihood that economic necessity would force Ulster into an all-Ireland parliament.[11] It is little wonder that Neville Chamberlain suspected that Lloyd George gave Collins reason to think 'he would get Fermanagh and Tyrone and at the same time allowed Craig to believe that no such transfer would take place'.[12]

There can be little doubt that without the prospect of major boundary adjustment seemingly intended by Article 12, the Irish delegates would not have signed. This was later emphasised by those who were in a good position to interpret the minds of the Irish negotiators. In March 1924, when T. M. Healy, the Governor General of the Free State, wrote to the British Secretary for Colonies officially requesting that the boundary commission be set up, he pointed out that 'the Treaty would never have been accepted' without Article 12.[13] Here, Healy was thinking of the Article as a vehicle for the transfer of large territories to the south. In 1924, when some British signatories of the Treaty were publicly suggesting that Article 12 could involve only minimal transfers of territory, and certainly not entire counties, Cosgrave pointed out that had the same signatories made this clear during the negotiations, the Irish plenipotentiaries would never have signed the Treaty. He described recent British interpretations of the boundary article as 'opinions which were carefully concealed when the negotiations which resulted in the Treaty were being undertaken', thus implying that the crucial Ulster clause of the agreement had been negotiated by the British in bad faith.[14] According to the Nationalist politician William O'Brien, T. M. Healy told him during the Treaty negotiations that Winston Churchill had assured him [Healy], that the boundary commission would be so constituted 'as to ensure the transfer to the Free State of the counties of Tyrone and Fermanagh, south Armagh, south Down, together with the towns of Londonderry, Enniskillen and Newry'.[15] J. M. Curran remarks that Healy, along with Thomas Jones, Assistant Secretary to the British Cabinet, was made the conduit for informal and oblique

11   Cabinet Minutes and papers, 23/27 C 89(21), Public Record Office, London, 5 Dec. 1921.

12   Kevin Matthews, *Fatal Influence: The Impact of Ireland on British Politics 1920–1925* (Dublin, 2004), p. 174.

13   Frank Gallagher, *The Indivisible Island: The History of the Partition of Ireland* (London, 1959), p. 156.

14   Dáil Debates, Vol. 12, Col. 2502, 15 Oct. 1924.

15   Frank Callanan, *T. M. Healy* (Cork, 1996), p. 578. O'Brien did not put this claim in writing until some years later in his *Irish Free State: Secret History of its Foundation*, which he had not completed at his death in 1928.

indications from the British side in the Treaty negotiations 'that the boundary commission would leave to Northern Ireland only three or four counties and that the drastically diminished Northern Irish state would in consequence find itself compelled to accede to its inclusion in the Irish Free State.'[16] Another contemporary source points in a similar direction. P. S. O Hegarty, who was close to Collins, recalled a comment made in the presence of both of them during the period of the Treaty debates by Seán Ó Muirthile, Secretary of the Supreme Council of the IRB. 'Before they signed,' Ó Muirthile declared, with Collins assenting, 'Griffith and Collins got a personal undertaking from Smith [Birkenhead] and Churchill that if Ulster opted out they would get only four counties and that *they* [the British] would make a four-county government impossible.' A problem with some of the testimony which relied on witness recollections of what Collins said about the genesis of the boundary commission, is the lack of supporting evidence. An example is the Dáil statement by Denis McCullough TD in November 1925, by which time it seemed obvious that only relatively minor changes in the boundary were in prospect. McCullough recalled that in company with Commandant Joe McKelvey, he was sent from Belfast to Dublin on St Stephen's Night, 1921, to clarify the position of northern Nationalists under the terms of the boundary clause. Collins, he recalled, assured McKelvey and himself that Article 12 'would enable every part of the Six Counties near the borders of the Saorstát, and where the majority of the people desired, to come under the jurisdiction of the Saorstát Government'. Collins had explained at length to McCullough in particular how this article was arrived at, and why economic and geographic considerations were included. Unfortunately for the historical record, McCullough failed to provide details of what Collins had explained to him, although his account suggests that Collins believed that the wishes of Nationalist inhabitants would govern the extent of the boundary changes. Of the three parties to the St Stephen's Night meeting of 1921, two were dead by the time of McCullough's speech: Collins had been killed in an ambush in August 1922, while McKelvey was the victim of the notorious reprisal shooting ordered by Cosgrave's Cabinet in December 1922.[17]

There is further evidence that Griffith, at any rate, was led to believe that a boundary commission would mean much more territory for the south, and a Northern Ireland whose viability would be in jeopardy. Robert Barton, a fellow signatory of the Treaty with Griffith, and a prisoner in Mountjoy Jail during the Civil War, heard a rumour that British Law Advisers had just pronounced the boundary clause of the Treaty *ultra vires*. Writing from the

16   J. M. Curran, *The Birth of the Irish Free State 1921–23* (Alabama, 1980), p. 133.

17   For McCullough's account see Dáil Debates, Official Report, Vol. 13, Col. 614, 19 Nov. 1925.

jail to a fellow Republican, Barton declared that: 'Poor A. G. (Arthur Griffith) would turn in his grave. He looked upon the Boundary Commission as the grave of Carsonism', which in this context meant the inability of Unionism to resist an all-Ireland settlement because a truncated Northern Ireland would not be able to survive alone.[18] In a speech delivered in Cork in September 1924, de Valera substantiated Barton's claim in respect of Griffith. During the Treaty negotiations and particularly in November 1921, Griffith was keeping de Valera regularly informed of British concessions relating to Ulster. In his speech, de Valera quoted extensively from Griffith's letters to him throughout the period. These demonstrated that Griffith, the leader of the Irish delegation, would be willing to accept Article 12 only on the clear understanding that it would lead to very substantial transfers of territory to the south.[19] In one of the letters quoted by de Valera, Griffith had suggested that the boundary commission would give the south most of Tyrone and Fermanagh and parts of Armagh, Derry and Down.[20] Twelve years after Griffith wrote this letter, Barton was still emphasising Griffith's anxiety to convince his fellow Irish delegates that the findings of a boundary commission would convince the Northern Ireland Government of the necessity of unity. In the course of a speech at Enniscorthy in January 1933, Barton recalled that when Griffith returned from meetings with Lloyd George, Chamberlain and Birkenhead, he would declare, 'over and over again', that 'if they [Ulster Unionists] do not come in they will lose half their territory and they can't stay out'.[21]

More persuasive evidence is found in the testimony of John Chartres, the English-born son of Irish parents, and a convert to Sinn Féin after meeting Griffith and Collins. Chartres was joint Chief Secretary, along with Erskine Childers, to the Irish Treaty delegation, and Provisional Government publicity agent in Ireland in 1921 and 1922. In a letter to Richard Mulcahy, Free State Minister for Defence, in February 1924, he described the whole of the Irish case on Ulster as a protest against the exclusion of large bodies of Nationalist Irishmen and their subjection to alien rule. He was adamant that it was not in order to secure 'minor rectifications' that Griffith made his conditional offer 'to recommend some form of recognition of the British Crown', and that self-determination, not boundary adjustment, was the essence of the Irish position. Referring to the Ulster component of the Conference on 17 October 1921, Chartres recalled Collins's warning that if 'our people' were

18   Robert Barton to Adjutant General Con Moloney, de Valera Papers P. 150/760 UCDA, 24 Feb. 1924.
19   *Irish Times*, 15 Sept. 1924.
20   Griffith to de Valera, Dáil Éireann Papers, NAI, 2/304/8, 9 Nov. 1921.
21   Macardle, *Irish Republic*, p. 567.

forced to remain under the Northern Ireland Government, there would be civil war. 'The case thus stated,' he pointed out, 'was illustrated by maps drawn and coloured to show, not minor frontier disadvantages but the wrongful cutting off of large communities from National rule', and that no single instance of 'minor rectification' was ever mentioned, let alone discussed. With the Irish case 'thus emphasised and fully in mind Lloyd George informed Craig that the area already placed under the jurisdiction of the Northern Ireland Government would have to be discussed, and referred to the fact that large communities were included in the Northern Ireland jurisdiction contrary to their wishes'.[22]

On 16 November, a draft treaty was submitted by the British negotiators. In this Treaty, Chartres observed, 'the wishes of the inhabitants are made subject to no limitations whatever', and there is 'not a word about economic or geographical considerations'. Why then, it may be wondered, did the Irish negotiators finally subscribe to a wording of the boundary commission clause which imposed just such limitations on the wishes of the inhabitants? Chartres had his answer: the limiting words were introduced in case the commission should feel itself obliged to transfer small districts remote from the border, such as the largely Catholic Glens of Antrim, to the south. This kind of case, according to Chartres, was mentioned by Lloyd George to illustrate possible exceptions to the general rule that the wishes of the inhabitants were paramount, and the Prime Minister stressed the point 'in the presence of all the British, 'none of whom made any demur correction, exception or addition.' Chartres was adamant that the Irish delegates' recognition of the Crown was expressly contingent upon British acceptance of a commission which would involve not slight rectification of the boundary but the transfer to the Free State of substantial areas. Chartres recalled that Collins and himself were present, as were 'the English delegates in full force', at the conference at which 'the Boundary Question in this particular aspect was discussed'. When Collins, with the aid of detailed maps, presented his argument for a large territorial claim, 'this position was fully accepted by the English representatives.' From all these circumstances, Chartres drew two possible conclusions. The first was that the British delegates deliberately tricked the Irish delegates in order to avert action by Lloyd George on his promise to see justice done to the Irish case, and possibly in the hope that once the Treaty was signed, the refusal of the Northern Government to appoint a commissioner would render the whole boundary commission transaction invalid. Chartres's alternative

---

22   For Chartres see Brian P. Murphy, *John Chartres: Mystery Man of the Treaty* (Dublin, 1995), pp. 154–5.

conclusion was that 'the English delegates are deliberately lying now about what took place during the negotiations'.[23]

Even anti-Treaty Republicans seem to have shared the view impressed on the Irish negotiators by their British counterparts that the boundary commission would transfer to the South a considerable proportion of Northern Nationalists and undermine partition. Article 12 was not a Republican target during the Treaty debates, and Document Number 2, de Valera's alternative to the Treaty, incorporated Article 12 verbatim, although he omitted it from a revised version of his alternative Treaty, circulated a few days after the first one.[24] Maureen Wall argues that de Valera had been convinced by the Treaty delegates that the Boundary Commission would solve the problem of partition.[25] Seán MacEntee, one of the few Dáil deputies with an intimate knowledge of the north, was not so convinced. He regarded the Treaty as a partitionist document, in the sense that Article 12 was an instrument which would re-partition the six counties. His contribution demonstrates his conviction that Article 12 was bound to have major territorial consequences. It was, he declared, 'going to remove from under the jurisdiction of the Northern Government that strong Nationalist minority which every day tries to bring Northern Ireland into the Irish Republic.' He imagined these liberated Nationalists being replaced by Unionists from Cavan, Monaghan and Donegal, with the purpose of securing a homogeneous population for the northern state.[26]

Three years later, de Valera, President of Sinn Féin, was expressing fears that the boundary commission would substantially reduce the Nationalist population of the north, and thus leave the remaining Nationalists even more vunerable to Unionist discrimination. This was at a time when Tyrone and Fermanagh Nationalists were hoping to use the October 1924 General Election to the Westminster Parliament as a demonstration of their numerical strength and of their determination to become citizens of the Free State. Nationalist leaders in the two counties were angered by de Valera's suggestion that by looking to the boundary commission to detach themselves from the northern state, the Nationalists of Tyrone and Fermanagh were showing a selfish disregard for their fellow Nationalists elsewhere in the six counties.[27] In the immediate aftermath of the Treaty, those who had supported it argued that its intention 'was to recognise the unity of Ireland and to provide that the whole

23   Chartres to Richard Mulcahy, Department of the Taoiseach Files. S/1801/E, NAI, 5 Feb. 1924.
24   See T. P. Coogan, *De Valera: Long Fellow, Long Shadow* (London, 1993), pp. 317–20.
25   Cited in T. D. Williams, *The Irish Struggle 1916–26* (London, 1966), p. 87.
26   Treaty Debates, 22 Dec. 1921, p. 155.
27   De Valera's comments were reported in the *Irish Independent*, 20 Oct. 1924.

of Ireland should become the Free State'.[28] Given that this ideal outcome was unlikely, champions of the Treaty insisted on reading the boundary clause in Article 12 as 'involving a penalty which the Government and Parliament of Northern Ireland were to suffer in the event of their deciding to remain outside the Free State'.[29] No representative of the Provisional or Free State administrations publicly interpreted Article 12 as promising anything less than a radical reduction in the area governed by the six-county Parliament. Collins, for example, professed the belief, and spoke as if Lloyd George shared it, that by means of the boundary commission the Free State would gain so much territory that the northern state might even be unable to maintain a separate existence. Neither he nor the other southern politicians who encouraged such hopes among border Nationalists seemed aware of the fact that the actual wording of Article 12 established no single principle whose operation was bound to fulfil the expectations thus raised.[30] They seemed unable to apprehend the sinister significance of the qualifying phrase, 'so far as may be compatible with economic and geographic conditions', and its potential to nullify, as a whole, the provision on which they concentrated their almost exclusive attention 'in accordance with the wishes of the inhabitants'. The qualifying phrase was to become the trap which enabled the Boundary Commission to disregard the wishes of large border majorities; a more benign interpretation made of it a second principle to check the operation of the first. De Valera subsequently blamed Griffith and Collins for not submitting Article 12 for scrutiny by legal experts before they signed. Had they done so, he told Lord Longford in 1963, 'some serious problems which later transpired might have been avoided.' However, in de Valera's own speeches on the Treaty there is no reference to the dangers lurking in Article 12, and he seemed less interested in the Ulster aspects of the Treaty than in the nature of the oath to the British monarch.[31]

Griffith did in fact submit the British draft Treaty, incorporating the final version of Article 12, to the kind of scrutiny which de Valera thought desirable. On his return to Dublin on 3 December 1921 for the final meeting between the Treaty delegates and the Dáil Cabinet, Griffith was accompanied by John O'Byrne, a legal adviser to the delegation, and later Attorney General of the Free State. Griffith discussed all the Treaty articles in detail with O'Byrne, explaining his view that the implementation of the boundary clause in Article 12 was bound to result in a major reduction of the territory controlled by the

28 Hand, *Report* (1969), pp. 40–1.

29 Ibid., p. 38.

30 See W. K. Hancock, *Survey of British Commonwealth Affairs. Vol. 1: Problems of Nationality 1918–1936* (Oxford, 1937), pp. 148–9.

31 See de Valera to Longford, Childers Papers TCD MS 7814, 302/10, 27 Feb. 1963.

Northern Ireland Parliament. O'Byrne expressed deep reservations about this reading, explaining that the clause as it stood did not necessarily mean what Griffith thought it did, and that it was too vague to admit of a single unequivocal interpretation. He suggested an alteration in the clause which would at least delimit the territorial units to be considered in applying it. Griffith was impressed by this argument. Padraig Colum, who recorded this episode, was puzzled that Griffith did not argue for the kind of alteration suggested by O'Byrne when the plenipotentiaries met with the Dáil Cabinet on 3 December. The only explanation Colum could think of was that the meeting was so preoccupied with the oath, the crown and the Empire that nobody present adverted to the unsatisfactory formulation of the boundary clause.[32] It may also be considered surprising that de Valera, who told a friend in June 1923 that he would never have 'placed a particle of dependence' on Article 12,[33] did not express such misgivings to the negotiators or other members of his Cabinet on 3 December 1921, while there was still time to negotiate a more acceptable version.

Collins's apparent willingness to believe, or desire to convince others, that the boundary commission would transfer substantial territory to the Free State is evident in his letter of assurance to Bishop Mulhern of Dromore in early 1922. Mulhern was troubled by reports that Craig had been telling Unionists from Newry that south Down would be retained under the Northern Parliament. He made his fears known to Collins through an intermediary. Collins seemed to believe that the boundary would be adjusted, 'on a basis of obvious fairness', as he put it. He expressed optimism that any boundary commission would be obliged to act in accordance with the principle of self-determination. 'Quite clearly,' he told Mulhern, 'the Irish Government would have the allegiance of the people of such places as south and east Down and a great part of Armagh. Newry is included in this territory. Therefore, no action and no desire of the Northern Parliament could take this territory away from the Irish Government.'[34] Collins and Griffith understood from the words of Lloyd George that Article 12 'was weighted in their favour and that the British Government had taken a definite political decision to give them the two counties [Fermanagh and Tyrone] provided their contention as to the wishes of the inhabitants proved correct'.[35] Had Mulhern or Collins studied Lloyd George's contribution to the Commons debate on the Treaty on 16 December

32   Padraig Colum, *Arthur Griffith* (Dublin, 1959), pp. 295–8.
33   John Bowman, *De Valera and the Ulster Question 1917–1973* (Oxford, 1982), p. 89.
34   Collins to Mulhern, NAI S 1801/2, 28 Jan. 1922.
35   Nicholas Mansergh, *The Government of Northern Ireland* (London, 1936), p. 121.

1921, either or both might have been less optimistic about the likelihood of large scale transfers of territory to the south. Among the Prime Minister's more conspicuous talents was his ability to introduce subtle refinements into his discourse, the import of which could be lost on his less attentive listeners. He suggested in Parliament ten days after the Treaty was signed that the economic and geographic qualifications in Article 12 would act as a brake on the commission's ability to transfer large territories from Northern Ireland.[36] It is difficult to believe that he could have advanced this interpretation to Griffith or Collins during the negotiations.

Optimistic interpretations of the effect of Article 12 were constantly canvassed by agents of the Free State. In the course of a formal presentation of the Free State case in London in August 1925, the Attorney General John O'Byrne, asserted that the governing factor in the boundary clause in Article 12 was 'the wishes of the inhabitants', while the qualifying reference to 'economic and geographic conditions', had not been intended to have the same force.[37] In a document submitted to his fellow members of the Provisional Government in August 1922, in which he suggested that the northern entity could still sustain a government and parliament even after the loss of the substantial territory the boundary commission was certain to deprive it of, Ernest Blythe argued that Article 12 of the Treaty gave the Free State 'a clear claim to at least two and a half counties of the six, and urged his colleagues to use every means to secure the last tittle of what the Treaty entitles us to'.[38] Like Collins, Blythe expressed faith in what he called 'the fair carrying out of Clause 12', by the boundary commission, believing that it was bound to give the Free State 'a very substantial amount' of territory. In his view, a just application of the terms of Article 12 would leave the northern state with 'in addition to Belfast and Co. Antrim, the greater part of Co. Down, Armagh and Derry, and possibly a portion of Tyrone'.[39]

Blythe's publicly expressed expectations were in general accord with those of Griffith and Collins. Griffith, hoping that the principle of self-

---

36 *Hansard*, House of Commons Debates, Vol. 149, Cols 314–5, 16 Dec. 1921.

37 Hearing of Counsel for the Irish Free State, Boundary Bureau Papers, NAI, 3/489 Carton 30, 25 Aug. 1925.

38 Blythe to Cabinet colleagues, Blythe Papers, UCDA P24/70/6, 9 Aug. 1922.

39 Blythe Papers UCDA, P24/621(a). Later, Blythe revised his views on the value of a boundary commission. He came to regard its establishment as an act of folly, and felt ashamed that a government of which he had been a member had been a party to its proceedings. Blythe's reassessment was based on his conviction, reached upon mature reflection, that any territorial award made to the south by a boundary commission was bound to consolidate partition and to perpetuate a further partition by dividing counties. See Ernan De Blaghad, *Briseadh na Teorann* (Baile Átha Cliath, 1955), pp. 55–62.

determination would govern the deliberations of the boundary commission and that each district would be considered separately according to the wishes of its inhabitants, suggested that the parts of Tyrone and Fermanagh with Unionist majorities would remain in the control of the northern Parliament. However, as he told de Valera in November 1921, he believed that this would be offset by the transfer to the Free State of large parts of Down, Armagh and Derry.[40] Collins expressed confidence that two entire counties would be transferred to the south, along with substantial parts of other counties contiguous to the border.[41] The views expressed by Griffith and Collins, if sincerely held, would provide essential evidence about the expectations they were encouraged by their British counterparts to entertain with regard to the significance of Article 12. Many leaders of northern Nationalist opinion considered the implications of Article 12 self evident. In his Lenten pastoral for 1922, Bishop McKenna of Clogher, a diocese divided by the border, insisted that 'the wishes of the people in all those large areas in the six counties which under the Treaty are fully entitled to remain in the Free State shall be given effect to'.[42] Like other Nationalists, McKenna assumed that the wishes of inhabitants would be the overriding concern of any boundary commission. A similar assumption was evident in the submissions later made by Nationalists to the Boundary Commission now established. It should be borne in mind, however, that McKenna and other optimists were merely repeating what they had been told by Collins and others identified with the negotiation of the Treaty, who were naturally anxious, on political grounds, to persuade Irish Nationalists of the value of what they had achieved. To underplay the significance of Article 12 so soon after subscribing to it would have damaged them politically, and exposed them to ridicule.

In February 1922, when representatives of the Provisional Government presented what became known as the maximum Irish demand to the British authorities in London, the newspapers published a map showing the areas in the six counties included in this demand. This map was based on the 1911 Census returns and the results of the 1918 Westminster General Election. The Irish case was that the transfer of these areas to the south would be required if the wishes of the inhabitants were to prevail. The downsizing operation contemplated in this map was a massive one, involving most of counties Tyrone and Fermanagh, all of south Down, south Armagh and Derry City.[43] In this matter, care must be taken to distinguish between public positions and

40   Griffith to de Valera, Dáil Éireann Papers 2/304/8, 8–12 Nov. 1921.
41   Gwynn, *Partition*, p. 214.
42   *Freeman's Journal*, 27 Feb. 1922.
43   The map was reproduced in the *Irish Times* and *Freeman's Journal*, 6 Feb. 1922.

the private views of those who advocated them. Collins, who presented his Government's territorial demands to the British, had deep misgivings about what any significant downsizing of the six counties might ultimately involve for the southern authorities. More importantly, if the Provisional Government were to pursue the claim to northern territory with vigour, and the result was a permanently truncated Northern Ireland, this would conflict with the fundamental aim of Nationalist statesmanship, which was a united Ireland. Collins and Griffith, at any rate, had been induced to sign the Treaty primarily on the basis of its inclusion of a boundary clause and consequently felt obliged to make public defences of its supposed downsizing implications.

Collins, however, was acutely aware that Article 12, no matter how it was implemented, had a profoundly disturbing significance. On the day after the appearance of what he called 'the most argumentative map we used in the [London] conference', he confided his fears to one of his closest associates. As a result of the findings of a boundary commission, Collins wrote, 'we may reduce the North East area to such limits that it cannot exist without us, and that it will be forced in.' This prospect, however, was not a source of complete satisfaction, since, as Collins realised, 'there would be much rancour in the train of this action,' as only a united Ireland 'will not leave minorities which it would be impossible to govern.'[44] Another argument against the downsizing of the northern state through a boundary commission, commonly deployed by anti-Treaty Republicans, was that the greater the extent of the territory to be ceded by Northern Ireland, the smaller would be the likelihood of successful pressure to end partition from within, given the overwhelming preponderance of Loyalists in a truncated state.

In the light of such circumstances, it is easy to appreciate the difficulties in which the Free State Government found itself as it faced the prospect of a boundary commission. There was no escaping the problem that even the most generous award of territory to the south would tend to make the official aim of southern statesmanship – the unity of Ireland – more difficult to bring about. It was not, however, politically expedient for members of the Free State Government to give public expression to this point of view. To do so would be to call into question their reiterated commitment to border Nationalists, and to risk charges of betrayal of their trusteeship. This makes it necessary to distinguish between southern ministerial rhetoric on the subject of the commission and the real views of members of the Free State Government. Sometimes the conflict between the two is dramatic. Consider, for example, Cosgrave's firm assertion in the Dáil on 20 July 1923, on his appointment of

---

44 Collins to Lughaidh Breathnach, 7 Feb. 1922, private possession. Copy shown to the author by Michael McEvilly, Dublin.

Eoin MacNeill as Free State Boundary Commissioner, that the southern Government 'cannot possibly ignore the discontent and dissatisfaction of those supporters of the Free State in the north who are kept against their will and wish out of the jurisdiction of the State to which they do not belong.' Among these inhabitants, Cosgrave included the entire populations of Fermanagh and Tyrone, as well as parts of Armagh and Down.[45] Three days before he made this commitment to border Nationalists and to the defence of their rights under Article 12 of the Treaty, Cosgrave was taking to Craig in a radically different vein. On 30 July 1923, Craig reported to his Cabinet on a meeting he had with Cosgrave on 17 July. Craig said that 'during his interview with Mr Cosgrave the latter referred personally to the Boundary Commission and stated that in view of the coming [Free State] elections it was necessary for him [Cosgrave] to have a political cry etc.'[46]

11 ARTICLE 12 REINTERPRETED: REVISED BRITISH VIEWS

By 1924, the year in which the Boundary Commission was set up, senior British politicians and political commentators, Liberal as well as Conservative, were engaged in the process of reinterpreting the Treaty, especially Article 12, in a radical way. They were suggesting that the Irish signatories, particularly Griffith and Collins, had, after all, been mistaken in their claim that Article 12 was designed to bring about large transfers of population from north to south. Much of this comment, however, must be interpreted in the light of the changing realities of British political life in the post-Treaty period. Between 1922 and 1925, there was considerable and growing disaffection within the British Conservative Party in particular over the northern boundary issue, much of this centred on the threat to Unionists posed by Article 12 of the Treaty. In the period immediately before the Treaty, the Conservatives had seen themselves as champions of the 1920 boundary arrangement, and defenders of the integrity of the six-county territory. The preservation of the Unionist position was 'the minimum price for Conservative support' for whatever settlement Lloyd George might make with Sinn Féin.[47]

The boundary clause of the Treaty represented an obvious threat to this position. Those Conservative members of Lloyd George's Coalition Government, Birkenhead, Chamberlain and Worthington-Evans, who negotiated and signed this Treaty on the British side, soon became targets of

45   Dáil Debates, Vol. 4, Col. 1226, 20 July 1923.
46   Northern Ireland Cabinet Conclusions, CAB 4/84/9, PRONI, 30 July 1923.
47   Callanan, *T. M. Healy*, p. 571.

Conservative Party anger, as betrayers of the cause of Ulster, which had been sacrificed on the altar of British politics. Far from appearing as the instrument which would permanently resolve the Anglo-Irish problem, the Treaty failed to settle the Ulster question, led to wholesale violence in both parts of Ireland, civil war in the south and the threat of hostilities between disaffected units of the IRA and British forces. As the Treaty settlement began to fragment, so too did the Lloyd George Coalition. On 19 October 1922, at a meeting in the Carlton Club, a majority of Conservatives voted to wreck the Coalition and force the resignation of Lloyd George whose aim was to lead the Coalition into the future as a political movement in its own right and thereby split the Conservative Party. Bonar Law, elected Conservative leader three days later, formed a cabinet of 16, which did not include those Conservatives most intimately involved in the Treaty negotiations: Birkenhead, Chamberlain and Worthington-Evans. After only seven months in office, the mortally-ill Bonar Law was succeeded as Prime Minister by Stanley Baldwin, whose Cabinet included Worthington-Evans. Baldwin's first administration lasted from May 1923 until January 1924, when Ramsay MacDonald's first Labour Cabinet took office.

Throughout MacDonald's first term as Prime Minister, which ended in November 1924, the Irish boundary question occupied much parliamentary time. The most troublesome issue arising was that the Northern Ireland Government refused to appoint its representative to the boundary commission as the Treaty required. This meant that if the Commission was to function, the British Government would be obliged to appoint a representative on behalf of Northern Ireland. Making this possible involved the passage of a special boundary bill, which was debated at considerable length by the House of Commons on the first two days of October 1924. In November, MacDonald was out of office. There followed a period of political stability. Baldwin's second Conservative administration remained in office for five years, during which time the Irish boundary question was finally disposed of. Baldwin's main domestic political task was to mend the division in the Conservative Party arising chiefly out of the Irish question. This involved moves to reunite those who had supported the Lloyd George Coalition and facilitated the passage of the Treaty, and those who had brought about the downfall of the Coalition. As part of the process of reunification, leading Coalition Conservatives who had been instrumental in dictating the terms of the now unpopular Treaty were restored to high government office by Baldwin. His second Conservative Cabinet included Chamberlain, Worthington-Evans and Birkenhead. Winston Churchill, a Liberal when he signed the Treaty, was adopted as a Conservative candidate for the safe seat at Epping at the General Election of October 1924, and was returned with a huge majority.

Baldwin, impressed by this, offered him the Treasury, which he accepted with alacrity.

Almost three years after the Treaty was concluded, four of its signatories again held high office. For this, all four were expected to pay a price, by offering a tangible token of reparation for what they had helped to bring about in December 1921, above all the Ulster clauses of the Treaty, which were yet to be implemented. As Taylor observes, people like Birkenhead and Chamberlain 'were laboriously working their way back into the Conservative Party which they had deeply offended by their surrender to Ireland.'[48] Their rehabilitation was to be effected through their renunciation of two key elements in the Treaty they had signed, both of which had been designed to push northern Unionists in the direction of an all-Ireland settlement: the boundary and financial clauses. Redressing the balance in favour of Northern Ireland was an essential Conservative aim. They only way in which this could be achieved was to undermine the force of the punitive boundary and financial clauses as threats to the integrity of the northern state. This helps to account for the steady flow of assertions by the British signatories of the Treaty that the purpose of the boundary clause was to facilitate minor rectification of the border, and not to leave open the possibility of large transfers of territory from north to south. It also helps to account for the steady dismantling of the financial clauses, in breach of the Treaty, by Bonar Law and Churchill, Baldwin's Chancellor of the Exchequer.

The fate of the Treaty settlement, in particular its Ulster dimension, was thus determined by the exigencies of British domestic politics in the post-Lloyd George era. Liberals, as well as Conservatives, pressed the Ulster boundary issue into service for party ends. Viscount Grey of Fallodon, Foreign Secretary in a variety of Liberal administrations from 1905 to 1916, made a remarkable intervention in the House of Lords debate on the Irish Boundary Bill in October 1924. He was not interested in the argument that the boundary clause involved mere rectification of the border. Instead, he suggested that Parliament was confronted with what he called 'an honourable understanding' reached with Ulster in 1920 that whatever happened after that, its boundaries as determined by the Government of Ireland Act would be inviolable. Against this, Grey set 'a definite engagement with the Free State' under the terms of the Treaty providing for a boundary commission which had the potential to alter these 'inviolable' boundaries. A choice now had to be made between these two conflicting commitments. Grey had no doubt as to the nature of the choice he would make. To cheers from his fellow peers, he declared that he would 'rather face a demand from the Free State to be a

48   A. J. P. Taylor, *English History 1914–1915* (Oxford, 1965), p. 162.

Republic than see the understanding with Ulster broken'.[49] What is most extraordinary about Grey's intervention is that he should have been prepared to afford superior status to an 'honourable agreement' with Unionists of which there was no public record, over those of a treaty ratified by parliament and registered with the League of Nations. The substance of Grey's affirmation is less important than the political impulse behind it. As Matthews points out, 'Grey was prepared to use the boundary dispute as a defining issue with which he might separate himself from the rest of the Liberal leadership and from Lloyd George in particular. His speech was an attempt to do that.'[50] It was also in tune with what Baldwin had told the House of Commons a few days before. Baldwin claimed that the British Parliament owed a 'double debt of honour, since pledges had been made to Northern Ireland as well as to the South, and that these earlier commitments [to the Ulster Unionists] should be upheld'.[51] He did not advert to the consideration that to follow the latter course, by honouring the earlier secret commitment at the expense of a later solemn and formal one which had been ratified by parliaments in two states, would constitute a major violation of the Treaty.[52]

In 1922, with Collins proclaiming that a boundary commission finding could only result in large reductions of the territory assigned to the northern parliament, senior Conservatives, with a growing commitment to Ulster Unionism, were troubled that this might indeed be the outcome unless the boundary clause of the Treaty could be amended in such a way as to prevent the commission from transferring substantial territories to the Free State. Chamberlain, one of the British signatories of the Treaty, speaking in 1924, declared that he and his fellow signatories did not have in mind a boundary commission that would have the power to transfer substantial areas of northern territory to the jurisdiction of the southern government.[53] Indeed, the opinion of 'the great lawyers' who had advised Lloyd George and the other British negotiators in 1921 was that Article 12 provided 'not for the creation of a new boundary, but simply for the rectification of the existing boundary'. Chamberlain claimed that Article 12 had been framed under a form of words which had been deliberately adopted to exclude such a dismemberment of

49 *Hansard*, House of Lords Debates, Vol. 59, Cols 550–3, 7 Oct. 1924.

50 Matthews, *Fatal Influence*, p. 187.

51 House of Commons Debates, Vol. 177, Col. 43, 30 Sept. 1924.

52 See comment made by Worthington-Evans to the effect that if the Commission were to transfer even one Ulster county, the British Government would be foolish if it tried to enforce this. See note 71 below.

53 Chamberlain's view in 1924 contradicts his earlier contention in March 1922 that Britain would have to redraw the boundary in a substantial way.

Northern Ireland as would be created by cutting out entire counties or large slices of counties.[54] Chamberlain repeated this claim after the collapse of the Boundary Commission in November 1925, telling Cosgrave at a meeting in London that he and the other British Treaty negotiators 'always spoke of an adjustment' and 'excluded the drawing of a new boundary apart from and independent of the existing boundary'. He also made the claim that 'every British signatory spoke of territory being given not only by Ulster to the Free State, but by the Free State to Ulster', that Griffith and Collins must have clearly understood this, and that he [Chamberlain] and other signatories had advanced a similar interpretation during the House of Commons debate on the Treaty, an interpretation not challenged by either Griffith or Collins in the Dáil.[55]

It is true that during the House of Commons debate on the Treaty, one of its signatories, Sir Laming Worthington-Evans, in an apparent though not conclusive concession to Unionists, declared that 'this Commission is a Boundary Commission to settle boundaries, not to settle territories'.[56] It is also true that Birkenhead, who had, immediately after the Treaty was signed, promoted the view that the commission would decide upon major territorial changes, including even the transfer of entire counties,[57] seemed to have second thoughts some weeks later. In March 1922, he told the House of Commons that Collins had recently put forward a novel interpretation of the boundary clause 'in relation to which no trained lawyer up to that moment had ever hinted there lurked ambiguity'.[58] Chamberlain, however, made a speech on the boundary commission during the Treaty debate which could only be interpreted in a sense quite opposite to what he would say in 1924 and 1925. He told MPs in 1922 that they could only retain the Nationalist areas of Ulster by resuming the war. Not to redraw the boundary, he declared, would mean that they would have to fight 'for no great issue of national honour, for no great issue of imperial strength, but in order that you may preserve within the

54   *The Times*, London, 11 Aug. 1924; 3 Oct. 1924.

55   Draft notes of a conference held at No. 10 Downing Street, NAI S 4270 A, 26 Nov. 1925.

56   *Hansard*, House of Commons, Vol. 150, Col. 1326, 16 Feb. 1922.

57   When the County Councils of Tyrone and Fermanagh declared allegiance to the Free State, the Belfast Government replaced them with Commissioners. Birkenhead looked forward to the time when a boundary commission would rescue the Nationalists of these counties from injustices such as this. He told a meeting in Manchester that the boundary commission would 'examine into the boundary lines with a view to rendering impossible such an incident as that a few days ago, in which the popularly elected bodies of one or two of these districts [Fermanagh and Tyrone] were excluded from their habitations by representatives of the northern Parliament on the ground that they were not discharging their duties properly.' *The Times*, London, 7 Dec. 1921.

58   *Hansard*, House of Lords, Series 5, Col. 685, 22 Mar. 1922.

boundary of the northern government populations the majority of which desire to leave their sway'.[59]

Also in 1924, on 6 September, Lord Balfour, a veteran Imperialist, published, at the instigation of Winston Churchill, a confidential letter which he had received from the Earl of Birkenhead, another signatory of the Treaty, on 3 March 1922, explaining the meaning of the boundary clause in Article 12. Churchill sent copies of this letter, doctored to make Collins look more ridiculous than the original did, to Craig and to the Press. His motive for doing so was to convince Ulster and British Unionists that he and his fellow negotiators had not betrayed their interests in framing the Treaty and had not induced the Irish delegation to believe that Article 12 would lead to significant boundary changes. Birkenhead's 'secret' letter was, according to Balfour, intended to allay the recipient's anxiety that the Treaty might have 'inadvertently done an injustice to Northern Ireland in respect of its boundary'. Birkenhead explained that the Clause meant 'merely a rectification of the boundary', and if anything else had been intended, Article 12 would have been drafted in very different words. He assured Balfour that Collins was promoting the contrary view for political reasons, and that it had no foundation 'except in his over-heated imagination'. It appeared to him 'inconceivable that any competent and honest arbitrator could take the opposite view', which would, as he put it, involve the kind of 'fantastic reading' of Article 12 promoted by Collins,[60] the same reading which Birkenhead himself had supported in a speech at Liverpool on 6 December 1921.[61] Birkenhead's letter to Balfour did not mark the end of his equivocations. On 10 September 1924, he issued a statement to the Press Association claiming that his secret letter to Balfour had 'repeated the view [on Article 12] I held then: it represents the view which I hold now,' adding that 'reflection indeed on this point only strengthened and deepened my conviction.'[62]

Less than three weeks before this, however, Birkenhead wrote to Chamberlain, also on the subject of Article 12, offering an interpretation of what was agreed between the Treaty delegates, contradicting that in the 1922 letter to Balfour and the September 1924 statement to the Press. In his letter to Chamberlain, Birkenhead acknowledged what so many Nationalists suspected: that the Irish Treaty delegates were encouraged to believe that the boundary commission was designed to bring about a considerable reduction in the territory of Northern Ireland, and furthermore, that the Irish would not

59 *Hansard*, House of Commons, Vol. 151, Col. 553, 2 Mar. 1922.
60 *The Times*, London, 8 Sept. 1924.
61 Ibid., 7 Dec. 1921.
62 Ibid., 11 Sept. 1924.

have signed without the assurance that this would be so.[63] In December 1925, Birkenhead confirmed what he had told Chamberlain in 1924. In a speech to the House of Lords on 9 December 1925, Birkenhead implied that the Treaty was signed by the Irish plenipotentiaries in the belief that Article 12 would lead to major alterations in the boundary, and that the Treaty would not have been signed on any other basis. He also implied that the British signatories acquiesced in the Irish interpretation because if they had not, there would have been no Treaty. 'I state plainly to your Lordships,' Birkenhead declared, 'that there was no signatory of the Treaty but knew that in Article XII there lurked the elements of dynamite. We knew it well. It was forced upon us in this sense, that whether it was good or bad that the Treaty should be signed, it never would have been signed without Article XII.' 'Supposing,' he asked, 'that we had proposed to stereotype the existing boundary, what do you think the prospects would have been of a settlement.'[64]

Winston Churchill, soon to become a member of a new Conservative government under Baldwin, professed to share Birkenhead's views as expressed to Balfour. He was glad that Birkenhead's letter to Balfour had been published, since, as he told Lionel Curtis, Adviser on Irish Affairs at the Colonial Office, it should 'reassure Ulster'. The essential task of the British Government, Churchill added, was 'to protect Ulster from extravagant claims on her territory'.[65] He went even further when he told his Epping Conservative constituency association that any change in the boundary should be subject to the consent of the Northern Ireland Parliament, even though this would violate Article 12 of the Treaty.[66] Sir Harry Goschen, Chairman of the Epping Conservative Association, insisted that Churchill's selection as a party candidate was conditional on his giving a pledge not to endorse any change in the Irish boundary that did not have the support of Craig's Government. This pledge, which made an absurdity of the boundary clause, and of the Treaty Churchill had signed on behalf of his country, was the price he willingly paid for a return to the centre of political power. About the same time, a leading Conservative politician, Sir Robert Horne, who had been Chancellor of the Exchequer in Lloyd George's Coalition Government in 1921–2, suggested to a Unionist demonstration at Perth that Article 12 could only have whatever effect the northern Unionists decided that it should have. There was, he

---

63 Birkenhead to Chamberlain, Winston Spencer Churchill Papers, Churchill College, Cambridge, 2/570, 22 Aug. 1924, pp. 50–6.

64 *Hansard*, House of Lords, Vol. LXII, Cols 1232–3, 9 Dec. 1925.

65 Churchill to Curtis, 8 Sept. 1924, Curtis MSS 89, Bodleian Library Oxford. Henceforth cited as Curtis MS.

66 M. S. Gilbert, *Winston S. Churchill: The Wilderness Years 1922–39* (London, 1976), Vol. 5, p. 46.

declared, 'enshrouded in British law the principle that territory of a sub-ordinate legislature under the Crown could not be altered without the consent of the people, and Ulster had a right to plead that nothing should be done to alter her Constitution without previous consultation with her.'[67]

Horne's view was in accord with the one Craig had been offering as far back as 1921. Craig, like Horne, argued that the northern state was a constant, not to be altered in shape without the consent of its parliament. In support of this view he and other Unionists fell back on such considerations as British Dominions' practice and the Colonial Boundaries Act of 1895. The latter Act provided that 'the consent of the self-governing Colony shall be required for the alteration of the boundaries thereafter'.[68] Craig's and Horne's position is undermined if we accept Hand's view that the northern state established under the Government of Ireland Act of 1920 was not a dominion or a self-governing colony, but a constitutional anomaly, an entity *sui generis*.[69] On the other hand, it could be argued that Northern Ireland was not *sui generis* but was in the same constitutional position as a provincial parliament within a dominion. If that were to be accepted as the real position, the dominion parliament could not diminish the territory of its northern province without its consent. However, account should be taken of the fact that in the 1920s, the conventions that were later to limit British parliamentary sovereignty over the six-county state did not operate. More significantly, it should be pointed out that the Unionist attempt to fall back on constitutional convention theory was a contradiction of the terms of the Anglo-Irish Treaty, Article 12 of which made explicit provision for interference with Northern Ireland territory without the consent of its government. On 2 March 1922, when the Treaty was debated in the British House of Commons, the Ulster Unionist MP Captain Charles Craig sought to have an amendment to the Treaty passed which would have prevented a boundary commission 'from being allowed to deal with the territory belonging to the Northern Ireland Government without its consent'. Craig's amendment was heavily defeated.[70]

Another signatory of the Treaty, Worthington-Evans, seemed to offer moral support to any Ulster Unionist whose resistance to an unfavourable boundary commission report might take aggressive and illegal forms. He

67 *Irish Times*, 8 Sept. 1924.

68 See House of Commons Debates 2 Mar. 1922. Extracts from parliamentary debates relevant to questions arising out of Article 12 of the Articles of Agreement for a treaty between Great Britain and Ireland. London, HM Stationery Office, 1924, p. 49.

69 Geoffrey Hand, in F. X. Martin and F. J. Byrne (eds), *Eoin MacNeill, The Scholar Revolutionary 1867–1945* (Shannon, 1973), p. 205.

70 See House of Commons Debates, referred to in note 63 above, 2 Mar. 1922, pp. 48–9.

suggested that the transfer by the commission of even one Ulster county 'would not be acceptable to the Ulster people', and that the British Government would be committing an act of 'supreme folly' in 'enforcing such a decision upon them'.[71] Worthington-Evans was reflecting the increasingly influential British view that if the Government were forced to choose between a boundary commission award unacceptable to Unionists and the breach of the Treaty involved in refusing to accept such an award, the Treaty would have to be violated. No such violation was contemplated on the British side if the commission's award did not meet Nationalist expectations. There was always a possibility that unless the boundary clause in Article 12 was implemented quickly, its original force would be blunted, and its application inhibited, by developing political circumstances. On 6 December 1921, the British and Irish negotiators subscribed to 'Articles of Agreement for a Treaty between Great Britain and Ireland'. Those who signed the document did so on behalf of Britain, not on behalf of the Conservative-Liberal Coalition Government of which they were members. The Treaty thus had the status of an international agreement, and as such its integrity should not have been at the mercy of the changing fortunes of British political parties.

The British Coalition Government depended on two disparate groupings, Conservatives and Lloyd George's National Liberals. Asquith's Independent Liberals were not part of the Lloyd George Coalition, being so called because they were outside this coalition, and were extremely critical of Lloyd George's Irish policy. On the second reading of the Government of Ireland Bill in 1920, the opposition was led by the Asquithian leader in the Commons, Sir Donald Maclean. The Lloyd George Coalition had been formed in 1918, and by the time the Treaty was ratified by both sides, its term of office was drawing to an end. There were justified fears among political elements in Britain who favoured a vigorous British implementation of the Treaty, particularly Article 12, that the forthcoming General Election, called for on 15 November 1922, would result in the formation of a Conservative government sympathetic to Ulster Unionism and consequently reluctant to implement Article 12 in a sense favourable to the Nationalist interpretation of its meaning. Sir Alfred Cope, Chief British Liaison Officer with the Provisional Government for much of 1922, and a member of the National Liberal Party, told Desmond FitzGerald, Minister for External Affairs, on the eve of the 1922 British General Election of the desire of National Liberals to ensure that the next British government would not renege on its obligations to Nationalists under the Treaty. Cope thought it essential, 'if the Treaty was to be kept in spirit by my country', that Tory diehards 'should not get into power with a working

71   *The Times*, London, 27 Sept. 1924.

majority'. Cope believed that people of Irish birth and background in Britain could help to combat this threat by recording their votes for National Liberal candidates supporting Lloyd George and Winston Churchill as well as for the Conservative Austen Chamberlain, who signed the Treaty and had lost office partly on this account. Cope reasoned that these three, along with Birkenhead, as architects of the Treaty, were 'the best people to see it through'. He wanted the names and addresses of influential Irish people in Britain. FitzGerald, conscious of the 'respective merits of parties and individuals' in Britain, quickly supplied Cope with the information he wanted.[72]

R. J. Purcell of Newcastle, one of several Irish expatriates who agreed to become involved, told FitzGerald that he felt he could influence the large Irish vote in Dundee in Churchill's favour, and reported that all the candidates in another constituency had replied 'in very favourable terms to the pledge submitted to them, to honour the spirit and letter of the Treaty, particularly Clause 12'.[73] The result of the General Election of 15 November 1922 disappointed the expectations of those who, like Cope and Fitzgerald, had looked to a strong National Liberal grouping to defend the fair implementation of Article 12. All the National Liberal leaders were defeated except Lloyd George. Churchill lost his seat at Dundee. With 345 seats, the Conservatives had a majority of 77 over the other parties combined, while the National Liberals won 62 seats. Cope's confidence in Austen Chamberlain and Birkenhead as likely advocates of a generous application of Article 12 as a means of meeting the grievances of border Nationalists was to prove misplaced: both, in conformity with Tory policy, became advocates of the minimalist interpretation of the boundary clause in the Article which Mr Justice Feetham's Commission was to enforce.

When, after the Boundary Commission had failed to perform the task of border rectification Cosgrave thought it was obliged to according to the terms of Article 12, he suggested that its proper operation had been impeded by 'persistent and unscrupulous use of threats of violence and political pressure'. Cosgrave had two forces in mind: what he called 'an influential section of the British Press',[74] and British politicians 'in the highest positions' who had lent themselves to the campaign of whittling away, by misinterpretation, the rights which a large number of Irishmen had acquired 'by Treaty and Statute, to be returned to the government of their choice'. Cosgrave was certain that this campaign had only one purpose: to prejudice the Commission in its interpretation of its terms of reference, to exert 'an improper influence upon the minds

---

72 See Desmond FitzGerald to Cope, FitzGerald Papers, P80/ 391, 6 Nov. 1922, p. 4.
73 R. J. Purcell to Desmond FitzGerald, FitzGerald Papers P80, 391/7, 12 Nov. 1922.
74 Speech by W. T. Cosgrave at Emyvale, Co. Monaghan, NAI S1801 C, 22 Nov. 1925.

of British nominees on the Boundary Commission'.[75] The revised British Conservative view of the meaning of Article 12 was articulated by a Special Correspondent in *The Morning Post* in February 1924. *The Morning Post* was the paper of the Tory diehards who opposed the Treaty. Collins, formerly admired in Tory circles as one of the two great architects of the Treaty, which would not have been concluded without his support, was now criticised for the 'fantastic' interpretation of Article 12 which the British negotiators had encouraged him to entertain as a means of getting the Treaty signed, and which, according to Birkenhead, they themselves accepted on 6 December 1921.[76]

In March 1922, in an interview with the Hearst Press, Collins described Article 12 as embodying 'forces of persuasion and pressure' to induce northeast Ulster to join a united Ireland. The latter course would guarantee Unionists 'a generous measure of local autonomy'. If, on the other hand, the Northern Parliament voted to stay out, 'the decision of the Boundary Commission arranged for in Clause 12 would be certain to deprive Ulster of Tyrone and Fermanagh'.[77] *The Morning Post* correspondent ridiculed Collins for having proclaimed such views, based as they were on an assurance from Lloyd George that Article 12 might be construed as involving *inter alia* the transfer of Tyrone and Fermanagh. Collins and Griffith, the correspondent suggested, 'knew as well as Mr Lloyd George that the latter was promising something not in his power to perform.' He argued that the boundary clause in Article 12 had no legal foundation, since, as he put it, no agreements 'signed in panic between parties can validly curtail the rights, or alienate the territory, of a third party which is no party to the agreement.'[78] From a Nationalist perspective, the problem with this argument was that if valid, it could be used to raise fundamental doubts about the treatment of northern Nationalists by the 1920 Government of Ireland Act. While Article 12 of the Treaty was framed without the consent of Unionists, it was nevertheless the outcome of negotiations which took account of their general political interests. The 1920 Act, on the other hand, divided the country in such a way as to alienate hundreds of thousands of Nationalists from the jurisdiction to which they clearly preferred to belong without any consideration of their wishes or interests. This argument is difficult to answer in moral terms. However, the basis on which Nationalist wishes were not considered when the 1920 legislation was being formulated was not a moral, but a legal and constitutional one. Northern Nationalists did not have a government of their own, and were therefore not a

75   Emyvale Speech, 22 Nov. 1935.
76   Gallagher, *Indivisible Island*, p. 157.
77   Interview reproduced in *Michael Collins: The Path to Freedom* (1996 edn, Cork) p. 80.
78   *The Morning Post*, 4 Feb. 1924.

'legal person' with rights of negotiation. This consideration underlay Craig's insistence on a separate Northern Ireland government which would fight for Unionist interests, rather than direct rule from Westminster.

The Morning Post correspondent was reflecting the contemporary British political climate in 1924–5, which was decidedly more favourable to the Unionist cause than it had been at the time of the Treaty, when the Cabinet contained a number of Liberal ministers, and public opinion was moderately sympathetic to Irish Nationalist aspirations. In July 1924, Baldwin, soon to become Prime Minister in a purely Conservative government, betrayed a widely-shared disillusionment with Irish Nationalism in his party and in Britain generally, when he remarked to Thomas Jones, the British Cabinet Secretary, of the southern Irish that it was 'difficult to forgive assassination and to forget their behaviour in the war'.[79] It was also difficult to forget Collins's attempts to destabilise Northern Ireland in early 1922, which were bound to diminish sympathy for the Free State's territorial claims based on the boundary clauses of Article 12 of the Treaty. Baldwin, in common with his party colleagues, found it much easier and politically more expedient to look kindly on northern Loyalists. More than political expediency was involved in the attitudes of Baldwin and many other British statesmen in 1924. Patriotic Britons, surveying the record of increasingly militant Irish Nationalist hostility to British rule in the wake of 1916, could scarcely have been expected to show forbearance. It would have been surprising had British politicians not been influenced in their attitude to the recent conduct of rival Irish parties to the Boundary Commission. Irish Nationalists had, after all, risen in arms against Britain in time of war, and subsequently waged a ruthless guerrilla campaign against Crown forces. Northern Unionists, on the other hand, had loyally supported the war effort throughout. Unionists had thus accumulated a considerable stock of credit with British public opinion since 1914; since 1916, Nationalists had dissipated much of whatever credit they had.

Something of the temper of British feeling on the boundary question was conveyed to Cosgrave in May 1924 by Sir Alfred Cope, who claimed that his comments were made 'in perfectly good faith'. The influence of the British press, he told Cosgrave, was hostile to the Nationalist interest. The special boundary articles in *The Times* were 'very misleading indeed', and the Free State point of view on the boundary was not being stated because 'the bulk of the press here is pro-Craig and do not want your side of the case'. Cope believed that British public opinion tended to the view that the Treaty and the setting up of the Free State Government had 'accomplished everything', and that whenever it thought of Ireland it was inclined, under the influence of the

79   Thomas Jones, in Keith Middlemas (ed.), *Whitehall Diary* vol. 3 (London, 1971), p. 233.

press, to think that Craig was 'doing his best for a peace settlement on a reasonable basis'. Craig was enjoying considerable success in using 'half the truth' to manipulate public opinion, maintaining 'the reputation he has among the uninitiated of being a man of intense patriotism, great courage and wise statesmanship'.[80] He was also able to assert that by striving to retain the 1920 boundary he was defending not only the Ulster boundary but the boundary of the British Empire, a position congenial to British politicians of all parties.[81]

III IRISH EQUIVOCATION ON THE TREATY

Much of the discussion of the boundary clause in Article 12 tends to focus on Irish criticism of British public figures for dishonouring the spirit of the clause and ignoring its original interpretation and context. On the British side there was, within days of the signature of the Treaty, a resentful and growing consciousness that the spirit, as well as the letter, of the agreement was being violated by the southern authorities, including some of those who had signed it, and was being rejected with contempt by leading members of the political movement under whose auspices it was negotiated. Two days after the Treaty was signed, de Valera, with whose assent Lloyd George had initiated the negotiations which led to it, and who had appointed the Irish negotiators who assented to it, issued a proclamation to the Irish people repudiating it as being 'in violent conflict with the wishes of the majority of this nation'.[82]

It soon became clear that Collins, anxious to avoid a civil war in the south and to reconcile anti-Treaty opinion, was preparing to preside over the preparation of an Irish constitution that would mention neither the British Crown nor the Anglo-Irish Treaty. The draft constitution, presented to the British on 27 May 1922, provoked fundamental objections, being, in Churchill's words, 'wholly inconsistent with the Treaty signed by the Irish plenipotentiaries and endorsed by their Parliament.' Under British pressure, Griffith was forced to agree to amending the draft to reconcile its terms with those of the Treaty of 1921.[83] In the preamble to the amended Free State Constitution it was affirmed that 'these presents shall be construed with reference to the Articles of Agreement for a Treaty between Great Britain and Ireland . . . hereinafter

80   Cope to Cosgrave, Blythe Papers, P24/129 (12), 13 May 1924.

81   Parliamentary Reports, Northern Ireland Commons, Vol. 4, Cols 1206–7, 7 Oct. 1924.

82   Macardle, *Irish Republic*, p. 596.

83   See D. H. Akenson and J. F. Fallin, 'The Irish Civil War and the drafting of the Free State Constitution', *Éire-Ireland* Vol. v, No. 4 (Winter 1970), p. 28; pp. 55–8.

referred to as the Scheduled Treaty, which are hereby given the force of law, and if any of the provisions of this Constitution or any amendment thereof is in any respect repugnant to any of the provisions of the Scheduled Treaty, it shall, to the extent only of that repugnancy, be absolutely void and inoperative.' Despite this, even in early 1922, Collins had been displaying a cavalier attitude to the Ulster clauses of the Treaty, and to the letter and spirit of the agreement in general. In April 1922, he told members of the northern IRA that he would never recognise Partition, 'even though it meant smashing the Treaty.'[84] By then, as Regan points out, 'he represented a semi-autonomous power-structure within the revolution.'[85] He was soon prepared, in his self-assumed role of a one-man government, to take up Churchill's proposal for direct discussions with Craig. Churchill, Chairman of the new 'Provisional Government of Ireland Committee',[86] believed that a boundary commission could not provide a permanent settlement of the problem. The direct discussions resolved themselves into a meeting between Craig and Collins in January 1922, which resulted in an immediate draft agreement, the Craig–Collins Pact, the most significant detail of which, as Collins explained, involved scrapping the boundary clause: 'It was agreed, that we ourselves could deal with the question of boundaries without help or interference from any British authority. . . . We both agreed that a commission on the boundaries would be bound to cause bad feeling.'[87] The northern and southern Governments were to nominate representatives with a view to reaching mutual agreement on the borders. Collins's diplomatic efforts soon went awry when it emerged that Lloyd George 'had given completely different impressions to the Northern and Southern leadership as to how much territory was likely to be involved in any border changes'. Collins told Craig of the impossibility of there being two governments in Ireland, while Craig ruled out Collins's scheme for an all-Ireland constitution.[88]

The confusion generated by Collins's Northern policy arose from his triple role as head of the Provisional Government, charged with the implementation of the Treaty, as Director of Organisation at IRA General Headquarters and President of the IRB Supreme Council. After Collins's death, one of his admirers, Kevin O'Shiel of the Boundary Bureau and a key government

84 Cited in Matthews, *Fatal Influence*, p. 250.

85 J. M. Regan, *The Irish Counter-Revolution 1921–1936* (Dublin, 1999), p. 7.

86 M. S. Gilbert, *Winston S. Churchill: The Stricken World 1917–1922* (London, 1975), Vol. 4, p. 686.

87 Michael Hopkinson, 'The Craig-Collins Pacts of 1922: two attempted reforms of the Northern Ireland Government', *IHS* Vol. xxvii, No. 106 (Nov. 1990), p. 147. The terms of the agreement may be studied in full in NAI, 5 PO, S1801.

88 Ibid., p. 149.

strategist on northern policy, commented on the consequences for Northern Ireland, and for peace in the country as a whole, of Collins's divided and incompatible allegiances: to his colleagues in government, to implementing the Treaty he had helped to negotiate, to the IRB, the IRA and even to his old comrades now on the anti-Treaty Republican side. The most egregious instance of Collins's destructive essay in statesmanship during the post-Treaty period was identified by O'Shiel two months after his death, when he recalled that while he himself was urging a policy of 'peaceful do-nothingness in Northern Committees, two branches of the IRA, with the active support of Collins, a signatory of the Treaty, were actively making united preparations to invade the north in alliance'.[89] O'Shiel, who observed that 'the army for a long time had one policy and the civilians another', was here referring to the two-pronged policy pursued by Collins, simultaneously involving conciliation and coercion of Northern Ireland. Without consulting his 'political' colleagues, he was behaving more as a warlord than as the head of a civilian government, sanctioning 'a renewal of operations by pro-Treaty IRA divisions within Northern Ireland in conjunction with anti-Treaty units in the South'.[90]

This was only one of the breaches of the Treaty in which one of its main architects was involved. From early 1922 until the onset of the Civil War at the end of June, Collins was primarily responsible for making the border region the location of continual violence, involving state approval for kidnappings of Unionists. This could only dissipate whatever hopes there might have been for Irish political unity and, as Churchill reminded Collins on 13 February, could only help those 'who wish to see Ireland partitioned permanently.' It also influenced the attitudes of some Conservative politicians to the course that should be adopted by a boundary commission. One of these, Lord Bayford, believed that no large-scale handover of northern territory to the Free State should be countenanced, and that the only way to achieve this aim seemed to be 'to appoint as Chairman [of the Commission] someone who is sure to decide what we want'. On 9 February, Austen Chamberlain, who had signed the Treaty only two months before, warned Griffith that unless those kidnapped were returned and border violence brought to an end by the Provisional Government, he would 'consider himself absolved' from its provisions.[91] Chamberlain was really suggesting that Collins and those who acted with him had placed the boundary commission in jeopardy.

89   O'Shiel to each member of the Provisional Government, Mulcahy Papers, P7/B/287 UCDA, 6 Oct. 1922.

90   F. S. L. Lyons, *Ireland since the Famine* (London, 1974), p. 457.

91   Cited in Matthews, *Fatal Influence*, p. 69.

Collins's blundering efforts yielded no benefit for Nationalists, north or south. Instead, Craig had good reason to be pleased, and border Nationalists, who regarded Collins as their champion, dismayed, by the implications of the pacts signed by the two leaders. The wily Craig realised, as Collins appeared not to, that the first pact, by inference, had two important results favourable to Northern Ireland. In his report to his Cabinet on 26 January 1922, Craig pointed out that by entering into an agreement on behalf of the Provisional Government destructive of the Boundary Commission, Collins had recognised that the Treaty was no longer inviolable, and that further amendment would be possible in the British House of Commons. Equally significantly, Collins, whose policy was to make Northern Ireland ungovernable, had effectively recognised the Northern Ireland Government. This gave Craig the confidence to reassure the Ulster Unionist Council that the document signed by Collins and himself was an admission by the Free State that 'Ulster is an entity of its own' and that he would never agree 'to any rearrangement of the boundary that leaves our Ulster area less than it is under the Government of Ireland Act'.[92] Border Nationalists in south Down and south Armagh, alarmed that Collins appeared to be setting their interests aside, sought reassurances from Collins and Griffith.[93]

On 20 May, the Collins–de Valera Pact represented a significant attempt to unite pro- and anti-Treaty factions; its main objective was to use the forthcoming General Election as an instrument for the establishment of a government of national unity, consisting of four Republicans and five supporters of the Treaty. The setting up of such a government would, the British correctly argued, be contrary to the letter as well as the spirit of the Treaty, since all its members would be obliged to take an oath to the King to which Republicans could not subscribe.[94] The British view was shared by Erskine Childers, who told fellow-Republicans that the Pact violated the Treaty.[95] Collins realised this. Three days after the Collins-de Valera Pact was signed, it was unanimously approved by the Sinn Féin Ard Fheis, and Collins was wildly applauded when he declared that 'unity at home was more important than any Treaty with the foreigner, and if unity could only be got at the expense of the Treaty, then the Treaty would have to go.'[96] Collins saw the Pact as a necessary affirmation of southern unity in dealing with the northern problem. 'The north,' he told the Ard Fheis, 'could not ignore the voice of a united

92 *Irish Times*, 28 Jan. 1922.
93 See Hopkinson, 'Craig-Collins Pacts', *IHS* for details.
94 Paul Canning, *British Policy Towards Ireland 1921–1941* (Oxford, 1985), p. 40.
95 See FitzGerald Papers, UCAD, p. 80/1,371.
96 See Michael Hopkinson, *Green against Green: The Irish Civil War* (Dublin, 1988), p. 98.

Ireland.' One month later, on the eve of polling in the Free State General Election, he repudiated the Pact, and encouraged his followers to do likewise.[97]

In response to the Pact, an angry Churchill, who saw it as preventing an expression of southern opinion on the Treaty, summoned Griffith and Collins to London, and made a belligerent and threatening public comment. De Valera responded with a statement to the United Press denying the right of any English authority 'to prescribe what Irishmen shall and shall not do.'[98] British anger was further inflamed by the assassination in London on 22 June 1922 of Field Marshal Sir Henry Wilson, military adviser to the Northern Ireland Government, by an IRA gunman, for long afterwards believed to have been acting on the orders of Collins.[99] Many historians attribute responsibility for the Wilson assassination to Collins, either directly or indirectly, among them T. P. Coogan.[100] Leon O'Broin thinks it 'not inconceivable that Collins was responsible,' but is not satisfied that there is sufficient evidence. F. S. L. Lyons, on the other hand, thinks that 'the bulk of the evidence points towards Collins, who was not only ruthless enough to give the order, but who was also at that time particularly incensed by the attacks upon northern Catholics made by the very Ulster Unionists with whom Sir Henry Wilson had always identified himself.'[101] Peter Hart, acknowledging that 'the lion's share of suspicion has fallen on Collins, to the point where his guilt has been widely accepted as fact' argues that 'there isn't any convincing evidence to this effect.'[102]

The British response to this was an ultimatum to Griffith and Collins to end the continuing Republican occupation of the Four Courts. When Collins moved to accomplish this, with the help of armaments supplied by the British and thus precipitated civil war, Churchill rejoiced that prospects of a *rapprochement* between the Republicans and the supporters of the Free State were now at an end, with the likelihood that a victorious provisional government would honour the terms of the Treaty without equivocation. It should be noted in this connection that Churchill, in earlier encouraging Collins and Craig to violate the terms of the Treaty by effectively scrapping its boundary clause, had made himself an unlikely champion of its integrity. Having sanctioned

97   Macardle, *Irish Republic*, p. 721, prints the repudiation as reported in the press.

98   Childers Diary, TCD. 7 816, 1 June 1922.

99   See Peter Hart, *Mick: The Real Michael Collins* (London, 1992), pp. 150–70.

100 Coogan, *Collins*, p. 72ff; Robert Kee, *The Green Flag, Vol. 3: Ourselves Alone* (London, 1972), p. 165.

101 Lyons, *Ireland since the Famine*, p. 460.

102 Hart, *The Real Michael Collins*, pp. 396–7. For a detailed examination of the evidence, see Hart, 'Michael Collins and the assassination of Sir Henry Wilson', *IHS* Vol. xxviii, No. 110 (Nov. 1992), pp. 150–70.

unsuccessful military action against Northern Ireland, thus violating the Treaty, and embarked on hostilities against the anti-Treaty Republicans, Collins decided at the end of June 1922, that a new, more conciliatory policy towards Northern Ireland was advisable. It was also imperative, since Civil War in the south rendered military activity against the north impossible. Southern preoccupation with civil war resulted in the restoration of relative tranquillity to Northern Ireland. Four months previously, Collins had been working for the collapse of government in Northern Ireland in the interest of Irish unity. On the eve of civil war, he was declaring that there could be no question of 'forcing Ulster into union with the twenty-six Counties', and that he was 'absolutely against coercion of this kind'. If Ulster was going to join, it must do so voluntarily, and this kind of union was the final goal.[103] With the death of Collins in August 1922, in his native county at the hands of a Republican marksman, the southern government showed itself determined to desist from encouraging military action against the north. Southern Irish attitudes to the Treaty between December 1921 and August 1922, and the civil war to which it led, strengthened the political influence of the diehard elements in British politics, who had regarded the 1921 settlement as a betrayal of Unionism and of Imperial unity and too accommodating to the demands of Irish revolutionaries.

There was a corresponding abatement of political sympathy for Irish Nationalism. Writing to Churchill, Lionel Curtis of the Colonial Office declared himself convinced 'that Collins's early death alone saved the Treaty' and was glad that 'Cosgrave in substance reversed his [Collins's] policy'.[104] Despite frequent and irritating breaches of the letter and spirit of the Treaty by the south, Lloyd George's Coalition Government had tried to promote the ultimate reunion of Ireland, albeit within the British Empire. The coming to power of a Conservative government under Bonar Law in November 1922 brought about a radical change: British policy would henceforth be based on the preservation of the 1920 settlement and solid support for northern Unionism. In the new Prime Minister, Ulster Unionists had an ally who shared and understood their political outlook, above all their determination not to be ruled from Dublin. After the British General Election of 6 December 1923, the Free State Government could argue that southern breaches of the Treaty belonged to the past. Republican opposition to the Treaty had been quelled at considerable human and economic cost, in a civil war waged in its defence. Kevin O'Shiel, Secretary of the Boundary Bureau, a body set up to promote the Free State case for boundary revision, believed that the results of

103 Cited in Patrick Buckland, *A History of Northern Ireland* (Dublin, 1981), p. 48.
104 Curtis to Churchill, Curtis MS 89, 19 Aug. 1924.

the December 1923 Election in which the Conservatives lost over 90 seats and a Labour government under Ramsay MacDonald emerged with Liberal support, heralded a more promising era for northern Nationalist hopes. 'The last election,' Kevin O'Shiel wrote at Christmas 1923, 'altered the composition of the British House of Commons in our favour and left the Conservatives too weak to give much support to the Belfast Government.'[105] Those who shared O'Shiel's optimism failed to take account of the fact that there was no marked difference of approach between British political parties on the boundary issue.

Ramsay MacDonald, the first British Labour Prime Minister, exhibited a sympathetic attitude to Unionists, combined with a distaste for both Irish Nationalism and Catholicism as well as for southern Irish people in general, some of whom he seems to have regarded as less than fully human. Becoming convinced in 1931 that the current high British crime and unemployment rates could be alleviated only by the forced repatriation of Irish immigrants to the Free State, he remarked that 'we should not be a dumping-ground for Dominion refuse'.[106] This outlook was shared by Baldwin, the Conservative Prime Minister who was in office when the Boundary Commission made its determination in 1925, as well as by many influential members of his party. In 1924, Baldwin and MacDonald had a common policy on the Northern Ireland question: to keep it out of British politics. To this end they collaborated in ensuring that their respective parties did not permit the Boundary Commission to become an issue of contention between them.

IV ARTICLE 12: A BRITISH DECEPTION?

The pronouncements of British public figures in support of a restrictive interpretation of Article 12 showed northern border Nationalists how vulnerable the 1920 Partition Act had made them to changing political circumstances in Britain. They were also reminded how dependent they were on the goodwill and political integrity of British statesmen. These, as Nationalists understood it, or were led to understand it by Collins, Blythe and other southern politicians, had originally proposed and formulated the boundary clause in Article 12 as a means of affirming their right to self-determination. In 1924, many of their leaders began to sense that their hopes of living under a government of their choice were not going to be fulfilled. At this stage, influential British statesmen were publicly interpreting the boundary clause in a restrictive sense. These included a large majority of the membership of the House of

105 MacNeill Papers UCDA, LA/1/96/1.
106 MacDonald Papers, 30/69/358, PRO, London, 14 Aug. 1931.

Lords, which in October 1924 adopted a non-binding resolution endorsing the opinions of Birkenhead, Lloyd George and Worthington-Evans. The resolution was to the effect that 'this House, having taken note of the opinions expressed in parliament and elsewhere in connection with the passage into law of the Irish Free State (Agreement) Act, 1922, by the members of His Majesty's Government who were signatories of the Irish Treaty, that Article 12 of that instrument contemplated nothing more than a readjustment of boundaries between Northern Ireland and the Free State, and believing that no other interpretation is acceptable or could be enforced, resolves that . . .'.[107] Kevin O'Higgins, Free State Minister for Home Affairs, condemned this resolution as 'a very deliberate attempt to influence the Commission on an international question such as they would not attempt in the lowliest Petty Session Court in their own country'.[108] These British politicians had raised a fundamental and disturbing political issue. The current British view of Article 12 would restrict its scope to the making of minimal boundary adjustments, and this was radically contrary to Free State and Nationalist interpretations of the Article as a licence for major transfers of territory.

Not all Unionist commentators accepted the British re-interpretation of Article 12. W. Alison Phillips, a Trinity College history professor, suggested in 1925, while the Boundary Commission was sitting, that the restrictive inter-pretation of the Article could not easily be reconciled with the understanding which prevailed when the Treaty was signed. Phillips argued that a study of the Treaty negotiations and of the debates which followed 'leaves no such clear impression of the limited scope of the Commission'.[109] Cosgrave discussed 'the alleged ambiguity in the proviso of Article 12,' with the Minister for Justice, Kevin O'Higgins, who had a legal background. If there really was an ambiguity, O'Higgins asked, what agency was to resolve it? O'Higgins was clear that the British Government could not have the right to interpret an Article to which it was but one of a party of two. He went further, arguing that 'what the British Government cannot do, the British nominee on the Boundary Commission ought not to be allowed to do'. All O'Higgins could then hope for was that the British Government should state whether there was disagreement between it and the Free State 'as to the proper meaning and interpretation of the Article'. If there was such disagreement between the Governments as to the meaning of an Article in an international document originally subscribed to by representatives of both of them, O'Higgins

107 *Hansard,* House of Lords, Vol. LIX, Col. 664, 8 Oct. 1924.

108 *London Evening News,* 12 Oct. 1924.

109 Phillips was writing in the *Edinburgh Review.* See Geoffrey Hand, in Martin and Byrne, *Scholar Revolutionary,* p. 206.

wondered whether the Free State Government should be prepared to allow the matter at issue to be decided, 'as it will in fact be decided, by the vote of one of these governments, i.e. the British, or the Commission.'[110]

In the event, there was to be no escape from the difficulty posed by O'Higgins, since the Treaty gave no scope to the Free State Government to restrict the power of the Commission's Chairman to interpret Article 12 in whatever sense he chose. This meant that border Nationalists were going to have their political future decided, not by Article 12 as they had understood it, but by whatever interpretation of it the Chairman might decide upon, which turned out to be the current British one, and the one most in accord with British interests. From the Nationalist point of view, the Boundary Commission debacle was the high price to be paid for the political errors and omissions of the past. The Treaty negotiators whose self-imposed function was to win the maximum degree of self-determination for those northern Nationalists converted into an artificial minority by the Government of Ireland Act of 1920, could, from the perspective of late 1925, be seen to have been guilty of poor judgement and neglect of duty in respect of some fundamental issues. It is difficult to understand how the Irish plenipotentiaries could have subscribed to the border clause in Article 12 in the form it finally took. O'Higgins's 'alleged ambiguity' was in fact a real ambiguity, whatever private understanding of its meaning may have been shared by Lloyd George, Collins and Griffith. Such private understandings could have no statutory effect. The words alone remained, and it was for the Chairman of the Commission to interpret them. Their ambiguity was recognised almost from the beginning by those qualified to pronounce. In March 1922, Lord Buckmaster, a constitutional lawyer, told the House of Lords that Article 12 was 'full of ambiguity, full of grave and dangerous ambiguity, and I think the Commission will have a very difficult task'.[111] Buckmaster was an Asquithian who might, therefore, be expected to sympathise with the Irish Nationalist position. His recognition of the ambiguity is thus significant. The unfortunate formulation of the Article has in more recent times been remarked upon by F. S. L. Lyons, who refers to its 'vague terms' and to the qualifying phrase as offering 'an almost infinitely exploitable area of disagreement'.[112]

The history of Article 12 of the Treaty, from its initial status as a proposal to redistribute territory on the basis of the consent of its inhabitants to its final

---

110 O'Higgins to Cosgrave, Blythe Papers, UCDA P24/129 (6), 10 May. 1924.

111 House of Lords Debates 22 Mar. 1922.

112 Lyons, *Ireland since the Famine*, p. 491. The phrase 'wishes of the inhabitants' was similarly vague, as there was no indication in Article 12 as to the nature or location of the inhabitants whose wishes were to be ascertained, or how these wishes were to be ascertained.

shape in British hands as an instrument for minor boundary rectification, raises the question, posed in acute form by Cosgrave in the Dáil in October 1924, whether the British Treaty negotiators had fraudulently induced the Irish delegation to agree to a form of words for Article 12 which, as Carty puts it, they 'hoped later to interpret in a way opposed to that which they had led the Irish negotiators to understand the same words'.[113] The allegation of fraud centres on whether the Irish negotiators were induced to conclude the Treaty because they were assured that Article 12 would give primary consideration to the wishes of the inhabitants, and because they were not apprised of the real British position which emerged only after the Treaty was signed, that the Article could not have the effect of interfering with the essential integrity of the six counties, irrespective of what the wishes of the inhabitants might be. If consent to the Treaty, and especially to the terms of the boundary clause on which Irish consent to the agreement as a whole was based, was obtained by deceit, this could be held to bring the validity of the Treaty into question. International law commentators have long accepted the principle enunciated by McNair, that 'a Treaty concluded as a result of a fundamental mistake induced in one party . . . by the fraud of another party is void, or at least voidable'.[114] In the case of the Anglo-Irish Treaty, however, the 'fundamental mistake' was that of Irish delegates in failing to discern, or to contemplate in detail, what they were actually subscribing to in the case of Article 12, a failure induced by British misrepresentation to them of its actual thrust and intent. The main difficulty that the Free State Government would have experienced in bringing an allegation of fraud as a ground for rendering the Treaty void is suggested in the proceedings of the Vienna Convention on the Law of Treaties in 1968–9. Sinclair, commenting on Article 49 of the Vienna Convention, which covers deceitful proceedings by one state to induce consent to a treaty by another, drew attention to the lack of state practice in the matter, observing that 'the scarcity of precedents means that there is little guidance to be found either in the practice or in the jurisprudence of international tribunals as to the scope to be given to the concept'.[115] Whatever may be thought of the bearing of international law on the subject, any Irish attempt to demonstrate British breaches of faith in relation to the Treaty would have been confounded by the formidable obstacle that those who come seeking equity must come with clean hands. The immediate post-Treaty period was remarkable for the contempt shown on the Irish side for the Treaty in general and for the boundary clause

---

113 Anthony Carty, *Was Ireland Conquered? International Law and the Irish Question* (London, 1996), p. 140.

114 Cited in I. M. Sinclar, *The Vienna Convention and the Law of Treaties* (Manchester, 1973), p. 93.

115 Ibid.; Carty, *Was Ireland Conquered?*, pp. 135–6.

in particular. Republicans fought a civil war in opposition to the settlement, Collins tried to set the boundary clause aside, made a pact with de Valera which would have violated the Treaty and connived at an abortive military offensive against the six counties in a clear breach of Irish Treaty obligations.[116] The British could thus defend their own revised views on the significance of the boundary clause by arguing that circumstances had changed significantly since their representatives had signed the Treaty. They could invoke the international law principle of *rebus sic stantibus*, according to which a treaty is subject to an implied condition that if present circumstances are substantially different from those obtaining when it was concluded, a party to that treaty is entitled to be released from it. A similar condition might apply if a change of circumstances has rendered the objective of the treaty difficult or even impossible.[117]

From the time of its formulation in 1921 to its abandonment at the close of 1925, the boundary clause accumulated as many interpretations and shades of meaning as there were parties with a vested interest in the outcome of the Commission's deliberations. Representatives of northern border Nationalism consistently saw it as the vehicle for the delivery of many of their number from the control of the Belfast Parliament. Northern Ireland Unionists could only regard it as an unwarranted threat to the integrity of their state in which they were not obliged to acquiesce: what they got in 1920 they were entitled to hold. The Free State authorities, the official upholders of the northern Nationalist cause, publicly affirmed the belief that the boundary clause was designed as a mechanism to increase the territory and population of the south at the expense of the North: privately some of them were not so sure of this. The general body of northern Unionists doubted the legality of the clause insofar as it was imposed on them without their consent, and in breach of solemn British undertakings given to their leaders in 1920. Some British statesmen, including those who negotiated the Treaty, professed not to know what the clause meant or what boundary alterations it might facilitate, preferring to leave its interpretation to the Commission. Later, a number of these statesmen, in changing political circumstances, discerned one significant import of the clause, namely that the British negotiators had never intended to permit more than minimal transfers of territory. Again, differences arose over the direction in which such transfers could be made. Nationalists were adamant that they could operate in only one direction: from north to south, while the British interpretation was that they must operate in both directions.

116 Hopkinson, *Green Against Green*, pp. 83–4.

117 The Vienna Convention on the Law of Treaties [Articles 61 and 62, 1969] differentiates between supervening impossibility of performance and a fundamental change of circumstances. See *Oxford Dictionary of Law* (Oxford, 2006), p. 441.

Satisfactory answers to three interrelated questions, which persisted to the end of the Boundary Commission process, would help to clarify most of the issues in dispute between 1921 and 1925. These questions seem relatively straightforward. The first is whether the Northern Ireland leadership was given solemn assurances, conveyed by the British Government through Walter Long at the end of 1919, that the six-county area, denominated in the Government of Ireland Act of 1920, would remain inviolate. When Parliament was debating the Irish Boundary Bill at the beginning of October 1924, this question received close attention. Lloyd George must be regarded as an expert witness here, since he was Prime Minister when the pledges regarding boundaries were supposed to have been given to Northern Ireland with unanimous Cabinet approval. The main source of evidence for the pledges was Walter Long, later Lord Long, who in 1919–20 acted as intermediary between the British Government and the northern Unionist leadership. A few days before his death, Long placed his recollections of the matters on record in September 1924 in a letter to Lord Selbourne.

Unionist support for the 1920 Act, he told Selbourne, was given on the clear understanding, unanimously sanctioned by Lloyd George's Cabinet, 'that the Six Counties, as settled after the negotiations [on the Act] should be theirs for good and all, and there should be no interference with the boundaries or anything else, excepting such slight adjustments as might be necessary to get rid of projecting bits, etc.' In the same latter, Long recalled that the British Cabinet had assured Carson and Craig that the six counties 'should be theirs for good and all and there should be no interference with the boundaries'.[118] During the Commons debate on the Irish Boundary Bill in October 1924, Lloyd George did all he could to undermine Long's account. He roundly declared that 'no pledge was ever given [in 1920] as regards boundaries', and that 'Lord Long did not say that there was any pledge [to Unionists] that the present boundary should be adhered to'. He went on to suggest that Long's memory could not be trusted: after all he 'was recalling something that was said four years ago, and how many of us can recall every word that was said four years ago . . . how can you remember what was said?'[119] Lloyd George's position on the pledge to Unionists was, however, undermined when his attention was drawn to a statement published two days before over the signature of Lord Carson in which the latter declared that in 1920 he had received a letter from Lloyd George assuring him 'that the six counties area would be permanently excluded' from any arrangement made with the

---

118 Cited in John Kendle, *Walter Long: Ireland and the Union 1905–20* (Dublin 1992), p. 191, p. 198.
119 *Hansard*, House of Commons, Vol. 177. Col. 185, 1 Oct. 1924.

rest of Ireland.[120] Lloyd George was technically correct when he asserted that Long never made a pledge to Unionists that their 1920 border would not be interfered with: after all, he did qualify his assurance to the Unionist leadership, and told Selbourne so, by mentioning 'slight adjustments' and 'projecting bits'.

The second question to be dealt with arises from the first. Even supposing that the Lloyd George Government had, in 1920, solemnly assured Carson and Craig that their six-county unit would not be diminished in the future even in the smallest particular, could such an assurance have any constitutional standing after the Treaty of December 1921? In March 1922, Birkenhead, an acknowledged authority in such matters, told Balfour in a letter made public that Article 12 of that Treaty 'contemplates the maintenance of Northern Ireland as an entity already existing, not a new State to be brought into existence upon the ratification of the Articles of Agreement of 1921. This meant, in Birkenhead's view, that post-Treaty Northern Ireland was to be regarded 'as a creature already constituted, having its own Parliament and its own defined boundaries'.[121] A similar analysis was to form the basis for Feetham's interpretation of the boundary clause when the Commission deliberated in 1924–5. However, writing to Chamberlain later in August 1924, Birkenhead took a view of the relation between the 1920 Act and the Treaty fundamentally at odds with the one he had communicated to Balfour over two years before. His new view was, as Matthews observes, that 'after December 6, 1921, the 1920 Act was irrelevant when it came to determining Northern Ireland's frontier'.[122] In the course of his letter to Chamberlain, Birkenhead drew attention to a vital constitutional point arising from the decision of the Belfast Parliament to invoke the first part of Article 12 of the Treaty as the basis for excluding itself from the all-Ireland arrangement on which the first 10 articles of the Treaty were based. Birkenhead made the important observation that by taking this action, 'The Northern Ireland Government had in fact already so far recognised the Treaty as to avail itself of an option which can only come into existence in virtue of the Treaty.'[123] Matthews draws some pertinent conclusions from Birkenhead's analysis, which 'made it plain that the Treaty and its ratifying legislation superseded the 1920 Act just as that legislation repealed the 1914 Home Rule Act before it'. If, as Matthews argues, following Birkenhead, 'Northern Ireland's Parliament gained the right to vote itself out of a single Irish State only through Article 12, the entity created by the 1920 Act was irrelevant, and so were its boundaries.' This meant

120 Ibid., Col. 190.
121 Birkenhead's letter, dated 3 March 1922 is printed in full in Matthews, *Fatal Influence*, pp. 288–90.
122 Ibid., p. 171.
123 Birkenhead to Austen Chamberlain, Churchill Papers 2/570/50–6, 22 Aug. 1924.

that the North's boundaries were not protected by the 1920 Act or by promises or bargains made at the time it was passed. It also meant that the Boundary Commission was in no way prohibited by the arrangements made in 1920 from making extensive changes to the size and shape of Northern Ireland.[124] The full significance of this last point was to become clear when Feetham took a contrary position by suggesting that the 1920 Act still had validity in 1925, and that the interpretation of Article 12 of the Treaty had to be based on what the Act had given Northern Ireland.

The third question, more pressing than the first two, bears on the meaning and intention of the boundary clause in Article 12. When they signed Articles of Agreement for a Treaty on 6 December 1921, what did the signatories think this vital clause meant? More to the point, did all or any of them believe that it limited the Commission to making minor adjustments to the boundary or that it was more extensive in scope? By the time this became an issue for widespread political debate, Collins and Griffith, the two Irish signatories most intimately concerned with the acceptance of the clause, were dead. The evidence they left after them, however, suggests that the British negotiators, particularly Lloyd George, either interpreted the boundary clause, or encouraged them to interpret it, as involving more than minor rectification of the frontier. Winston Churchill, addressing the Commons on the issue two months after the Treaty was signed, interpreted the clause in a similar sense. Referring to unspecified districts in Fermanagh and Tyrone in which the majority of inhabitants would probably wish to join the Free State, he felt that 'the tremendous arguments which protect the freedom of Protestant Ulster have, in these districts, lost their application and have possibly the opposite application'. More significantly, he added that 'the Boundary Commission to be set up under Article XII affects the existing frontiers of the Ulster Government and may conceivably affect them prejudically'.[125]

For a well-weighted, fair-minded and balanced judgement of what was in the minds of the principal negotiators in relation to the boundary clause, it is wise to turn to Lord Longford's *Peace by Ordeal*, published in 1935, when some of the principal actors in the events of 1921 were still alive, of whom two were particularly helpful: Robert Barton and Sir Austen Chamberlain, the latter reading to him his contemporary notes of the crucial meetings. Longford raises the vexed question whether the British Government knew what the Sinn Féin delegates thought was the intention behind the clause. He contends that neither Chamberlain nor Birkenhead knew, but that 'unless all our documents are fabrications, all our deductions childish, Lloyd George must

124 Matthews, *Fatal Influence*, p. 172.
125 *Hansard*, House of Commons, Vol. 150, Cols 1271–2, 16 Feb. 1922.

have known'. The basis for this conclusion is that from two months' conversations with Griffith and Collins, Lloyd George knew that they would never have been prepared to give up the Republic on the mere chance of the chairman of the Commission proving favourably inclined to them, and that if the possibility of a 'Feetham decision' was even allowed to cross their minds 'the Treaty never would be, never could be signed.' Longford had no doubt that Collins and Griffith 'unquestionably believed as a result of two months' conversations, as a result above all of Michael Collins's last conversation with Lloyd George', that the boundary clause was weighted in their favour, drawn up with the intention of giving the Free State Tyrone and Fermanagh, provided that the Commission found that there were large areas in the north running down to the frontier whose populations would prefer incorporation with the south.[126]

It may, or may not, be over cynical to suggest that the boundary clause was not designed to express any specific intention in relation to the transfer of territory, but that its nebulous formulation reflected the need to avoid a breakdown of the Treaty negotiations, something both sides were anxious to prevent. A more detailed clause confirming the expectations of Nationalists might well have seemed impossible to the British negotiators, conscious as they were of the danger of a violent Ulster Unionist and British Conservative response to any significant reduction of Northern Ireland territory. Just as a boundary clause was necessary to having a treaty signed, the form the clause took satisfied Nationalists in the short term, and did not provoke Unionists to mount the militant campaigns that had characterised their response to Home Rule.

V THE STRENGTHS OF UNIONISM

By 1924, when the Boundary Commission was established, Unionist political leaders could act and speak in the growing assurance that no British government would, or perhaps could, permit any but the most minimal adjustment of the boundary, with such adjustment not necessarily all in favour of the Free State. Nationalist non-recognition of the Northern State might be a principled position with a good democratic foundation, but those who persisted with it did not have the leverage or the outside support at their disposal to make non-recognition the means for achieving any of their major goals. In this kind of context, after military attacks on the northern state were abandoned in 1922,[127]

---

126 Longford, *Peace by Ordeal*, pp. 303–4.
127 Hopkinson, *Green Against Green*, pp. 77–88.

the Nationalist case, however well documented and ethically justifiable, could amount to no more than impressive rhetoric echoing in a void. A disinterested observer from some headquarters of reason and sound political morality might find much of this case persuasive, and sanction the assertions that the six-county state was not a normal historic, religious, political or economic entity, that it was neither a nation nor a province, that it was an arbitrarily gerry-mandered area designed to secure religious and civil ascendancy for a favoured minority in Ireland as a whole, and that it had been established contrary to the principle enunciated by Asquith in 1912 that 'you can no more split Ireland into parts than you can split England and Scotland into parts'.[128] Unionists, over whose heads such arguments were addressed, did not tend to rebut them or even to address them. They could afford to ignore them, for as Lee observes, 'Craig held almost all the cards',[129] and based his tactics not on the demands of political morality, minority rights or contemporary self-determination theory, but on the hard facts of possession, dominance, superior force, determination to retain possession at any cost, British sympathy and the consciousness of the support of a unified, well disciplined movement. Apologists for Ulster Unionism might confront such hostility to its claims by arguing that the Nationalist counter-claim was based on the erroneous assumption that while Irish Nationalists and Republicans had a perfect right to self-determination and to secede from the United Kingdom, Ulster Unionists had no similar right to refuse to be part of an Irish state, and to remain part of the United Kingdom. The Unionist argument here might seem perfectly reasonable to an impartial observer.

Another of Craig's strengths was his knowledge that at worst he and his supporters would have to face only minor border changes. With the Boundary Commission imminent, Craig was privately told in May 1924 by J. H. Thomas, Colonial Secretary in MacDonald's first Labour Government, and was able to tell his Cabinet, that 'the Boundary Commission was merely concerned with an adjustment of the actual boundary and not with the transfer of significant territories'.[130] This comforting reassurance to Craig raises a number of questions. It was provided exactly a month before the British Government appointed a chairman of the Boundary Commission. Since the interpreta-tion of the boundary clause in Article 12 was exclusively a matter for the Commission, it is difficult to understand how Thomas could be so confident of the outcome of the Commission's deliberations even before it met, unless, perhaps, he was privy to an understanding already reached with the man

128   Asquith cited in Notes on Ulster, FitzGerald Papers UCDA P80/ 363/C 1–5.
129   J. J. Lee, *Ireland 1912–1985: Politics and Society* (Cambridge, 1989), p. 141.
130   Cabinet Conclusions, PRONI CAB, 4/112/4, 5 May 1924.

appointed chairman that the latter would interpret the clause in a restrictive sense, or that Thomas was certain that no British government would honour any award which was unacceptable to Unionists. The Thomas-Craig under-standing also illustrates the helplessness and isolation of Northern Nationalists as they prepared their thoroughly documented cases for transfer to the south under the terms of Article 12, unaware that the great majority among them were merely wasting their time, since the destination of all but a few small areas was almost certainly already predetermined.

Article 12, so widely canvassed as the Magna Carta of border Nationalism, proved a major liability to the Nationalist cause, by diverting it into futile paths and squandering its resources. Paradoxically, it was of significant benefit to the Unionists it was supposed to penalise. While its implications helped to fracture Nationalist unity, the Unionist leadership made skilful use of the putative threat it represented to the integrity of the northern state as a unifying force and consolidating political device, a means of quelling dissent within Unionism by focusing attention on the overriding need to repel the common danger, the supposed threat to the 1920 settlement. Captain Charles Craig, brother of the Unionist leader, told the House of Commons in February 1922 that if a boundary commission were to make 'anything more than the minutest change in our boundary', the inevitable result 'would be bloodshed and chaos of the worst description'.[131] From the beginning of 1922, Sir James Craig had been taking his stand on the principle that his Government had ultimate control over its own boundaries which would not be changed without its compliance. When he wrote to Churchill on 26 May reviewing border developments, he told him that 'the Boundary Commission has been at the root of all the evil', while a few days before he had told his Parliament that Unionists would not yield to any unfavourable findings the Commission might make: 'What we have now we hold, and we will hold against all combi-nations.'[132] His speeches became more and more unyielding on the issue, particularly after he and his parliament had formally excluded themselves from the jurisdiction of the Free State on 7 December 1922. In a debate on the boundary question on the same day, Craig made it clear that he would have nothing to do with the Boundary Commission, declaring that there could be no boundary adjustments 'unless agreement existed between North and South and the border counties were satisfied'. In a plea for patriotic British support for the integrity of the six counties, he declared it unthinkable that his Government could be dragged into the Boundary Commission and that the fixing of the boundary could rest in the hands of one man who might, 'by a

131 *Hansard*, Vol. CLIX, Col. 2149, 16 Feb. 1922.
132 Hopkinson, *Green Against Green*, p. 79.

stroke of the pen hand over the houses, the homes, the cottages of those gallant men who had spilled their blood for the safety of their own country.'[133] He was able to assure the northern House of Commons, however, that no British troops in the border areas would be withdrawn without consultation with his Government.[134]

Craig also made extensive inspirational tours of border areas, with the object of stiffening local determination to preserve the six-county territory intact. In April 1923, strong moral and material British support for Craig's resistance to boundary adjustment was afforded by Lord Derby, the British Secretary of State for War, on a visit to the A and B Specials in County Fermanagh. Derby promised to help the Unionist cause, 'not only from the military point of view', should help be required. Craig justifiably interpreted Derby's assurance to mean that any call Unionists would make on the British Government would be 'honoured without any more hesitation in the British Parliament' and, more significantly, 'that the great question of the border is thrown practically altogether into the background and probably will never arise again'.[135] In July 1923, accompanied by members of his Cabinet, he visited 'threatened' areas in Tyrone and Fermanagh, including Omagh and Enniskillen, inspecting the defenders of these areas, the Special Constabulary.[136] In August, he designated the members of that force in Tyrone and Armagh as 'those upon whose shoulders fell the burden of protecting the border'. What they were protecting it from he made clear in a further comment: 'No matter what might have been said, or what rumours might be circulated, the determination of the northern government to maintain and preserve their status in their Parliamentary area was unchanged.' A member of the Special Constabulary, who was present, was 'perfectly satisfied from the assurance of Sir James Craig, that they would never be brought under a Free State government'.[137] Significant British moral support for Unionist resistance to border change came in the summer of 1924, when it was officially announced that the Duke of York would visit the six counties. The prospect troubled Kevin O'Shiel of the Boundary Bureau, who told Cosgrave that the Duke would be used, as Lord Derby had the year before, as an instrument of Orange propaganda. A royal visit to Enniskillen would, O'Shiel believed, be 'a great demonstration of the loyalty of Fermanagh to the Royal Family and to the

---

133 *Freeman's Journal*, 8 Dec. 1922.
134 Northern Ireland House of Commons Debates, Vol. 3, Cols 22–3, 27 Feb. 1922.
135 For Derby's and Craig's speeches, see *Fermanagh Times*, 12 Apr. 1923.
136 *Irish Times*, 30 July 1923.
137 Ibid., 1 Aug. 1923.

Empire' at the very time when the Boundary Commission would be considering disputed territories in the county.[138]

Craig's public acknowledgement of the Ulster Special Constabulary as the force that would protect the six counties against any border adjustments made by a boundary commission recalled the very effective invocation in 1912 of the threat of paramilitary force to defeat the imposition of Home Rule on Ulster. The appointment in August 1924 of a Chairman of the Boundary Commission was marked by the mobilisation of the Special Constabulary along the border. Almost a thousand men assembled on the eastern boundary of Fermanagh in September, while on the same day a similar number paraded in south Tyrone, to be addressed by officials of the northern Government.[139] Such shows of strength and determination were undertaken with the purpose of convincing both the Boundary Commission and the British Government that significant alteration of the boundary would result in massive Unionist resistance, bloodshed and even civil war.

With the return of a Conservative government under Baldwin in October 1924, Churchill, a defector from the Liberals, now a powerful defender of northern Unionism and ally of Craig, was Chancellor of the Exchequer. Craig's threats of violent resistance to boundary changes were reinforced and given greater credibility when Churchill agreed to pay £1,250,000 for the Special Constabulary for 1924–5, contrary to advice from his own officials.[140] This, he made clear, was in the context of what the Boundary Commission might do. With the Commission now in session, Churchill considered it 'all the more necessary that the Northern Government should be solidly supported and militarily in a strong position'. Churchill told his Treasury officials that throughout the 'difficult period' during which the boundary was being adjudicated on, it was the British Government's duty to sustain the northern Government either by troops or subvention or both.[141] The military support for Craig's Government referred to by Churchill was also provided by the British, again in the context of the Boundary Commission: the British Army authorities in the north were instructed to discuss cooperation with the RUC and the Special Constabulary to allay 'the apprehensions of the population along the border', as the British Commander in the north put it.[142] As Farrell points out, the close military cooperation between the British

---

138 O'Shiel to Cosgrave, Blythe Papers P24/192(2) UCDA, 9 May 1924.

139 *Irish Times*, 3 Sept. 1924; *Belfast News Letter*, 5 Sept. 1924.

140 Michael Farrell, *Arming the Protestants: The Formation of the Ulster Special Constabulary and the Royal Ulster Constabulary 1920–27* (London, 1983), p. 233.

141 Ibid., p. 234.

142 Ibid.

Government and Craig had important implications for the boundary question. 'By aligning itself so firmly with the Northern authorities the British Government was abandoning the role of neutral arbitrator between North and South implied in Article 12 of the Treaty.'[143]

The supposedly impending threat posed by the Boundary Commission became a weapon in the hands of Craig and other Unionist politicians which they wielded with impressive effect to reinforce their hold on power and even to increase it. Regarding the Nationalist population as inherently disloyal clients of a Free State determined to take a major share of their territory by the device of the Boundary Commission, the northern Government embarked on a series of measures to undermine the political rights of Nationalists. Harkness argues persuasively that to Nationalists, the threat of the Boundary Commission to the northern state 'held out their best hope of reunion with Dublin and, while this hope existed, there was every reason to withhold support from the new state at every level, and indeed to work actively to bring its downfall'. He also suggests that 'it was at least in part because of the Boundary Commission . . . that the four crucial years of Northern Ireland were so divided, with Protestant determination moulding its every institution, and Catholic aloofness refusing every opportunity to contribute.'[144] The threat of a boundary commission led to heightened fear among border Unionists that their 1920 frontier might no longer be secure, and that many of them might become unwilling inhabitants of the south. On the other hand, it generated unfounded expectations among Catholics that the northern state would soon cease to exist. The volatile political situation in Britain from October 1922, when Lloyd George's unstable Coalition Government lost office, to November 1924, when the Conservatives, under Baldwin, came to power, was on the whole, favourable to Craig in his determined resistance to the Boundary Commission. In that two-year period, there were three British administrations, two Conservative under Bonar Law, the friend of Ulster Unionism, and Baldwin, and a Labour one under Ramsay Macdonald. The longer Craig could resist the establishment of the Boundary Commission, the more entrenched his six-county state would become and the more difficult it would be to adjust its boundaries in a substantial way. The unstable British political situation until November 1924 facilitated Craig's purposes in this respect.

As the formation of the Commission became inevitable, Craig used the reassembly of the Northern Parliament in 1924 to denounce the Commission idea once more, threatening that if it produced a report hostile to the six counties, he would resign as Prime Minister and, as a chosen leader of

143 Ibid., p. 235.
144 David Harkness, *Northern Ireland since 1920* (Dublin, 1983), p. 36.

Unionism, defend in a manner he did not specify, but which implied menace 'any territory which we may consider has been unfairly transferred from under Ulster, Great Britain and the flag of our Empire.'[145] J. M. Andrews, the Northern Minister for Labour, told a Unionist rally in Newry that the Unionist Government would not concede the town to the Free State 'even if the Boundary Commission recommended it'.[146] The considerable armed force at the disposal of the Unionists was an added reassurance in case the Commission failed to follow the Conservative and Unionist line on what it had to do. When it did finally gratify Unionist expectations, Kevin O'Higgins stressed the significance of well-armed Unionism in helping to bring about this outcome. O'Higgins talked bitterly of 'an army of Special Constables paid and maintained by the British Government' to impress the Boundary Commission members 'with an idea of the terrible things to happen if they acted strictly and fairly on their terms of reference. . . . The Commission has been influenced by Specials standing with their fingers on the trigger.'[147]

The problems to be resolved by the Boundary Commission hung over Unionist electoral politics from 1922 to 1925, and dictated Unionist electoral strategy. Unionist politicians saw to it that the Northern Ireland campaign for the Westminster General Election in November 1923 was dominated on both Nationalist and Unionist sides by the boundary issue, the Unionist objective being to use a siege mentality to maximise the Party vote.[148] A more extreme example of the overwhelming political importance of the Boundary Commission issue was the six-county General Election called by Craig on 3 April 1925. Craig made this a specifically border election which, officially at any rate, would give Unionists an opportunity to reject any boundary commission transfer of border populations to the south. 'I believe,' Craig declared, 'that a pronouncement by the people while the Commission is sitting in their midst will go a long way to assure [it] that the feeling throughout the length and breadth of Ulster is that they will remain steadfast inside the ambit of Great Britain.'[149] This was a cynical exercise, since Craig's ulterior object was to try to ensure 'maximum Unionist solidarity at a time when his administration was vulnerable and the Unionist Party in danger of

---

145 St John Ervine, *Craigavon: Ulsterman* (London, 1949), p. 492.

146 Bryan Follis, *A State under Siege: The Establishment of Northern Ireland 1920–1925* (Oxford, 1995), p. 169.

147 Meeting of O'Higgins and other Free State representatives with Baldwin at Chequers, NAI, DT S4720A, 28 Nov. 1925.

148 Follis, *State Under Siege*, p. 159.

149 Farrell, *Arming the Protestants*, p. 239.

splitting on educational and administrative issues'.[150] Craig's campaign slogan, 'Not an Inch', was a defiant message for the Boundary Commission. His political use of what he interpreted as its threat to border territory met with some success. In four border counties, Armagh, Derry, Fermanagh and Tyrone, his party increased its vote. In Belfast, however, where he found it difficult to make the Boundary Commission an issue, and was obliged to fight on social and economic policies, his party lost seven seats to Labour and Independent Unionists.[151] Craig was even-handed in suppressing dissent. His 1925 election experience prompted him and the Ulster Unionist Council to abolish Proportional Representation (PR) in order to disfranchise Protestant minority interests.[152]

It was greatly to the advantage of Northern Ireland that the establishment of the Boundary Commission was delayed until the autumn of 1924. The longer the delay, the more time Craig's administration had to consolidate itself as a credible working entity, progressively less vulnerable to dismemberment. On 7 December 1922, the boundary provisions of the Treaty came into operation, and there was, in theory, no constitutional obstacle to the appointment of a boundary commission. The practical obstacle was that the Government of Northern Ireland, in keeping with its principled objection to having its 1920 boundaries subjected to possible alteration, refused to appoint its Commissioner as provided for in the Treaty.

The arguments advanced by Northern Ireland politicians and their British Conservative allies in favour of this refusal may be studied in detail in the proceedings of the British House of Commons debate on the Irish Boundary Bill at the beginning of October 1924. The most fundamental objection to appointing a commissioner was outlined by Captain Craig, brother of Sir James. Having been given 'a definite piece of territory', over which Unionists 'were to be supreme', they were afterwards told that a commission was to alter the boundaries of that area. 'It does not matter,' he declared, 'whether they were only allowed to alter it by a few hundred yards on either side. They have no right to do this without our consent.'[153] There was the further argument that the Northern Ireland Government was not obliged to appoint a commissioner to serve on a body provided for in an agreement to which it had not been a party, and which might well interfere with its territory. Worthington-Evans, who declared at a public meeting in September 1924 that he approved

---

150 Denis Kennedy, *The Widening Gulf* (Belfast, 1988), p. 137; Harkness, *Northern Ireland since 1920*, p. 39.

151 Follis, *State Under Siege*, p. 176.

152 David Fitzpatrick, *The Two Irelands 1912–1939* (Oxford, 1998), p. 178.

153 *Hansard*, House of Commons, Vol. 177, Cols 224–5, 1 Oct. 1924.

of Craig's refusal to appoint a commissioner,[154] argued that if the British Parliament appointed a commissioner on behalf of a northern government which had declined to do so, this amounted to a treaty additional to that of 1921, 'turning what was a voluntary submission to arbitration into a compulsory submission' by the Belfast Parliament. If MacDonald's Government proposed to alter the Treaty in this way, it ought, Worthington-Evans believed, put in a declaration of the powers it intended to give the Commission in respect of territorial adjustment.[155]

Earlier in the course of the same debate, Worthington-Evans made it clear what he believed such a declaration should involve. It should conform to what he now understood to have been the intention of the British negotiators in 1921, when he and those who framed the boundary clause deliberately adopted a form of words 'to exclude such a dismemberment of Northern Ireland as would be created by cutting out whole counties or large slices of counties'. The form of words adopted in the boundary clause 'directed the Commissioners to readjust an old boundary, and not to create a new one regardless of history or existing conditions'.[156] If Worthington-Evans was being truthful here, his words take on a considerable significance. If he and the other British negotiators really framed the boundary clause to involve merely minor rectification, did they convey this meaning of a vital component of the Treaty to their Irish counterparts, and if not, why not? The obvious answer is that they did not because otherwise there would have been no Treaty. It is stretching credibility to suggest since the Irish delegation could have yielded so much in return for what they could only have regarded as a trivial concession on the north.

The Irish Boundary Bill debate yielded other interesting arguments in favour of the refusal of the Belfast Parliament to nominate a commissioner. Captain Eden, a future Prime Minister, stressed the debt in honour and in law owed by Britain to Northern Ireland: 'Ulster did not want to be a self-governing community, but the people of this country asked her to accept that responsibility, and she did so, and it would be an injustice . . . if we were to deprive her of territory which was solemnly guaranteed to her by an Act of Parliament.' Eden believed that Ulster had sacrificed much by accepting self government and giving up three of the nine counties.[157] He also appeared to believe that the 1920 Act retained the full force of law and had not been superseded by the Treaty. Another Conservative MP, Sir John Marriott, the author of a standard work on British Constitutional history, was anxious to

154 *The Times*, 27 Sept. 1924.
155 *Hansard*, House of Commons, Vol. 177, Col. 392, 1 Oct. 1924.
156 Ibid., Col. 166.
157 Ibid., Col. 403, 2 Oct. 1924.

divorce Northern Ireland from the terms of the Treaty, on the ground that this was an agreement made between the British Government and representatives of southern Ireland. This was clear to him from the fact that he could not find appended to the Treaty the name of a single Irish representative written in a tongue which he could understand. 'Did these gentlemen, he asked, 'who wrote their names in what is to me, I regret to say, a foreign tongue, sign on behalf of the six North-eastern counties of Ulster?' If they had, he observed, 'they would have signed in a different tongue.'[158] Marriott made a more serious observation when he distinguished two treaties, one embedded in the Government of Ireland Act of 1920, the other agreed with Southern Irish representatives in 1922. His substantive, though highly contestable, point was that 'the second Treaty did not and could not abrogate the first'.[159]

Craig's adamant stand on the issue is one of the minor ironies of Ulster history. While the Commission was a threat to Unionists, it was also, as Nicholas Mansergh observed, 'a product of their own political imagination.'[160] While the Government of Ireland Bill was being negotiated in 1919, Craig raised the possibility that a boundary commission should be set up 'to examine the distribution of population along the boundary of the Six Counties' and further suggested that such a commission might take a vote of the population 'on either side of and immediately adjoining the Boundary'.[161] After much legal argument, an Agreement dated 4 August 1924 was signed by Cosgrave on behalf of the Free State and MacDonald on behalf of Great Britain by virtue of which the Treaty was amended to permit the British Government to appoint a representative for Northern Ireland. This agreement was ratified by the Parliaments at Dublin and Westminster, and the Boundary Commission duly set up.

Although the two-year delay in appointing the commissioners suited Northern Ireland, its Government's refusal to collaborate was not the only cause. The Irish Civil War, which lasted until the late spring of 1923, necessarily postponed the Free State application for its institution. Kevin O'Shiel, Assistant Legal Adviser to the Executive Council, urged the postponement of the Commission until the end of the Civil War, because 'we must be in a position to maintain public order and to guarantee the protection of the lives

158 Ibid., Col. 407.

159 Ibid., Col. 408. See Matthews, *Fatal Influence*, p. 172, for Birkenhead's view communicated to Austen Chamberlain on 22 Aug. 1924, that the Treaty and its ratifying legislation superseded the 1920 Act.

160 Nicholas Mansergh, *The Unresolved Question: The Anglo-Irish Settlement and its Undoing 1912–1972* (London, 1991), p. 130.

161 Craig to L. S. Amery, 4 Oct. 1924. Cited in Alvin Jackson, *Home Rule: An Irish History 1800–2000* (London, 2003), p. 209.

and property of possible future citizens'.[162] On 2 October 1922, Cosgrave, successor to Collins as President of the Executive Council, had appointed O'Shiel, a Northerner, as Director of the Free State North-Eastern Boundary Bureau, with responsibility for reporting regularly to the Executive Council 'in connection with the forthcoming Boundary Commission'.[163] O'Shiel recruited several talented people as advisers to his Boundary Bureau, including Patrick Lynch, KC, who had contested East Clare on behalf of the Irish Parliamentary Party against de Valera in the groundbreaking by-election of 1917. Some of the most impressive of these advisers were Protestants, among them Bolton C. Waller, J. M. Stephens and Joseph Johnston. Serjeant Hanna, described by Hand as 'the ablest of the Counsel retained by the Free State' to argue its case before the Boundary Commission[164] was an Ulster Presbyterian. He compiled a memorandum on the international law question. As part of its work, the Bureau made detailed studies of European post-war boundary settlements, including those of Silesia, Schleswig-Holstein, Klagenfurt and Hungary. It gathered much useful information from qualified northern Nationalist sources on local circumstances in Ulster.[165] As a key part of his work O'Shiel published a handbook on the Ulster question replete with detailed statistical tables and a range of arguments in favour of the Nationalist case focusing on three elements of the boundary clause of Article 12 of the Treaty: wishes of inhabitants and geographic and economic considerations. In January 1923, Waller submitted alternative revised boundary lines to the Executive Council, representing the maximum and minimum Nationalist demands.[166] If even the minimum demand were to be conceded, Northern Ireland would lose all of Fermanagh, most of Tyrone, one third of London-derry including the City, one third of Armagh and a quarter of Down, reducing the length of the 1920 border from 280 miles to 124, and leaving a Catholic minority of 27 per cent.

The Boundary Bureau also dedicated itself to achieving adjustments to the boundary by the use of propaganda, but, as O'Halloran points out, 'avoided the fundamental issues, notably the refusal of Northern Unionists to entertain any notion of either unity or the reduction of their territory.'[167] The range and volume of Free State propaganda concealed the deep reservations felt by even

---

162 O'Shiel Memo, Richard Mulcahy Papers P7/B/288, 10 Feb. 1923.

163 NAI Provisional Government Minutes, 2 Oct. 1922.

164 Hand, *Report* (1969), Introduction, p. xiii.

165 These may be studied in the voluminous Boundary Bureau Papers in NAI.

166 Blythe Papers, UCDA, p. 24/171, Jan. 1923.

167 Claire O'Halloran, *Partition and the Limits of Irish Nationalism: An Ideology under Stress* (Dublin, 1987), p. 13.

those responsible for it, about the Commission as a vehicle for an equitable settlement of boundary problems. O'Shiel expressed these reservations
in December 1923 to members of the Free State Executive Council. 'The
Boundary Commission,' he wrote, 'is not an ideal solution because it does not
necessarily lead to national union and might easily lead in the opposite direction.'
He made the perceptive comment that a commission 'would be no solution at
all if it was not carried out in the spirit in which it ought to be carried out [i.e.
generous transfers of territory to the Free State] and it is extremely doubtful
if a Conservative Government would ever carry it out in that way'.[168] A similar
communication from O'Shiel at about the same time makes one wonder how
the man entrusted with the task of directing the Free State case for the incorporation of substantial Northern Ireland territory could, in a memorandum to
his Government argue in a sense which fundamentally undermined his brief.
He defined 'our object' as 'not the setting up of a Boundary Commission with
the intention of wresting as much territory as possible from Craig, but a much
more lasting thing than any temporary arrangement of purely arbitrary and
utterly absurd boundaries, *viz.* National Union.'[169]

O'Shiel's uncertainty and ambivalence should be interpreted in the light of
the new Ulster policy formulated by a Free State Government committee
shortly before the death of Collins on 22 August 1922. This committee
consisted of Patrick Hogan, Desmond FitzGerald, Michael Hayes, J. J.
Walsh and Ernest Blythe. Four of these were members of the Government
following the death of Collins. In a eight-page memorandum reflecting
conclusions reached by its members, Blythe, an Ulster Protestant, insisted
that 'it was no more than bare sanity' to assume a 'pacific and friendly disposition immediately'. This, he pointed out, meant recognition of the northern
Government and encouraging Northern Nationalists 'to acknowledge its
authority and refrain from any attempt to prevent its working'.[170] Fanning
observes that although Blythe's memorandum made not a single mention of
Collins, 'every line of it constituted a stinging indictment of Collins's policy.'[171]
The significance of the memorandum, which can be taken to represent the
revised Free State policy on Northern Ireland, is that it 'logically implied the
abandonment of any territorial claims on the North'.[172] If this was the case, it
is difficult to discern the purpose of the work of O'Shiel and the North-

168 O'Shiel to each member of the Executive Council, MacNeill Papers, UCDA, LA/1/96/1,
Dec. 1923.
169 O'Shiel Memo, Blythe Papers, P24/171, UCDA, early Dec. 1922.
170 Blythe Memo, P24/70 UCDA, 9 Aug. 1922.
171 Ronan Fanning, *Independent Ireland* (Dublin, 1983), p. 34.
172 Lee, *Ireland 1912–1985*, p. 142.

Eastern Boundary Bureau. It is also difficult to refrain from admiring the firmness of purpose characteristic of Craig and his followers.

If Northern Unionists were largely the engineers of their own success, Nationalists on both sides of the border contributed generously to their own misfortunes. Between the signing of the Treaty in December 1921 and the death of Collins in August 1922, the response of the leadership of northern Nationalism, with the support of the Provisional Government in the south, was to work to undermine the northern state through a combination of military force and widespread refusal to become involved in its political and civic agencies or to acknowledge their legitimacy. The Irish Catholic bishops described the Unionist Government as 'not for Catholics any more than the Turk has government for the Armenians', refused to recognise the Belfast Parliament, and condemned partition as a device for 'putting power into the hands of one section of the people remarkable for intolerance.'[173] Sinn Féin and Nationalist MPs refused to take their seats. Local authorities with Sinn Féin and Nationalist majorities refused to discharge their duties and professed allegiance to the Free State.

By April 1922, the futility of this policy became clear to the Provisional Government in Dublin when it was realised that no money was available to support local authorities maintaining allegiance to the Dáil. The refusal of Nationalists to participate in the operation of local government gave the Unionist administration a ready excuse to dissolve local authorities which refused to recognise the Belfast Parliament. The boycotting strategy was futile in the short term and ill-advised in the longer term: the response of the Unionist administration was to reduce the political power of those who refused to accept the logic of the partition settlement. It would have better served the interests of Nationalists had councils on which they had majorities continued to perform their functions and recognised the Belfast Parliament, in order as Harkness puts it, 'to be in command of their areas when the Boundary Commission came to take its soundings.'[174] Continued Nationalist boycotting frustrated the sensible objective outlined by Harkness. A commission to determine the new county council and rural district areas, approved on 31 October 1922, was largely boycotted by Nationalists.

At a time when maximum Nationalist political representation would have major significance during the period leading to a boundary commission, Nationalists reduced their own capacity to control local authorities even in areas where they predominated. In the short term, following Leech, a combination of new local government arrangements arrived at in their absence, and

173 *Irish Catholic Directory, 1922*, pp. 605–6.
174 Harkness, *Northern Ireland since 1920*, p. 26.

their boycott of elections, reduced by half the number of Nationalist-controlled councils in 1920, including the County Councils of Tyrone and Fermanagh, the latter an issue of central importance during the Boundary Commission hearings of 1924-5. The abolition of PR in local government elections in 1922, combined with widespread gerrymandering and other Unionist responses to Nationalist non-recognition policies, contributed to further Nationalist disadvantage. Thirteen Councils, and two evenly divided, were won by Unionists. These Councils were mostly large and significant ones in terms of population. They included Londonderry County Borough, Fermanagh and Tyrone County Councils, Cookstown, Lisnaskea, Omagh, Dungannon, Magharafelt and Strabane Rural Districts, as well as Omagh and Enniskillen Urban Districts. Unionists concentrated their gerrymandering on large council districts, allowing non-Unionists to administer relatively small ones.[175] The significance of Unionist control of major public bodies, largely but not exclusively, as a result of short-sighted Nationalist tactics, became manifest during the proceedings of the Boundary Commission, when a Unionist mayor was in a position to put the case for the predominantly Catholic and Nationalist City of Londonderry, and a Unionist Chairman was able to make submissions on behalf of Fermanagh County Council.

Long before Home Rule became a *fait accompli*, commentators from diverse backgrounds, assuming some form of partition as a consequence, were alert to the predicament of the Catholic minority in such a situation. As early as 1916, the Protestant Home Ruler R. J. Smith urged Nationalists to concentrate on keeping whatever partitioned areas emerged under London control to save the Nationalist minority from an Ulster parliament governing by 'seventeenth-century Orange ideas'.[176] Two years earlier, Winston Churchill, then a Liberal, had warned of the consequences for Nationalists of a northern state controlled by Unionists. 'What treatment,' he asked, 'do you suppose these Orangemen would mete out to their fellow-countrymen in their midst . . . We know the treatment that they would consider quite appropriate to Nationalists to-morrow if they obtained a majority.'[177] Churchill's comment must be seen in the light of his then membership of the Liberal Party. His change of view was later forced upon him by the need to repent for his past utterances. Nationalists of every shade throughout Ireland rejected partition

---

175 See J. Whyte, in Tom Gallagher and James O'Connell (eds), *Contemporary Irish Studies* (Dublin 1983), pp. 5–6; Denis O'Hearn, 'Catholic grievances, Catholic nationalism: a comment', *British Journal of Sociology* Vol. XXXIV, No. 3 (1983), p. 438.

176 *Irish Opinion*, 25. Nov. 1916. Cited by Patrick Maume, *The Long Gestation: Irish Nationalist Life 1891–1918* (Dublin, 1999), p. 188.

177 *Irish Times*, 16 Mar. 1914.

tout court. Many border Nationalists, however, found themselves in the contradictory position of being opposed to partition on principle and at the same time being ready to work, through the Boundary Commission, for a modification of the border which would still leave some form of partition intact in a form which would result in a numerically weaker Nationalist minority and a consolidated Unionist grip on power.

Hesitation and uncertainties harboured by members of Cosgrave's Government and their advisers may explain why the Free State had still not pressed for the setting up of the Commission by Christmas 1923. Cosgrave believed that it was in the interest of the Free State to postpone the setting up of a commission until a new customs barrier between Northern Ireland and the Free State had been completed. This belief was based on O'Shiel's advice that this customs barrier, which would cause economic distress in the north, would soon induce traders in Northern Ireland to seek an end to political as well as the customs partition.[178] John D. Nugent, Nationalist MP for South Armagh, saw an altogether more sinister significance in the customs barrier. He interpreted its introduction on 1 April 1923 as an indication that the Free State Government was implicitly forfeiting any claims which its Boundary Bureau was preparing for the transfer of Tyrone, Fermanagh, Derry City, Newry and south Armagh.[179] The customs barrier might further be seen as a sign that Cosgrave and his Cabinet were acquiescing in the reality of partition and that they lacked faith in a boundary commission as an agent of major change in territorial distribution. The barrier had the obvious effect of making the existing border appear stable, functionally entrenched, and even permanent. As Fanning observes, the day on which the barrier was erected, 'partition was further consolidated.'[180] On the 60th anniversary of the event, Dennis Kennedy recalled how 'the arch-partitionists of the Cosgrave Government' evoked some strongly anti-partitionist comments from Craig, who 'denounced the decision to establish the Customs Barrier as partitionist,' telling the Belfast Wholesale Merchants' Association that 'partition was nothing; there was no such thing as partition if the customs wall was not built'.[181] At the same time, *The Northern Whig*, in an editorial headed 'The Arch Partitionists', claimed that Craig 'had shown the Southern barrier to be the spiteful blunder it was'.

---

178 O'Shiel to the Irish Executive Council, NAI, S2. D27, 19 Feb. 1923.
179 Nugent's view is recorded in *The Ulster Gazette*, 19 May 1923 and cited in K. J. Rankin, 'County Armagh and the Boundary Commission', *Armagh History and Society* (Dublin, 2001), p. 955.
180 Fanning, *Independent Ireland*, p. 86.
181 Cited in Dennis Kennedy, 'The first customs barrier', *Irish Times*, 31 Mar. 1983.

Free State scepticism about the utility of the Boundary Commission was reflected in a memorandum circulated by Kevin O'Higgins to his fellow Ministers on 25 and 29 September 1924, on a possible offer to the northern Government of a joint settlement of the boundary question between the Free State and Northern Ireland to be arrived at independently of the Boundary Commission. O'Higgins reminded his colleagues that the Boundary Commission had never been regarded in Dublin as the most satisfactory solution, and argued that any new boundary would leave untouched the alienation of supporters of the Free State who would still be left in Northern Ireland. At this late stage, O'Higgins argued for the setting aside of the Ulster provisions of the Treaty and the establishment of an all-Ireland authority with the powers enjoyed by Westminster under the 1920 Act transferred to it, while under its auspices common matters affecting north and south would be dealt with tariff barriers ended, PR restored in the north, gerrymandering abolished and the B Specials disbanded.[182] By this time, the Free State Government felt obliged to proceed with the arrangements for a boundary commission mainly because not to have done so would further alienate a northern minority increasingly critical of the approach of the Free State Government. It would also have led to a political crisis in the south and given the opposition party a means of discrediting Cosgrave and his colleagues.

182 O'Higgins to Executive Council, 25 Sept. 1924; 'Notes on possible offer to Northern Ireland', 29 Sept. 1924; McGilligan Papers, UCDA/P35b/138, [1], [2], [3]; FitzGerald Papers, P 80/947. UCDA, 29 Sept 1924.

FOUR

THE COMMISSION IN SESSION

—

I PRELIMINARIES

The activities of the Commission may be divided into three distinct phases. The first four months were taken up with informal meetings and visits, the next four, ending in early July 1925, with formal hearings, after which the Commission adjourned to London. By 17 October, it had formulated its award. Between 9 December 1924 and 3 March 1925, its members met informally with representatives of a wide range of public bodies, visited the principal points on the border likely to be in contention, met MPs for the districts they passed through, and called on the leading ecclesiastics whose seats lay in disputed border counties. On 9 December 1924, Mr Justice Feetham and Eoin MacNeill visited Archbishop Patrick Joseph O'Donnell in Armagh, while Feetham and the Secretary to the Commission, Mr Joseph Fisher visited the Church of Ireland Archbishop, Charles D'Arcy, who was hostile to the purposes of the Commission and would have found a visit from MacNeill unwelcome. D'Arcy, Carson's friend and a sturdy defender of Northern Ireland, was reputed to have said that 'if any of the Commission visited him, he would take steps to have them removed from his house'.[1] The Commissioners visited Bishop Mulhern of Dromore, Bishop McHugh of Derry and Bishop McKenna of Clogher. They were advised by Bishop McKenna to visit two of the most outspoken political priests in Northern Ireland, Archdeacon John Tierney of Enniskillen and Philip O'Doherty of Omagh, who could provide them with unpublished records of all parishioners, compiled by priests. They also accepted resolutions, written submissions and enquiries from interested parties. On 9 December 1924, the Commission arrived in Armagh, where it established its headquarters, and spent three nights at each of four centres: Armagh, Enniskillen, Newtown Stewart and Londonderry. It met with the town councils of Armagh,

---

1   Geoffrey Hand, 'MacNeill and the Boundary Commission', in F. X. Martin and F. J. Byrne (eds), *Eoin MacNeill: The Scholar Revolutionary 1867–1945* (Shannon, 1973), p. 233.

Monaghan, Newry, Enniskillen, Omagh, Strabane and Londonderry and also with senior police officers in Armagh, Down, Monaghan, Tyrone, Londonderry and Donegal.[2] It was significant that the Commissioners' preliminary tour of the border area did not encompass east Tyrone: this boded ill for Nationalist claims on the entire county.

The Commissioners used Armagh as their base until 13 December, proceeding along the boundary line before returning to London on 22 December. As they were holding their first formal meetings with local groups, they had not settled a vital question: how they would apply Article 12 of the Treaty, above all, how they would ascertain the wishes of the inhabitants, as the first element of the boundary clause of the Treaty required them to do. The brevity of the clause, its ambiguity and the lack of clear direction, precluded definitive judgement on its meaning. Thomas Jones, Assistant Secretary to Lloyd George's Cabinet in December 1921 when the Treaty was signed, a constant presence at the negotiating sessions, and frequently a facilitator of the compromises which made agreement possible, later offered a helpful, if sometimes tendentious gloss on the genesis of the troublesome boundary clause. The Treaty, he observed, was not drafted as meticulously as an act of parliament might be drafted, and was signed in a hurry, since the British were 'under a pledge to let Craig know whether it was to be peace or war'. Another problem was that officials were frequently excluded from the negotiations, chiefly because of Childers, and though there were half a dozen famous lawyers among the plenipotentiaries, 'it is notorious that a lawyer cannot draft his own Will clearly.'[3] Both sides, the Irish to a greater extent than the British, were happy to exclude the meticulous and precise Childers, the most accomplished draftsman on either side, who would, had he been permitted to play a part in the drafting of the boundary clause, not have tolerated the loose, ambiguous formulation that finally emerged. For practical purposes, the most fruitful source of confusion was the appropriate method of ascertaining which inhabitants were to have their wishes satisfied. On this, Nationalist representatives were agreed that there was only one equitable way of proceeding. When northern legal agents and leading clergymen met in Dublin on 12 November 1924, they agreed that a plebiscite based on Poor Law Unions should be insisted upon by the Free State government, while Cahir Healy, the leading Fermanagh Nationalist, declared that the Nationalists

---

2   Eoin MacNeill's Diary of the Boundary Tour, MacNeill Papers, LAI/H/114, UCD Archives, 9–22 Dec. 1924.

3   Friction between Childers on the one side and Collins and Griffith on the other are discussed in chapter 2. Thomas Jones, in Keith Middlemas (ed.), *Whitehall Diary* vol. 3 (London, 1971), p. 238.

should leave the Commission if a plebiscite were refused.[4] On 1 December, the Free State Government decided to seek a plebiscite in border areas on the basis of Poor Law Unions.[5] Sentiment in favour of a plebiscite was so strong among Fermanagh Nationalists that they decided not to meet the Commissioners in protest against the failure to hold a plebiscite.[6]

Nationalists were anxious for plebiscites based on Poor Law Unions because many of these would have yielded Nationalist majorities. Feetham, having weighed this and other considerations, including constitutional ones, came to the conclusion that plebiscites were not feasible. Although in mid-September 1924 he had mooted the idea of legislation to permit the taking of a plebiscite, he came up against resistance from the Colonial Office, which was influenced by the belief that apart from the danger of civil unrest in border areas, it might prove impossible for the British Government to enforce an award based on a plebiscite in the face of anticipated Ulster Unionist resistance. Both the Cosgrave ministry and border Nationalists were kept in ignorance of these exchanges between Feetham and the British authorities.[7] Feetham told a Nationalist deputation in Derry that the Commission did not have the powers necessary to order plebiscites: instead, 'all records, including census figures and the results of elections, would be taken into account.'[8] Another question of considerable potential significance was whether the Commission was entitled to transfer territory from the Free State to Northern Ireland. This was the subject of an enquiry received on 20 December 1924, from residents in County Monaghan. Any such transfer would be contrary to the Free State interpretation of the purpose of the boundary clause, which was seen by Nationalists as a penalty on Northern Ireland, involving some loss of its territory, for refusing to be part of an all-Ireland settlement. The Commission informed the Monaghan residents that it would be willing to hear evidence on the subject of their enquiry in the course of their formal hearings beginning in March 1925.[9]

Although, officially at least, the future configuration of Northern Ireland was in the hands of the Commission, Craig and his Government had decided in advance not to afford recognition to its mandate under the Treaty, and

4   Eamon Phoenix, *Northern Nationalism, Nationalist Politics, Partition and the Catholic Minority in Northern Ireland 1890–1940* (Belfast, 1994), p. 310.

5   Free State Executive Council Minutes, S1801/L, NAI, 1 Dec. 1924.

6   *Irish News*, 12 Dec. 1924.

7   Hand, in Martin and Byrne, *The Scholar Revolutionary*, pp. 228–9; Memorandum from Sir Geoffrey Whiskard of the Colonial Office to Justice Richard Feetham, Feetham Papers, Rhodes House Library, 18 Sept. 1924.

8   *Irish News*, 22 Dec. 1924.

9   Geoffrey Hand (ed.), *Report of the Irish Boundary Commission* (Shannon, 1969), p. 10.

adopted a policy of non-cooperation with its work.[10] At the beginning of 1925, Feetham suggested that the Enniskillen Urban District Council should give evidence before the Commission. The membership of this all-Unionist body unanimously declined to do so. They explained their decision by reference to the interpretation placed on Article 12 of the Treaty by three of its British signatories; Birkenhead, Chamberlain and Worthington-Evans that 'only a mere rectification of the border-line was at any time contemplated'. This expert view, the Council implied, should be of sufficient weight to convince the Commission of the limitations of its mandate. The Town Clerk explained that 'as Enniskillen is ten miles from the nearest part of the Free State, we are of the opinion that the Treaty does not apply, and was never intended to apply, to the territory under our control', and that the Commission in consequence had no jurisdiction over the town.[11] In the event, Feetham was to come to a similar conclusion. Before the Commission began its investigations, Sir Wilfred Spender, Secretary to the Northern Ireland Cabinet, informed F. B. Bourdillon, Secretary of the Commission, that the Government of Northern Ireland did not wish to present any statement 'with reference to the work with which the Commission is charged, nor to appear before the Commission by Counsel, or by accredited representatives, nor to submit to the Commission any evidence dealing with the question'.[12] It must be noted, however, that despite this, Craig and his colleagues found ways of making their views known to the Commission, and to influence the course of its proceedings. In July 1924, Craig had two meetings with Feetham in Belfast to alert him to 'the gravity of the question he was handling and the very grave dangers that would come from any mistakes'. Among such mistakes would be 'the compulsory transfer of any Loyalists or any Roman Catholics against their wish'.[13] The transfer Craig was warning against was of either Loyalists or Catholics from Northern Ireland to the Free State: his fundamental requirement was to keep the 1920 boundary intact with minimal adjustments.

The Northern Ireland Government, while holding to the principle of not recognising the Commission *de jure*, was nevertheless obliged by force of circumstances to acknowledge its significance *de facto*, and was therefore concerned that the Ulster Loyalist case should be thoroughly prepared and presented by an agency other than the Government. The most effective instrument to hand for this purpose was the Ulster Unionist Council, which was given a role by Craig somewhat similar to that of the Free State Boundary

---

10   CAB, PRONI CAB 4/129/20, 10 Nov. 1924.

11   A. W. G. Ritchie to the Irish Boundary Commission, CAB 61/62, 13 Jan. 1925.

12   Hand, *Report* (1969), p. 7.

13   CAB, PRONI, CAB 4/117/4, 4 July 1924.

Bureau. Its task was to take and compile evidence from the Loyalist community and to submit this evidence, which was assembled by Unionist constituency associations, to the Commission. This operation was overseen at Unionist Party Headquarters in Belfast by Herbert Dixon, Chief Whip of the Unionist Parliamentary Party. Dixon was an ideal choice: as Parliamentary Secretary to the Ministry of Finance he was in a position 'albeit unofficially, to liaise with the Cabinet'.[14] There were other vital links between members of the Northern Ireland Cabinet and members of the Ulster Unionist constituency associations which were working to influence the Commission in the Loyalist interest. Craig and two members of his Cabinet, John Andrews and Edward Archdale, were members of constituency associations which included disputed border areas: Craig and Andrews were active in the County Down Joint Unionist Association, and Archdale in a similar body representing Fermanagh and Tyrone. The Northern Cabinet could further monitor and influence the work of the Commission as a consequence of Craig's suggestion that the submission of evidence by Loyalist-controlled public bodies would not embarrass his Government.[15]

In accordance with Northern Ireland Government policy on Loyalist dealings with the Commission, on 20 December 1924, the Secretary of Fermanagh County Council forwarded a resolution proposed by Sir Basil Brooke, a future Prime Minster, seconded by another Unionist member, H. Kirkpatrick JP and passed by the Unionist Party majority to the effect that 'if an assurance is given by the Boundary Commissioners that their duties are confined to the mere rectification of anomalies on both sides of the existing border only', the Fermanagh County Council would prepare a case and submit evidence.[16] The Commission, understandably enough, refused to give any such assurance, but offered to accept a submission from the County Council, and to hear representatives appointed to urge this interpretation. On foot of this, Sir Basil Brooke persuaded the Unionist County Council of Fermanagh, which represented a population of which Unionists formed less than 44 per cent, to prepare a submission, supported by numerous witnesses from all parts of the county, which was heard by the Commission from 27–29 April 1925.[17] Districts bordering the Free State were particularly strongly represented: Clonelly, Belleek, Garrison, Door, Crum, Newtownbutler, Roslea and Brookeborough.[18]

14   Bryan Follis, *A State Under Siege: The Establishment of Northern Ireland 1920–1924* (Oxford, 1995), p. 166.
15   Ibid.
16   Hand, *Report* (1969), p. 10.
17   E. M. Stephens to Free State Minister for Justice, NAI S/1801/L, 19 Feb. 1925.
18   PRO CAB 61/64.

The County Council was a Unionist body owing to the abstention of the Nationalist Party from the last election, in protest against gerrymandering. This practice involved the manipulation of local boundaries so as to give unfair advantage at elections to a particular party, in this case the Unionist Party. For some Nationalists, the willingness of so large a Unionist body in a contested county like Fermanagh to present its case was welcome to the extent that it suggested a widespread Unionist acknowledgement of the Commission and its mandate.

Craig and his Cabinet colleagues were thus in the fortunate position of being able to direct Unionist strategy in an informed way in private, at the same time remaining free to take a public stand should the Commission make an award that they did not like. The Ulster Unionists thus enjoyed the same kind of freedom of action as they did at the time of the Treaty. That agreement was reached without their direct involvement, while at the same time Craig was briefed by Lloyd George about the negotiations and permitted to influence these. In the case of the Boundary Commission, Craig's Government was not officially consulted on its direction on proceedings, but supplied with an abundance of information by Unionist Party members and even from within the Commission itself.[19] In both cases, Craig's Government could reject disagreeable outcomes by asserting that since it was not an official party to the negotiations leading to these, it had no obligation to be bound by them.

Ulster Loyalists enjoyed a further advantage arising from the fact that almost all the investigative and evidential work of the Commission was necessarily carried out in Northern Ireland. The police force, overwhelmingly Loyalist in composition, was as much an arm of the Unionist Party as of the State. Among the functions handed over to Craig's Government on 22 November 1921 was the unfettered control of law and order, including supervision of the Special Constabulary. One of the duties of the police was to escort the Commissioners during their tours of border areas. In the course of this work, the police were able to report on the movements of the Commissioners to Craig's Government, supplying the names of those they met in the areas they visited.[20] A more significant contribution to the Loyalist engagement with the Commission was made by RUC detectives. Throughout the winter and spring of 1925, they infiltrated meetings at which northern Nationalists discussed the evidence they were preparing to submit to the Commission. Reports on the proceedings of these meetings, including lists of participants, were forwarded to Craig's office, and then circulated to the Ulster Unionist Council. E. M. Stephens, Secretary to the Free State North-Eastern

19   St John Ervine, *Craigavon: Ulsterman* (London, 1949), pp. 499–500.
20   Follis, *State Under Siege*, p. 167.

Boundary Bureau, and nephew of the dramatist J. M. Synge, found it difficult to resist the conclusion that this information was used to intimidate Nationalists, and this reality could explain the difficulty experienced by the Bureau in obtaining witnesses for the Commission hearings.[21] Almost two years before this, Kevin O'Shiel was reporting to the Executive Council of the Free State on 'Ominous Activities on parts of the North-Eastern Border' involving all elements of the police force: RUC, B Specials, and C Specials.[22] These 'offensive and provocative' activities included watching the movements of Nationalist agents of the Boundary Bureau. O'Shiel believed that the B Specials, 'acting very obviously on instructions from some superior quarter', were trying to create 'a position of actual warfare along the border, trying to create the impression that they were being attacked from the south, so hoping to prejudice the Commission's findings in their favour'.[23]

The divided allegiances of northern Nationalists, and the deep division of opinion among them on the value, or even desirability, of a boundary commission, gave the united Loyalist front a distinct advantage in presenting a coherent case to the Commission. On the one hand, Nationalists of every shade were anti-partitionists opposed in principle to any kind of border. Those among them who gave evidence to the Commission were however, obliged, by its terms of reference, to argue for some kind of border, thus compromising their principles. Six-county Unionist participants, on the other hand, unanimously dedicated to the preservation of the existing border, faced no such dilemma. Northern Republicans, abetted by their southern counter-parts, anti-Treaty Sinn Féin, regarded the Commission, whatever its findings might be, as a death-blow to a united Ireland, and withheld cooperation from it. Nationalists in Belfast and other areas of Northern Ireland remote from the border, whose political destinies were not going to be affected by whatever findings the Commission might announce, could not be expected to exhibit a lively interest in its proceedings. Hugh A. McCartan, an agent of the North-Eastern Boundary Bureau, was sent to Northern Ireland to assess Nationalist feeling on the Boundary Commission. In Derry, he found widespread eagerness to come into the Free State. In Belfast, he was struck by the 'disorganised and

---

21   E. M. Stephens to Kevin O'Higgins, NAI DT S1801/6, 21 Jan. 1925.

22   There were three categories of Special Constabulary; A, B, and C. The A Special Constables were a full-time body based in barracks and attached to the RUC. The B Specials, a more numerous group, selected their own officers. They were armed and uniformed, and served in their home districts. The C Specials were a reserve force. They were unpaid, and were called out only in an emergency. The Special Constabulary was exclusively Protestant, with many members in the Orange Order.

23   Memorandum on the boundary question to each member of the Executive Council by Kevin O'Shiel, NAI DFA Box 16 File 106 (4), 19 July 1923.

apathetic condition' of the population. He reported that Belfast Catholics had lost faith in the Boundary Commission, and that many of them thought that it would do more harm than good. In the immediate post-Treaty period, they were 'almost wholly in favour of it', but he met many Republicans 'who had become so [had become Republicans] on account of the Free State's lack of interest in their position and the humiliations heaped upon them'.[24] On the contrary, the general attitude among north-eastern Catholics was that the fewer northern Nationalists the Commission transferred to the Free State, the better it would be for those who would have to remain in Northern Ireland, since, as they saw it, a large Catholic population would feel safer, and less beleaguered and isolated, than a smaller one. Republicans had a similar interest in the maintenance of a large proportion of Catholics in Northern Ireland, believing that this would increase the likelihood of a United Ireland in the longer term. What Nationalist divisions could mean in practice, when preparation for the Boundary Commission was in question, is illustrated in the case of the Carlingford Lough Commission. Control of this important body would have given border Nationalists the right to argue on its behalf before the Boundary Commission. In August 1923, however, H. J. McConville JP, a Nationalist extremely hostile to Sinn Féin, voted with Unionist members to give the Belfast Government a majority on the Carlingford Commission.[25]

II HEARINGS AND SUBMISSIONS

The Boundary Commission, which began its work in November 1924, travelled widely during the course of its deliberations. The Commission had asked the interested parties to submit written representations by the end of January 1925, to enable it to begin its formal hearings early in March. By February 1925, the Commission had received 130 separate submissions: 50 from private individuals and business firms, 44 from local political groups, 23 from local authorities, and 13 from other public bodies. In advance of the formal hearing of evidence in March, which involved the examination of a thousand witnesses, Nationalists and Unionists were engaged in the intensive preparation of their respective cases. While the Unionist communities and public bodies were able to frame their submissions in a spirit of unity, on the Nationalist side personal animosities and ideological differences made this impossible. When, for example, an agent of the Free State North-Eastern Boundary Bureau, E. M. Stephens visited Newry on 19 December 1924,

24 H. A. McCartan to Kevin O'Shiel, NAI S2027, 31 Oct. 1923.
25 Phoenix, *Northern Nationalism*, p. 291.

he encountered a 'bad-tempered meeting' at which Patrick Donnelly, a former Nationalist MP for south Armagh, signified his refusal to present the Nationalist case. This refusal may have been prompted by scepticism on Donnelly's part about the willingness of the Commission to gratify Nationalist wishes in Newry and Armagh.[26] There was the further problem that many Nationalists in the area were Republicans, and thus hostile to the work of the Commission. In contrast, when Stephens visited Fermanagh in January 1925, he found much greater Nationalist enthusiasm for the process. The two outstanding Fermanagh Nationalists, Cahir Healy and Archdeacon Tierney, who appeared as witnesses before the Commission, supervised the arrangements for the presentation of a demand for the inclusion of the entire County of Fermanagh in the Free State. The Nationalist position in County Derry was less hopeful. Outside Derry City, Free State officials found it difficult to obtain witnesses in outlying Nationalist areas, and encountered apathy in districts which seemed unlikely to be transferred to the Free State.

The proceedings of the Boundary Commission, particularly as these related to the Nationalist case, were strongly influenced by the character and outlook of Eoin MacNeill, the Commissioner nominated by the Free State Government. His interpretation of his role as a member of the Commission was not in accord with that of the Government which had nominated him. The conflict involved here is well described by Geoffrey Hand, who points out that MacNeill refused to take a political view of his functions, instead regarding the Commission as a quasi-judicial body: he thus regarded his loyalty in that connection 'as owed to his fellow commissioners rather than to his political colleagues'. As a consequence, he felt it his duty to preserve a scrupulous discretion about the proceedings of Feetham and Fisher, and to resist attempts by the Free State Government, or its agents, to induce him to pursue 'particular lines of action or argument'.[27] Thus, in December 1924, when E. M. Stephens, with the support of Kevin O'Higgins, tried to get him to supply information of use to the North-Eastern Boundary Bureau, MacNeill was not forthcoming. Even when he was given confidential material by a Nationalist informant which would have been useful to the Bureau, he circulated this to Feetham and Fisher. While the latter had little scruple about passing details of the Commission's work to a Unionist confidante, the wife of a Unionist MP, MacNeill preserved his impartiality, a stance which those who appointed him had not contemplated. His relatively few interventions during the examination of Unionist witnesses were neither probing nor forceful, giving the impression that he was a disinterested, aloof spectator. He

26   Ibid., p. 312.
27   Hand, in Martin and Byrne, *The Scholar Revolutionary*, p. 211.

seemed to become actively engaged only when objections to the compulsory teaching of Irish was at issue. While the two other Commissioners acted in a full-time capacity, MacNeill was obliged to absent himself from Commission meetings to attend to his duties as Minister for Education. He tended to deal with Commission correspondence only at the last minute.[28]

MacNeill was to observe during the Dáil debate following the collapse of the Commission that his own interpretation of the boundary clause differed in essentials from Feetham's. For him, 'it was a case of restoring a denied franchise [to Nationalists], and the wishes of the inhabitants were the dominant consideration.' In Feetham's view, in stark contrast, the Commission was competent, 'in one part of our award, to make economic considerations dominant, and, in another place, to make the wishes of the inhabitants dominant.'[29] In a moving admission of his own failure as a commissioner, MacNeill revealed a fundamental flaw in the procedures adopted under Feetham's chairmanship. 'There was,' he declared, 'at no time any debate between the members of the Commission as to the principles of interpretation and no definite decision taken which could lead to an application of such principles and to their application in the same [consistent] way in different districts affected by the award'. He acknowledged that it was remiss of him when he did not 'demand, require and challenge, at the earliest convenient stage, a discussion of the general principles of interpretation and a decision upon those principles'.[30] Instead, he allowed Feetham to enforce his own interpretations, and the decisions based on these, 'in a very gradual and a very piecemeal manner, and each in the form of a *fait accompli*.'

III PROCEEDINGS

Analysis of the entire range of written submissions to the Boundary Commission and of the evidence given at its oral hearings makes it possible to isolate the predominant concerns which preoccupied the minds of the participants. Of even greater importance are the responses of the Commissioners, above all Feetham, to the arguments raised by witnesses. Some of Feetham's interventions gave a clear indication of the way in which he interpreted the brief of the Commission on such central questions as the extent of territory it was empowered to transfer, whether such transfer should be in one or both directions, the degree to which economics and geography should be permitted

28 Ibid., p. 212.
29 *Dáil Debates*, Vol. 13, Col. 802, 23–4 Nov. 1925.
30 Ibid.

to override the wishes of inhabitants and what kind of majority would be necessary to make these wishes count. The massive evidential records of the Commission are an indispensable guide to the views and attitudes of a representative range of people from all walks of life north and south of the border. They also have considerable sociological importance, and are a source for the economic history of the period. The confidential nature of the proceedings facilitated a degree of frankness in the expression of opinion, not easily achieved in a more public forum. Feetham imposed one qualification on confidentiality which should be noted. In many instances, he permitted the contending parties to have access to each other's submissions, and to submit countervailing arguments.

At the centre of most Nationalist submissions was the contention that the boundary clause made the wishes of inhabitants the predominant consideration in the disposal of people and territory, bringing geography and economics into play only when these were of overwhelming significance. In areas such as Derry City, Newry and south Down generally, south Armagh and large parts of Fermanagh and south Tyrone, there were considerable Catholic majorities. This meant that it had to be assumed that the majority of such inhabitants were in favour of transfer to the Free State. One Unionist strategy to counter the majoritarian argument was to emphasise the adverse economic consequences which would flow from such transfers. Another strategy, employed with equal frequency, had two strands. One was to try to establish that Catholic majorities, based on the 1911 Census returns on which Nationalists based their case, were not true majorities, since there had been significant demographic changes between 1911 and 1924–5. Furthermore, an element in the Unionist case was that inhabitants might be divided into two categories: transitory and permanent, the former exclusively Catholic. A Tyrone Unionist submission, for example, drew attention to 'some labouring men coming and going who might remain for only six or twelve months', and who could therefore not properly be regarded as inhabitants for the purposes of the Commission.[31] Another Unionist submission, from William Thomson Smyth, a resident of Bournemouth, drew attention to population changes since the First World War, involving a considerable increase in the proportion of transitory Catholic inhabitants. 'Swarms of Roman Catholic labourers,' Smyth claimed, 'have joined the local population during and since the Great War – replacing loyal Protestants who left and wore His Majesty's uniform in the Great War and never returned – hence the big Roman Catholic population.'[32] In Unionist eyes, these Catholic labourers did not merit the same status as

31   PRO CAB 61/63.
32   PRO CAB 61/134.

those inhabitants with a permanent stake in the country. Many other Unionists distinguished between transitory Catholic inhabitants and permanent Unionist ones. Captain Scott, on behalf of the Donegal Protestant Registration Association, asserted that migratory labourers, especially unmarried servant boys, should not be entitled to be reckoned as inhabitants, who should have a permanent home of some sort.

In their submission, a group of Donegal Unionists complained that their electoral strength was adversely affected by the Free State Electoral Act of 1923, which gave the franchise to a 'migratory servant-boy class, almost entirely Roman Catholic, on whom Protestant farmers must rely for agricultural labour'.[33] Feetham, curious about such submissions, asked Archdeacon Tierney of Enniskillen about the extent to which 'the work on the land is done in this country [Northern Ireland] by men who do not belong to this country'. Tierney, who claimed an intimate acquaintance with these matters, acknowledged that 'some migratory labourers, commonly called servant boys, came to Fermanagh for half-year periods from Leitrim or Cavan: these were mainly Catholics, but few in number'.[34]

The second strand in the Unionist strategy of undermining Nationalist majority arguments was to suggest with considerable emphasis that the views of those with the greater financial stake in trade, business and land should prevail against those with lesser economic standing. Alfred McCall, a Unionist member of Armagh County Council, stressed the economic and financial dominance of Unionists in Armagh City, urging that because they were 'strenuously opposed to any transfer', this should be decisive even though the majority of the population in the city was Catholic, and thus assumed to favour transfer.[35] The thrust of this and similar Unionist submissions was that some extra consideration should be given to property valuations. The general case put forward by Armagh County Council, while acknowledging a numerical Nationalist majority, was based partly on the premise that the key element in the Nationalist position, the majoritarian one, could be undermined by one based on ownership: three quarters of the property in Armagh City was owned and occupied by Protestants, who also constituted the vast majority of employers.[36] The superior claims of property over mere head counting was a common theme of Unionist submissions from Donegal and Monaghan. This was allied, on both sides of the border, with an affirmation of the superior rate-paying and tax-paying capacities of the generality of Unionists. The

33 PRO CAB 61/51.
34 PRO CAB 61/68.
35 PRO CAB 61/21.
36 Ibid.

authors of a general submission from Unionists in east Donegal were anxious that if a plebiscite were to be taken, the wishes of farmers and other owners of property, 'who pay practically all the rates', should be ascertained separately from those of 'the migratory portion of the population', who had no stake or interest in the country, and could not be regarded as 'electors' properly so called. 'It cannot be denied,' the authors claimed, 'that the welfare and prosperity of a county like Donegal depend almost entirely on the owners of property, and that it is unjust and inequitable that they should be swamped by their labourers.' This latter grievance was based on the fact that in the Free State, a property owner had only one vote, while, according to the Donegal Unionists, his labourers and their families, who paid none of the rates, and many of whom might be merely temporary residents, could have 20 votes between them.[37] The east Donegal Unionists calculated that in the Manorcunningham area, 83.4 per cent of the Poor Law Valuation was on Unionist property.[38] Two Monaghan Unionist farmers, who wanted Drumully in the northern state, admitted to a slight Catholic majority in the area or a near equality, but implied that this should be overridden by the consideration that Protestant farmers paid seven eighths of the rates and owned the greater and most valuable portion of the land.[39] William McGuffin, Clerk to two Unionist bodies, Dungannon Board of Guardians and Dungannon Rural District Council, stressed that all factories and businesses in the area were owned by Protestants, who paid 'the vastly greater proportion of rates and taxes', and did not want to be incorporated in the Free State.[40] Again, this was considered by the two local bodies a sufficiently strong argument for retention in Northern Ireland.

In the most ardently contested counties, Fermanagh and Tyrone, Unionist reliance on property-based arguments was a standard component of most submissions. These arguments featured even when the transfer of territory on the basis of the wishes of inhabitants was not directly in question. Hugh Duff, a Unionist farmer from Coagh in Cookstown Rural District, was asked by Feetham whether he was aware that Catholics were 'not particularly fond of the special police'. Duff replied that Catholics had told him that the special police were 'the saving of the country', adding that these were farmers in his neighbourhood, but not 'the people who have no stake in the country'.[41] W. Copeland Trimble from Enniskillen had recourse to historical events to explain the Unionist emphasis on property. These seventeenth-century events

37   PRO CAB 61/51.
38   Ibid.
39   PRO CAB 61/56.
40   PRO CAB 61/59.
41   PRO CAB 61/44.

left 'this land of marshes' very largely to the incoming planters, who reclaimed the land and made it what it is today. The descendants of these settlers, he explained, pay from two thirds to three quarters of the rates in the County of Fermanagh, the majority of the native or Catholic population 'being in great part farm servants, many of them from the County of Cavan, whose social and economic conditions are not so favourable as in County Fermanagh'. Trimble described Catholic-Protestant numbers as 'almost equal', but relied on the fact that the chief owners of land, employers of labour, professional classes, merchants and the farming community were in the strongest sympathy with the northern Government.[42] William Miller, Unionist MP from Newtownstewart, County Tyrone, when reminded by Feetham that Catholics formed three quarters of the population of Strabane, replied that valuation was the other way: 60:40 for Protestants. Miller argued for ownership as the test to be applied by the Commission, since many residents in Tyrone from Donegal were merely casual ones: occupancy was not a reliable indication of legitimate habitation, but ownership and saleable interests were.[43] In his submission, Mr Ross, a Protestant farmer from Scribby, County Fermanagh, expressed a wish to have his district retained in Northern Ireland but when Feetham remarked that the district as a whole appeared to be strongly Catholic, Ross replied, 'The mountain side of it is.'[44]

Many Unionist submissions reflect impatience with the presence in Northern Ireland and on its borders of lower-class Catholic interlopers, vagrant farm boys and labourers paying little or no rates or taxes and masquerading as proper inhabitants. Charles Monteith, an Omagh Unionist, remarked that in the West Ward, 'which is the working-class Ward of the town, and contributes less in rates than the other two, there is a Nationalist majority of about 400.'[45] The Fermanagh Unionist MP William Miller was even more forthright: 'Labourers don't count; they can get up and move if they don't like the Government under which they are living.'[46] Mr Mills, a Church of Ireland Minister representing the parish of Urney, distinguished between real and virtual inhabitants. Feetham recalled that the district in which Mr Mills ministered was one in which Catholics were in the majority. Mills replied: 'I think so – a labourers' majority.' Mills identified these labourers as people imported from the Free State, 'mostly Roman Catholics, [who have] come from a backward part of Donegal.' He would like to incorporate Protestant

42 PRO CAB 61/45.
43 PRO CAB 61/152.
44 PRO CAB 61/69.
45 PRO CAB 61/143.
46 PRO CAB 61/152.

parts of east Donegal with Tyrone, 'and bring in the [Protestant] sheep together and leave the [Catholic] goats by themselves.'[47] The owner of a farm in County Monaghan named Condle gave evidence that the 'vast majority' of his north Monaghan neighbours wanted to be transferred to Northern Ireland. When asked by Feetham what this vast majority was, Condle replied: 'I do not mean the majority in population: I mean the majority in land-owners and ratepayers.'[48] The Earl of Enniskillen, of Florence Court, County Fermanagh, testified that on his estate the larger farms, almost without exception, were owned by Protestants, while 'the majority of [his] Nationalist tenantry are often hired men living in houses who do not actually belong there'.[49] This latter claim could not be made in respect of the Earl himself, who pointed out that his family had been in Fermanagh since 1764.[50] Major Sir Charles Falls claimed that if Nationalists had a majority, this was made up of 'servant boys from the Free State who have come across the border to work for Unionist farmers'. Falls was anxious to stress that Fermanagh Unionists owned 75 per cent of the land and paid 75 per cent of the rates in the County, and that the drainage of Lough Erne was financed at a loss of £200,000 to riparian owners, every one of whom were Unionists, who also paid three quarters of the cost of the public buildings in Enniskillen.[51] The Raphoe Presbytery, comprising the central portion of east Donegal and representing over 900 Presbyterian families, petitioned the Commission for the inclusion of east Donegal in Northern Ireland 'in view of the fact that the Protestant population owns a preponderating proportion of the land and pays a corres-pondingly larger proportion of the rates'.[52] The Guardians of the Kilkeel Union in County Down and the Unionist majority on the Kilkeel Rural District Council, based their desire, and their right, to remain within the jurisdiction of Northern Ireland on the assumption that the wishes of those inhabitants who paid the largest proportion of the rates in the district were entitled to have those wishes gratified, even at the expense of local Nationalist majorities.[53]

47   PRO CAB 61/153.
48   PRO CAB 61/39.
49   PRO CAB 61/66.
50   PRO CAB 61/64.
51   Ibid.
52   PRO CAB 61/128.
53   PRO CAB 61/85; 61/86. Similar arguments were made by Strabane Traders' Association, PRO CAB 61/137; Hardmans Flax Spinners, Sion Mills, PRO CAB 61/75; Warrenpoint Unionists, PRO CAB 61/157; Rev B. Naylor, Belleek Rectory, PRO CAB 61/64; Matthew Neil, Presbyterian Minister, Urney and Sion Mills, PRO CAB 61/36.

An interesting aspect of this Unionist body of evidence is its tendency to turn on its head the traditional Nationalist view of Unionists as non-indigenous inhabitants of Ireland, alien interlopers who imposed their will on the native population and occupied their lands. In their evidence to the Commission, very many Unionists stressed their own indigeneity, based on their fixity of tenure, their economic and financial status, their overwhelming contribution to the rates and taxes levied on the community and consequently to the prosperity of Northern Ireland, their ownership of the preponderance of productive assets. In Unionist eyes, all this was in contrast to the relatively unstable Nationalist population, whose members contributed significantly less to the general welfare, whose stake in the country was not at all comparable to that of Unionists, and large elements of which were transitory inhabitants. On the basis of such contrasts, Unionists felt justified in assuming control of the important local government bodies, by reducing the value of Nationalist votes relative to their own. The latter principle informed their view that the Commission should attach greater weight to the views of owners of property, largely Unionist, than to the views of people, largely Nationalist, with little or no property. Major General H. F. de M. Montgomery, Fivemiletown, County Tyrone, explained to the Commission how arrangements had been put into effect after 1920 to give greater relative weight to Unionist votes in local elections. Feetham observed that it took 496 Nationalist voters to elect one member of local authority, while 284 Unionist voters could also elect one member. Montgomery clarified the process which produced this kind of result. 'Of course,' he told Feetham, 'if you take the valuation and the size of the farms into account, the situation is considerably modified.' As an example, he cited the Ballygawley division, which had 232 Catholics and 193 Protestants. However, the valuation figures favoured Protestants at £1,600; Catholic valuations amounted to only £1,000. Feetham elaborated by referring to the Northern Ireland Local Government Act of 1922, which took account of rateable valuation as a condition for getting a vote. Montgomery declared himself open to having this arrangement reconsidered once the boundary had been settled, acknowledging that 'there had been a certain amount of unfairness and that the Protestants by this bargaining succeeded beyond what they had expected'.[54] T. J. S. Harbison, a Nationalist member of the Imperial Parliament for Fermanagh and Tyrone, explained what the rateable valuation clause in the 1922 Local Government Act meant for Catholics in Tyrone. The Act had based the franchise on a £5 Poor Law Valuation qualification, which, Harbison ruefully remarked, 'means a very respectable farm, the kind Catholics were deprived of by planters when driven to the hills and bogs'; the average holding in Tyrone was about £3 or under.[55]

Montgomery, an enlightened landlord, had dedicated himself by March 1919 to the cause of ensuring Unionist control of local government bodies in Tyrone. His motive was clear. Writing to Baron Farnham, the leading Cavan Unionist, Montgomery recalled that at the Buckingham Palace Conference in July 1914, 'the fact that in County Tyrone the Unionists were able to control the County Council and five of the district councils was taken together with the evidence that the Protestants in Tyrone paid more than two thirds of the rates, as a strong argument for including Tyrone in the Ulster Pale.' He feared that if the Tyrone County Council and most of its district councils went to the Nationalists, the case for the inclusion of Fermanagh inside the northern Pale would be much weakened. To prevent this outcome, Montgomery suggested the abolition of PR, a move which, after 1922, was to facilitate the result he desired. He explained to Farnham that keeping such a large area as Tyrone under Unionist political control would extend 'the only too small section of Ireland where Unionists and Protestants have any chance of obtaining appointments as Dispensary doctors, County Officials, Clerks of Unions etc.'[56]

Some few Nationalist witnesses tried to counter the Unionist emphasis on their superior property ownership. Cahir Healy claimed that Unionists 'base their claim to Fermanagh rather on the possession of bullocks and grass than on the goodwill of human beings'. Asked by Feetham to explain this, Healy noted that the Local Government Register, 'which is based entirely on a property franchise' put Unionists in a particularly favourable position, since they owned a greater portion of the land of Fermanagh. Healy also pointed out that there were a number of Unionists who owned more than one farm, and in all these cases the ownership of a farm meant the possession of a local government vote. The consequence was that 'you can have father and son occupying the same home with four Local Government Votes'.[57] Among other attempts to meet the Unionist property argument was that of Eugene Coyle, Parish Priest of Belleek, County Fermanagh, who believed that a man who owned 10 acres had a bigger stake in the country than a man with 50 acres, because he had a harder job to live. Coyle also chose some extreme examples to undermine the notion that the views of large owners of property and financial assets should count for more politically than those of the majority of less prosperous inhabitants. If 2 per cent of Americans hold 60 per cent of the

55 PRO CAB 61/150.

56 Montgomery to Baron Farnham 25 Mar. 1919. Letter reproduced in Patrick Buckland, *Irish Unionism 1885–1923: A Documentary History* (Belfast, 1973), pp. 135–7.

57 PRO CAB 61/68.

wealth of America and 6 per cent of English people owned 90 per cent of English wealth, would this mean that minorities as small as 2 and 6 per cent should rule America and Britain, Coyle wondered. Coyle was ignoring the consideration, advanced by Feetham as well as by Ulster Unionists that 'the really permanent population' of disputed areas consisted of people like the Protestant landowners of east Donegal, and that the Catholic population consisted partly of people moving about fairly frequently, 'and who are therefore not in the same way permanently rooted to the district and who do not permanently belong to it in the same sense as the landowners.'[58]

Those who formulated and presented the Unionist submissions to the Commission, and gave evidence under questioning before it, were conscious that they should avoid undue emphasis on the first element of the boundary clause (the wishes of the inhabitants) since Nationalists seemed to enjoy the advantage here. Instead, they focused strongly on economic and geographical arguments. The main thrust of these dubious Unionist arguments was that the economic, ideological, sentimental and religious links of disputed areas were overwhelmingly with other areas within Northern Ireland or with Northern Ireland as an entity and only minimally with the Free State. This was the approach adopted even by some Unionists in Donegal and Monaghan, although to a much lesser extent. One instance is the submission of a group of Donegal Unionists. They observed that the major portion of the trade of east Donegal was with the City of Derry, the distributing centre for County Donegal, where many females were employed on outwork from the shirt factories in Derry City. Donegal traders depended on supplies from Derry, and on credit from Derry merchants. There was the further point, with the geographical aspect of the boundary clause in mind, that the land boundary of Donegal was almost exclusively with three of the six Northern Ireland counties, Derry, Fermanagh and Tyrone.[59] It was evident to Revd Frederick Torrens, a Donegal Presbyterian minister, that if there was to be partition, County Donegal should be with Northern Ireland: apart from being almost entirely cut off from the Free State, its economic fortunes depended on its Northern Ireland neighbours, especially Derry.[60]

Northern Ireland Unionists witnesses constantly emphasised the organic wholeness of the six-county economy, and the interdependence of its regions. A joint committee representing the Church of Ireland and the Presbyterian and Methodist Churches in Ardstraw, Sion Mills and Castlederg submitted that the congregations they spoke for were economically and geographically

58   Feetham answering Rev. John O'Doherty PP, Letterkenny, CAB 61/50.
59   PRO CAB 61/51.
60   PRO CAB 61/142.

attached to County Tyrone, depending for their markets on Castlederg and other towns in Tyrone, and never had any commercial relation with County Donegal. Their district was flax spinning and potato growing and depended entirely on the spinners in Northern Ireland for the purchase of its flax and on cities such as Belfast and Derry, and locations in England and Scotland for the export of its potatoes. The local Sparmount Woollen Mill depended on the market for its manufactures on Belfast and Northern Ireland generally.[61] Almost all witnesses involved in the linen industry emphasised its reliance on Belfast, with its 'quick and expeditious means of export'.[62] Two directors of a firm of flax spinners in Castletown, County Tyrone, observed that over 99 per cent of their business was done through Belfast, and that a customs barrier separating Cookstown from Belfast would be 'an intolerable nuisance'. They were in an economic unit in the UK to which they were accustomed, whereas they would expect trouble if transferred to the Free State which was 'still in an experimental state'.[63]

The absence of significant economic connection with the Free State was central to the Unionist economic argument. This argument was not confined to industrial and agricultural enterprises. The Bessbrook, County Armagh, and Newry, County Down Tramway Company explained that it had no connection, either economic or geographical, with the Free State. Its operations were inseparably connected with Belfast and the linen trade of Northern Ireland, and 'it would be quite incompatible with economic conditions' to transfer any part of the undertaking of the tramway to the Free State: a new boundary line north of Bessbrook and Newry would divide the large industrial centre of Bessbrook from its natural base at Belfast and expose imports and exports to intolerable delay.[64] The Trustees of Camlough, County Down Waterworks disclaimed all economic connection with the Free State: the economic connections of the undertaking were exclusively with Northern Ireland. Camlough supplied water to Newry, and 80 per cent of its revenue came from the extensive mills and factories of the Bessbrook Spinning Company on the Camlough River.[65]

Not all attempts to demonstrate the absence of economic connection between regions and enterprises in Northern Ireland and the Free State were allowed to go unchallenged. When representatives of Dungannon Urban Districts Council argued along these lines, Feetham was not convinced. 'I am rather surprised,' he remarked 'to hear this attempt to make out that there is no trade between Dungannon and the Free State.' Feetham added that the

61 PRO CAB 61/36.
62 Thomas Montgomery, Armagh County Council, CAB 61/21.
63 PRO CAB 61/44.
64 PRO CAB 61/31.
65 PRO CAB 61/35.

Dungannon representatives were so anxious to establish their exclusive connection with Northern Ireland that they occulted the considerable trade in potatoes to the Free State.[66] T. A. Montgomery, Chairman of Armagh County Council, emphasised the indispensable link between County Armagh and Belfast, with particular regard to the linen industry, declaring that his county was 'a self-contained economic unit depending on, and trading almost entirely through, Belfast'[67] and that almost all the trade in cattle passed through the Port of Belfast to England and Scotland. This contention was declared 'absolutely inaccurate' by Patrick McGarvey of Armagh Urban District Council, who pointed out that most of the cattle going from Armagh to England were shipped via Greenore in the Free State.[68] McGarvey, a journalist representing *The Manchester Guardian*, *The Daily Herald* and *The Irish Times*, was in a good position to know.

Judging on the basis of the volume of evidence submitted to the Commission, two areas in particular were of vital importance to both Unionists and Nationalists: Derry City and south Down. For Unionists, Derry had immense sentimental and patriotic importance, while the Silent Valley in south Down was the source for much of the water supply to Belfast. Witnesses on both sides, and in the case of both areas, mounted impressive cases, while Feetham's interventions were also telling. The Derry situation was complicated by the fact that if Derry City were to be transferred to the Free State in response to the wishes of a substantial majority of its inhabitants, the wishes of a number of east Donegal Unionists to be in Northern Ireland could not be gratified. One representation from the latter, submitted by Captain Scott of the Donegal Protestant Representation Association, was to the effect that economic conditions compelled reckoning Inishowen with Derry no 2 Rural District as part of Northern Ireland. The difficulty with this proposal, as Feetham pointed out, was that the figures for the resulting unit gave an overwhelming majority of Catholics: to include Inishowen with Derry no 2 would, *prima facie*, 'involve the over-riding of the wishes of the great majority of the population in the district taken as a whole.' Scott cannot have been pleased when Feetham speculated that joining Inishowen with Derry no 2 might involve having both in the Free State. Scott, however, found it unthinkable that Derry City could be separated from the County of which it was an essential part, claiming that even Catholics had told him that it could not be regarded as practical politics to separate the City from the Waterside.[69]

66 PRO CAB 61/60.
67 PRO CAB 61/21.
68 PRO CAB 61/23.
69 PRO CAB 61/63.

Twenty-five members of the Derry Shirt Manufacturers' Federation signed a representation calling for the retention of the City in Northern Ireland on economic grounds. On the face of it, this representation was impressive. The raw materials for the shirt factories were purchased in Great Britain, and over 98 per cent of the goods manufactured were shipped to Great Britain, the colonies and abroad. The principal factories were branches of firms carrying on business in Great Britain. Interference with the British connection would 'reflect disastrously' on factories in Derry. If Derry were to become part of the Free State, the principal factories and many of the smaller ones would transfer their business to territory under Loyalist control and close down their factories in Derry.[70] An independent Derry shirt manufacturer, John McKimm, offered countervailing testimony, however, remarking that before the erection of the Free State customs barrier, he had sold three quarters of his output to Free state customers. He was certain that unless Derry City were transferred to the Free State he would have to transfer all of his business there, where the recent budget had imposed levies on goods from Northern Ireland.[71]

A very strong case for the transfer of Derry City to the Free State was made by Charles O'Neill, who leased the only public customs warehouse in Derry. His qualifications as a witness were formidable: he had been in control of a distributing business for 30 years and was Senior Deputy Lieutenant in the City, and High Sheriff on the occasion of the visit of the late King Edward. He also was an ex-City Alderman, an ex-President of the Chamber of Commerce and a large ratepayer. He did a considerable volume of business all over the hinterland of the Free State adjoining Derry. Unlike the shirt manufacturers of the City, he regarded Derry as the natural commercial outlet and inlet for the Free State. In support of this, he suggested that of the present volume of Derry trade, both import and export, the greater proportion came from the Free State or eventually went there through the distributing houses of the City. No other port could so well serve the needs of the northern territory of the Free State than that of Derry. O'Neill believed that Derry was retrograding economically, or at best standing still. Its two distilleries had closed; its shipyards, once employing 2,000 men, were shut down. Its monopoly of the shirt and collar trade had ceased owing to competition from English and continental factories. Belfast was exerting a malign influence: its tendency was to reduce Derry to 'the status of a mere village'. Should it lose its distributive trade, and the traffic coming through its port from the Free State, it would cease to exist as a business centre. In the Free State, O'Neill believed it would have a new lease of prosperity, and could not be worse off than at

70   PRO CAB 61/92.
71   PRO CAB 61/93.

present.[72] On the opposing side the Honourable Irish Society, far from contemplating the loss of Derry to the Free State, was anxious to have part of the Donegal shore of Lough Foyle included with Derry in Northern Ireland, thus preserving the Foyle fishery from predation by Donegal fishermen.[73]

The retention of south Down in Northern Ireland was a matter of urgency for Unionists, since the case for transferring Newry, with its three to one Catholic majority, to the Free State was overwhelming if the wishes of the inhabitants were permitted to prevail over economic and geographical circumstances. It was on the last two that Unionists were compelled to base their submissions. The overwhelming geographical consideration was that the Belfast water supply depended largely on waterworks begun as recently as 1923 in the Mourne Mountains, and not yet completed. This new geographic and economic entity, aside from its practical utility, could be seen as an impressive counterweight to the large majority presumed, on religious grounds, to favour inclusion in the Free State. The contention of the Belfast City and District Water Commissioners was that in order to provide the maximum security for the Belfast supply, the present boundary should be retained. When asked by Feetham about the wishes of inhabitants, the representative of the Belfast Water Commissioners suggested that the vital interests of 500,000 people in the Belfast region should take precedence over the wishes of the larger part of the population of south Down. The safety of the water works was the all-important issue. The real fear in Belfast was that if the works were under the authority of the Free State, the supply might be cut off altogether by a hostile southern administration or by terrorist elements living in the Free State. Feetham was reminded that in 1921 the Mourne works were seriously damaged 'by disorderly persons' and must be guarded day and night.[74] The Camlough Lake Water Trustees had similar concerns about the transfer of their undertaking to the Free State. The practical problem this would cause was explained to the Boundary Commission by their representative James Bowes, who also represented the nearby Bessbrook Spinning Company. Bowes told Feetham that if he devised a new boundary separating Camlough Waterworks from Northern Ireland, he would 'place the power over our water power in the hands of an alien country', whose government might 'at any time divert that water and deprive us of the benefit due to us by the money we have spent and the taxes we have paid'.[75] Bowes did not want Bessbrook and its spinning company transferred to the Free State, since this would mean that the present

72 PRO CAB 61/124.
73 PRO CAB 61/78.
74 PRO CAB 61/28.
75 PRO CAB 61/32.

Protestant customers in Northern Ireland would place 'a black mark' against the firm. He explained that 'if you go to Belfast at present and you have a business house very strongly [Loyalist] Ulster and they ask for quotations, if a firm from the Free State and an Orange firm in Belfast tender for the same price, the Orange man would get the contract on political preference, since Northern Ireland customers would not like to deal in the Free State'.[76]

The Newry Chamber of Commerce submitted that 'if Newry were thrown into the Free State', the coal trade of Newry would be severely affected, because the towns remaining in Northern Ireland whose coal supplies were always derived from Newry, would get their supplies elsewhere. The representative of the Newry Chamber, F. D. Russell JP made the point that, those who guided the linen industry in Northern Ireland would retaliate against the coal industry in Newry should it be located in the Free State. Russell took it for granted that the commercial decisions of the linen manufacturers in Northern Ireland would inevitably be determined by political and ideological considerations. 'If by any means,' he told Feetham, 'Newry were thrown out of their [Northern Ireland] territory, because they [the linen manufacturers] are all loyal men in those places – there is not a linen factory in the north that is not guided by loyal men; I have no hesitation in saying that those firms who take their coals from Newry would place their orders elsewhere.'[77] Feetham, however, drew attention to the economic advantages which would accrue to Newry and other regions in its neighbourhood if they were in the Free State: a large new area to trade in and a large new volume of business for its port in respect of Free State grain and flour.[78]

The Newry Chamber claimed to represent the significant business interests in the town. In a reply to its submission, a special committee of Newry UDC described the Chamber as 'a Unionist political body masquerading as non-political', and actuated by political, not economic considerations. The Chamber, the Committee pointed out, was not entitled to speak for the Port of Newry, but the body that was, the Newry Port and Harbour Board, supported the inclusion of Newry in the Free State. The UDC Committee, outlining its own case for the transfer of Newry, argued that its imports and exports would not be adversely affected; indeed its future prospects depended on its severance from Northern Ireland. Increasingly, the northern Government would naturally favour the port and city of Belfast as against Newry, its rival town and port. The Chamber had maintained that those who desired to remain in Northern Ireland paid the greater part of the rates in Newry, but the

76   Ibid.
77   PRO CAB 61/115.
78   Ibid.

records showed that Catholics paid 45.2 per cent, non-Catholics 41.3 per cent, and public utilities 13.3 per cent. The UDC submission observed that aside from the linen industry, nothing whatever was manufactured in the town or the hinterland of Newry. The requirements of daily living were met largely by imports from England, and under the Free State these same goods would still come into Newry Port. Under the Free State, such protected industries as boot making, might be developed in response to the duty on imported footwear.[79] In support of the UDC submission, a number of Catholic businessmen in the town stressed the advantages Free State Government aid to farmers and businesses would confer on Newry, and the absence of negative consequences associated with a transfer to the Free State. Thomas Magee, representing the hardware trade, pointed out that his supplies were imported from England and would still come from England no matter what government they were under.[80]

Unionist witnesses associated with manufacturing pointed to one grave disadvantage of operating in the Free State. James Bowes of the Bessbrook Spinning Company spoke for many other employers in drawing attention to the considerable disparity between costs of production in the two parts of Ireland. Bowes pointed out that his firm paid labourers 26 shillings per week, but claimed that a linen house in Dublin paid 45 shillings. This disparity would place a Bessbrook manufacturer at a double disadvantage if he was forced into the Free State, as Bowes explained: 'On sentimental grounds, even if prices were equal, preference would go to the Northern Ireland firm, but prices would be in favour of Northern Ireland because Free State costs would be higher.'[81] The Nationalist inhabitants of the Newry and Kilkeel Unions, counteracting the Unionist emphasis on the importance of keeping the linen industry in Northern Ireland, pointed out that the industry was not an example of Northern Ireland self sufficiency: flax grown in Cavan and even in Russia was transported into the six counties to be processed. If the mills of Bessbrook Spinning Company were in the Free State, its flax demands could be satisfied there, attain dominance in the Free State and concentrate on fostering the US market.[82]

Further attempts to undermine the Unionist case for the retention of Newry were made by Nationalist residents of the Newry Union, the Secretary of the Newry Port and Harbour Trust and Joseph Johnston, an economist retained by the Free State Boundary Bureau. The Nationalist residents drew

79 PRO CAB 61/119.
80 Ibid.
81 PRO CAB 61/82.
82 PRO CAB 61/112.

attention to the huge volume of produce from Newry and its hinterland for export per Greenore in the Free State in 1922, including 35,313 head of cattle and other agricultural produce, while exports from Newry Quay included 25,677 head of sheep and 6,415 tons of potatoes. Most of the agricultural produce of the Union of Newry and Crossmaglen was marketed in Newry, the balance being disposed of in Dundalk and Castleblaney.[83] Edward Lamb, Secretary of the Newry Port and Harbour Trust, explained that his organisation would prefer to see Newry in the Free State because it would then get sufficient funds to carry out Port development: such assistance would be denied by the Belfast Government because it was determined to develop Belfast Port at the expense of Newry. As Lamb put it, 'Belfast would do all they could to destroy us.'[84] Joseph Johnston argued that under present conditions, the commercial hinterland which sustained Newry's activities was to a greater extent in the Free State area than in Northern Ireland. Great Northern Railway figures showed that in 1924, 24,000 tons of merchandise originating in Newry went to the Free State and only 10,000 tons to Northern Ireland.[85] Johnson also made the point that the greater part of Newry's grain and flour trade was with Cavan and Monaghan. A deputation from the Nationalist inhabitants of the Union of Newry believed that the transfer of south Armagh to the Free State would help the Belfast Government to save considerable money on policing. At present, they pointed out that south Armagh was being policed by the armed Special Constabulary, 'for the purpose of forcing the laws of the Northern Ireland Parliament on those who do not desire to live under them.'[86]

Given the apparently primary status of the wishes of inhabitants in the boundary clause, and the strong belief among Nationalists that these wishes would prove decisive, it is not surprising that much Nationalist evidence focused on this aspect. There is a sense in which evidence on these placed before the Commission was beside the point: Feetham, inhibited from arranging a plebiscite to ascertain the wishes of inhabitants, felt obliged to assume that these wishes were adequately reflected in the figures for religious denominational membership in the 1911 Census. During the hearings, he frequently cited these figures to settle arguments about support for the Free State or Northern Ireland in individual areas. The map published with the final report of the Commission was coloured pink to indicate non-Catholic majorities and green to indicate Catholic majorities, in accordance with calculations

83   Ibid.
84   PRO CAB 61/120.
85   Ibid.
86   PRO CAB 61/112.

based on the 1911 Census. In these circumstances, it made little sense for Bishop Mulhern of Dromore to tell the Commission that 'the overwhelming majority of Catholics' in Newry and its Poor Law Union 'favoured inclusion in the Free State'.[87] The same might be said of the observation of Canon Felix McNally, Upper Killevy, County Armagh, that the boundary line separating County Armagh from Free State territory passed through one of the most Catholic districts in Ireland, and that the Catholic percentage was higher on the Armagh side of the boundary than on the Louth-Monaghan side.[88] A procession of Nationalist witnesses made virtually the same kind of statement as that of Patrick Conroy, Greenore, County Armagh: 'Catholic inhabitants claim incorporation with the Free State.'[89] Frequently this was elaborated on, as in the testimony of Arthur Rafferty of Cladymore, County Armagh, whose Catholic neighbours were 'all for going into the Free State' because they were Irish, and were 'looking to be with Irishmen'.[90] Some witnesses, like S. O'Reilly from Armagh, went so far as to assert that they wanted to be in the Free State even if it meant economic ruin for them.[91] The Commission got many assurances from witnesses from strongly Nationalist areas that virtually no Catholic wanted to remain in Northern Ireland. Richard O'Hagan, Chairman of Newry UDC testified that 'there would not be two in every thousand Catholics who would vote against inclusion in the Free State'.[92]

During the hearing of evidence, Feetham made efforts to explore the possibility that the classification in 1911 of people into Catholics and non-Catholics might no longer be a sure guide to their political wishes. In this enterprise, he received some unsolicited help from Unionist witnesses, several of whom assured him that northern Catholic loyalty to the Free State was by no means solid. T. A. Montgomery, Major Sir Charles Falls, W. Copeland Trimble, Thomas Hegan, a farmer from Cookstown, Dr Robert Mowbray of Castlederg, Douglas Hughes and Hugh Hunter, farmers from north Monaghan, Canon T. G. Rudd, Castleblaney, John Park, Chairman of Newry no 1 RDC and a group of Donegal Unionists all testified that they knew of many Catholics who wanted to live under the jurisdiction of the Belfast Government. Hughes and Hunter had Catholic acquaintances who would be glad to get out of the Free State; Hunter even suggested that several of these wanted to be associated with the Unionist testimony to that effect. Park had

---

87 PRO CAB 61/113.
88 Ibid.
89 PRO CAB 61/72.
90 PRO CAB 61/26.
91 PRO CAB 61/20.
92 PRO CAB 61/120.

spoken to about 20 of 'our chief Roman Catholic neighbours', who were 'perfectly satisfied' to stay where they were.[93] Canon Rudd had detected a distinct movement in Monaghan Catholic opinion away from nationalism, having reason to believe that 'many in the townlands of north Monaghan who before the birth of the Free State were non-Unionists are now ardent Unionists and anxious for transfer to Northern Ireland'.[94] Mowbray testified that of all the Catholics he questioned, 'not one single one would say they wanted to go [to the Free State].'[95] Copeland Trimble claimed that 'many of the Roman Catholics' preferred the peace and security of Northern Ireland to the 'raids, arsons and robberies' in the Free State.[96] Montgomery declared that 'as regards the Roman Catholic minority', of those whose opinions he had heard expressed, all were not merely reconciled to the Northern Ireland Government, but were now opposed to any transfer.[97]

Another Unionist witness, Edward Pedlow, argued that some Nationalist voters did not share the opinions of those who made representations on their behalf.[98] James Morrison, a Protestant farmer from Kiltubrid, in the electoral division of Middletown, County Armagh, told the Commission that many Nationalist farmers in the district had expressed a preference for Northern Ireland. Those Catholics who favoured incorporation in the Free State were 'a small discontented section having little, if any, stake in the country'.[99] It may, or may not, be significant that none of the Nationalist farmers in the Middletown area came before the Commission to signify their preference for living in Northern Ireland. In his evidence, the Earl of Belmore, Killyhelvin, Enniskillen, clarified the issue when asked by Feetham whether the religious division still matched the line of political division. The Earl had little doubt that it did, suggesting that few Protestant Home Rulers or Catholic Unionists could now be found. Even the few Protestants or Catholics voting 'for the other side' at the time of Home Rule agitation had 'very much disappeared now'. His conclusion, based on close observation over a long period, was that 'religion and politics very much go together'.[100] In determining the wishes of the inhabitants, Feetham employed Belmore's rule: a Catholic was a Nationalist and a Protestant a Unionist, in the absence of evidence to suggest

93   PRO CAB 61/111; 61/117.
94   PRO CAB 61/111.
95   PRO CAB 61/36.
96   PRO CAB 61/45.
97   PRO CAB 61/21.
98   PRO CAB, 61/157.
99   PRO CAB, 61/21.
100 PRO CAB 61/30.

cross cutting. Feetham was not impressed by the evidence of Unionists purporting to interpret the wishes of Catholic inhabitants. He told Montgomery, for example, that the Commission had not so far heard a single Catholic witness say he wanted to remain in Northern Ireland.[101]

The views of John Tierney, Parish Priest of Enniskillen, on what Article 12 meant, and how he assumed it would operate, were representative of general Nationalist expectations. The kind of case he believed would impress the Boundary Commission, where members visited him on 15 December 1924,[102] was one firmly based on the desire of the majority of the inhabitants of Fermanagh to be part of the Free State. He told a Nationalist meeting in Enniskillen in December 1924 that in the absence of a plebiscite, the chief available index to the wishes of the inhabitants was the Census of 1911, which showed that the population of Fermanagh numbered 34,740 Catholics and 27,096 Protestants. Tierney quoted the report of the northern Minister of Education for 1923–4, which showed that 57 per cent of those attending Public Elementary Schools were Catholics. He wanted the Commission to operate the old county option scheme, whereby the political destiny of an entire county would be decided by a simple majority of its inhabitants. The Nationalist claim, Tierney pointed out, was that Fermanagh should be treated as a unit for the purpose of ascertaining the wishes of the inhabitants, which in the case of Fermanagh and Tyrone would have given Nationalists a distinct advantage.[103] On the one hand, considered in isolation, the Nationalist claim that Fermanagh should have been considered as a unit, its territorial destiny to be decided by the majority in the county as a whole may or may not have been justified in the circumstances, but cannot be deemed absurd. On the other hand, if the claim is examined in the light of another fundamental Nationalist one, that south Down and south Armagh should go into the Free State although there were Unionist majorities in both counties, the inconsistency becomes troubling.

In the case of Fermanagh, at any rate, even if Feetham were to treat it as a unit, the argument based on a considerable Catholic numerical advantage on the evidence of the 1911 Census was not as strong as Tierney and other Nationalists seemed to think it was. In 1925, a private census was carried out as part of the Unionist case and its details presented to Francis Bourdillon, Secretary to the Boundary Commission by James Cooper and Sons, a family

---

101 PRO CAB 61/21.

102 Eoin MacNeill, Diary of Irish Boundary Tour, MacNeill Papers, UCDA LAI/H/114, 9–22 Dec. 1924.

103 Report of Revd John Tierney's address at Enniskillen, Boundary Bureau Papers, NAI Carton 30, 3/489, 10 Dec. 1924.

solicitors firm from Enniskillen, on 15 May 1925.[104] The Census showed that during the years from 1920 to 1925, just over 2,100 Protestants had migrated to County Fermanagh from the 26 counties. In a covering letter to Bourdillon, Cooper pointed out that many of these migrants, including farmers and ex-RIC men, had purchased farms in County Fermanagh, and were permanently settled there, as were those migrants who had joined the RUC. The list also included names and addresses of southern shopkeepers who had bought premises in Fermanagh, and of railway officials 'cleared out of the Free State'. Cooper, a Unionist MP, pointed out that 'the Protestant people have been pouring into County Fermanagh during the past few years', and that this trend showed every sign of being maintained. What was convincing about Cooper's submission was that every migrant named could readily be identified.[105] The submission also partially confirmed the view, strongly urged by Bourdillon to Lionel Curtis at the British Colonial Office, that a census of religious affiliation, given its exposure to changing circumstances over time, did not offer a trustworthy, credible basis for gauging political preference.[106]

A substantial body of Nationalist evidence was devoted to explaining that Catholics could not be expected to give allegiance to Northern Ireland because since partition they had become the victims of a radically unfair electoral system devised by the Unionist administration with the purpose of depriving them of a fair share of representation on elected bodies throughout the six counties. The case put by one Nationalist witness, Michael Lynch of Omagh, is typical of very many. Lynch made the usual claim that majorities in Tyrone, Fermanagh, Derry City, Newry, south Armagh and south Down wanted to be under a Free State government. The main reason for this, he asserted, was that 'they had been deprived of their legitimate share of representation in Local Government and administrative bodies by a system of gerrymandering of electoral areas unparalleled in any civilised country'.[107] Dozens of witnesses had, between them, compiled an impressive body of evidence to suggest that what Lynch claimed was not an exaggeration. The imbalance in the electoral system which favoured Unionists had its source in the abolition of Proportional Representation in 1922 and the alteration of electoral areas in the same year by the Government-appointed Leech Commission. The proceedings of this body were boycotted by Nationalists with the result that electoral boundaries were almost

---

104 Details of this transaction are given in Terence Dooley, 'Protestant migration from the Free State to Northern Ireland, 1920–25: a private census for Co. Fermanagh', *Clogher Record* 15:3 (1996), pp. 87–132.

105 PRO CAB 61/64.

106 Bourdillon to Curtis, PRO CO 739/25/60802, 7 Dec. 1923.

107 PRO CAB 61/98.

exclusively based on Unionist schemes. Most of these schemes were designed to ensure that even in electoral areas where Catholics were in the majority, they could not elect a majority of the public representatives. Several witnesses explained to Feetham how this was brought about; Feetham in turn summarised what they told him: 'The effect of the scheme of division has been to herd a number of Nationalist voters into 3 or 4 areas so as to waste their strength and so give to the other party a very unfair share of the power.'[108] The best way to explain the gerrymandering process is to give an example, Fermanagh being a convenient one. The Nationalist Parliamentary electorate of the County was 29,400, the Unionist 23,500. The electoral boundaries were so drawn as to make one overwhelmingly Nationalist constituency, south Fermanagh, with 12,200 Nationalists and 3,700 Unionists. Unionists guaranteed themselves the two other divisions, Lisnaskea and Enniskillen, in which they had small but sufficient majorities. In Lisnaskea, the Unionist electorate was 9,200 as against 8,300 Nationalists, and in Enniskillen 10,600 as against 8,900. Thus, the minority got twice the parliamentary representation of the majority, while 8,499 Nationalist votes were wasted, compared to 2,589 Unionist ones.

Judge John Leech, the Deputy Recorder of Belfast, whose local public enquiries were the basis for the rearrangement of local government ones, made it clear that the Ministry of Home Affairs was anxious that everybody had the right to submit a scheme, and that all would be on a equal footing.[109] The attendance at all but five of Leech's enquiries was exclusively Unionist. Nationalists boycotted the great majority of hearings because they professed to believe that the Leech Commission was a meaningless operation since its outcome was predetermined. In two cases, Irvinestown and Ballycastle, where Nationalists cooperated, however, they had a significant say in the final schemes. Unionists could, and did, argue that Nationalists had only themselves to blame for failing to have their say in the rearrangement of areas, and leaving the reorganisation of controversial districts to be dictated by local Unionists. They could also suggest that Nationalist non-participation could be interpreted as consent to the justice of the process. To a large extent, however, the Nationalist boycott can probably be accounted for by the fact that many of them believed that any rearrangement Leech might endorse would, in a relatively short time, not concern them, since they would be transferred by the Boundary Commission to the Free State. It is impossible to say what arrangements Leech might have decided upon had Nationalists participated in the process with the same enthusiasm as Unionists did, and presented convincing, well documented, evidentially-based submissions. It is

108 Feetham to Cahir Healy, MP, CAB 61/68.
109 *Fermanagh Herald and Monaghan News*, 3 Mar. 1923.

certainly going too far to attribute bias to Leech, as many Nationalists did or to represent him as a pliant instrument in the hands of the Belfast Government or of local Unionists.[110] The general Nationalist attitude to Leech and his Commission is conveyed in Gallagher's comment that 'the Minister for Home Affairs, who was Sir Dawson Bates, a Tory and leading member of the Orange Order, appointed as a Commissioner, Mr John Leech, KC, a fellow Tory'.[111]

The decision by the Northern Ireland Government to rearrange local electoral areas should not be seen as part of a scheme to deprive Nationalists of equitable representation, although it is fair to say that the Government hoped that the outcome would be favourable to its own Party. The arrangement of rural district boundaries was defensible because of the serious anomalies which had long been obvious under the old system, based as this was on schemes dating back to the 1840s. There is no question that huge changes in the distribution of population since the Great Famine necessitated a radical re-drawing of electoral boundaries to take account of these. The fundamental purpose of the 1922 Local Government Act was to apportion rural districts with due regard 'to the equality of the population in every division'. The old system had been generally advantageous to Nationalists. Examples of this were cited by the Ministry of Home Affairs in a memorandum prepared in 1934 to answer Nationalist charges of gerrymandering: where there were at one time Nationalist majorities, these were obtained because of the anomalies which allowed in some instances 600 people to have the same representation as 3,100 and in others where 2,158 obtained the same representation as 105.'[112] Reform of such a system was therefore desirable. However, before a much more questionable provision of the 1922 Act was the inclusion of a provision making the right to vote in local elections depend to some extent on property valuation.

From several parts of Northern Ireland witnesses brought carefully documented evidence of the political effects of gerrymandering combined

---

110 Frank Gallagher, for example, calls the Leech Commission 'an elaborately staged judicial tribunal'. Commenting on the fact that the only scheme presented for Strabane Rural Council was from William Millar, the local Unionist MP, Gallagher remarks: 'If Judge Leech, who knew who Mr Millar was, had been an impartial judge, he would of course have been asked how was it that in so important a matter involving the representation of all parties he had received but one scheme and that from the minority party [The Unionists].' Frank Gallagher, *The Indivisible Island: The History of the Partition of Ireland* (London, 1959), p. 230.

111 Ibid., p. 229.

112 Patrick Buckland, *The Factory of Grievances: Divided Government in Northern Ireland, 1921–39* (Dublin, 1979), p. 239.

with the abolition of PR on their level of representation. Cahir Healy showed that under PR and before gerrymandering the distribution of local government seats in County Fermanagh approximated with mathematical accuracy to the relative strengths of Catholic and non-Catholic electors. Under PR, Nationalists had elected 11 members as against 9 Unionists, reflecting precisely the demographic position: 55 per cent Nationalists and 45 per cent Unionists. With the gerrymandered areas, Healy calculated, 27,096 Protestants would have elected 13 Unionist councillors, while Catholics could have elected no more than 7, making one Unionist vote equal to 2 Nationalist ones.[113] The consequence of this kind of arrangement, as Collins had predicted in 1922, was to give a false impression of the real wishes of the people, and to paint Fermanagh, Tyrone and other Nationalist areas orange for the benefit of the Boundary Commission.[114] Healy observed that for every 211 votes, Unionists could get one District Councillor, while it took 367 Nationalists to achieve the same result. Archdeacon Tierney, pointing out that the local government franchise, based as this was on property, inevitably favoured Unionists who, as a community, tended to own the more valuable properties. A man with two or three small farms could divide these among his three sons, thus making extra local government votes. The consequence, Tierney explained, was that the people with the largest amount of property could have the largest number of votes. He made the significant remark that in areas known to him 'this manufacturing of votes is almost a fine art'.[115] The disproportionate value of Unionist votes was illustrated by Revd B. O'Kane of Magharafelt, where 1,600 Catholics got one representative and 2,400 Protestants got four.[116] A more extraordinary situation was revealed by Richard Vance, of Aughnacloy. There, the arrangement for elections was based on a Unionist submission to the Leech Commission: town commissioners were elected on the vote of the town as a whole; there were no separate wards. This meant that the majority party could fill all the seats.[117] Feetham was concerned that in the area represented by the Clogher Board of Guardians, Unionists had 11 elected representatives and Nationalists only five, meaning that Unionists got one member for every 284 voters and Nationalists got one for every 496.[118] Feetham also remarked that in elections to the Fermanagh County Council under the

113 PRO CAB 61/67.
114 Jonathan Bardon, *History of Ulster* (Belfast, 2005), p. 500.
115 PRO CAB 61/68.
116 PRO CAB 61/104.
117 PRO CAB 61/25.
118 PRO CAB 61/40.

Unionist Redistribution Scheme, in a county where Catholics had a numerical advantage, Unionists could elect 13 members and Nationalists only seven.[119]

Nationalist representatives who lamented the abolition of PR in local Government elections might have expected that the Free State Government would share their concern in this respect. The contrary was the case. Cosgrave was just as determined an opponent of PR as Craig and his colleagues were. This is illustrated in a curious exchange between Cosgrave and Craig at a meeting in London on 29 November 1925, during which the two agreed to bury Feetham's report. When Kevin O'Higgins, Free State Minister for Home Affairs, suggested to Craig that Nationalist dismay might be ameliorated if PR were restored in Northern Ireland, Craig dismissed the suggestion out of hand: 'I can't stick PR. Does not seem to be British.' Cosgrave supported Craig: 'For my part I'd like it out of the way.'[120] Cosgrave disliked PR as a feature of the Free State electoral system because it posed a threat to his own electoral majority. In this respect, he had much in common with Craig.

In evidence before the Commission, James Cooper MP, Chairman of the Fermanagh County Council, who was active in gerrymandering schemes and vote manufacturing, acknowledged that people got votes who were not entitled to them. 'It all depends', he told the Commission, 'who went round the country in a motor car at night the longest and got bogus agreements signed.' This activity gave 'an unfair advantage' to the side which was 'more energetic'.[121] The lack of dynamism on the Nationalist side was explained by Revd P. McQuaid, Catholic Curate in Clogher: 'In districts where people saw there was no chance of doing anything, they became apathetic in regard to revision, because they looked upon it as though they were playing against a loaded dice. This is a commonplace now in these counties. Everyone knows the thing was fixed and that Catholic votes would be ineffective because we have too many votes in one place and not enough in another.'[122] What would be achieved by gerrymandering, the abolition of PR for local elections and vote manufacture is dramatically illustrated in the results of electoral changes in the Omagh Rural District with its 61.5 per cent Catholic majority. In 1920, Nationalists won the Council with 26 seats to 13; after gerrymandering Unionists were assured of 21 seats for 5,381 votes, compared with 18 Nationalist seats for 8,459 votes.[123] These results were based on a Unionist scheme presented at Leech's Omagh enquiry on 21 February 1923, attended by 40 Unionist representatives, but boycotted by Nationalists.

119 PRO CAB 61/60.
120 Jones, *Whitehall Diary* vol. 3, p. 244.
121 PRO CAB 61/60.
122 PRO CAB 61/151.
123 Phoenix, *Northern Nationalism*, pp. 275–6.

The wholesale gerrymandering complained of by Nationalists was engaged in with the connivance and involvement of Craig's Government. This is clear from a communication from James Cooper, the Fermanagh MP to Craig on 9 August 1922. Making the extraordinary claim that Fermanagh was 'absolutely Unionist all over except in two or three mountain areas', Cooper explained the measures taken by himself and Fermanagh Unionists to ensure that the County would never again be controlled by a Nationalist majority on the main local authority. 'We took steps last Winter,' he told Craig, 'and went through all these [County Council] divisions and manufactured votes wholesale.' Cooper took much of the credit for these efforts: 'Personally I have gone to very considerable trouble just over the manufacture of the new votes and then in carving up the county vote into new divisions and arranging the different areas. This meant going into the [Catholic-Protestant] composition of every townland in the county and fitting them together.' Cooper also revealed that William Miller, Unionist MP for Tyrone, was equally involved in the gerrymandering process. He had called on Miller a few days before, 'and found him plodding away on the Tyrone maps. He has a very big job to tackle and the [Unionist] people all over are most enthusiastic about the whole thing.' One of the fruits of Miller's labours was the reconstitution of the Strabane Rural Council area in the Unionist interest. Miller produced a proposal on this in the Leech Commission on 24 February 1923. Leech announced that Miller's scheme was the only one submitted, and was therefore accepted.[124] The thoroughness with which Cooper had applied himself to his work is indicated in his offer to give Craig the names of 36 townlands round the borders of Fermanagh in which 'there is not a single Protestant which, or portion of which, he would be quite willing to exchange for the Pettigo area of Donegal and the Unionist town land of Cloghore at Belleek.'[125] The Secretary to the Tyrone Unionist Association had been preparing in advance of the Leech Commission, in the same way as Cooper and Miller had been. He wrote to his Fermanagh counterpart in April 1922: 'I suppose you are preparing a scheme to make Fermanagh boundaries safe [for Unionism]. I am gerrymandering at night. It is the hardest job I ever undertook . . . we have a big Nationalist majority against us.'[126]

An accurate reflection of the temper of many border Unionists is to be found in the evidence of two Protestant clergymen, one living in Northern Ireland, the other in Castleblaney, County Monaghan, in the Free State. The Revd W. B. Naylor, Rector of Castle Caldwell, Belleek, County Fermanagh was adamant that he would not under any circumstance live in the Free State

124 *Ulster Herald*, 3 Mar. 1923.
125 Cooper to Craig, PRONI CAB 9B/40/1, 9 Aug. 1922.
126 Cited in Brian Barton, *Brookeborough: The Making of a Prime Minister* (Belfast, 1988), pp. 63–4.

if Belleek were transferred, and that there were numerous clergymen in the Free State who would come north if they had a chance. He had told his bishop that if his parish was transferred to the Free State, his resignation was automatic, since he could not be loyal to the Government there. 'I can't,' he told the Commissioners, 'get over my bringing up.' This was because their churches were burned and desecrated. Southern Ireland, he believed, would always be disturbed, always be 'a second Mexico',[127] which Protestants should leave at the earliest opportunity. He characterised the inhabitants of Fermanagh as 'a restless and discontented people', their discontent in no way depending on 'the tyranny of the Northern Ireland Government or the British Government', but on their own bellicose tendencies. The native Irish displayed their unruly behaviour not only in Fermanagh: they were just as disturbed 'in the packing yards of Chicago and the Bowery in New York'. Naylor dissociated himself from most of the people among whom he lived. He was an Englishman first of all although his people had been in Ireland for 360 years. He had no Celtic blood, and was an Irishman by accident of birth. Being in the Free State would mean being governed by people who had achieved power by 'treacherous attack and murder'. He knew of no case 'where there was any bravery in Southern Ireland'.[128] He avoided answering one pertinent question: why Unionists would want to keep these troublesome Fermanagh Nationalists in the Northern Ireland state against their will.

Canon T. G. Rudd, Rector of Castleblaney, who claimed to be in tune with Catholics as well as Protestant opinion in the border areas of Monaghan, had come to the conclusion that 'a very large number of Roman Catholics here, what would be called Nationalists before, are now very strongly Unionists in the Free State', but would be reluctant to state this publicly. Canon Rudd was himself reluctant, or perhaps unable, to provide evidence for this contention. He attributed this change in attitude to the poor financial position of the Free State, resulting in a higher cost of living than in Northern Ireland and higher income taxes. Compulsory Irish in schools was a further irritant. It wasted the time of those who would emigrate or get posts in Northern Ireland, and make no use of it afterwards. Canon Rudd was arguing in favour of the transfer of parts of north Monaghan to Northern Ireland, thus anticipating a contentious element in the Commission's award.[129] Rudd, interpreting the views of fellow-Unionists in north Monaghan, explained that in 1920 they

127 At the time of the Boundary Commission hearings Mexico was half way through a 32-year revolutionary phase, marked by political turmoil, factional fighting, terrorism, religious persecution and assassination.

128 PRO, CAB, 61/66.

129 PRO, CAB 61/111.

had been compelled to remain under the Free State Government without their consent, and had reluctantly submitted to being cut off from Northern Ireland for the sake of the Empire. This sacrifice, Rudd argued, should be remembered by the Commission, and rewarded by the reinstatement of southern border Unionists under a government loyal to Imperial principles. The Revd T. F. L. Stack, a Tyrone landlord, explained that the Anglo-Irish Treaty had pushed back the boundary of the British Empire, the secession of southern Ireland having been brought about by the enemies of England, Germans and Bolshevists, whose object was the Empire's ruin. Stack was worried that the Commission might push back the Imperial boundary even further, and thus strike 'at the very heart of the Empire' which would be forced to retaliate by reconquering Ireland.[130] Here, the Revd Stack seems to have been thinking of the reconquest of Ireland as a whole. Representatives of the Protestant Churches of Castlederg district, County Tyrone, wanted to be left in Northern Ireland, and a Loyalist farmer, named Hunter, in Derrycreevy, County Monaghan, who wanted to be included in it, had a common motive: Castlederg Protestants objected to anything that would 'interfere with their loyalty to throne and Empire', while Hunter wanted to resume his status as 'a faithful and dutiful subject to the British government . . . a protection to honest men the world over'.[131] The Imperial motive was also strongly present to the minds of the members of The Honourable Irish Society[132] when they pressed for the retention of the City of Londonderry in Northern Ireland. In its submission, the Society emphasised the intimate links, historical and contemporary, between the imperial capital and the city; 'The City of London may take pride in the [seventeenth-century] Plantation of Londonderry, and the people of Derry on their part value highly their connection with the metropolis of the Empire.' Indeed, many of those educated in schools established by the Society 'had rendered eminent service both at home and abroad throughout the Empire'.[133] According to F. D. Russell, President of the largely Unionist Newry Chamber of Commerce, the Nationalist population,

130 PRO CAB, 61/135.

131 PRO CAB 61/36; 61/111.

132 Following the departure of the Earls of Tyrone and Tyrconnell for the Continent in 1607 the way was open for the English Government to Anglicise most of the province of Ulster. In 1613, the Common Council of the City of Derry agreed with the Crown to the plantation of the entire county of Londonderry and to a town-building programme at Derry and Coleraine. At the same time, the body known as the Honourable Irish Society was created by royal charter. The Society was a standing committee of the Common Council of Derry City and included representatives of the principal companies of London. Its task was to administer the establishment of the Londonderry plantation. Its purpose continued to be the advancement of Protestant and colonial interests in Londonderry.

133 PRO CAB 61/78.

before it was infected by Republican and working-class elements, was largely composed of people who conformed to the Unionist ideal, 'very decent, straightforward, honest men, many of them anxious to remain part and parcel of the great British Empire, whilst holding that Ireland should have a certain say in local affairs.'[134] Russell's claims may not have been altogether fanciful. There is some evidence of West British Catholics in Newry before 1914. The town was large enough to have a significant Catholic middle class.

Attachment to the imperial ideal went hand in hand with an abhorrence of the Irish language and what it had come to represent. Border Unionists in Donegal and Monaghan were particularly exercised by the imposition of compulsory Irish in Free State schools by the Cosgrave Government. The Gaelic League, the Irish-Ireland movement which provided the impulse for this was originally non-political and non-sectarian, although dedicated to the de-Anglicisation of Ireland by means of the revival and preservation of Irish as a spoken language. In 1915, Nationalist politicians and their followers took control of the League, making the political independence of Ireland one of its primary aims, thus establishing an intimate link between the Irish language and advanced nationalism, and disposing Irish Protestant Unionists to regard the imposition of Irish on their children as an affront to their British sensibilities as well as being a waste of time. These sentiments featured in many submissions from both sides of the border. Border Unionists on the Free State side told the Commission of the sacrifices they felt obliged to make by having their children educated north of the border to avoid the unwelcome burden of Irish. E. Y. Elliott, a property agent in Belleek, County Fermanagh, testified that practically all the Loyalists in the Free State portion of his area so resented the teaching of Irish in the Free State schools that they were sending their children across into Northern Ireland to avoid this imposition.[135] Others like Samuel Stoops of Castleblaney, were concerned at the waste of time involved in forcing their children to learn a language they would never use,[136] and at the prospect of seeing these same children denied employment in the Free State for lack of proficiency in Irish. One witness, Colonel F. T. Warburton of Portarlington, deplored the fact that money was being squandered in an attempt to revive 'a barbarous, guttural language without literature or commercial words', sounding like something 'between coughing and spitting', spoken only by 'the lowest, most uneducated and the poorest of Ireland'.[137]

134 PRO CAB 61/115.
135 PRO CAB 61/125.
136 PRO CAB 61/111.
137 PRO CAB 61/155.

W. B. Smyth, a Unionist mill-owner in Strabane, mentioned the distressed economy of the Free State and its policy of compulsory Irish in schools as his two principal reasons for preferring to live in Northern Ireland.[138] A north Monaghan Unionist named Condle, cited rates, taxes and 'this learning of Irish', a hardship without benefit, as his reasons for desiring inclusion in Northern Ireland.[139] Another Monaghan Unionist, Hugh Hunter, when asked why he wanted to be in Northern Ireland, answered that people like him 'were better used under the Imperial flag, and next, the educating the children in the Irish language . . . a language that will be of no service to our families when they grow up'.[140] Perhaps the most telling submission on the Irish language issue was made by John Gillespie of Castleblaney, a solicitor who was manager of a local Protestant school. The parents of those attending that school wanted to exclude Irish as a subject. Gillespie was concerned that these parents who were 'very large taxpayers', had to endure the hardship of seeing their school closed for a month while the teachers, 'who have never been so well paid as they are now', took time off to go to classes in Irish, 'which would never become a useful language for people in commerce or in the professions.'[141]

There is no escaping the impression that Unionist witnesses who raised the language issue were convinced that attempts to revive Irish through the educational system violated common sense and the rights and wishes of Protestant parents and of those West British Catholics who still lived in the North. It also seemed to represent a regression to more primitive, less civilised, standards than those enjoyed in Northern Ireland. Unionist contempt for Irish was merely one aspect of the general sense of superiority conveyed in evidence given to the Boundary Commission. For example, Dr William Thompson Smyth, a County Monaghan Unionist working in Bournemouth, contrasted the invasive swarms of Roman Catholic labourers with 'the loyal Protestants who wore his Majesty's uniform in the Great War'. He also lamented the fate of north Monaghan Protestants who realised 'their doom in being forced into a lower civilisation . . . with not the slightest physical, moral or financial betterment whatever'.[142] Much Unionist evidence is similarly informed by such question-begging assumptions as that of E. Y. Elliott of Belleek: 'The respectable Roman Catholics (of whom I am glad to say there are a few in number) . . . say they hope they will never see the day when they will go into the Free State. They say God

138 PRO CAB 61/138.
139 PRO CAB 61/39.
140 PRO CAB 61/111.
141 Ibid.
142 PRO CAB 61/134.

Forbid.'[143] A Roman Catholic is thus defined as 'respectable' when he or she is an admirer of the Empire, opposed to assimilation in the Free State and content to live in Northern Ireland. Those not so inclined must be assumed to belong to less desirable categories.

The record of the Boundary Commission hearings provides useful indications of Feetham's interpretation of the task imposed on him by the terms of the boundary clause in Article 12 of the Treaty. Archdeacon Tierney of Enniskillen was one of those witnesses who stimulated him to explore some of the larger questions involved, to tease out, for example, the relative importance of the wishes of inhabitants and economic considerations. Tierney first advanced his own interpretation, holding that the wishes of the inhabitants were clearly predominant, while economics and geography were secondary. He gave a balanced view of how an economic consideration might overrule the wishes of inhabitants. If, for example, the majority in Derry were Unionists who wanted to be excluded from the Free State, then on the ground that vital economic relations existed between Donegal and Derry, these relations might prevail against Unionists wishes. Feetham dissented from Tierney's central majoritarian argument: 'When you say predominant and secondary it suggests that it [wishes of inhabitants] is to predominate, whereas the terms used show that sometimes economic and geographic conditions are to prevail against the wishes.' Tierney disagreed, arguing that the wishes of inhabitants were in the principal clause of the sentence, and that the economic and geographic part was, subordinate. 'But,' Feetham explained, 'it is also qualifying.' Tierney refused to yield, telling Feetham that 'it is the people and not economics that decide the principle and the people living in a particular area know their economic conditions better than anyone else ... and it is they who will have to suffer if they are hit economically.'[144]

Feetham proceeded to give his interpretation of another vital concern: the choice of unit which might be considered for transfer. On this issue he had no doubt that he had to be careful not to adopt areas that were too large, because that would mean that 'the wishes of one part may be over-ridden by the wishes of the other'. On the other hand, he had no doubt that 'the smaller the units you take, the more close attention you can give to the wishes of the people'.[145] When Tierney argued for the transfer of the whole of Fermanagh to the Free State, Feetham rejected this because large districts there were Protestant. Tierney then suggested that the Poor Law Union, with a population of approximately 10,000, was the appropriate one, being the smallest unit of

---

143 Ibid.
144 PRO CAB 61/121.
145 Ibid.

administration. When George Leek, the Derry Nationalist MP, made a similar argument in relation to Derry Union, which had a Catholic majority of 4,483, Feetham was dismissive, telling Leek that the Union had Catholic majorities in one part, and Protestant majorities in other parts, and asking him: 'Is that your way of following out the wishes of the population?'[146] Other Nationalist witnesses including Revd Eugene Coyle of Garrison, County Fermanagh, wanted administrative units to be considered as the basis for transfer. Feetham told Coyle that the Treaty did not refer to administrative units.[147] Coyle might have replied that neither did the Treaty refer to the smallest possible or practicable units or indeed to any units. When dealing with Coyle's preference for administrative units, Feetham objected, as he had in Tierney's case, that this would mean allowing overall majorities to prevail over large local ones and bringing in 'an administrative consideration in order to override the wishes of these local majorities'. Feetham then declared that 'this [i.e. the choice of unit] is not to be dealt with on the basis of retaliation', by which he meant that the Treaty did not imply that the Boundary Commission was to impose a penalty on parts of Northern Ireland for not choosing to be part of the Free State.

In a lively exchange between Feetham and Alex Donnelly, who wanted Castlederg Union to be treated as a single unit, the integrity of which had to be respected, even if the Catholic majority there was only 175 out of a total population of 11,161, the question of the choice of unit came to a head. When Feetham argued that Donnelly's claim would involve 'disregard of the wishes of the population', Donnelly countered by remarking that it was only reasonable to say that the majority should count, and that Feetham's 'wishes of the population' really meant the wishes of 'a section of the population', the minority in fact. Feetham could not accept the proposition that he could set aside the wishes of a Protestant block 'because they were combined with another block with which they disagree'.[148] Essentially he was suggesting that the wishes of the majority of the population of Castlederg Union were not decisive enough to permit the Union as a whole to be considered for transfer: if the Union were transferred as a whole, over 5,000 unwilling Protestants would have to go into the Free State along with a slightly larger number of willing Catholics. Donnelly's principle that the integrity of a single administrative unit should be respected even if this involved overriding the wishes of a substantial minority was not a novel one. It had been put into practice by the framers of the 1920 Government of Ireland Act. In that case a county-based

146 Ibid.
147 PRO CAB 61/146.
148 PRO CAB 61/148.

unit was chosen in spite of the fact that in three of the counties involved, Derry, Down and Armagh, the wishes of very substantial minorities were disregarded, while in two counties, Fermanagh and Tyrone, a significant majority of the inhabitants had their wishes disregarded. Feetham's rejection of administrative units, whether counties or Unions, confronted the Commission with a problem: would not the same objections apply in the case of most lesser units he might consider as he discerned in the case of counties or Unions?

Rational consideration of this issue is bedevilled by the fact that no locus is provided in the boundary clause for the whereabouts of those inhabitants whose wishes are to be ascertained. Thus, the choice of any unit within which these wishes were to be determined was bound to be quite arbitrary. Thomas Elliott, representing the Congregational Committee of the Strabane Presbyterian Church, believed that the terms of the boundary clause left the Commission with an impossible task. He argued that since it was dealing with 'a boundary to be determined, an unknown boundary', the question arose, 'How are the wishes of the inhabitants contiguous to an unascertained boundary to be ascertained?'[149] It is difficult to unravel this conundrum. What can be said, however, is that the smaller the units Feetham settled upon to determine these wishes, the smaller the chance was that substantial amounts of territory would be transferred.

IV THE COMMISSION'S FINDINGS

The Commission decided on its award on 17 October 1925. This would have transferred 31,319 people to the Free State and 7,594 in the opposite direction. The award of a relatively large portion of south Armagh to the Free State was counterbalanced by the transfer of a rich portion of east Donegal to the north.[150] Amid public outrage in the Free State and the Nationalist north[151] after the Tory *Morning Post* carried a reasonably accurate forecast of the recommendations on 7 November, Eoin MacNeill resigned as Free State Commissioner. Another kind of protest threatened to be more robust. Patrick McCartan reported 'on good authority' to a Republican militant that following the signing of the Boundary Agreement, de Valera had prevented the

---

149 PRO CAB 61/136.
150 For the full details of Feetham's two-way transfers, see Appendix II(A) and II(B), p. 319-20.
151 Dorothy Macardle, *The Irish Republic* (Dublin, 1937), p. 807.
152 John Bowman, *De Valera and the Ulster Question* (Oxford, 1982), p. 93.

assassination of Blythe, MacNeill and O'Higgins.[152] There appears to be no evidence to corroborate McCartan's statement.

Cosgrave moved quickly to avert the serious damage to his Government's position threatened by the Commission debacle. From his point of view, the potential loss of the southern territory to the north and the accompanying danger to the stability of his administration weighed more heavily than the failure of the Boundary Commission to meet the Nationalist demand for self-determination. With the collusion of Baldwin, Churchill, Feetham and Fisher, he succeeded in having the Report of the Commission suppressed, acquiesced with relief in the preservation of the status quo and pledged 'neighbourly comradeship with Craig's Government'.[153] A boundary agreement signed on 3 December 1925 by the Governments of the Free State, Northern Ireland and Great Britain and registered with the League of Nations, gave the 1920 partition a permanent, instead of a provisional, status. The first article of the agreement involved the Free State not only in the abrogation of Article 12 of the Treaty of 1921, but in the formal recognition of the terms of the 1920 partition, and in the apparent recognition of the status of Northern Ireland as equal to that of the Irish Free State.[154] The decision of Cosgrave's Government to seek the suppression of Feetham's report and to have its findings set aside was questionable. While it is true that southern acceptance of these findings would have involved formal recognition of partition, and its final confirmation, it is equally true that the Tripartite Agreement he signed as the alternative also recognised partition. In choosing between two versions of partition, that of 1920 and the more equitable one proposed by Feetham, he settled for the less equitable one. Feetham, after all, had proposed giving more Irish people, including 35,000 Nationalists, the opportunity of living under a government of their choice.[155]

Cosgrave's curious pledge should be seen in the light of the close, if expedient, relationship that developed between Craig and himself during their talks with Baldwin on the boundary issue in December 1925 where they found common cause on essential issues. Cosgrave, as Fanning points out, 'was now in total agreement with Craig in wanting no change in the border.'[156] Cosgrave believed that the Tripartite Agreement represented the best possible outcome in all the circumstances. Craig supported Cosgrave in his successful attempt to have Free State liability for part of the British war debt under

153 David Harkness, *Northern Ireland since 1920* (Dublin, 1983), p. 40.

154 Anthony Carty, *Was Ireland Conquered? International Law and the Irish Question* (London, 1996), p. 149.

155 Alvin Jackson, *Home Rule: An Irish History 1800–2000* (London, 2003), pp. 213–4.

156 Ronan Fanning, *Independent Ireland* (Dublin, 1983), p. 61.

157 T. P. Coogan, *De Valera: Long Fellow, Long Shadow* (London, 1993), p. 379.

Article 5 of the Treaty waived.[157] The subsequent Dáil debate on the London Agreement of 1925 is also illuminating and suggests that Cosgrave and his ministers were indeed the partitionists Craig had sensed they were when they had customs barriers erected on 1 April 1923. The tone and content of the Government contribution to the debate suggests the haste of Cosgrave and his ministers to complete the process of distancing the Free State from northern nationalism and, as O'Halloran points out, 'to divest themselves of the embarrassing burden of the northern minority' and to withdraw 'behind the boundary and into a wholly Free State context'.[158] All Cosgrave could offer northern Nationalists was 'the goodwill and neighbourly feeling of the people among whom they live', while Kevin O'Higgins suggested that northern Nationalists, 'the inhabitants of a particular set of square miles', should sacrifice their interests to 'the best interests of the whole country', just as Carson had hoped that the Unionists of Cavan, Donegal and Monaghan would understand that the best interests of North-Eastern Unionists would be best served by a northern state limited to six counties.[159] The Free State Government put its symbolic seal on its view that the northern minority were, in effect, citizens of a foreign country by refusing to let a deputation of their representatives address the Dáil on 9 December 1925 on the boundary agreement.[160] With the collapse of the Commission and the acquiescence of the Free State, the northern Nationalists were cut adrift, and a potential danger to the 1920 partition settlement was averted.

Border Nationalists, the overwhelming majority of whom had supported the Treaty and the Free State Government on the basis of Article 12, mounted angry protests at what they saw as their betrayal by Cosgrave and his Cabinet. De Valera led a southern Nationalist demonstration.[161] The general response of those who felt betrayed was best expressed by Cahir Healy, the Fermanagh MP, in December 1926:

> The Free State leaders told us that our anchor was Article 12: when the time of trial came, they cut our cable and launched us, rudderless, into the hurricane, without guarantee or security, even for our ordinary civic rights.[162]

158 Claire O'Halloran, *Partition and the Limits of Irish Nationalism: An Ideology under Stress* (Dublin, 1987), pp. 71–2.
159 *Dáil Debates*, Vol. 13, Cols 1306–7; 1368–9, 7 Dec. 1925.
160 Irish News, 10 Dec. 1925.
161 *Irish Independent*, 7 Dec. 1925.
162 Healy in a letter to *The Irish Statesman*, 18 Dec. 1926, cited in Phoenix, *Northern Nationalism*, p. 447.
163 Buckland, *Factory of Grievances*, p. 228.

Healy's fear that Northern Nationalist civic rights would be compromised proved justified: in 1929, Craig's Government abolished Proportional Representation in parliamentary elections and re-drew the constituencies in the interests of Unionism.[163]

FIVE

PROCEDURES AND FINDINGS

—

I THE CHAIRMAN: AN IMPARTIAL ARBITER?

The composition of the three-member Boundary Commission provided for in Article 12 of the Anglo-Irish Treaty meant that for practical purposes it was bound to be controlled by its Chairman, Justice Richard Feetham, of the South African Supreme Court. This was because the views of J. R. Fisher,[1] nominated by the British Government to represent the six-county state, which had refused to nominate a commissioner, and Eoin MacNeill, nominated by the Free State, were bound to cancel each other out on all substantive matters. Eoin MacNeill, the largely ineffectual nominee of the Free State Government, whose integrity was to prove his greatest single liability, had, even before the Treaty was agreed to, but when a boundary commission was in prospect, warned de Valera against accepting a chairman nominated by the British Government.[2] The provision in Article 12 to allow the British to appoint the chairman was not contested by the Irish negotiators of the Treaty settlement, nor did the Free State Government challenge Feetham's appointment. Indeed, the initial response of the Secretary of the Free State Boundary Bureau was that this was 'a good appointment' from the Nationalist point of view,[3] a response which echoed the mistaken view of the Cosgrave Government that Feetham would be favourable to the Free State, because the members of that Government assumed that, as an imperial federalist in the mould of Lionel Curtis,[4] he would be more inclined to preserve the unity of the Empire by making concessions to the Free State than to preserve the territorial integrity

---

1   A staunch Ulster Unionist who had for many years been editor of *The Northern Whig*.

2   See John Ryan, 'Eoin MacNeill, 1867–1945', *Studies* (1945), p. 34. MacNeill himself was Ryan's source.

3   E. M. Stephens to H. A. McCartan. McCartan File, Boundary Bureau Papers, NAI, 6 June 1924.

4   Curtis was Adviser to the Colonial Office on Irish Affairs and a member of the British delegation which negotiated the Anglo-Irish Treaty in 1921. He was opposed to the award of Ulster territory to the Free State.

of the 1920 northern State. Why both Curtis and Feetham took the opposite position is uncertain but that they would do so was not necessarily inevitable on *a priori* grounds. Fitzpatrick, however, suggests that 'there was no sound reason to expect that the casting vote of a British-appointed chairman would support any but the most minor alterations'.[5]

On the other hand, doubts existed in some Unionist quarters about the view Feetham was likely to take on Irish boundary adjustment. In September 1924, Sir James Craig received a memorandum on Feetham prepared by a correspondent[6] in Johannesburg, who purported to be friendly to the Northern Ireland cause. The purpose of the Memorandum was to let the Ulster people know how Feetham was regarded in South Africa, and what his position on the boundary was likely to be. The correspondent acknowledged that 'on paper' Feetham was an impartial colonial judge, chosen from South Africa because of its small Irish vote, a circumstance which made him less likely to be influenced by Irish matters than would a Canadian or Australian judge. He could therefore be made to appear 'the just man, calculated to hold the balance' between the two Irish parties. The correspondent went on to suggest some significant divergences between the foregoing estimate of Feetham and a less flattering one, at least from an Ulster Unionist point of view. 'Feetham's conversation in my presence,' he remarked, 'has always been on the basis of self-determination all over Europe, and I have heard him remark that it was a fatal mistake to have allowed Ulster her independence [in 1920].'

Feetham's political career in South Africa as a member of the Legislative Council of the Transvaal from 1907 to 1910 and of the South African Union Parliament from 1915 to 1923 did not inspire confidence in the correspondent. He seemed to discern a sinister significance in the fact that Feetham was elected by the Parktown Division of Johannesburg. To hold this division, the wealthy area of the town, where three out of four householders were wealthy Jews, he had to be *persona grata* with Jewish finance: 'in other words, he is not objectionable to the elements that put Isaacs and Montague [*sic*] into India, Samuel into Palestine, and Hamar Greenwood into Ireland: elements which have always been revolutionary and separatist for financial motives.' Two further considerations were calculated to arouse misgivings in Ulster Unionists. The first was that Feetham enjoyed the approval of the Anglo-Catholic movement which dominated the Anglican Church in South Africa, an element described by Disraeli as 'the disloyal section of the High Church Party that always use, and are used by, Irish sedition'. The second consideration

5   David Fitzpatrick, *The Two Irelands 1912–1939* (Oxford, 1998), p. 108.
6   Unnamed correspondent to Craig, CAB 6/97; Memorandum on Mr Justice Richard Feetham, Sept. 1924. Cited in Alvin Jackson, *Home Rule: An Irish History 1800–2000* (London, 2003), p. 211.

was even more disturbing. The correspondent saw Feetham's appointment as Chairman of the Irish Boundary Commission as part of a complex web of intrigue involving General Smuts, Prime Minister of South Africa from 1919 to 1924; an Irish separatist element in Johannesburg led by two IRB men called Foley and MacDonald, and a compliant Feetham. Smuts, confident that he could lead his Party back into power if he could hold Johannesburg, had to detach votes from the Labour Party to achieve the latter goal. To this end, he promised the Irish element that in return for its electoral support 'he and they would nominate the Boundary Judge; both Foley and MacDonald spoke of Feetham as safe to come down on their [Irish] side' in the boundary dispute. To facilitate these arrangements, Feetham resigned his seat in Parliament a few months before the election, and his speedy appointment as a judge in 1923 'came as a shock'.[7] In June 1924, Craig had made it clear to a fellow-Unionist MP that he cared very little who was appointed, but suggested that 'perhaps on the whole it is well that it is not a man of more outstanding reputation'.[8] The views of Craig's Johannesburg correspondent, however, appear to be out of accord with almost everything we know about Feetham's background and his British connections. The correspondent's suggestions about Feetham, in particular that he was biased in favour of Nationalists, are undermined by the internal evidence from his memo that the correspondent himself was an obsessive anti-semite of a type not uncommon among the diehard fringe of the Conservative Party. His memo may be considered, not as a piece of reliable evidence about Feetham's outlook on nationalism or anything else, but about his own. He and those who thought like him believed that there was a worldwide Jewish conspiracy to undermine the British Empire by encouraging Nationalist movements. They believed that evidence for this conspiracy was to be found in the creation of the Palestine Mandate[9] and the role of such Jewish statesmen as Lord Reading and Edwin Montagu in the Government of India. The correspondent's mistaken belief that Hamar Greenwood was a Jew who, in his role as last Chief Secretary for Ireland, betrayed the British fighting men and gave Sinn Féin a winning position, reveals the real import of his letter as an unconvincing effort to recruit Feetham to bolster his far-fetched theories.

Feetham, who had been a member of the South African Unionist Party, retained close friendships with many prominent Conservatives in England.[10]

7   Memorandum on Mr Justice Feetham – Chairman of the Boundary Commission, PRONI CAB 6/97, Sept. 1924.
8   Sir James Craig to D. D. Reid, PRONI CAB 92/11/1, 6 June 1924.
9   After the First World War a mandate was granted to the United Kingdom to administer Palestine.
10   Paul Canning, *British Policy towards Ireland 1921–1941* (Oxford, 1985), p. 93.

When Lord Selbourne, who later emerges as a Conservative diehard on the boundary issue, was British High Commissioner in South Africa, Feetham was his legal adviser. It was Curtis who had put forward Feetham's name for the chairmanship of the Boundary Commission,[11] and when he first arrived in England on the business of the Commission, Feetham stayed with Curtis.[12] It was commonly recognised that Curtis and Feetham held similar views on imperial consolidation. As a South African witness put it, 'These two hunt in couples, and are politically sympathetic.'[13] Following Feetham's appointment, Curtis could not disguise his gratification that the choice of chairman was in perfect accord with converging Unionist and Conservative interests. 'Feetham,' he wrote to Churchill, 'is just the Chairman you wanted, of conservative temperament, a man who could be relied upon to reject the preposterous and extravagant claims being advanced by the Free State.' Upon Feetham's appointment, Curtis sent him a three-word telegram the import of which could not be mistaken: 'England expects. Moot.'[14] In March 1924, one of its agents, A. H. McCartan, told the Free State Boundary Bureau that Curtis held the view, with grave implications for the Nationalist case, that the Boundary Commission would be obliged to operate on the basis of conditions as they were when it was actually in session, not as they had been at the time of the Treaty.[15] The distinction drawn by Curtis between the political and economic circumstances of late 1921 and those prevailing in 1924 and 1925 proved to have a considerable effect on the interpretation by Feetham of the weight to be attached to the qualification to be placed on the wishes of the inhabitants by

11   On 5 June 1924, David Reid, Ulster Unionist MP for Down told Sir James Craig that 'we may take it that Feetham was the nominee of Curtis'. Reid to Craig, PRONI CAB 9 Z/1/1. See Jones, 27 May 1924: 'Saw Cope who tells me that Curtis has got the PM's consent to telegraph to South Africa inviting Feetham to act as chairman of the Boundary Commission', Thomas Jones, in Keith Middlemas (ed.), *Whitehall Diary* vol. 3 (London, 1971), p. 232.

12   Geoffrey Hand in F. X. Martin and F. J. Byrne (eds), *Eoin MacNeill: The Scholar Revolutionary 1867–1945* (Shannon, 1973), p. 220.

13   Memorandum on Feetham, PRONI CAB 6/97, Sept. 1924.

14   Curtis to Churchill, Curtis MS 89, Bodleian Library, Oxford, 19 Aug. 1924. The telegram is a reference to Lord Nelson's celebrated order to his fleet before the Battle of Trafalgar: 'England expects every man to do his duty.' The suggestion was that Feetham knew his duty to those who appointed him. 'Moot' was a reference to the meetings of the 'Round Table' which concerned itself with imperial unity, and of which Feetham and Curtis were members. Before 1914, Feetham had been involved 'to a modest extent' in its deliberations on Irish affairs. See Hand, in Martin and Byrne, *Scholar Revolutionary*, p. 220.

15   Report of A. H. McCartan to Boundary Bureau, Boundary Bureau Papers, NAI, McCartan File, 11 Mar. 1924. For Curtis, see Deborah Lavin, *From Empire to International Commonwealth: A Biography of Lionel Curtis* (Oxford, 1995).

'economic and geographic conditions'. Feetham's dependence on the views of Curtis is most plainly suggested in the decision by the former not to hold plebiscites. Before he left the Colonial Office, Curtis expressed his opposition to plebiscites in the border counties in a memorandum which came into Feetham's hands.[16] In this memorandum, Curtis urged that Feetham be advised by the British Government of the dangers that would attend the holding of border plebiscites. The final report of the proceedings of the Boundary Commission shows Feetham resolutely defending the position espoused by his friend Curtis and preferring to ascertain the wishes of the inhabitants by having recourse to any expedient to avoid plebiscites: census returns, the results of elections and listening to what 'the representative people of districts say'.[17]

Among the economic and geographic conditions which had been generated since the Treaty, were the appearance of a Free State customs barrier on 1 April 1923, and the construction in the Mourne Mountains of the Silent Valley reservoir to supply water to Belfast, Portadown and Banbridge. The Silent Valley scheme had been in contemplation since 1893, and minor work on it had proceeded through the years without urgency. In 1923, however, with a boundary commission in prospect, the contract was signed, and Carson travelled from England to lay the foundation stone.[18]

In her perceptive discussion of Feetham's interpretation of the boundary clause, Margaret O'Callaghan finds it incredible that the location of a new reservoir to supply Belfast, not yet finished, could have become an argument for maintaining the existing border.[19] Just as incredible was another Unionist argument based on the geography of the seventeenth-century plantation, and advanced by the Honourable Irish Society. This argument was what O'Callaghan describes as 'an alleged anterior geographic definition of the border, one laid down in the old parchment of plantation, [which] was used to claim parts of Donegal and counter the wishes of inhabitants for the inclusion of Derry City in the Free State.'[20]

A consideration of changed circumstances over four years would also influence the interpretation of the boundary clause as a whole. The lapse of

16   See Kevin Matthews, *Fatal Influence: The Impact of Ireland on British Politics 1920–1925* (Dublin, 2004), p. 108.

17   Geoffrey Hand (ed.), *Report of the Irish Boundary Commission 1925* (Shannon, 1969), Appendix 1, pp. 22–41.

18   A. T. Q. Stewart, *Edward Carson* (Dublin, 1981), p. 128.

19   Margaret O'Callaghan, 'Old parchment and water: The Boundary Commission of 1925 and the copperfastening of the Irish Border', *Bullán: An Irish Studies Journal* Vol. IV, No. 2 (Notre Dame, 1999), p. 40.

20   Ibid., p. 44.

time since 1921 had given the six-county state an identity it did not have when Article 12 was drawn up. Feetham would be impressed by the idea that by 1925, this entity had acquired prescriptive rights not envisaged by the architects of the Treaty, and that as it was four years in existence as a recognisable political entity, significant interference with its territory could not be justified. Feetham being a judge, as Oliver MacDonagh reminds us, he naturally tended to be 'crabbed in by statutory interpretation and respectful of visible institutions'.[21]

The temper of British politics in 1924 may well have influenced the appointment of Feetham. It may at first glance appear surprising that MacDonald's Labour Government should have appointed a Conservative and an imperialist unless it is realised that MacDonald's views on the Ulster question, were, like those of Curtis, Feetham, Churchill and Baldwin, firmly fixed within an empire and commonwealth framework. He was as anxious that Northern Ireland should be subject to only minimal changes to its territory. This is clear from a letter he wrote to Lady Londonderry, wife of the Northern Ireland Minister of Education, appealing to her to use her influence with the Northern Ireland Cabinet to facilitate the formation of the Boundary Commission by appointing a commissioner by the end of September 1924. Another purpose of the letter to Lady Londonderry, with whom MacDonald had formed a close relationship, was to reassure her that the Commission would represent no substantial danger to the territory of Northern Ireland, since only rectification of the boundary was contemplated. His Government could not, he told her, say this publicly, since this would 'only be jumping from the frying pan into the fire'.[22] Feetham's appointment, however, may be seen as an effective tactic in warding off criticism from a host of right-wing politicians and agencies becoming increasingly hostile to the idea of a boundary commission, whose findings might modify the 1920 boundary settlement to the detriment of the Unionist state. Prominent Conservative newspapers lent their support to Conservative politicians in their assault on Article 12 as a betrayal of the northern state. In April 1924, Lord Rothermere's *Daily Mail* carried editorials openly advocating the breaking of the Treaty in respect of the Boundary Commission. In May, *The Times* warned the British Government that any suggestion that 'Ulster is going to cede counties or towns' should be ruled out in advance, although this course of action would have violated the Treaty.[23] The appointment of a man with Feetham's credentials was to deprive Tory attacks of much of their force. The impartiality or otherwise of Feetham's discharge of his duties as Chairman of the Boundary Commission did not

21 Oliver MacDonagh, *Ireland: The Union and its Aftermath* (Dublin, 2003), p. 117.

22 Hugh Montgomery Hyde, *The Londonderrys: A Family Portrait* (London, 1979), p. 159.

23 *Daily Mail*, 30 Apr. 1924; *The Times*, 2 May 1924.

become a matter of urgent public debate until after the broad outlines of his award were revealed in an inspired 'forecast' published by *The Morning Post* on 7 November 1925. A proper evaluation of Feetham's work was not possible until 1969, when the full report of the Commission was published for the first time, having been suppressed in 1925 by agreement of the three governments at the insistence of Cosgrave.[24]

Some versions of his role as chairman present Feetham as a compliant instrument of British policy. Frank Gallagher, perhaps his most trenchant critic on the basis of circumstantial evidence, describes him as acting throughout 'as he had been told to act by the most influential British statesmen, many of them of the party which had given him his first chance in life'.[25] Nicholas Mansergh, on the other hand, dissents from the idea, common in Nationalist accounts, that 'Feetham deliberately weighted the scales against the Irish Free State and its representative on the Commission'. Mansergh finds the key to Feetham in 'high integrity allied to inflexibility', and devotion to right principles as he conceived them. In common with Geoffrey Hand, Mansergh argues that no direct evidence has been brought forward to throw doubt on the integrity of Feetham's conduct. Far from being susceptible to behind-the-scenes British pressures, he was, Mansergh asserts, 'concerned above all to insist upon his own only too well-weighted restrictive interpretation of the Commission's terms of reference.'[26] In the absence of further evidence, it is impossible to pronounce definitively on whether Feetham was subject to direct political persuasion in his general interpretation of Article 12 and in his ultimate decisions. It is, however, difficult to be as confident as Mansergh was that he was not susceptible to such British influence as was, for example, exerted by men like Curtis.

Eoin MacNeill, who had worked with Feetham on the Commission, did not question his personal integrity, but he had no doubt that Feetham, in interpreting the boundary clause, 'imported . . . a new governing and dominant condition into Article 12, a political one, a political consideration which was made a dominant consideration . . . and which he could only read into it by a kind of constructional effort'. MacNeill was referring to Feetham's decision, which was utterly to undermine the Nationalist case, that if accommodating the wishes of the inhabitants were to place the Government of

24 Eamon Phoenix, *Northern Nationalism: Nationalist Politics, Partition and the Catholic Minority in Northern Ireland, 1890–1940* (Belfast, 1994), p. 330.

25 Frank Gallagher, *The Indivisible Island: The History of the Partition of Ireland* (London, 1959), p. 175.

26 Hand, *Report* (1969), Introduction; Nicholas Mansergh, *Nationalism and Independence: Selected Irish Papers* (Cork, 1997), p. 218.

Northern Ireland 'in a distinctively less advantageous position than it occupied under the Act of 1920, then the political consideration was to override the wishes of the inhabitants'.[27] MacNeill was arguing, plausibly enough, that the text of the Treaty gave no warrant for Feetham's introduction of a gratuitous political argument. The approach adopted by Feetham here was bound to generate suspicion that he was determined to use any arguments, even bad ones, to justify his restrictive interpretation of Article 12. This suspicion is reinforced by the consideration that when it suited the latter purpose, he could insist that the only basis for judgement was the wording of Article 12, taken in isolation from the context in which it had arisen.

MacNeill made an impressive case when he challenged Feetham's canons of construction, both in principle and in detail, but only months after these had become the basis for the final Commission report, and Feetham's decision had become a *fait accompli*, almost totally destructive of the Free State's position. MacNeill's case would have been more impressive, and more effective, had it been made on 11 September 1925, when Feetham provided him with a memorandum outlining his interpretation of Article 12. This Memorandum[28] effectively demolishing the Free State case for significant boundary change, contained all the detail MacNeill needed to make him aware of the shape the final report would take. It is one of the enigmas surrounding MacNeill's role as a Commissioner that he did not put in a series of detailed objections to Feetham's Memorandum. By not doing so, he could be deemed to have given both Fisher and Feetham reason to assume that he approved of its general outline. His only recorded observation, made just over a week after he received Feetham's Memorandum was that he did not accept the Commission's right to transfer Free State territory to Northern Ireland.[29] Then, in mid-October, he and the other two Commissioners acted together to give the Commission report its final form. It was only on 20 November that MacNeill resigned from the Commission, to the surprise of Feetham and Fisher. His unsuitability for the post of Commissioner was thus made manifest. After his resignation from the Commission, Cosgrave told Baldwin and other members at a meeting in London in November 1925 that 'MacNeill's conduct [had been] deplorable. He was a philosopher and had been out of touch with the feeling on the border'.[30] Unlike Feetham and Fisher, MacNeill was no more than a part-time commissioner, at the same time functioning as Free State Minister for

27 *Dáil Debates*, Vol. 13, Col. 801, 24 Nov. 1925.
28 Feetham's Memorandum to MacNeill and Fisher is reproduced in full in Hand, *Report* (1969), pp. 32–68.
29 MacNeill Memorandum, MacNeill Papers, LAI/119, 7–25 UCDA, 19 Sept. 1925.
30 Jones, *Whitehall Diary* vol. 3, p. 238.

Education, and as a consequence 'erratic in attendance' and 'unpredictable in his attendance to the Commission's business'.[31] Cosgrave does not seem to have realised that he himself, as head of the Free State Executive Council, had questions to answer. It was, after all, he who had appointed MacNeill and retained his services as a government minister while expecting him to accomplish a task for which he was not qualified by training or expertise.

II THE ROLE OF FRANCIS BOURDILLON

The staffing of the Commission might well have given rise to justified uneasiness among Nationalists, in particular Feetham's appointments. Major Boger, the British member of the Commission for Upper Silesia from 1920 to 1923, became Feetham's Chief Technical Assistant. Much more significant in this regard was the emergence of Francis Bourdillon as Secretary to the Commission. His appointment to this post gave him a central role in its deliberations, and a significant influence on their outcome.[32] Bourdillon, by then a leading authority on boundary disputes, had represented the Foreign Office on the Commission that determined the German-Polish frontier, in Upper Silesia (1920–2). In 1923, he wrote a paper, which he hoped to publish, casting doubt on the case being put forward by the Free State Boundary Bureau in its *Handbook of the Ulster Question*, for substantial territorial adjustments involving major reductions in the territory of Northern Ireland. He was anxious to give the British Colonial Office the benefit of his expert advice on an appropriate response to the Irish boundary question. With this in view he sent his paper to Lionel Curtis in December 1923. He was anxious that Curtis and others with responsibility for Irish affairs should have the benefit of the experience he had gained since early 1920, as such experience was not available in any form other than Foreign Office dispatches.[33] Bourdillon's main criticism of the Irish Boundary Bureau case, prepared under the direction of Kevin O'Shiel, Secretary to the Bureau, was that it was based on the assumption, not

31 Nicholas Mansergh, *The Unresolved Question: The Anglo-Irish Settlement and its Undoing, 1912–1972* (London, 1991), p. 236.

32 Eoin MacNeill tried to offset the preponderance of vital Commission personnel from backgrounds scarcely likely to make them receptive to Nationalist points of view. He suggested the appointment of an Irish parliamentary draftsman to the staff of the Commission. He reported to his colleagues on the Free State Executive Council that Feetham had rejected this proposal. MacNeill felt this rejection merited a letter of protest. NAI, D/T S1801K, 1 Dec. 1924.

33 Bourdillon's paper may be studied in the Colonial Office Papers, PRO CO/739/25/60802, dated 7 Dec. 1923.

well-founded, that the Irish Boundary Commission was intended, by the terms of Article 12 of the Anglo-Irish Treaty, to take into consideration the wishes of the inhabitants of extensive areas of Northern Ireland (but not of the Free State) in which there was any doubt about their wishes. Bourdillon took the much more restrictive view of the scope of Article 12, a view later to be taken by Feetham, that 'clause 12 of the Treaty as it stands might equally be interpreted as implying that the scope of the Boundary Commission should be restricted to the neighbourhood of the boundary'. Drawing on his European experience of the terms of reference and operation of such bodies, Bourdillon drew a distinction between a boundary commission, which was concerned 'with the drawing of a convenient frontier, and a plebiscite commission which was intended to apply self-determination to a large area'.[34]

Since European precedents and terms of reference for commissions were persuasive in the Irish case, Bourdillon made the significant observation, inimical to the Free State claims on large tracts of Northern Ireland, including counties (Tyrone and Fermanagh) and significant areas of others (south Armagh and south Down), that 'a transference of territory covering as large an area a whole county, or localities as important in themselves as Derry or Newry, would have been quite outside the scope of the boundary commissions set up under the treaty of Versailles, St Germain, etc'. He pointed out that the German-Polish Boundary Commission, on which he had served, took the view that it had no power to displace any village or any property of national importance such as a coal mine or an important factory, except with the agreement of the two interested states. This view, he recalled, was upheld by the Conference of Ambassadors, acting in the name of the principal Allied Powers. On Bourdillon's reasoning, it followed that if large territorial changes were proposed by an Irish commission with European precedents in mind, these changes would need the agreement of the two interested parties, Great Britain and the Irish Free State. Bourdillon was, however, prepared to acknowledge that the terms of Article 12 of the Anglo-Irish Treaty, with its primary emphasis on the drawing of a border 'in accordance with the wishes of the inhabitants' seemed to indicate that an Irish commission 'must have wider powers than an ordinary Boundary Commission'.

Bourdillon made his own preference clear. Again, this was fundamentally contrary to what the Free State Boundary Bureau had in mind. The interpretation, he suggested, that 'will be found to interpret most truly the

---

34 The year after Bourdillon submitted his paper to Curtis, the Marquess of Salisbury was to make a similar distinction: between a commission which deals 'with the mere adjustment of boundaries', and one which deals with the transfer of territory, which he described as 'another and a different thing'. *Hansard*, House of Lords, Vol. 59, Col. 595, 8 Oct. 1924.

intention of Article 12' would be realised in a commission 'empowered to deal with an area of limited extent on either side of the existing frontier'. The area in question would be 'a frontier zone, from 5 to 15 miles on both sides of the present boundary, inside which a new frontier map would be drawn as nearly as possible in accordance with the wishes of its inhabitants'. Such an interpretation of Article 12, which Bourdillon considered fair, balanced and in conformity with the intention of the framers of the Article, would mean, as he put it, 'the application of self-determination to the boundary area, but quite frankly not mean its application to the whole of the area in which a majority for the Free State might result.' It would thus not mean general self-determination.

A few observations on the advice tendered to Curtis by Bourdillon in this document are pertinent. Firstly, if followed, it would undermine, if not demolish, the two main foundations on which the Free State case to the Commission were to be based: the transfer of large areas, possibly up to 35 per cent of Northern Ireland, to the Free State, and the non-interference with the territory of the Free State. Secondly, the restrictive interpretation of Article 12 advanced by Bourdillon and his argument for a two-way transfer of territory, were to form the essential basis for Feetham's determination of the boundary. There is a sense in which no important difference would have been made to the outcome had Bourdillon framed Feetham's report.[35] Thirdly, Bourdillon's advice on the scope of the Irish Commission was taken extremely seriously by Curtis. He asked Sir Geoffrey Whiskard of the Colonial Office to circulate confidential copies to Sir Mark Sturgis, Assistant Under-Secretary of State for Irish Services; Sir James Masterson Smith, Permanent Under-Secretary of State for Colonies; Sir John Anderson, Permanent Under-Secretary of State at the Home Office and Thomas Jones, Deputy Secretary to the Cabinet. Whiskard described Bourdillon's document as 'valuable and interesting'; Sturgis found it 'most interesting'; Masterson Smith, having read it thoroughly, described it as 'a document of exceptional interest'; and Anderson considered it 'very interesting'.[36]

These first readers took exception to only one element in the Bourdillon document: its dismissal of the notion that a new frontier, based on the wishes of inhabitants could be credibly based on religious statistics. Bourdillon's experience in Europe had convinced him of the impossibility of doing this. Instead, he suggested that plebiscites in the areas under review constituted the only appropriate means of proceeding fairly. Whiskard, however, rejected this idea, finding it impossible to conceive that 'the holding of a plebiscite in a neutrally controlled area . . . will ever be possible', and claiming that the discussions

35   Bourdillon's report should be compared to Hand, *Report* (1969), especially 'Chairman's Memorandum', pp. 32–68.
36   PRO CO 739/25/60802.

of the methods of such a plebiscite 'merely confuses the issue'.[37] Whiskard's view was to prevail in 1924–5 when the Colonial Office rejected the notion of border plebiscites, taking the view that these could not be undertaken without grave risk of riot and disorder. Bourdillon completed his analysis with a pertinent comment which would prove to be sadly prophetic: 'The acceptance by both parties of the interpretation which is to be finally placed on Article 12 will obviously depend entirely on the confidence in the impartiality of the persons selected to give it.' This measure of acceptance was never to be realised. Neither was Feetham able to match in full the description of the ideal boundary commission chairman provided by Austen Chamberlain in February 1922: 'Some man of high standing, of unimpeachable reputation, of known sagacity, who must command the confidence of all parties.'[38] The disappointment of Nationalists with Feetham's performance came early. As they observed the trend of his questions and observations, many of them came to believe that whatever the evidence from witnesses might suggest to him, he was, from the start, as E. M. Stephens of the Free State Boundary Bureau expressed it, 'bent on mere rectification', and 'intended to use gerrymandered District Electoral Divisions to their [the Nationalists'] disadvantage'.[39] It seemed to many Nationalist observers that Feetham tended to find overwhelming obstacles in the way of their proposals for self-determination, as when he remarked, for example, that the transfer of the predominantly Nationalist city of Londonderry to the Free State would be 'a serious surgical operation.'[40]

III DOUBTS AND UNCERTAINTIES

Given the difficulty of divining Feetham's motives with certainty, his role as Chairman is best examined by considering his lengthy report on the work of the Commission, particularly the considerations which led him to formulate the conclusions he did, and the conflict in every significant respect between his interpretation of Article 12 and the construction placed upon it by those who argued the Nationalist case. It is fair to recognise that there could not be any interpretation of the boundary clause which could have enjoyed the general assent of even constitutional lawyers, nor was there any provision in the Treaty or elsewhere, which might have provided definitive guidance on its meaning or application. After he had ceased to be a member of the Boundary

---

37 Whiskard Memo., PRO CO 739/25/60802, 7 Dec. 1923.
38 Hand, in Martin and Byrne, *Scholarly Revolutionary*, p. 219.
39 Report of E. M. Stephens to the Free State Executive Council, NAI S1801 M, 22 May 1925.
40 Ibid.

Commission, and was therefore able to speak freely on a subject with which he had been closely and frustratingly engaged for well over a year, MacNeill reflected dispassionately on the problems associated with the interpretation of Article 12. From his experience, 'the thing that made the Boundary Commission fruitless was the defective character of Article 12 of the Treaty.' What MacNeill was suggesting was that Article 12, as formulated, was not an adequate instrument for dealing with the situation which made its inclusion in the Treaty necessary. The fact that an Article covering a boundary revision was included 'admitted by implication that the boundary fixed in the Act of 1920 was indefensible and unconstitutional'. MacNeill regarded it as a major flaw in the Article that it gave the British Government the central role in determining the nature of the remedy to be applied. By Article 12, he remarked, the British Government, 'itself responsible for the Act of 1920 and a principal in the controversy, was made the umpire and the deciding judge.' MacNeill remarked on another 'grave defect' in Article 12. This concerned the fact that the wishes of the inhabitants were to prevail in so far as these were compatible with economic conditions as well as geographical ones. 'This,' he pointed out, 'did not allow the inhabitants to be judges of their own economic advantage, and made it possible to hold that some undefined economic condition could override the wishes of inhabitants.'[41]

MacNeill amplified this point later, in memoirs he dictated between 1932 and 1940. He observed that the will of the inhabitants was ascertainable, but that the economic and geographical considerations 'were left entirely to be decided by the Commission in accordance with any opinion that its members might happen to hold'. He added that any decision was bound to be 'dominated by the voice of the Chairman representing the British Government'.[42] A third defect in Article 12, also bearing on the question of interpretation, was that in the absence of any specific provision for a plebiscite, the Boundary Commission was 'to draw across the north of Ireland a political boundary based chiefly on religious statistics', to MacNeill's mind 'a barbarous contrivance'.[43] He might well have observed that even the wishes of the inhabitants were to be decided not by themselves but by the Commissioners, which for practical purposes meant Feetham, on the basis that religious affiliation was a sure indication of political preference. He might also have drawn attention to two further defects in Article 12. The first, a vital one, was that the Article failed to

41 Statement by Eoin MacNeill about his intention to contest a Senate seat, MacNeill Papers, UCDA, LAI/F/2, 16 Oct. 1925.
42 Extracts from the memoirs of Eoin MacNeill, Hand, in Martin and Byrne, *Scholarly Revolutionary*, p. 270.
43 Statement, UCDA, LAI/ F /2, 16 Oct. 1925.

indicate who exactly were the inhabitants whose wishes were to be considered, and where exactly they lived. Newspaper comment on the first sessions of the Commission made it evident that there was general public confusion about this subject. The London correspondent of the *Freeman's Journal* had no doubt that the first task of the Commissioners would be to decide the manner in which the wishes of the inhabitants were to be ascertained. 'Dr MacNeill,' this Correspondent remarked, 'will presumably demand that a plebiscite shall be taken in the whole six-county area, while Mr Fisher will probably insist that only the wishes of the parishes which are situated immediately along the present frontier line are to be consulted. . . . Much will depend on the unit of area selected for taking a plebiscite.'[44] The second defect was the omission of a timetable for setting up the Commission. All these considerations were bound to mean that northern Nationalists were likely to be treated as arbitrarily as they had been by the Partition Act of 1920. A thorough application of the principle of self-determination in 1925 as a compensation for its setting aside in 1920 was not easy to visualise under the terms of Article 12.

It is difficult not to suspect that the ambiguity surrounding the meaning and effect of Article 12 was a calculated thing on the part of the British signatories of the Treaty. A clear and explicit formulation of a boundary Article, with precise terms of reference for a commission and clear definitions of such key terms as 'the inhabitants', the means to be employed in ascertaining their wishes, the areas and sizes of units to be considered, of the relative weight to be attached to democratic choice, geography and economics, would have eliminated the conditions for possible controversy, discouraged false hopes, and inhibited fruitless political activity. It would also, however, as the British negotiators were certainly aware, have irrevocably alienated either the Ulster Unionists on the one hand, or the southern authorities and northern Nationalists on the other. Indeed, all the evidence suggests that the very ambivalence of Article 12 was its greatest asset in the view of British politicians who negotiated the Treaty. Had the transfer of counties or other large units of territory been provided for in a boundary clause, there was the virtual certainty of violent Unionist outrage and resistance of an extra-legal kind. Had a minimalist rectification been specified, it would have been politically impossible for the Irish plenipotentiaries to sign the Treaty, something which was of paramount concern to the British Government. The actual formulation of Article 12 made it possible to get a treaty and leave the problems of interpreting its most troublesome Article to be solved by a commission meeting in an unspecified future time. It also made it possible for both Unionists and Nationalists to claim that its terms were essentially in accord with their

44 *Freeman's Journal*, 6 Nov. 1924.

respective points of view. The Unionists could make their claim with greater assurance, because successive British Government representatives privately intimated to their leaders that the restrictive interpretation of Article 12 was the only sensible one, indeed the only feasible one. The fact that the British negotiators' claim to know what the Article meant was at odds with public confessions that they did not, raises large questions about the *bona fides* of those involved in these exercises. This applies to Lloyd George in particular. In his anxiety to get an Anglo-Irish treaty, and to be hailed as the man who had thus achieved what no British Prime Minster had even come close to doing, he had devised a formula which passed muster in the short term, without undue concern for its future consequences, which he left others to face.

Other circumstances surrounding the Commission suggest that the majority of British Conservative politicians, as well as the Commissioner appointed on behalf of Northern Ireland, when they found this expedient, in the light of changing political circumstances in Britain, were determined to modify the role originally assigned to it in Article 12, and conventionally understood to belong to boundary commissions elsewhere. Eoin MacNeill pointed out that 'the duties of the Boundary Commission were entirely of a judicial character, and had no proper concern with negotiations or diplomacy'. The judicial character of the Commission required that its members kept their deliberations confidential. At the first formal meeting of the Commission in London, 6–7 November 1924, all three Commissioners formally decided that none of them would make any statement as to the work of the Commission 'either to any government or any individual without first consulting his colleagues'.[45] J. R. Fisher, the Northern Ireland member, in contravention of his obligation to preserve secrecy, kept his friends in the Unionist Party informed of significant developments while the Commission was still sitting. He provided valuable and frequent reports on the progress of the Commission to the wife of Sir David Reid, Unionist MP for east Down and Chairman of the Ulster Unionist Party at Westminster. Reid had an interesting and suggestive background: he had been a contemporary of Feetham and Curtis at New College, Oxford.[46] In the course of a Commons debate on the Irish Boundary Bill in September and October 1924, Reid proposed two amendments to Article 12 of the Anglo-Irish Treaty. One would have ruled out the transfer of any territory between the two parts of Ireland 'without the consent of the parliament to whom jurisdiction over that territory has been granted by the Imperial Parliament'. His second amendment would have defined the phrase 'in accordance with the wishes of the inhabitants' in Article 12 as meaning 'the

45   Hand in, Martin and Byrne, *Scholarly Revolutionary*, p. 232.
46   Alvin Jackson, *Home Rule: An Irish History 1800–2000* (London, 2003), p. 211.

consent of the parliament of the Irish Free State and of the parliament of Northern Ireland'.[47] In the summer of 1925, however, Fisher had written to Mrs Reid that all was 'going smoothly' from the Unionist point of view, and that 'the more extravagant (Nationalist) claims have been practically wiped out'. He told her that the Commission would be transferring 'border townlands for the most part', and that as a result of its work 'a stronger and more compact' northern state would enlarge, 'with not inconsiderable bits added'.[48]

As late as September 1925, Craig told the northern House of Commons that he knew nothing of what was happening in the Commission although however much he knew, he would scarcely have considered it opportune to say so.[49] In late October 1925 with the proceedings nearing their end, the British Government did not appear to have been as well informed as Mrs Reid. On 25 October, L. S. Amery, Colonial and Dominions Secretary, submitted a memorandum to the Cabinet in which he suggested that the town of Newry and appreciable areas of Tyrone and Fermanagh might be transferred to the south.[50] Around the same time, according to Keith Middlemas, 'the British Cabinet remained under the impression, which they shared with the Free Staters, that the report would be very favourable to the south.'[51] Even after the Commission had decided on its award, Austen Chamberlain, British Secretary of State for Foreign Affairs, told Cosgrave that the British Government 'had no information as to the new boundary line proposed'.[52] It seemed, however, that the northern Unionist leadership was more enlightened. When Sir William Joynson-Hicks, British Home Secretary, visited Belfast on 4 November 1925, he found Craig in an uncharacteristically cooperative mood. Craig 'not only agreed to abide by a reasonable settlement, but urged the Unionist members of the northern parliament from the border areas to do likewise'. The only conclusion one can come to from this, as Canning observes, is that Craig's surprising good humour 'was based on the knowledge that Ulster had nothing to fear from the Commission'.[53] As early as mid-September 1923, Craig had been assured by Sir David Reid, on the basis of 'very private' information that could have come only from a source within the Commission, that 'the Free State contentions as regards the construction of the boundary

47 *Hansard*, House of Commons, Vol. 177, Col. 50, 30 Sept. 1925; 2 Oct. 1925.
48 St Ervine, *Craigavon: Ulsterman* (London, 1949), pp. 499–500.
49 Hand, in Martin and Byrne, *Scholarly Revolutionary*, p. 231.
50 Canning, *British Policy*, p. 103.
51 Jones, *Whitehall Diary* vol. 3, p. 236.
52 Conference at No. 10 Downing Street, NAI DT S4720 A, 26 Nov. 1925.
53 Canning, *British Policy*, p. 105.

clauses of the Treaty have been definitely turned down and that it is now a question of alterations of frontier'.[54]

The outcome described by Fisher and Reid was fortunate for more than the Unionists. British Cabinet papers show that had Feetham's report significantly favoured the Nationalist case, Baldwin's Government would have dishonoured or deferred its Treaty obligations in respect of Article 12. In the course of a visit to Belfast during the Parliamentary summer recess of 1924, Baldwin promised as much to Craig, telling the latter that if he practised public moderation, the British Government would support him if the decision of the Boundary Commission proved unacceptable to northern Unionists.[55] As early as 6 September 1924, two months before he succeeded Ramsay MacDonald as Prime Minister, Baldwin had told Edward Wood, the Conservative politician who later became Viscount Halifax, that 'if the Commission should give away counties, then of course Ulster couldn't accept it and we should back her'.[56] Baldwin, however, was sure that provision could be made for a boundary determination which would meet with the approval of northern Unionism. 'The Government,' he assured Wood, 'will nominate a proper representative for Northern Ireland and we hope that he and Feetham will do what is right.'[57] The last phrase suggests that Baldwin saw Feetham and the representative for Northern Ireland as having a duty to act jointly less in a judicial than in a political capacity to protect the essential integrity of the 1920 Unionist state.

On 28 October 1925, the British Cabinet decided that if Feetham's award were so favourable to Nationalists that it could not be implemented without 'grave risk of widespread disorders and possibly bloodshed' arising from a Unionist revolt, the Government would be free to inform the Free State

> that in the interests of Ireland as much as of this country decisive action could not immediately be taken [to enforce the award] and that, while fully recognising our obligations, we must have time to cast about for means of discharging them without entailing such consequences as no responsible Government could deliberately contemplate.[58]

Whatever Feetham did, short of satisfying Unionist demands, it is likely that the wishes of the inhabitants, qualified as these were in Article 12, by

54 Reid to Craig, PRONI CAB 9Z/11/1, 16 Sept. 1925.

55 Canning, *British Policy*, p. 98.

56 Ibid., p. 86.

57 Ibid.

58 Hand, in Martin and Byrne, *Scholarly Revolutionary*, pp. 244–5; see also Jones, *Whitehall Diary* vol. 3, p. 236.

economic and geographical constraints, would have been subject to a third, more decisive consideration: the political interests of the British Government as these were conditioned by the close ties of kinship and political outlook between northern Unionists, British Conservatives and Liberal Unionists, and by Unionist militancy, backed as this was by the considerable armed force supplied by the British authorities. The Boundary Commission, which had been envisaged as a strictly judicial tribunal by Article 12, acquired, over time, a political character, as British statesmen continued to anticipate how the Commission would have to interpret the Article, and in the end decided that its findings might have no practical effect in the face of political and military resistance. The strength of Unionist determination to ignore local majority wishes had been conveyed by Craig when he met Collins in February 1922. While Collins insisted that majorities must rule, 'Craig made it clear that Unionists would never abandon places such as Derry City and Enniskillen; he stressed their historic and sentimental importance to Protestants and ignored their Catholic majorities.'[59] In the Free State Senate on 17 October 1924, the Unionist Lord Glenavy recognised that whatever a judicially-based boundary commission might decide, the actual outcome would be politically determined. Glenavy could see 'no hope of finality in the findings of this Commission', because it seemed to him impossible that any government 'will be able to accept or submit to them'.[60] All of this reflects the variety of new political realities which had come to pass since 6 December 1921, when the Treaty was signed. The likelihood of merely minor changes to the boundary steadily increased in proportion to the length of time during which the boundary question was left in abeyance, to the growth of pro-Unionist sentiment in Great Britain, and of indifference and hostility to Irish Nationalism among influential British politicians.

IV FEETHAM'S PRINCIPLES OF INTERPRETATION AND THEIR APPLICATION

Feetham's role as boundary arbitrator had two aspects. The first of these concerned his enunciation of the general principles he believed should govern the interpretation of Article 12. The second was the application of these principles to the particular areas to which the Article appeared to him to refer. In the course of the Commission hearings over which he presided, some of these in London, some in the north, Feetham provided a detailed analysis of

59   Michael Laffan, *The Partition of Ireland 1911–25* (Dundalk, 1983), p. 93.
60   *Seanad Debates*, Vol. 3, Col. 1055, 17 Oct. 1924.

the contested questions Article 12 raised, and a series of answers to these questions. These answers formed the basis on which Feetham reached his conclusions about what Article 12 permitted and did not permit him to do, and which determined the nature of his final award. His interpretation of all the major issues to which Article 12 gave rise was uniformly unfavourable to the Nationalist point of view. One of his most vital decisions, conveyed at a hearing in London on 25 August 1925, confounded the expectations of those who put the Nationalist case. This decision was that Article 12 gave the Commission the power to transfer parts of the area within the jurisdiction of the Government of the Free State to 'the area under the joint jurisdiction of the Government of Great Britain and the Government of Northern Ireland'.[61] The significance of this decision, in its grave implications for the Nationalist demands, can scarcely be overestimated. If, as a consequence, any areas in east Donegal, north Cavan and north Monaghan were to be transferred to the northern jurisdiction, the portions of six-county territory bordering these would have to remain under the control of the northern government, whatever the wishes of their inhabitants might have been, or whatever economic considerations might have come into play. The transfer, for example, of the large portion of east Donegal, stretching from Muff in the north to below Saint Johnston in the south, which Feetham finally recommended, on the basis of his interpretation, meant that no part of Derry City or its western hinterland could be awarded to the Free State without converting the political map of north-west Ireland into an absurdity.

Feetham's interpretation of Article 12 as giving him power to shift the existing boundary line in either direction, and as providing him with no more and no less authority to take territory from the six-county side of the existing boundary and give it to the Free State than he had to take territory from the Free State and give it to Northern Ireland, seemed to the Free State side to rest on a mistaken reading of the Treaty as a whole. The conflict arising from Feetham's decision in this case suggests either an extreme lack of clarity in Article 12, or an inability or unwillingness on the part of one side or the other to discern its true meaning. Eoin MacNeill, at any rate, had no doubt that neither the terms of the Treaty as a whole, nor the purposes for which Article 12 had been included, gave a warrant for transferring any part of southern territory to the northern state. In a letter to Cosgrave in October 1925, MacNeill explained that Article 12 had been devised to solve the problems caused by the coercion since 1920 of Nationalist populations 'put against their will under the Ulster Unionist Government'. This, MacNeill suggested, was the only Ulster problem to be solved during the Treaty negotiations: there was

61   See Memorandum on the Boundary Question, Kennedy Papers UCDA P4/424, 19 Sept. 1925.

no claim 'for the transfer to Northern Ireland of any other part of the area of Ireland'. The area of Northern Ireland alone was in dispute. MacNeill's argument depended on a recognition of the intention of the parties to the Treaty negotiations, which was to give the Ulster Unionists the choice between an all-Ireland settlement which they rejected, and a boundary commission whose task would be to adjust the six-county territory as a remedy for Nationalist grievances. Such, MacNeill argued, was the context of fact in which the boundary provisions of the Treaty were to be read.[62] A careful reading of the relevant Treaty clauses tends to support MacNeill's position. The Treaty purported to set up a new state encompassing the entire island. It also permitted the six counties represented in the Northern Ireland Parliament to exclude themselves by invoking the earlier part of Article 12. It therefore seemed logical to conclude that the Treaty offered no justification for excluding from the Free State any area outside the six counties represented by the Northern Ireland Parliament, and that any transfer of territory had to be from north to south.

When on 7 November 1925 *The Morning Post* leaked the information that the Commission had recommended the transfer of Free State territory to the six counties, President Cosgrave, reflecting the view of his Government, told the Dáil that the provisions of Article 12 of the Treaty did not empower the Commission to do this. Cosgrave relied, as MacNeill was to do, on the circumstances with which the Commission was originally intended to deal, specifically the grievances of border Nationalists assigned by the 1920 Government of Ireland Act to a state they believed to be hostile to their welfare. Cosgrave, however, based his case against two-way transfers of territory mainly on the text of the Treaty. This gave the whole of Ireland recognition as the Irish Free State. It also contained a provision (Article 12) that if the Parliament of Northern Ireland elected to dissociate itself from the Free State, the Boundary Commission envisaged in the same clause was to determine the limits over which its powers should be exercisable. Until that determination was made, the powers of the Parliament and Government of the Free State remained in suspension over Northern Ireland, but would come into instant operation in any area assigned to the Free State by the Commission. Cosgrave's major point was that there was no corresponding arrangement 'whereby the powers of the government were in a state of suspension over any Free State territory and that therefore Northern Ireland could have no lawful claim on territory in the 26 counties, nor could the Boundary Commission act as if it did'.[63]

62   MacNeill to Cosgrave, MacNeill Papers UCDA LAI/F/299, 10 Oct. 1925.
63   *Dáil Debates*, Official Record, Vol. 13, Col. 635, 7 Nov. 1925.

As Cosgrave saw it, if the northern parliament wished for a complete dissociation from the jurisdiction of a 32-county Irish legislature, the area in which they had power under the Treaty to exercise jurisdiction should be 'cut down as nearly as possible to the area inhabited by those who desired the arrangement'. This, Cosgrave suggested, was what the high contracting parties to the Treaty had intended, but since the Commission had been set up 'a most scandalous campaign of intimidation and misrepresentation', a 'most indecent and flagrant violation of judicial procedure', had been engaged in by 'important personages in public life both in Great Britain and in the Six Counties' to influence the Commission to ignore the clear meaning and intent of the boundary clause.[64] If the Commission were a Court of Justice, Cosgrave added, 'it would be incumbent upon it to commit personages of very high station to imprisonment for flagrant contempt.'[65] Cosgrave made a further interesting point against the transfer of 26-county territory to Northern Ireland. His argument was based on the provisions of Article 15 of the Treaty. This outlined a set of arrangements to be made in the event of Northern Ireland electing to remain in the Free State system with its entire territory. The most significant of these was the provision of 'safeguards for minorities in Northern Ireland'. The minorities in this case would be Unionist. There was no comparable provision in the Treaty for the Nationalist, in case Northern Ireland elected to exclude itself. The reason for this, Cosgrave explained, was that in that event, a boundary commission was to be set up 'for the purpose, as was clearly indicated at the time, to consider what portions of Northern Ireland inhabited by those [Nationalist] minorities should be excluded from Northern Ireland'.[66] In effect, Cosgrave was arguing that the Boundary Commission should be regarded as a mechanism for upholding the rights of Nationalists who desired to be governed by a Dublin parliament, and had no relevance to those Loyalists in the 26 counties who did not. Feetham thought otherwise.

In emphasising the need to have regard to the intention of the Treaty-makers when interpreting Article 12, MacNeill and Cosgrave were arguing in conformity with the norms of international law. Cukwurah, in his study of the international law of boundaries, boundary tribunals and commissions writes:

> There are certain considerations which such a tribunal must regard as paramount to an effective settlement of a boundary question. The principal and controlling one should be to interpret and give effect to the boundary Treaty between the parties, if any, in the way it was mutually understood by its original negotiators. In other

64   Ibid., Col. 638.
65   Ibid., Col. 639.
66   Ibid., Col. 637.

words, the tribunal should not attempt to rely in great detail on every point advanced by the contending parties, especially if it is evident that these are largely hearsay in character, or that they reflect simply the present conditions in the boundary area. The tribunal should, therefore, seek in the boundary Treaty as a whole the general idea or scheme of compromise upon which the original negotiators were able to agree.[67]

Feetham's emphasis on the circumstances prevailing in 1924–5, rather than on the original context of Article 12, should be considered in the light of Cukwurah's comments.

In his memorandum on Article 12 Feetham had addressed the kind of argument advanced by MacNeill. Such an argument, Feetham pointed out, suggested that the boundary commission proviso to the Article 'should be read in effect as involving a penalty which the Government and Parliament of Northern Ireland were to suffer in the event of their deciding to remain outside the Irish Free State'. This, it must be said, is the interpretation that seems most in accord with common sense, and the one favoured by most impartial commentators up to the present. The British constitutional expert Hancock and the Irish historian F. S. L. Lyons saw the boundary clause in Article 12 as both a penalty on Unionists and as involving a one-directional process. Hancock wrote: 'If they [Unionists] should decide to maintain their separation from the Free State and their existing connexion with the United Kingdom, they must resign themselves to a rectification of their boundaries in accordance with the decision of a specifically constituted Boundary Commission.'[68] Lyons explains: 'On 12 November [Lloyd George] saw Griffith and explained that Ulster would be offered an all-Ireland Parliament with the right to opt out of it within 12 months. But if this right was exercised then Craig would have to accept a boundary commission.'[69] It must be noted that immediately following the Treaty even Craig seems to have seen the boundary clause in Article 12 as a penalty to be imposed on a recalcitrant six-county state. He wrote to Austen Chamberlain on 15 December 1921 that 'had it not been for the inclusion in the terms [of the Treaty] of a proposal to set up a Boundary Commission', he could have carried 'the people of Ulster' with him towards a peaceful settlement. He also regarded the boundary clause as 'tearing up' the 1920 partition.[70]

67 A. Oye Cukwurah, *The Settlement of Boundary Disputes in International Law* (Manchester, 1967), p. 231.

68 W. K. Hancock, *Survey of British Commonwealth Affairs Vol. 1: Problems of Nationality 1918–1936* (Oxford, 1937), p. 148.

69 F. S. L. Lyons, *Ireland since the Famine* (London, 1974), p. 434.

70 Jones, *Whitehall Dairy* vol. 3, pp. 189–90.

Feetham was able to sustain the contrary interpretation by concentrating his emphasis not on what the Treaty signatories intended to express, but mainly on the actual words of the Article, 'taken in their grammatical and ordinary sense', in which he remarked, there was nothing which limited the transfer process to the territory 'included within Northern Ireland by the Government of Ireland Act 1920'.[71] It was here that proponents of the Nationalist case found his arguments vulnerable. In a memorandum on the Boundary Commission prepared by Hugh Kennedy, Feetham was criticised for applying a too rigid, too narrow and literal canon of construction to the Article, such as might be appropriate to the interpretation of English private contracts, but not to an international instrument like the Treaty. Kennedy was able to cite the work of leading English authorities on international law to show that the generally-accepted rules for the interpretation of treaties were at odds with those Feetham had applied to Article 12. One such authority, Westlake, had pronounced that in interpreting treaties the important point was 'to get the real intention of the parties', and not to allow 'enquiry to be shackled by any rule of interpretation which may exist in a particular national jurisprudence but not generally accepted in the civilised world'.[72]

Another of Feetham's verdicts represented a decisive rejection of the Nationalist case that large transfers of territory, even involving entire counties and significant areas of others, were contemplated in Article 12 by those who had inserted it in the Treaty. On this central issue, whether Article 12 was minimalist in scope or whether it permitted extensive territorial revision, Feetham left no room for doubt. He decided that the scope of the Article was restricted to making relatively minor modifications of the existing boundary. Feetham nowhere explained how he had arrived at the conclusion that the remit of the Commission was confined to making relatively minor adjustments to the boundary as it stood. O'Callaghan describes Feetham's position on this core issue as deriving from a 'quasi-legalistic ruling based on highly dubious, indeed non-existent alleged legal precedents'.[73]

One Nationalist territorial demand prepared for the Commission by the Free State representatives was outlined in detail in a document composed for the Boundary Bureau by Kevin O'Shiel and the economist Joseph Johnston.

71   Hand, *Report* (1969), p. 39.

72   Cited in MacNeill to Cosgrave, UCAD, LAI/ F/299, 16 Oct. 1925. Hugh Kennedy: Legal Adviser to the Provisional Government (1922). Member of the Committee appointed to draft the Irish Free State Constitution (1922); Attorney General (1922–4). Chief Justice of the Irish Free State (1924–36). John Westlake (1828–1913): Liberal MP (1885–6) and social reformer. Professor of International Law at Cambridge (1888–1908) and one of the founders of The Institute of International Law.

73   O'Callaghan, 'Old parchment and water', p. 39.

What the document termed the 'Minimum Line' represented not only the minimum territory the Free State Government thought it was entitled to, but also the line most in accord with the three considerations in Article 12: the wishes of the inhabitants as well as geographic and economic considerations.[74] The minimum claim would diminish the area under the Northern Government by about a third, and its population by about a fifth. The adjustment would have placed 179,421 residents of the Belfast parliamentary area under the Dublin Government, while 266,135 Nationalists would remain under the Belfast Government. Feetham considered another Nationalist territorial claim formulated and signed by senior lay and clerical leaders from all the six counties apart from Antrim.[75] This claim, based primarily on the wishes of the population and on geographical factors, suggested the transfer to the south of an area comprising the whole of the counties of Tyrone and Fermanagh, the city and most of the county of Derry, more than half the county of Armagh and portions of county Down. This area, taken as a whole, comprised 258,617 Catholics and 205,528 members of other denominations, according to the Census of 1911.

Feetham dismissed both of these claims because they violated another principle he had decided upon. This principle provided that when the wishes of the inhabitants were to be ascertained, this was not to be done using large units of area such as counties or parliamentary divisions, or large, clearly-defined geographical regions such as Poor Law Unions, which ranged in population from 11,000 to over 50,000. Instead, Feetham decided to use 'the smallest areas which can fairly be entitled . . . to be considered separately'. These were district electoral divisions, about half of which had a population of over 1,000, with some having fewer than 500 people. Since there were Nationalist majorities in Tyrone and Fermanagh, and in other large geographical regions such as Derry and its hinterland, the larger the units used to measure the wishes of the inhabitants, the better it suited the Nationalist case. In the case of Fermanagh and Tyrone the relatively complex geographical distribution of Catholics and Protestants ensured that the use of a great number of small areas would make it impossible to transfer anything more than a series of small enclaves near the border. Feetham did not consider it appropriate that overall majorities in regions such as council or Poor Law Unions should be allowed to overrule the wishes of the majority of the inhabitants of large areas within these, even if, 'when the whole group of areas is taken together, the wishes of the majority of the inhabitants are shown on

74 'Our territorial demand at the Boundary Commission', Kennedy Papers P4/391/(7).
75 See Boundary Bureau Papers NAI Carton 31, 3/489.

the basis of regional statistics, to be in favour of . . . a transfer of jurisdiction'.[76] It would be difficult to show that this kind of reasoning and its consequences was in accord with the general tenor of Article 12, since it would render any reasonable implementation of its terms impossible.

Feetham's refusal, contrary to the expectations of many Nationalists, to consider at least some counties as units for determining the wishes of inhabitants had major implications for the Nationalist populations of Tyrone and Fermanagh. In the case of Tyrone, there were blocks of Catholic districts and blocks of Protestant districts, but the Catholic blocks, as he pointed out, 'are in the interior of the county, while the Protestant blocks are mostly near the borders of the county.' On the western side of County Tyrone along the Donegal border, districts containing Protestant majorities were continuous; the Catholic area at the western end of the Castlederg division was, Feetham observed, 'the only area which is conveniently placed from the point of view of making it possible to meet the wishes of the inhabitants by transferring them to the Free State without at the same time transferring Protestant districts.'[77] Had these Protestant districts been transferred to facilitate the wishes of Tyrone Catholics, they would have experienced on a smaller scale what the 1920 partition had done to large local Catholic majorities throughout the six counties.

Feetham's decision to concentrate on small, rather than large, units of measurement affected Nationalist claims in Fermanagh as well as in Tyrone. There was a Protestant majority in the northern and central parts of Fermanagh adjoining the southern border of Tyrone, and Feetham was adamant that 'it would be unjustifiable to use Catholic majorities in adjoining areas for overwhelming the Protestant majority in this area'. This Protestant district, he decided, must by virtue of its geographical position be recognised as a governing factor 'not only in respect of Co Fermanagh but also in respect of Co Tyrone'.[78] The inclusion of large Nationalist areas of Tyrone would, on geographical grounds, involve the inclusion in the Free State of the whole of County Fermanagh.[79]

In rejecting the large Nationalist claim, Feetham introduced a further refinement of the implications of the wishes of the inhabitants in Article 12. He observed that the adoption of the line suggested in the claim would, based on the 1911 Census figures, in turn based on religious affiliation which he himself had chosen to employ as reflecting the wishes of the inhabitants, gratify the wishes of 258,617 Nationalists and be contrary to the wishes of

76   Hand, *Report* (1969), p. 78
77   Ibid., p. 95.
78   Ibid., p. 99.
79   Ibid., p. 96.

205,528 Unionists. On this basis he suggested that on balance the number of persons whose wishes would be gratified would be 53,089. Thus 'in order to achieve the net result of pleasing 53,089 persons, it would be necessary to transfer 464,145 persons'.[80] This kind of formula could, and did, prove to be a double-edged weapon in Feetham's hands and could be used against him when he came to implement his own awards, particularly when these involved the transfer of areas from south to north. He transferred 30,295 acres with a population of 5,149 in east Donegal, adjacent to the Liberties of Derry, to the Northern Government. The result of this exercise, using his own cancelling formula, was that the net number of persons who would be pleased was 1,311, and that to achieve this net result, 5,149 persons had to be transferred, or nearly 3.92 times the net number pleased. The same kind of calculation would lead to similar statistics in the case of people transferred from north Monaghan to the northern jurisdiction. In this case he transferred 995 people, 660 of them Protestants, thus gratifying the presumed wishes of a net 325. The number transferred was therefore over 3 times the net number pleased. The total number of people Feetham thought it reasonable to transfer to the northern state was 7,594. Of these, 2,764 were Catholics. Applying Feetham's cancelling formula, 7,594 were transferred to please 2,066. This meant that the number transferred was 3.65 times the net number pleased. The same formula might be applied to the partition of 1920, which left the northern state with a population of 1,250,531. This was composed of 430,161 Catholics and 820,370 others. The net number pleased by this arrangement, according to Feetham's formula, was 390,209. To achieve this result, the British Government transferred 1,250,531 or 3.2 times the net number pleased, from Ireland as a whole to a new jurisdiction. Taking another view, 430,161 Catholics were placed in a jurisdiction they did not choose, to please a net 390,209 persons or 1.1 times the net number pleased. It may be significant that when Feetham came to make his final award, the Protestants he transferred to the north would have brought half as many Catholics with them, whereas the Catholics going to the Free State would have brought only one tenth of their number of Protestants.[81]

V MATHEMATICAL MAJORITIES MUST NOT PREVAIL

A related issue also had a large bearing on the Nationalist case. This concerned the question of what majority of inhabitants, estimated on the basis of census figures, should be regarded as sufficient to justify the alteration of

80 Ibid., p. 78.
81 Ibid., p. 146.

the existing boundary. The greater the majority required for transfer the less likelihood there was of the major change desired by Nationalists. Since Article 12 provided no guidance on this subject, although the practice adopted in other boundary settlements might have, Feetham decided that the determination of what constituted a sufficient majority of inhabitants to justify particular transfers was 'a question to be determined by the Commission'.[82] To answer this question Feetham laid down the principle, remarkable for its vagueness, that no case made to the Commission for transfer on the basis of the wishes of the inhabitants could succeed 'unless the majority in favour of the change appears to be a substantial majority, i.e., a majority representing a high proportion of the total number of persons entitled to rank as inhabitants'.[83] Feetham doubted that it was possible to lay down a definite rule 'for general application as to the percentage figure which should be regarded as sufficient to constitute a substantial majority'.[84]

In 1917, the British War Cabinet had taken a much less restrictive and more decisive view than Feetham was to take of the percentage of inhabitants that would be required to justify transfers, and of the units of territory to be considered. The War Cabinet instructed a committee of three to prepare a draft bill to amend the 1914 Home Rule Act. The Cabinet had initially decided that each of the six northern counties should have the option of remaining aloof from a Home Rule settlement. No county would be included under a Home Rule parliament unless 55 per cent of its electors voted for this in a plebiscite. The Committee appointed to draft the bill considered that a 55 per cent majority in the county plebiscites was open to obvious objection from the point of view of equity, since it represented 'an apparently trifling departure from ordinary constitutional procedure for the transparent purpose of enabling a minority in Tyrone and Fermanagh to decide the issue in those counties'. The minority the Committee had in mind in each case was likely to be Unionist. The Committee decided that a bare majority in each county should determine its political fate.[85] By contrast, Feetham's explicit abandonment

---

82   Ibid., p. 31.

83   Ibid., p. 32.

84   Ibid., p. 52.

85   Minutes of War Cabinet 16 Apr. 1917 (Cab 23/2); Cabinet papers 29 Sept. 1919 (Cab. 24/89) at Munich in 1938, Hitler asserted the right of Sudeten Germans to become citizens of the Third Reich. He persuaded the British and French Governments, anxious as they were to avoid war over the issue, to confront the Czechoslovak Government with their joint decision that Czechoslovakia 'must cede to Germany all territory where over 50 per cent of the inhabitants were Sudeten Germans'. The British Government would have been happier with 65 per cent as a guide. See Telford Taylor, *Munich: The Price of Peace* (London, 1979), pp. 804–6.

of the majoritarian principle became an essential means of restricting the scope for change.

His two arguments in justification of this procedure are worth examining. He first considered a case where there is a majority of one out of a unit of 2,000 people, and found it unreasonable to regard this as decisive,[86] ignoring the fact that respect for mathematical majorities, however slight, is an essential feature of electoral practice in democratic states: the alternative would involve giving mathematical minorities the right to prevail over majorities. Feetham's second, and more significant, general principle was the exponential one that the more territory to be transferred, 'the higher the percentage of inhabitants who can be regarded as supporters of the change which should be required to justify it'.[87] It should be noted that nothing in Article 12 of the Treaty gives warrant for the notion conveyed here that minorities should decide the fate of the territories they inhabit. It is of course true that the 1920 Government of Ireland Act, based on the assignment of whole counties, provided for the inclusion in the northern state of two counties, Fermanagh and Tyrone, with clear Catholic majorities, thus facilitating the wishes of the Protestant minorities in these cases. However, if due weight is given to the context in which it evolved, it is clear that a fundamental purpose of the boundary clause in Article 12 of the Treaty, which constituted the basis for Feetham's task, was to remedy the democratic deficit which had resulted from the 1920 partition. In defence of Feetham's rejection of the principle that bare majorities should be sufficient when the transfer of units of territory was in question, the argument might be invoked that in many states a bare majority was not decisive on constitutional issues. It might thus be suggested that this applied to the decision made by a particular district as between one state and another. The latter position, however, implicitly assumed that membership of the United Kingdom was the *status quo* for Northern Ireland while the Boundary Commission was deliberating: that any transfers of territory would be from one established state (the United Kingdom incorporating the six counties of Northern Ireland) and another (the Irish Free State). However, to assume that two established states were involved in the transfer process was to ignore the fact that if the boundary clause of the Treaty of 1921 meant anything, it had made Northern Ireland a provisional entity until after the Boundary Commission had made an adjudication on its territorial extent. Feetham's decision that the boundary clause covered nine rather than six counties, thus permitting two-way transfers, also made the Free State a provisional entity subject to boundary alteration on the same conditions as Northern Ireland

86   Hand, *Report* (1969), p. 52.
87   Ibid., p. 53.

was. If this interpretation is valid, transfers made by the Commission were not from one state to another, but from one as yet not fully defined territory to another.

Feetham also introduced a consideration which understandably troubled Nationalist observers: the importance, as he saw it, of 'bearing in mind any distinctions which could fairly be drawn between different classes or sections of the population whose wishes were being taken into account'.[88] Having speculated whether all inhabitants were entitled to 'an equal voice', he conceded that had a plebiscite been decided upon, 'every voter would count for one and no voter for more than one', but since the wishes of inhabitants were, as he himself had decided, to be considered in 'some less direct way', he thought it right to operate on the principle that 'the more permanent elements of the population of a particular area have a greater interest in the destiny of that area, and their wishes are therefore entitled to greater weight'. These 'more permanent elements' were owners and lessees of land or house property for example. Feetham decided that the wishes of a number of persons having such interests deserved greater consideration than the wishes of an equivalent number of persons who have no such interests.[89] There could be no doubt that the effect of implementing such a principle would, on balance, tend to give Unionist inhabitants of disputed areas a considerable advantage over their economically less well-endowed Nationalist neighbours. Here Feetham was reflecting a practice which was a distinguishing feature of local democracy in the north: the political advantage held by property-owning electors in local government areas over other elements in the population. The use of the property franchise was not unique to Northern Ireland at this time: it existed in the United Kingdom until 1945.

The pronouncements by Feetham that the views of some inhabitants should be considered more significant than those of others in determining the boundary, while finding no justification, directly or indirectly, in the terms of the Treaty article he was supposed to be interpreting, were nevertheless an important concession to the Unionist case. Ulster Unionists in Fermanagh and Tyrone, invoking the politics of ownership, also argued forcibly that majoritarian arguments should not be considered decisive in the handing over of border territory to the south, since the opinions of the typical Nationalist voter could not be considered equal in value or significance to those of the typical Unionist voter. A strong Unionist contention was that the force and credibility given to any voter's opinion should depend on whether that voter was a ratepayer, a taxpayer or property owner, on the amount of rates and taxes

88   Ibid., p. 52.
89   Ibid., p. 61.

he/she contributed, and on the amount of property one owned. Thus, the wishes of the majority of ratepayers and taxpayers could be seen as more significant than the wishes of mere democratic majorities, however large.

Unionist emphasis on the need to discriminate between the weight to be given to the collective voice of the propertied class, by and large a Unionist one, and that of the much larger class of inhabitants with a demonstrably smaller economic and financial stake in the community, was not a distinctively twentieth-century phenomenon. When Daniel O'Connell's campaign for the repeal of the Act of Union was at its height, Unionist thinkers like William McComb feared that if the legislative Union between Great Britain and Ireland were dissolved, the effect would be to give Irish Roman Catholics 'an ascendant preponderance in the councils of the state', thus depressing Protestants 'to the level of their numbers, as compared with the bulk of the general population'. At a time of an extremely limited franchise based on property, McComb deplored the demand of repealers 'for household, and even for universal, suffrage', which proved to his satisfaction that advocates of Repeal 'look mainly to the counting of heads in their contemplated reorganisation of Ireland'. For nineteenth-century Unionists who thought like McComb, Repeal, and its insidious agenda of political equality, opened up a dangerous prospect for the possessing classes: 'If a numerical majority is to rule the destinies of this country, without any counteracting influence arising from comparative property, or the expediencies necessarily generated by Imperial, as distinguished from . . . local interests, then it is evident that Roman Catholicism must triumph in the exclusive ascendancy of its professors, and that Protestantism must suffer in proportion.'[90] Over 80 years after McComb expressed these views, the Chairman of the Irish Boundary Commission and Fermanagh and Tyrone Unionist representatives were articulating essentially similar ones, stressing the need for giving a role to the 'influence arising from comparative property' in counteracting numerical majorities.

In Fermanagh and Tyrone, while it was clear that Nationalists were in a numerical majority, Unionists could be shown to own the bulk of the property and to contribute more to public funds than Nationalists. Fermanagh Unionists, as the Fermanagh-Tyrone MP, James Cooper, told Craig in late 1921, claimed that they paid 75 per cent of the rates and 90 per cent of the income taxes in the county.[91] Tyrone Unionists, like those in Fermanagh, had been conducting economic research with a view to preventing the transfer of their county to the Free State long before the Boundary Commission was set

90 William McComb, in Patrick Maume (ed.), *The Republic Repealed* (Dublin, 2003), pp. 4–5.
91 Bryan Follis, *A State Under Siege: The Establishment of Northern Ireland 1920–1925* (Oxford, 1995), pp. 171–2.

up, or even formally agreed to in London. On 3 November 1921, a Unionist from Fivemiletown told the Secretary of the Ulster Unionist Council, the body which in 1924 was asked by the Northern Cabinet to compile evidence for the Commission from the Loyalist community, that Unionist-owned property in Tyrone was worth £280,663, with Nationalist property worth only £146,100; while Unionists paid £54,495 annually in rates, Nationalists paid only £25,090.[92]

It is not clear whether Feetham's misgivings about giving an equal voice to all inhabitants were reflected in his final determination of what the 'substantial' majority would have to be before change could come about. In the event, the lowest majority in any area he transferred which could be deemed in favour of change was 62 per cent. The desire to safeguard Unionist interests, implied in Feetham's principles of interpretation, and more openly expressed by leading British politicians, had already been apparent in one of the suggestions made by the drafting Committee which worked on the war Cabinet's abortive Home Rule Bill from 1917 on. The Committee determined that provision had to be made for the possibility that Tyrone and Fermanagh might vote for Home Rule. In that case, as long as an excluded northern area existed, any inhabitant of Tyrone and Fermanagh would, for all civil and criminal purposes, be entitled to insist that any case in which he was involved would be dealt with in a court in the excluded northern area under Unionist control. What this meant in practice was that Unionists in Tyrone and Fermanagh would, if their counties voted by simple majority for Home Rule, have been able to claim extra-territorial status.[93]

VI WISHES OF INHABITANTS NOT DECISIVE

The effect of another major decision made by Feetham was to compound the problems faced by the Nationalist case. This concerned the relation between the three different factors mentioned in Article 12 as governing the determination of the boundary: the wishes of inhabitants and economic and geographic considerations. It had always been a central part of the Nationalist case that the wishes of the inhabitants would be the determining factor in any award, on the basis that the Article had been drawn up to facilitate the wishes of those in the six counties who desired to become citizens of the Free State. In discussing the weight to be attached to 'the wishes of the inhabitants', however, Feetham drew a semantic distinction whose force might well have been lost

92 Ibid., p. 172.
93 R. B. McDowell, *The Irish Convention 1917–18* (London, 1970), p. 75.

on even the most acute analyst. He decided that under the terms of the Article, 'the wishes of inhabitants are made the primary but not the paramount consideration.'[94] Feetham decided that the Commission would take into account the economic and geographic relations between different areas and would overrule the wishes of the inhabitants in cases where a boundary line based on these would involve serious economic detriment, or their geographic isolation, to communities on either side of it. It did not seem important to him that some inhabitants might, in the interest of having their political wishes gratified, have been prepared to endure at least 'economic detriment' if not 'geographic isolation', or even have preferred to be the judges of their own economic interests.

The major significance of Feetham's decision may be seen in his treatment of Newry and its hinterland. Here, he enunciated one of his central principles, that where the wishes of the inhabitants 'were found to be definitely in conflict with economic and geographic conditions, the latter should prevail under the terms of Article 12'.[95] If the wishes of the inhabitants were, in Feetham's own terms, to be made 'paramount' or even 'primary', Newry Nationalists had an overwhelming case for inclusion in the Free State. On the figures supplied by Feetham himself, the town of Newry and the areas associated with it in counties Down and Armagh, had a population of 24,645 Catholics out of a total of 35,677, which was 69 per cent. This clearly fulfilled Feetham's criterion for a 'substantial' majority, but he came to the conclusion that the economic interests of Newry were so bound up with the industrial life of Northern Ireland that to transfer it to the Free State 'would be to separate it from the country to which in an economic sense it belongs, and to expose it to economic disaster'. He clearly believed either that those agitating for incorporation with the Free State had little sense of their own economic welfare, or that they were prepared to sacrifice this to their Nationalist principles, something he was not prepared to permit. Feetham pronounced that except in the northern part of Monaghan, Newry had no hinterland in the Free State which it could effectively serve as a port, so that its prosperity depended on its trade with the six-county area.[96]

Feetham's economic analysis of Newry was fundamentally at odds with evidence from other sources, including a representative conference of the merchants of the town, and the Trinity College economist Joseph Johnston.

94 Hand, *Report* (1969), p. 29. The Oxford English Dictionary defines 'primary' as 'of the first importance, chiefly, of the first order in any sequence or progress. That which is of the first order, rank or importance'. It defines 'paramount' as 'above in a scale of rank or authority; superior. Above all others in rank; order or jurisdiction, supreme, pre-eminent'.

95 Hand, *Report* (1969), p. 137.

96 Ibid., p. 135.

At the Newry conference, convened at the end of January 1922, there was general agreement that the economic interests of Newry and its hinterland, including south Armagh, would best be served if it were included in the Free State. A leading Unionist declared that 'from the viewpoint of hard business', continued inclusion in the north-eastern area 'would be a disaster for Newry'. Another speaker pointed out that under the partition arrangement the port of Newry which was 'the very life, not only of Newry, but of south Down and south Armagh, and was necessary for Monaghan, Cavan and Leitrim',[97] was in a very bad state. In his report on the economic aspects of partition, Johnston argued that while the boundary proposed by the Free State, incorporating much of south Armagh and south Down, including Newry, 'severs the hinterland of no important market town or distributing centre', the 1920 partition cut off Derry City and Newry from 75 per cent of their respective hinterlands and severed the hinterlands of Strabane, Enniskillen and Clones. Johnston also pointed out that the wholesale and retail trade of Newry was mainly with the 26 counties and with the areas of south Down and south Armagh claimed by the Free State. He also observed that the port of Newry was a rival to that of Belfast, which would not allow it to thrive in a six-county arrangement. There was the further consideration that Greenore, the out-port of Newry, was in the Free State, a factor which made for commercial dislocation.[98] Like Johnston, Lloyd George was acutely aware of the deleterious effects of the 1920 partition on long-established patterns of trade and commerce. When Craig suggested to him in November 1921 that the Northern State should have the same dominion status as a new Irish Free State, and thus be in all things independent of it, Lloyd George rejected 'so complete a partition of Ireland' in the light of European post-war experience of artificial boundaries. 'The existing states of Central and South-Eastern Europe,' he told Craig, 'were a terrible example of the evils which spring from the creation of new frontiers, cutting the natural circuits of commercial activity.' In the same letter, Lloyd George implicitly condemned as defective the 1920 boundary settlement over which he himself had presided when he pointed out that the frontier which Craig wanted to stereotype was based 'neither upon natural features nor broad geographical considerations'.[99]

Feetham's use of economic analysis to override the wishes of the inhabitants of south Down, debatable as it was, was further compromised by

97   *Freeman's Journal*, 30 Jan. 1922.

98   'Our territorial demand at the Boundary Commission', Kennedy Papers P4/391/, pp. 16–19.

99   *Irish Boundary, Extracts from Parliamentary Debates, Command Papers, etc, Relevant to Questions arising out of Article XII of the Articles of an Agreement for a Treaty between Great Britain and Ireland, dated 6 December, 1921*, H. M. Stationery Office (London, 1924), p. 25.

his failure to contemplate what the economic position of Newry might be outside the Northern State, particularly if this was in conjunction with south Armagh. Its economic dependence on that state, which Feetham used as an argument for leaving it there, was due to partition and the consequent Customs barrier erected on 1 April 1923. He failed to address the different position which would arise if Newry was to become a Free State port in conjunction with Greenore and in conjunction with the substantial portion of south Armagh that he was prepared to transfer to the Free State. He did speculate on the consequences of including the whole of Newry's market area in the Free State. This, he claimed, would mean that the boundary would have to run about 8 miles north of Newry near Poyntzpass and would absorb areas having substantial Protestant majorities which were within reach of northern market towns such as Banbridge and Tandragee. The logic of this seemed clear to Feetham: overriding the wishes of Protestant majorities in areas near Poyntzpass 'for the purpose of protecting the economic interests of Newry as a market centre would not be justified'.[100] At the same time, Feetham was prepared to override the wishes of Catholic inhabitants who were in the majority in an area of east Down in which the waterworks supplying Belfast, Portadown and Banbridge had been built in the post-Treaty period, for the purpose of protecting the economic interests of these places.[101]

On the one hand, Feetham was determined to prevent the 'economic disaster' which he claimed was facing Newry if he acquiesced in the wishes of the 69 per cent of its inhabitants who, on the evidence of census returns for religious affiliation which he accepted as conclusive, wanted to join the Free State. On the other, he was sympathetic to the Protestant inhabitants who formed the majority in the rural districts to the north of Newry, who preferred separation from Newry to inclusion in the Free State, although from the point of view of business convenience they would much prefer to be 'in the same jurisdiction as Newry'. The opposition of these Protestants to a boundary which would include them in the Free State was 'based on political views which are so strongly held as to lead them to disregard such business consider-ations'.[102] Feetham contrived to satisfy both the strong political views and the business needs of these Protestants by leaving Newry and its hinterland under the Northern Government. He protected what he claimed were the economic interests of Newry Nationalists without satisfying their wishes. It thus appears obvious that Feetham's treatment of south-east Ulster was notably devoid of even-handedness. He refused to allow the Nationalists of south Down to

100 Hand, *Report* (1969), p. 132.
101 Ibid., p. 133.
102 Ibid., p. 132.

prejudice what he saw as their own economic interests by transferring them to the southern jurisdiction. There was more to this strategy than a paternalistic solicitude on Feetham's part for the welfare of Catholics. One commentator remarks that even where the wishes of Nationalist inhabitants could be satisfied without compromising the wishes of Protestant ones, but where a transfer of Nationalists could cause anxiety to Protestants, 'then there could be no question of a transfer' since Nationalist wishes, as Feetham decided, 'must not be allowed to cause any anxiety to any sector of the Protestant population.'[103]

At a meeting with Baldwin, the British Prime Minister, in Chequers on 28 November 1925, Kevin O'Higgins professed particular surprise at the decision to leave Newry in the northern state and could not accept the reasoning behind the exclusion of parts of east Donegal from the Free State. 'I cannot understand,' he told Baldwin, 'how the award could leave Newry out', observing that its inhabitants were overwhelmingly Nationalist as was its economic hinterland. O'Higgins was conscious that the same arguments for the inclusion of Newry in the Free State applied with even 'fuller force' than those against putting east Donegal into the northern state.[104] Newry could be left out of the Free State because Feetham had decided that majoritarian arguments should not prevail against geographical and economic considerations. It is fair to say that Feetham had strong economic arguments to support his decision in this instance, however strong the countervailing democratic case. As Rankin observes, 'the preservation of Newry and its hinterlands [in Northern Ireland] was vital in uniting the supply, marketing and export aspects of the local linen industry.' The link between port revenues and coal supplies convinced the Commission that Newry was inextricably linked with its northern hinterland.[105] Sometimes, however, Feetham found it expedient to invoke the wishes of inhabitants as a decisive factor, most notably when it came to rejecting the possibility of county transfer, which would have been incompatible with his fundamental requirement that the northern state must retain its 1920 configuration subject to relatively minor modifications. He argued that if a county like Tyrone or Fermanagh were to be treated as indivisible, and if the inhabitants in one portion of a county 'were in opposition to

103 Anthony Carty, *Was Ireland Conquered? International Law and the Irish Question* (London, 1996), p. 47.

104 NAI DT S4720, 28 Nov. 1925. The British stenographer seems to have misinterpreted a vital sentence of O'Higgins's submission, reporting him as saying: 'The same arguments for leaving Newry out of the Free State were used against putting eastern Donegal into Northern Ireland and applied in full- or fuller-force.'

105 K. J. Rankin, 'The creation and consolidation of the Irish border', *Working Papers in British-Irish Studies* 48, Institute for British-Irish Studies (UCD, 2005), p. 24.

the wishes of the inhabitants of the whole county', the Commission would thereby be setting up a new factor, 'administrative considerations' as 'superior to the wishes of the inhabitants'.[106] This meant in practice that local Protestant majorities must prevail over Catholic majorities in each of two counties as a whole. Here for once Feetham was prepared to acknowledge the overriding importance of the wishes of the inhabitants as Article 12 suggested he should do, but perhaps because the inhabitants he had in mind were the Protestants of Tyrone and Fermanagh.

VII ANTICIPATIONS OF FEETHAM

Feetham's principles of interpretation, their application, and the language used in formulating them carry many strong and curiously suggestive echoes of earlier pronouncements on boundary determination advanced by sympathisers with the Northern Ireland case. Among the most significant of these was Francis Bourdillon's detailed paper, 'The Scope of the [Irish] Boundary Commission', submitted to Feetham's friend Lionel Curtis in December 1923, and discussed earlier in this chapter (see section II: The Role of Francis Bourdillon). Feetham's intimate association with Bourdillon, who served as Secretary to the Commission, and his long-standing intimacy with Curtis whose influence over him was, as Hand observes, 'unquestionably great',[107] and who was deeply impressed by Bourdillon's views on how Article 12 should be implemented, make it difficult to imagine that Feetham was unfamiliar with Bourdillon's paper. While the evidence here is at best circumstantial, it may be regarded as significant that Feetham's position on the major questions of concern in determining the application of the boundary clause, closely reflects Bourdillon's. Both concluded that the Boundary Commission should confine itself to the drawing of a convenient border, but was not intended to apply self-determination to a large area or to such important centres as Londonderry City or Newry. Again, they both argued that the limited transfers of territory were to be made in both directions, not merely from north to south as the Free State Government believed.

Feetham's final arrangement of the boundary also bears a resemblance to some elements of a border proposal made by Fisher to his close associate James Craig in January 1922. The context of Fisher's proposal, communicated in a personal letter, was a recent speech by Craig expressing concern for the thousands of Unionists in east Donegal severed from Northern Ireland by the

106 Hand, *Report* (1969), pp. 62–3.
107 Ibid., p. xiii.

1920 Act. Fisher suggested that since Craig had, by 1922, 'a self-contained, self-governing Ulster', he was in a good position to press for the inclusion of areas outside Northern Ireland and to cede troublesome areas within it. A willingness to absorb Donegal would show the world that Unionists were ready to share 'the burden of congestion and misery' which Fisher associated with that county. Fisher's detailed proposals are of considerable interest in the light of Feetham's treatment of the areas they incorporated. 'Ulster,' Fisher told Craig, 'can never be complete without Donegal. Donegal belongs to Derry, and Derry to Donegal. With north Monaghan in Ulster and south Armagh out, we should have a solid ethnographic and strategic frontier to the south.'[108] Fisher regarded Donegal as 'a hostile Afghanistan'[109] on the north-west frontier of the Unionist state which it would be desirable to place in the 'safe keeping' of Craig's Government. What he proposed was to draw the border along the Erne, including almost the whole of Donegal in Northern Ireland, while leaving Fermanagh south of Lough Erne to the Free State. His ideal frontier would take in a fair share of the 'passionately northern people' of north Monaghan and leave out the generally refractory inhabitants of south Armagh. Three years after Fisher made his suggestions to Craig, Feetham transferred parts of east Donegal and north Monaghan to Northern Ireland, and removed a substantial part of south Armagh from its jurisdiction.

It was a commonplace Free State and northern Nationalist criticism of Feetham that he was swayed by British Conservatives and Ulster Unionists to interpret the boundary clause in a restrictive way. W. T. Cosgrave was a leading spokesperson for this line of attack.[110] Hand, however, felt obliged to go on record to say that he found the evidence for Feetham's 'independence of mind and legal acumen too overwhelming to make this criticism plausible'.[111] It is not incoherent to argue that Feetham's independence of mind might not have been incompatible with his holding views on the Irish boundary question notably similar in nature and detail to those expressed by numerous Conservative and Unionist commentators. One of the striking things about his report on his findings is the number of close verbal parallels between his formulation of these and the expression of similar points of view by those who advocated, or came to advocate, the same restrictive interpretation of the boundary clause which he advanced. The central question raised by the contentions put forward by those who gave evidence to the Commission was, as Feetham put

108 Fisher's letter to Craig is printed in Ervine, *Craigavon*, pp. 481–2.

109 Afghanistan was a territory on the north-west frontier of India and presented the British authorities in India with serious military problems.

110 *The Times*, 23 Nov. 1925.

111 Hand, *Report* (1969), p. xiii.

it: 'Can the Commission make changes in the existing boundary which involve the transfer of large areas and populations to one side and or the other, or is its scope restricted to the making of minor modifications in the existing boundary?'[112] Feetham's answer to this question was unequivocal: 'Northern Ireland must, when the boundaries have been determined, still be recognisable as the same provincial entity; the changes made must not be so drastic as to destroy its identity or make it impossible for it to continue as a separate province of the United Kingdom with its own parliament and government for provincial affairs under the Government of Ireland Act.'[113] In the Commons debate on the Treaty in February 1922, one of its signatories, Worthington-Evans, spoke of the purpose of the Commission in language remarkably similar to Feetham's: 'This Commission is a Boundary Commission to settle boundaries, not to settle territories.'[114] Birkenhead's letter of assurance to Balfour, written in March 1922, that the boundary clause was restrictive in intent is a curious anticipation of Feetham's conclusion. 'The article,' Birkenhead explained, 'contemplated the maintenance of Northern Ireland as an entity already existing . . . It is regarded as a creature already constituted, having its own Parliament and its own defined boundaries.' Birkenhead also dismissed the notion that the Commission might 'conceivably wholly change the character of Northern Ireland by enormous reductions of its territory' as having no foundation whatever except in the 'overheated imagination' of Collins.[115]

Another question raised by those who argued before the Commission was whether it was its duty to make an entirely fresh determination of boundaries, and to lay down a new line of division without regard to the existing boundary. Feetham's answer was that the Commission must start its examination on the basis of the division marked by the existing boundary and 'must treat that boundary as holding good where no sufficient reason is shown for altering it'.[116] In the debate on the Free State (Agreement) Bill of 1922, Worthington-Evans anticipated this when, identifying the inhabitants whose wishes were to be consulted, he described them as 'the inhabitants through which the [existing] boundaries run'.[117] Another signatory of the Treaty, Austen Chamberlain, told Parliament in October 1924 that the intention of the British negotiators had been 'to readjust the old boundary, not to create a new one'. During the same debate, Lloyd George affirmed that a boundary commission did not

112 Ibid., p. 26.
113 Ibid., p. 29.
114 *Hansard*, House of Commons, Vol. 150, Col. 1326, 16 Feb. 1922.
115 Birkenhead's letter is reproduced in full in Matthews, *Fatal Influence*, pp. 288–90.
116 Hand, *Report* (1969), p. 28.
117 *Hansard*, House of Commons Vol. 150, Col. 1393, 17 Feb. 1922.

merely mean taking parishes out of Ulster and giving them to the south: it also meant taking parishes from the south, where they were contiguous and on the frontier, and putting them into the north. Lloyd George's use of 'parishes' and 'on the frontier' had dispiriting implications for the Nationalist case.[118] An interesting detail in Feetham's report is his decision not to admit into evidence the various statements on the interpretation of the boundary clause made by the signatories of the Treaty, both in the course of the negotiations and subsequent to the signing of the Articles.[119] Feetham did not give reasons for regarding such evidence as inadmissible. It is clear from the published record of the parliamentary debates on the Irish Boundary Bill that many of the British signatories professed to know what the boundary clause was, and was not, intended to achieve. Chamberlain emphatically declared in 1924 that there was no doubt what British intentions were when the clause was formulated, and that Lloyd George and Churchill were at one with him in this. So too was Worthington-Evans.[120]

In the debate in the House of Lords on the same Bill, the Marquess of Salisbury pointed out that all the British signatories of the Treaty, in their assessment of the boundary clause, 'were insistent upon the distinction between anything like a transfer of territory and the mere adjustment of boundaries.'[121] This would suggest that had Feetham called the British signatories as witnesses, they would have given powerful and convincing evidence in favour of a restrictive interpretation of the boundary clause. Birkenhead would undoubtedly have proved a most interesting witness, particularly if his testimony had followed the trend of his speech in the Lords in October 1924 on the Irish Boundary Bill.[122] Birkenhead most likely would have conceded that those like himself who had formulated the boundary clause lacked the advantage 'which is conceded to those who drew up great international instruments'. When the Treaty of Versailles was being fashioned, 'you would have found five or six skilled draftsmen whose whole lives had been spent in drafting and in giving true expression, in technical and highly competent language, to the sense desired by the negotiators'. Unfortunately, Birkenhead would have said, the nature of what he and others had to negotiate, 'the very secrecy of the discussions, made the inclusion of such expert draftsmen impossible.' They thus had to make do with men like himself, who though skilled in the law and famous as a practitioner, had 'never pretended to be a professional draftsman'.

118 Ibid., Vol. 177, Cols 166, 187–8, 1 Oct. 1924.
119 Hand, *Report* (1969), p. 27.
120 *Hansard*, House of Commons, Vol. 177, Cols 160–6, 1 Oct. 1924.
121 *Hansard*, House of Lords, Vol. 59, Cols 595–6, 8 Oct. 1924.
122 Ibid., Vol. 59, Cols 627–37, 8 Oct. 1924.

Judging by his House of Lords speech Birkenhead's evidence would have been to the effect that all the British signatories had known what was intended by the boundary clause, which contemplated nothing more than the adjustment of boundaries. However, he would also have told Feetham that the unanimous acceptance of this interpretation by the signatories was not properly reflected in the words of Article 12, due to 'incompetent and slovenly draftsmanship'. The Article, Birkenhead would have explained, 'was lacking in the clarity that could have been given to it, had the circumstances permitted more detailed consideration, an expression of, perhaps, more convincing lucidity'.[123]

This line of reasoning is similar to that accepted by Thomas Jones, intimately involved, as Birkenhead was, with the boundary clause when the Treaty was being negotiated. Jones observed that the Treaty was not drafted in the meticulous manner of an Act of Parliament.[124] Such a lack of clarity in the formulation of so central a component of the Treaty was, one might imagine, bound to make its interpretation extremely difficult for the members of the Boundary Commission. One might also imagine that those most qualified, perhaps uniquely qualified, to provide clarity of meaning would have been those who formulated the clause and who professed to know its intent. In the event, it would not have mattered if Feetham had called the signatories to give evidence, since his own conclusions were at one with what they would have told him. He was almost certainly well aware of their well-publicised views in any case. Birkenhead, though, might have made a problematic witness. He had, it is true, told the Lords that on every occasion when he was called upon to express an opinion on the meaning of the boundary clause, he had made his view 'absolutely plain as to the meaning of Article 12'.[125] His expression of meaning had not, in fact, been absolutely plain or consistent. In 1922, he had confidently offered a restrictive interpretation of the boundary clause to Balfour. In 1924, he admitted to Chamberlain that he and the other British negotiators had 'at the entreaty of the Irish negotiators', agreed 'upon a reference to the Commission which many of us knew to be disputable, but which we were certain could only be decided in one way'.[126] How could Birkenhead have been certain that something known to be 'disputable' could have only one outcome? Had he been called to give evidence, would he have chosen his Balfour version or his Chamberlain one?

123 Ibid., Vol. 59, Cols 633–4, 636, 8 Oct. 1924.
124 See Jones, *Whitehall Diary* vol. 3, p. 234.
125 *Hansard*, House of Lords, Vol. 59, Col. 636, 8 Oct. 1924.
126 Matthews, *Fatal Influence*, pp. 169–72.

VIII THE APPLICATION OF ARTICLE 12

Those who were obliged to deal with the application of Article 12 were inevitably conscious of the yawning gap between intention and drafting. Feetham was given the sole responsibility for filling this gap. It is fair to say that his five mutually reinforcing ground rules for the interpretation of Article 12 could not have been better calculated to facilitate the Unionist case and undermine the Nationalist one. These were: the restriction of the Commission's scope to 'minor modifications of the existing boundary'; the decision to concentrate on small 'convenient' units of area of unspecified extent rather than on counties or electoral districts; the insistence on undefined 'substantial majorities' as necessary if change were to be made; the granting of superior status to the presumed wishes of inhabitants with economic strength, mainly Unionist; and the vital principle that when the wishes of the inhabitants, however overwhelming, were found to conflict with economic and geographic considerations, the latter must prevail.[127] The first rule meant that the case for transferring all of Fermanagh and much of Tyrone was dismissed, and this dismissal was reinforced by the 'small units of area' procedure. The 'substantial majorities' requirement was sufficiently flexible, at least as interpreted by Feetham, to rule out any transfer, while the invocation of geography and economics could, and did, work to the same effect. In his discussion of the Protestants of Fermanagh, he upheld their right to remain 'on their present side of the border'.[128] This expression underlines the fundamental consideration that in approaching his task Feetham regarded the 1920 border as an established entity, not to be altered except on the basis of overwhelming reasons for doing so. In his 'Interpretation and principles of application relating to Article 12', he made it clear that the Commission could examine the question only 'on the basis of the existing boundary', and that no 'wholesale reconstruction' of the map of Ireland based on the wishes of the inhabitants was contemplated in the boundary clause of Article 12.[129]

It is here that Feetham's work is most vulnerable to criticism. The task assigned to him and the Commission he controlled was to implement the boundary clause of Article 12 of the Treaty: to reconstitute the 1920 boundary in conformity with the wishes of the inhabitants, at the same time taking account of whatever geographical or economic considerations might reasonably be held to override these wishes. It is not an exaggeration to say that Feetham's interpretation turned the Article on its head by starting from

127 Hand, *Report* (1969), p. 31, 35, 63, 137.
128 Ibid., p. 98.
129 Ibid., p. 29.

the premise that the six-county state was already a well-established legitimate political entity, and therefore must retain its essential configuration, so that no changes made to the boundary should affect its integrity. This reasoning was in turn based on Feetham's idea that the entire six-county entity specified in the Government of Ireland Act of 1920 had acquired a legitimacy, and a right to territorial integrity, prior to the negotiation of the Anglo-Irish Treaty with its boundary clause. In order to accommodate this interpretation, which separated the legitimacy of the 1920 State from the legitimacy of satisfying the wishes of its inhabitants which was the first requirement of the boundary clause in Article 12, Feetham had to change the essential meaning of the Article. Carty provides a fair summary of what Feetham had decided upon as the basis on which he would work: 'The north of Ireland is now an entity separate from the wishes of its inhabitants, and no expression of the wishes of these inhabitants must be allowed to undermine its integrity.'[130] The Chairman thus reversed the order of the elements in the boundary clause in Article 12, which put the wishes of the inhabitants first, by subordinating these wishes to the overriding need to maintain the integrity of the entity established in 1920. Feetham's decision to reify the 1920 territory established by an act of the British Parliament meant that, as far as the Boundary Commission was concerned, no expression of the wishes of its inhabitants must be allowed to effect a significant modification of its area.

In summary, the evidence points to the conclusion that Feetham had decided that his overriding duty was to conserve the integrity of Northern Ireland as a jurisdiction. He realised that this could not be achieved by acceding in any significant way to the unmeasured, though presumed, wishes of inhabitants. These wishes had to be substantially overruled. A mechanism for doing this lay in the very vagueness of the language: the qualifying phrase 'as far as may be compatible with economic and geographic conditions'. Feetham freely deployed this as if it enjoyed a status superior to the wishes of inhabitants when the two appeared to him to be in conflict. This line of thinking implied that those who framed the boundary clause had designed it with the object of avoiding any serious departure from the status quo.

The boundary clause had given Feetham intentionally vague terms of reference combined with sweeping, decision-making powers of interpretation. These permitted him to implement a wide range of essentially subjective judgements, inevitably conditioned by his intellectual, judicial and political background. Although the Boundary Commission had three members, it was, for all practical purposes, a single-member body. The special interests of the Imperial Government which appointed Feetham as the arbiter of Northern

130 Carty, *Was Ireland Conquered?*, p. 142.

Ireland's political destiny can be shown to have had a bearing on his appointment: his known conservative temperament was perhaps his most desirable qualification from a British perspective. It is difficult to imagine how he could have interpreted his brief as he did unless, as O'Callaghan puts it, this can be explained 'in terms of his inherent bias in favour of the by- then pre-existing'.[131]

Feetham was effectively starting from the position that 'a strict application of the consent of the governed constitutes a threat to the very existence of Northern Ireland',[132] a position which implied a decidedly unflattering view of the democratic credentials of the state whose integrity he was defending. Effectively, Feetham narrowed his problem of interpretation to a choice between what he saw as two conflicting principles: the right to self-determination claimed on behalf of border Nationalists and suggested in Article 12, and the territorial integrity of the existing six-county entity, something not considered in Article 12. In choosing to give pre-eminence to territorial integrity, he frustrated any possibility that serious consideration could be given to the wishes of Nationalist inhabitants since, if these had been substantially gratified, the territorial integrity of the 1920 northern state, which Feetham was determined to preserve, would have been compromised. Instead of implementing the obvious sense of Article 12, Feetham chose to attach a form of territorial integrity, a substantial pre-established identity, to the six-county entity, for which the Treaty gave no warrant: the whole point of the Article was to make the geographical extent of the entity depend on the Commission's work. Through this interpretation Feetham showed that he believed the boundary provisions of the Government of Ireland Act merited a status superior to those of the Treaty. Instead of adjudicating on the relative claims of the wishes of inhabitants on the one hand, and geography and economics on the other, as Article 12 required him to do, Feetham's fundamental area of choice was between self-determination and territorial integrity. In choosing territorial integrity as his governing principle, he was influenced by the consideration that wide application of the principle of self-determination to minority areas might threaten the survival of a separate northern state. To satisfy the wishes of the inhabitants would have been to give a substantially new shape to the six-county entity, in contravention of Feetham's prior conclusion that its essential shape, defined by the 1920 partition, was not subject to alteration.

Unlike its European precedents, the brief Irish boundary clause was unsupported by any kind of detailed directives as to its interpretation or implementation. It thus left itself open to two radically different canons of

131 O'Callaghan, 'Old parchment and water', p. 39.
132 Ibid.

construction. It could have been interpreted as the remedy provided by the Treaty-makers for the grievances of the northern minority. This kind of interpretation would have found its warrant in the history of the negotiations which led to its insertion in the Treaty. In contrast, it could have been read, if the record of its evolution and its context in the Treaty were set aside, as merely giving a licence to the Commission to effect minor adjustments to an existing boundary by removing obvious anomalies. This was how Feetham chose to read it. A careful examination of Feetham's report will show that he saw his task 'in the light of the Government of Ireland Act which set up the northern Irish state rather than in the light of the Anglo-Irish Treaty which set up the Boundary Commission'.[133] Since the instrument he was applying was part of the Anglo-Irish Treaty, which was an all-Ireland settlement, registered with the League of Nations, it is difficult to defend Feetham's concentration on the Government of Ireland Act as a support for his basic argument that after the Boundary Commission had done its work, the six-county state must remain 'the same provincial entity'. There is a strong case to be made for the proposition that in all the circumstances the Government of Ireland Act was an inappropriate foundation for the implementation of Article 12, something recognised by Birkenhead in August 1924[134] and that if it had any significance for the work of the Commission, this could be no more than a peripheral one. Feetham tended to read and apply Article 12 as if it was part of the 1920 Act rather than an indispensable component of the Treaty, particularly since the latter agreement involved significant modification of the arrangements made in 1920.

133 Laffan, *Partition of Ireland*, p. 101.
134 Matthews, *Fatal Influence*, p. 171.

SIX

THE BOUNDARY COMMISSION'S EUROPEAN CONTEXT

—

I RESPECTING SELF-DETERMINATION

The Irish partition settlement of 1920 was one of a series of contemporary attempts to fix boundaries between distinct ethnic groups and competing nationalities. In the same year that the Government of Ireland Act partitioned Ireland, territories in other parts of Europe were being partitioned and assigned to the states and peoples which laid claim to them, or to parts of them. The partitioning of territories all over Europe, and the assignment of regions to the victorious powers in the Great War, was the outcome of the provisions of post-war treaties which were essentially imposed settlements requiring a radical redrawing of the map of Europe. Leaders of the Allied and Associated Powers who framed the Peace Treaties of Paris made public declarations that the governing principle of territorial settlement was to be self-determination. This meant that the wishes of the inhabitants of regions in dispute, in the event frequently determined on *a priori* grounds, were to be the primary consideration in deciding the jurisdictions under which they were to live. The meaning of the term 'national self-determination', the most memorable slogan in President Wilson's wartime rhetoric, remained imprecise, but it was widely interpreted by Wilson's European admirers to imply that 'each national group, defined by a common cultural tradition, history and above all, language, deserved to constitute its own political unit and to conduct its own affairs without interference from powerful predatory neighbours'.[1] There was nothing, however, in Wilson's public declarations to indicate that the new political boundaries could or should coincide precisely with ethnic frontiers. Geography, economics, the untidy distribution of ethnic groups and territorial security made it impossible to form new states or to determine new boundaries purely on the basis of ethnicity without having recourse to the wholesale transfer of

---

1   M. F. Boemke, G. D. Feldman and E. Glaser, *The Treaty of Versailles: A Reassessment after 75 Years* (Cambridge, 1998), p. 475.

millions of people from their traditional homelands, a solution applied in Greece, Turkey, Belgium and Bulgaria in the early 1920s.

The post-war boundary settlements and the principles which informed some of these had a significant influence on the incorporation in the Anglo-Irish Treaty of a provision for a boundary commission. Even before the 1920 Act, they had already influenced the thinking of one senior British statesman. With the rhetoric of self-determination becoming more strident, and its application, however imperfect and inconsistent, becoming a feature of a variety of European settlements, Lord Balfour believed that Ulster Unionists should enjoy its benefits. With national aspirations being gratified in central and eastern Europe, Balfour, British representative at the League of Nations Council and a participant in its deliberations on European boundaries, thought it inconceivable that the Protestant north should be denied self-determination, which, for him, involved exclusion from the rest of Ireland and continued incorporation in Great Britain. 'No one can think,' he wrote on 25 November 1919, 'that Ulster ought to join the south and west [of Ireland] who thinks that the Jugo-Slavs should be separated from Austria. No one can think that Ulster should be divorced from Britain who believes in self-determination.'[2] The validity of Balfour's argument depends on the meaning to be attached to 'Ulster'. If he was arguing that the principle of self-determination could justify a nine, or six-county unit, he was clearly mistaken, whatever might be said for the exclusion of a largely homogeneous Unionist area. The Government of Ireland Act of 1920, however, with its generously inclusive interpretation of the principle from a Unionist point of view, was designed to meet Balfour's wishes.

The terms of reference of the boundary clause in Article 12 of the Anglo-Irish Treaty seemed to place the Boundary Commission firmly in the same category as the boundary commissions which were established by the Treaty of Versailles to resolve territorial disputes in five European regions. These were Upper Silesia, Allenstein and Marienwerder, all in dispute between Germany and Poland; Schleswig in dispute between Germany and Denmark, and Klagenfurt, in dispute between Austria and Yugoslavia, then known as the Kingdom of the Serbs, Croats and Slovenes. In all these areas, plebiscites, impartially conducted and supervised, were employed as the means of ascertaining the wishes of inhabitants with a view to assigning them to the jurisdiction of their choice. The wording of Article 12 in the Anglo-Irish Treaty was almost identical with that of the various boundary clauses in the Treaty of Versailles, and was clearly copied from them. The formulation for Allenstein (Article 95 of the Treaty of Versailles) provided that 'regard will be paid to the wishes of the inhabitants as shown by the vote and to the

2   T. G. Fraser, *Partition in Ireland, India and Palestine: Theory and Practice* (London 1984), p. 27.

geographical and economic conditions of the locality'. This was repeated word for word in the case of Marienwerder (Article 97) and Upper Silesia (Article 88, Annex 5). The Irish formulation provided that the boundary be drawn 'in accordance with the wishes of the inhabitants, so far as may be compatible with economic and geographic conditions'. There are, however, two significant differences between the five European precedents and what was provided for in Article 12. In the Irish case, no provision was made for determining the wishes of the inhabitants by plebiscite, nor, indeed, was any other method prescribed. Equally significantly, no area was demarcated within which the wishes of the inhabitants were to be ascertained. This meant that while European boundary commissions were able to do their work with the aid of precise guidelines, the Irish Commissioners were confronted with a minimalist wording fraught with ambiguity, which meant that its British-born and British-appointed Chairman was left to interpret it as he thought fit. While the awards made by the European Commissioners were almost universally regarded as equitable the award made by the Irish Commission was received with anger and dismay by the Government of the Free State and the representatives of Nationalist opinion in the six counties.

It is important to bear in mind that there was one fundamental difference between the partition arrangements made for Ireland by the provisions of the 1920 Government of Ireland Act and the Boundary Commission in 1925, on the one hand, and the arrangements for partitioning disputed areas in Europe made by the Treaty of Versailles, on the other. Unlike the European territories in which boundary commissions functioned in 1920 and 1921, Ireland had already been partitioned in 1920, five years before the Irish Boundary Commission reached its determination. The configuration of the Irish boundary in 1920 had no obvious warrant, and was out of keeping with the common contemporary practice of awaiting the results of the deliberations of boundary commissions before finally attempting to fix boundaries. Craig seems to have been conscious of the anomaly. In 1919, in conversation with the British politician Sir Laming Worthington-Evans, he proposed the establishment of a boundary commission to examine the distribution of population along the borders of the whole of the six counties, and to take a plebiscite on districts on either side whose political allegiance might be in doubt. On 15 December 1919, Craig's proposal was commended to the British Cabinet, 'as being in accord with the practice and principles adopted in the peace treaties.' It received much Cabinet support, but it was ultimately rejected on the argument that formal enquiries into the wishes of the inhabitants along the border, by way of plebiscite, 'would produce unrest'.[3] The consequence of this rejection was that the partition of Ireland,

3   Nicholas Mansergh, *Nationalism and Independence: Selected Irish Papers* (Cork, 1997), p. 19.

unlike the partitions effected in Europe in the 1920s, and the later partition of India, was carried through with no preliminary democratic enquiry into the delimitation of frontiers. This in turn meant that the Irish Boundary Commission was given the task of reconstituting boundaries drawn only a few years before it did its work, a task made all the more difficult by the fact that the 1920 boundary had acquired a quasi-legal *de facto* status, and by the determination of those pleased with it to resist any but the most minor alterations. There was the further problem that the absence of formal guidelines to the interpretation of Article 12 made the Irish Boundary Commission an oddity among bodies of its kind.

The Anglo-Irish Treaty failed to specify a time limit for the setting up of the Boundary Commission, thus departing from continental precedents. Another contested feature of the boundary clause of Article 12 was the right it conferred on the British Government to nominate the Chairman of the Boundary Commission, particularly since that Government was one of the contending parties. The British choice as Chairman was Justice Richard Feetham. This was out of keeping with the arrangements governing the adjudication of boundary disputes in other parts of Europe. While European boundary commissions included representatives from the parties involved, they were presided over by a person chosen from a country which had no vested interest in the disposition of the territory in dispute. In the case of the Polish boundary, the Treaty of Versailles (Article 27,7) made provision for a commission consisting of seven members, one each from countries not directly affected. The Commission appointed to settle the Aaland Island dispute between Sweden and Finland consisted of one member each from the countries in dispute, along with a Belgian, a Swiss and an American. In the case of Upper Silesia, when an elaborately supervised plebiscite failed to produce the basis for a clear-cut division between Germany and Poland, the League of Nations commissioned a report from representatives of four countries without a vested interest in the Silesian question: Belgium, Brazil, China and Spain. Their report formed the basis for the boundary settlement.[4] The Saarland plebiscite of January 1935 was supervised by an international Plebiscite Commission established to organise the voting. An Irish High Court judge, James Creed Meredith, was chosen as Vice President of the Saar Supreme Plebiscite Tribunal, which adjudicated on any disputes over alleged irregularities.[5]

---

4   Sarah Wambaugh, *Plebiscites since the World War: With a Collection of Official Documents*, Carnegie Endowment for International Peace Vol. 2 (Washington, 1933), p. 65, p. 268; Bolton C. Waller, Memorandum on European precedents for the North Eastern Boundary Bureau, Kennedy Papers UCDA P4/390, p. 14.

5   M. Kennedy and J. M. Skelly (eds), *Irish Foreign Policy 1919–1966: From Independence to Internationalism* (Dublin, 2000), p. 421.

Despite all the reservations that might be expressed about Feetham's suitability as chairman of the Commission, and the not entirely baseless suspicions about his political and intellectual background and associations as factors which might be deemed fatal to his capacity, or perceived capacity, to act impartially in the business assigned to him, a case can be made to justify his appointment, even if the terms of this case might not satisfy many Irish nationalists. On the British side there was the persuasive argument that the Imperial dimension had a decisive bearing on the choice of a chairman of an Irish boundary commission, as distinct from a European one. The British position would have been that since the dispute was between the Irish Free State and Northern Ireland, two members of the Empire, and not, as was the case in European disputes, where the disputing parties were fully sovereign states, it was quite appropriate that the chairman should be drawn from the Empire. There was the related point that the Westminster Government in appointing Feetham was not acting as the Government of Great Britain but as the Imperial Government. The 'imperial' argument, while theoretically convincing, is somewhat weakened by the *de facto* position that if the same government was acting in two capacities, as the Government of Great Britain and as the Imperial Government, it was not easy to distinguish or separate these functions. The Feetham issue draws attention to the anomalies involved in membership of the Empire and the extent to which this involved subordination to Westminster and its particular interests. If the 'imperial' argument is found plausible, objections to Feetham as chairman must be directed not to the constitutionality of his appointment or its supposed repugnance to international law and precedent, but to his English birth and past association with people and causes which might have impaired or prejudiced his function as an impartial chairman. There was a danger that a *post-factum* review of his performance as arbiter could, in the light of all the circumstances surrounding his appointment, lead to the conclusion that his findings were predetermined and shaped by an under-standing of the Irish Question circumscribed by an Empire and Commonwealth framework. It is not surprising that a common southern reaction to his findings was that impartial justice had not been served, or, at the very least, was not seen to be done. T. M. Healy's abusive catch-cry, 'Feetham-cheat 'em!' expressed a widespread Nationalist sentiment. Another common response was that Feetham's findings were not surprising since his career had been based on pleasing his British 'masters'.[6]

6   Kevin Matthews, *Fatal Influence: The Impact of Ireland on British Politics 1920–1925* (Dublin, 2004), p. 155. The comment about Feetham's British 'masters' was not Matthews's own. It formed part of the case made against Feetham by Thomas Johnson, leader of the Labour Party and Denis Gorey of the Farmers' Party in the course of a Dáil debate on 15 Oct. 1925. Dáil Éireann debates, Vol. 8, Cols 2505, 2558.

The interpretation of Article 12 by Justice Feetham, effectively arbiter of the decisions of the Irish Boundary Commission, ensured that its general tenor bore little resemblance to that of its European counterparts. His decision not to permit the holding of a plebiscite was one of the essential differences. Having rightly pointed out that Article 12 said nothing about the means by which the wishes of inhabitants were to be ascertained, he observed that 'the only means of arriving at precise figures with regard to the wishes of the inhabitants would be a plebiscite'. The grounds on which he excluded a plebiscite are seriously open to question: 'The Treaty makes no provision whatever for a plebiscite, and the Commission has therefore no power to carry out a plebiscite.'[7] The absence of a provision in the Article for a plebiscite did not, in fact, mean that no such thing was possible. Had Feetham decided on a plebiscite, he had the means at hand to arrange with the British Government for one, as he himself implicitly acknowledged: 'Legal provisions of a very stringent and comprehensive nature would be necessary in order to ensure that only persons entitled to vote as inhabitants took part, that all inhabitants were free to vote and that the security of the vote was maintained.'[8] Indeed at one point, in mid-September 1924, Feetham suggested to the British Government that legislation might be enacted to enable a plebiscite to be taken. There was, however, a view in the Colonial Office that such legislation 'would present political hazards for the British Government and that it might be impossible to enforce the resultant award in the teeth of Ulster Unionist resistance'.[9] In a memo dated 9 May 1924, Lionel Curtis suggested that a grave situation would arise if the Boundary Commission decided to conduct a border plebiscite. In such a case, the British were 'certain to meet with the armed resistance of the Protestant majority throughout Northern Ireland'. Commenting on the Curtis memorandum, the Army General Staff estimated that if a plebiscite were to be held, at least three divisions, a brigade of cavalry and some armoured cars would be needed to 'cordon off Tyrone, Fermanagh and Armagh, and prevent outside interference from either Northern Ireland or the Free State'.[10]

Such compelling considerations ensured that the Irish Boundary Commission would not facilitate the free expression of the popular will, as the European commissions strove to do. In the process, an opportunity was also lost to redress a grievance commonly expressed by Nationalists: that the 1920

7 Geoffrey Hand, *Report on the Irish Boundary Commission 1925* (Shannon, 1969), p. 59.
8 Ibid.
9 Geoffrey Hand, in F. X. Martin and F. J. Byrne (eds), *Eoin MacNeill, The Scholar Revolutionary 1867–1945* (Shannon, 1973), pp. 228–9.
10 Paul Canning, *British Policy towards Ireland 1921–1941* (Oxford, 1985), pp. 91–2.

partition had been ultimately implemented by the British Government without any gesture to popular consultation. Feetham drew another remarkable conclusion from the terms of Article 12 when he suggested that 'the absence from the Article of any provision for a plebiscite affords grounds for inferring that it was not the intention of the parties to the Treaty that the Commission should ascertain the wishes of the inhabitants in that manner'.[11] If, as he decided, the Commission could not have recourse to a plebiscite, he had to find some means of ascertaining the wishes of the inhabitants other than by asking them. His problem here was that if Article 12 did not mention a plebiscite, it did not mention any other method of satisfying the self-determination element in the boundary clause. Undeterred by this difficulty, Feetham found no problem in fixing on three: census returns for 1911, election results, and 'evidence of persons claiming to speak on behalf of inhabitants of different areas'.[12] In coming to this conclusion, he failed to advert to the fact that it was open to exactly the same objection he had just used to rule out a plebiscite: none of his three methods was mentioned in Article 12.

The value of using plebiscites as the sole means of ascertaining the wishes of inhabitants becomes evident when European boundary commission practice is examined in relation to the methods Feetham resorted to. In effect, this meant one method, as he explained when he dismissed the use of plebiscites. In his 'Interpretation and Principles of Application', he announced that 'the Commission has been invited by both parties to the boundary controversy to rely upon the census returns of 1911, showing the religious denominations to which inhabitants belong, as affording an indication of the wishes of the inhabitants'.[13] This gives an inaccurate impression of the attitude of one of the parties, the Free State Government, to the use of the 1911 Census as the means of establishing the wishes of inhabitants. It is true that initially those who advised Cosgrave and his ministers believed that, as B. C. Waller put it, 'a plebiscite is unnecessary as the wishes of the inhabitants are already well known by the results of elections and other indications, and where unnecessary the expense and possible danger of a plebiscite are best avoided.'[14] In 1924, however, both Free State and northern Nationalist leaders felt that the interests of the six-county minority would be served only if the Irish Boundary Commission followed the European example. In August 1924, the Fermanagh Nationalist leader, Cahir Healy, conscious that Article 12 bore 'a striking similarity' to boundary clauses in the Versailles Treaty, wrote that the border minorities

11   Hand, *Report* (1969), p. 30.
12   Ibid.
13   Ibid., p. 25.
14   B. C. Waller, Notes on a possible offer to Northern Ireland, NAI S4084, 25 Sept. 1924.

would be satisfied if the Anglo-Irish Treaty were 'interpreted in the same democratic way as the Commissioners interpreted the European document': there must, in other words, be an Irish plebiscite to ascertain the wishes of the inhabitants as there had been in Upper Silesia.[15] In September 1924, the Free State Executive Council decided that a demand should be made for a plebiscite in all Poor Law Unions which showed a Catholic majority in the 1911 Census.[16] In November 1924, Nationalist legal agents and northern Catholic clerical leaders agreed to insist on a plebiscite based on Poor Law Unions.[17] In December 1924, Healy, fearing that the vagueness of Article 12 might prove disadvantageous to the Nationalist case, told George Murnaghan, solicitor to the Boundary Bureau, that if the Commission did not define its terms of reference, Nationalists were going to be cheated. To avoid this, Healy urged that 'we should insist on a plebiscite, and if that is denied us, leave the Commission'.[18] By the end of 1924, Feetham, on political as much as judicial grounds, had decided that he was not going to follow European precedent. He told a meeting of Derry Nationalists that there would be no plebiscite, but that 'all records, including census figures and the results of the elections, would be taken into account'.[19]

II LESSONS FROM EUROPE

The fundamental deficiencies inherent in Feetham's scheme for ascertaining the wishes of inhabitants are suggested by a consideration of what happened elsewhere when plebiscites were used for this purpose. A good illustration is provided by the plebiscite conducted in the Klagenfurt Basin in 1920. The question of the disposition of the Klagenfurt Basin, which formed the southeastern part of Carinthia, became one of the most important minor disputes at the Paris Peace Conference. The plebiscite area contained about 755 square miles and a population of about 125,900.[20] The states in contention for Klagenfurt were Austria and Yugoslavia. For the purposes of a plebiscite,

15 Cahir Healy in *The Weekly Westminster*, 16 Aug. 1924, cited in Eamon Phoenix, *Northern Nationalism, Nationalist Politics, Partition and the Catholic Minority in Northern Ireland* (Belfast, 1994), p. 304.

16 Executive Council Minutes, NAI G 2/3, C2/128, 8 Sept. 1924.

17 North-Eastern Boundary Bureau Correspondence, Minutes of Conference in Dublin, NAI Boundary Bureau Papers, 12. Nov. 1924.

18 Healy to Murnaghan, North-Eastern Boundary Bureau Correspondence (Oct. 1924–Feb. 1925), NAI Boundary Bureau Papers, 5 Dec. 1924.

19 *Irish News*, 22 Dec. 1924.

20 Wambaugh, *Plebiscites since the World War*, Vol. 1, p. 163.

which was to be the sole means of determining the political future of the inhabitants of Klagenfurt, the Allied and Associated Powers decided to divide the region into two zones: Zone 1, the southern and larger zone, covering about 622 square miles, and with about 73,000 inhabitants who were predominantly Slovene in speech, and Zone 2, with a population of about 54,000 who were predominantly German-speaking. The only real question at issue between Austria and Yugoslavia was the future of Zone 1, since the Yugoslav Government did not claim jurisdiction over Zone 2. The plebiscite was administered by an international commission of four members, one nominated respectively by the United States, Great Britain, France and Italy. The contending parties were also allowed representation. The Allied Powers decided that if the vote in Zone 1 should be in favour of Austria, no vote should be taken in Zone 2.

Had the Allied Powers, in dealing with Zone 1 of Klagenfurt, worked on principles similar to those employed by Feetham, they might have decided that the Austrian Census of 1910 gave them all the evidence they needed about the wishes of the inhabitants, without having recourse to a plebiscite, since this showed that 68.6 per cent of the population of the zone was Slovene-speaking, and that the countryside had for the most part a Slovene majority, rising in a large area to 95 per cent, being even higher in some parishes.[21] On such evidence, they might have assigned Zone 1 to Yugoslavia without misgivings. The results of the plebiscite in Zone 1, however, dramatically confounded expectations based on the ethnographical preponderance of the Slovenes. Of 37,303 votes cast, representing 95.76 per cent of registered voters, 22,025 voted for Austria and 15,278 for Yugoslavia, Austria thus winning 59.04 per cent of the total vote. The Yugoslavs had been confident of victory: the winning of only 40.96 per cent of the votes was received by them with bitter surprise, since it meant that 10,000 Slovene-speaking voters and 21 of the predominantly Slovene communes had voted for Austria.[22] A legal adviser to the Irish Boundary Bureau, Patrick Lynch KC, had little doubt that 'economic and geographical factors played the largest part in the Austrian victory', and a factor 'that did sway a very great number of the inhabitants was the question of future markets for their produce'.[23] The Klagenfurt plebiscite suggests the inadequacy of Feetham's system of boundary drawing based on a fourteen-year-old census of religious allegiance. As that plebiscite showed, the wishes of inhabitants, when their political, economic and geographical futures were at stake, were not necessarily determined by merely ethnic, cultural, religious

21   Ibid., p. 166.
22   Ibid., pp. 198–200.
23   Boundary Bureau Papers, NAI, Carton 29.

or ideological preoccupations. In Zone 1 of Klagenfurt, many inhabitants were prepared to put convenience and closeness to advantageous markets in Austria before strong national sentiment. In the absence of a plebiscite, it was impossible to know whether Feetham's assumption that all border Catholics wanted union with the Free State and that all border Protestants wanted to be governed from Belfast might have had as little foundation as the assumption that Slovenes in Klagenfurt would naturally see their future in the Yugoslav Kingdom of the Serbs, Croats and Slovenes. David Fitzpatrick offers a minor piece of evidence to suggest that it was not always possible to equiparate confessional allegiance with political outlook. Of the Ulster Covenant Fitzpatrick remarks that 'not all signatories were Protestants: according to the RIC, the Covenant was signed by Catholics in every district of Antrim'.[24] Whether it was always freely signed is, of course, another question.

The plebiscites in Allenstein and Marienwerder in July 1920 offered further convincing evidence that census figures, whether as reflecting the religious, cultural, ethnic or linguistic composition of regions, did not constitute an adequate basis on which to pronounce on the political preferences of their inhabitants. What was of greater significance in Feetham's decision was that these examples afforded little justification for making a religious census the main guide to the fixing of the Irish boundary. The Allenstein plebiscite area measured 4,715 square miles, with a population of about 558,000, while Marienwerder measured about 1,000 square miles with a population of 160,720. Language statistics were available from the German Census of 1910 showing that almost 85 per cent of the population of the Marienwerder plebiscite area was German-speaking, the figure for the Allenstein area being 52.4 per cent. The five-member Boundary Commission calculated that Allenstein contained 279,600 Poles and 263,300 Germans.[25] When the German Government objected to plebiscites being held in Allenstein and Marienwerder, the Allied reply, transmitted on 16 June 1919 raised concerns which Feetham might well have pondered when he came to interpret and apply the provisions of Article 12 in the Irish boundary clause. The Allies pointed out that there was a considerable Polish majority in Allenstein. The Germans, on the other hand, suggested that the Poles would not wish to be separated from Germany. The Allied response to this was reasonable: 'It is precisely because there may be some doubt as to the political leanings of the inhabitants that the Allied and Associated Powers have determined to hold a plebiscite here. Where the affinities of a population are undoubted, there is no necessity for a plebiscite; where they are in doubt, there a plebiscite is enjoined.' The Allies went on to

24 See David Fitzpatrick, *The Two Irelands 1912–1939* (Oxford, 1998), pp. 245.
25 Wambaugh, *Plebiscites since the World War*, Vol. 1, pp. 99–105.

declare that a plebiscite was 'the most obvious means' of applying the principle of self-determination.[26] The results of the plebiscites in the two areas justified the belief that the wishes of the inhabitants could not be gauged from census figures, that these indeed were a most unreliable guide. Had the Commissioners relied on the ethnographic, religious and linguistic data for Allenstein, and not conducted a plebiscite, they would, prescinding from economic and geographic factors, have awarded the region to Poland. The result of the Allenstein plebiscite shows how mistaken this would have been. Of an estimated Polish population of 279,600 or 51.2 per cent of the region, only 8,018 people voted for Poland, which got 2.14 per cent of the total vote. In many areas where over 60 per cent of the inhabitants had Polish as their mother tongue, fewer than 2 per cent voted for Poland.[27]

The massive vote for Prussia in both Allenstein and Marienwerder was substantially influenced by the contrasting economic circumstances of Germany and Poland. As was the case with the Slovenes in Klagenfurt, many Polish voters put their economic interests before whatever patriotic sentiments their ethnic background might have inspired. Wambaugh observes that the Polish state, 'not yet organised and its stability doubted by a great part of Europe, was in no position to offer material advantages equal to those which the area had long enjoyed under Germany.'[28] An Irish border plebiscite would at least have given the opportunity to the participants to weigh their economic self-interest against their atavistic political inclinations, as Slovenes and Poles were allowed to do. Instead, Feetham withheld this choice, and made it for them himself, by deciding first where their economic advantage lay, and then giving it precedence over their likely political preferences in deciding the jurisdiction to which they were to belong.

Feetham's decision that where the presumed wishes of inhabitants were in conflict with economic and geographic conditions, the latter must prevail, contrasted sharply with the general European interpretation of clauses similar to the boundary clause in Article 12. One post-war settlement was, however, devised in a way that had something in common with Feetham's adjudication. This concerned Armenia, whose leaders had long complained of Turkish oppression. In 1916, when Britain was at war with Turkey, Asquith declared that his Government was resolved to secure the liberation from Turkey of what he called 'this ancient people'. It became British policy to do everything possible to determine the future of Armenia upon the principle of self-determination. Up to the beginning of 1917, neither the British nor the French

26 Ibid., p. 108.
27 Ibid., pp. 133–4.
28 Ibid., p. 140.

Governments had fully decided what they were fighting for. They realised, however, that if they were to involve the United States in the war, they would need to espouse some great principle: this they found in 'national self-determination'. This, among other things, would be expected to bring about 'the freeing of the populations subject to the bloody tyranny of the Turks'.[29] On 10 August 1920, the Allied and Associated Powers recognised the Armenian Republic *de jure* by admitting its representatives to sign a peace treaty with Turkey at Sèvres, Article 89 of which made provision for a new Turkish-Armenian frontier. This Treaty recognised Armenia as a 'free, independent state', and President Wilson was asked to fix the Turkish-Armenian boundary. On 22 November 1920, he announced the award of about 40,000 square miles of pre-war Turkish territory to Armenia. One element of Wilson's arbitration bears a curious resemblance to Feetham's approach to the relation between economic factors and self-determination. Wilson decided that 'the conflicting territorial desires of the inhabitants along the boundaries could not always be harmonised'. This being the case, he concluded that 'consideration of a healthy economic life for the future state of Armenia should be decisive'.[30] Wilson, however, made some minor concessions to geography and ethnicity when these were not in conflict with economic considerations. Districts along the border which were predominantly Kurdish or Turkish were left to Turkey rather than assigned to Armenia, 'unless trade relations with definite market towns threw them necessarily into the Armenian State.'[31] Feetham saw the six-county state in much the same light as Wilson saw Armenia: its economic survival took precedence over the application of the principle of self-determination to the overwhelmingly Nationalist population of Newry and south Down.

III THE UPPER SILESIAN MODEL

Of all the post-Versailles boundary settlements the one in Upper Silesia provides perhaps the most appropriate standard against which the work of the Irish Boundary Commission may be measured. Officials of the Free State Boundary Bureau were conscious of the possibilities inherent in the use of the Silesian Boundary Commission as a model for the Irish one. Lloyd George was intimately and influentially involved with setting the terms governing

29 A. J. P. Taylor, *The First World War: An Illustrated History* (London, 1981), p. 161.
30 A. Oye Cukwurah, *The Settlement of Boundary Disputes in International Law* (Manchester, 1967), p. 166.
31 Ibid.

both the Silesian and Irish Boundary Commissions. He was, when European boundary settlements were in question, anxious to uphold the political preferences of inhabitants in disputed regions, and the principles of nationality and self-determination. On such issues, A. J. P. Taylor argues, 'Lloyd George, so often despised as unprincipled, was the one man who stuck to his principles. He insisted on a plebiscite in Silesia, which turned out in Germany's favour ... He held out firmly against the incorporation into Poland of Danzig, a purely German town.'[32] The democratic principles which informed dealings with many European settlements were less in evidence in the formulation of the boundary clause of the Anglo-Irish Treaty. In 1920, Lloyd George presided over the incorporation into the northern Irish State of such predominantly Nationalist border towns as Derry and Newry and of other Nationalist areas such as south Down and south Armagh. The proximity of all these to the Free State would have facilitated their inclusion in the latter without violating either cartographic symmetry or the principles which governed the treatment of Upper Silesia and Danzig.

As early as October 1922, Kevin O'Shiel reported to the Executive Council that he had assigned a number of experts to the task of 'exploring every possible political aspect of the Silesian, the Schleswig-Holstein and the Hungarian plebiscites'.[33] In one respect, as B. C. Waller, the expert adviser to the Irish Boundary Bureau, recognised the Irish and Silesian situations were dissimilar. In a memorandum to Kevin O'Higgins, Waller saw an Irish boundary settlement based on permanent partition as something to be avoided. 'It is a very different thing,' he wrote, 'to draw a boundary in Upper Silesia between Germany and Poland which are two separate states, than to draw it between two parts of a country which we hope will eventually be one.'[34] Waller's observation draws attention to a troublesome dilemma which confronted all Irish Nationalists, north and south, who were working for a significant redrawing of the 1920 boundary and a territorially much larger Free State, and who regarded minor adjustment as an unacceptable interpretation of Article 12 of the Treaty. Those who believed that large-scale transfers of territory to the south were the likely outcome of the work of the Boundary Commission, and who still aspired to the traditional Nationalist goal of a unified independent Irish state, were bound to realise that the achievement of unity in the immediate or medium-term future depended on the failure of a much-reduced Loyalist entity to survive independently of the rest of the

32   Taylor, *First World War*, p. 267.

33   O'Shiel Memorandum, NAI S4743, 14 Oct. 1922.

34   B. C. Waller to Kevin O'Higgins Memorandum. Notes on possible offer to Northern Ireland, NAI, S4084, 25 Sept. 1924.

island, by no means an assured prospect. Republican Nationalists, whose fundamental aim was a united Ireland, tended to view the work of the Boundary Commission as an unwelcome diversion, whose end result, however much border territory it might transfer from one jurisdiction to another, could only strengthen the position of Ulster Unionists. From any kind of realistic Nationalist perspective, the Boundary Commission involved a sinister paradox. The greater the extent to which the Commission favoured the Nationalist case, the smaller would be the population of Nationalists remaining in the northern state. The impetus for national unity coming from within that state would thus be correspondingly diminished.

There is a paradoxical congruence between this point of view and the outlook of some British statesmen, notably Lloyd George, at the time when the measure which partitioned Ireland in 1920 was being framed. Members of Lloyd George's Cabinet were in general agreement that the six-county arrangement was not easy to defend in terms of the principle of self-determination, depriving as it did inordinate numbers of Nationalists of this right. Originally, the British Cabinet had been prepared to incorporate an even more considerable Nationalist population in a Unionist-controlled state by implementing a nine-county partition, in the belief that partition was, and ought to be, no more than a temporary expedient, and that the smaller the overall Unionist majority, the nearer the day of eventual Irish unity. The converse of this was that the greater the preponderance of Unionists over Nationalists, as might for example have emerged in 1925 if a boundary commission had reclaimed large Catholic areas for the Free State, the smaller would have been the likelihood of a united Ireland, the position taken by many Republicans when the Boundary Commission was doing its work. During the Treaty negotiations in 1921, Lloyd George defended the six-county unit on the ground that its relatively large Nationalist population made it more provisional, telling Griffith, with a degree of sincerity that remains uncertain, that 'in order to persuade Ulster to come in there is an advantage in her having a Catholic population'.[35] This argument might have carried even greater weight had the original scheme for a nine-county state, unacceptable to the majority of Unionists for the very reason advanced by Lloyd George, been enforced in 1920.

In other respects, the complexity of the problems which the Silesian Boundary Commission was required to solve, and the large measure of its success in doing this, made it a useful case study for advocates of the Irish Nationalist point of view. In Silesia, as in Ireland, there were powerful tensions between two ethnic groups. The Silesian plebiscite was delayed when a Polish force attempted to seize the disputed area, but the fact that in the face

---

35　Thomas Jones, in Keith Middlemas (ed.), *Whitehall Diary* vol. 3 (London, 1971), p. 131.

of a month's armed hostilities between Poles and Germans a plebiscite could be held and an award made[36] was evidence that a boundary settlement, largely reflecting the wishes of those affected, could be completed even in the most adverse circumstances, something which many people in Britain and Ireland doubted when they commented on the Irish situation. Apart from major ethnic conflict, an equitable partition of Silesia was made difficult by economic circumstances. Of much greater relevance to the Irish situation was the fact that the geographical distribution of the population involved such a haphazard mixture of racial elements that any division must inevitably result, as the Council of the League of Nations observed in October 1921, 'in leaving relatively large minorities on both sides of the line.'[37] An Irish boundary commission would have to face the same kind of problem if it decided that the principle of self-determination was to be thoroughly applied over wide areas. Large homogeneous districts without significant minority enclaves were as rare in Silesia as they were in Ulster border regions. In both cases, significant numbers of people were bound to be dissatisfied.

The Allied and Associated Powers, in dealing with Silesia, had to apply Article 88, Annex 5 of the Treaty of Versailles, which stipulated that 'regard will be paid to the wishes of the inhabitants as shown by the vote and to the geographical and economic conditions of the locality', a formulation only slightly different from that in Article 12 of the Anglo-Irish Treaty. Before the Silesian Boundary Commission could carry out its work, the Allied Powers had to deal with the German claim that Upper Silesia was not traditionally a part of Polish territory, and that separation from Germany was not in accord with the wishes or interests of the population as a whole. Against this, the Allied Powers advanced the view that while Poland had no legal claim to Upper Silesia, 'it is emphatically not true that she has no claim that could be supported on the principles of President Wilson', specifically the principle of self-determination. This claim had its basis in the fact that the majority of the population was indisputably Polish: the 1910 Census for the Silesian plebiscite area showed that there were 1,248,000 Poles and 673,000 Germans. Under the circumstances, the Allied and Associated Powers were willing 'to allow the question to be determined by those particularly concerned'.[38] It is important to observe that the Allies were anxious to place the predominant emphasis on

36   Roman Dyboski (ed.), *Cambridge History of Poland 1697–1935 Vol. 2: From Augustus II to Pilsudski* (Cambridge, 1951), pp. 515–7.

37   In many rural districts the Polish-speaking population numbered 80 or 90 per cent, but in the five industrial towns the German majority ranged from 54 to 58 per cent. Wambaugh, *Plebiscites since the World War*, Vol. 1, pp. 211–58.

38   Ibid., p. 216.

the wishes of the inhabitants, although geographical and economic conditions were also to be considered according to the terms of Article 88, the governing instrument. Balfour, the British Representative on the League of Nations Council, later to declare that the similar clause in Article 12 of the Anglo-Irish Treaty had a contrary meaning, had no doubt that those who framed the Peace Treaty 'put population first and industry second'. Acknowledging that there was a point at which the wishes of the population must give way to the needs of the district, in the industrial area, for example, Balfour was certain that the European treaty-makers 'desired that as far as possible the wishes of the population (of Upper Silesia), as exhibited by the plebiscite should afford the ground upon which the decision should be come to'.[39]

Feetham's decision on the balance between self-determination, geography and economics reversed Balfour's principle. This reversal, if considered in a European perspective, appears in need of greater explanation than Feetham offered. It is beyond dispute that the boundary clause of the Anglo-Irish Treaty derived directly from the Upper Silesian and other European models, and that Feetham was aware of this. By the time he came to determine the Irish boundary, the various European commissions had completed their work. Details of their decisions and of the principles underlying these were widely available. It was also easy to ascertain what those who framed the provisions governing the Commissions had in mind: such information was provided in detail in the reports submitted to the League of Nations by those whose task it was to settle disputed boundaries. The Silesian Report, compiled by a committee of experts, was placed before the League on 6 August 1921. From the Irish point of view, this Report was especially relevant in one significant respect. Its authors suggested how the guiding elements of the Silesian boundary clause, namely wishes of inhabitants, geography and economics, were to be applied to boundary determination and how they ranked in order of importance. On the ranking issue, which became central to Feetham's interpretation of the identical Irish boundary clause, the authors of the Silesian Report were unequivocal in their decision that no frontier could be based on the wishes of the inhabitants because of the intermingling of the racial groups. However, the experts also decided that economics and geography must be seen as secondary, not primary, elements, to be invoked on the condition that 'the wishes of the population held the foremost place in the elements to be taken into account'.[40]

39 *The Times* (London), 17 Oct. 1921.

40 'Report of the Committee of experts appointed to study the frontier to be laid down between Germany and Poland in Upper Silesia as the result of the plebiscite.' Copy submitted to the Irish Boundary Commission by a group of Nationalist residents in various parts of Northern Ireland, CAB 61/121, 6 Aug. 1921.

Feetham and the interpreters of the identical Silesian clause came to opposite conclusions as to what the three-part formulation meant and how it should be applied. The authors of the Silesian Report were firmly of the opinion that economic or geographical factors could not nullify the wishes of the inhabitants. Feetham, even in cases where the wishes of inhabitants were deemed overwhelmingly in favour of inclusion in another jurisdiction – in effect the Free State, ruled that economics and geography could, indeed must, prevail. Newry and its surrounding district provides the outstanding example of this. Newry's three districts, two rural and one urban, had Catholic, and in Feetham's terms therefore Nationalist, populations of 60.7, 67.5 and 74.6 per cent respectively. Feetham decided that even this incontrovertible evidence of democratic choice must yield to something essentially subjective: his own estimation of the extent to which the wishes of over two thirds of the people in the area in question must be given lesser weight than the possible adverse economic effects of acceding to these wishes. In favour of preserving the status quo, Feetham's main argument was based on Newry's position as a centre of the flax-spinning and linen-weaving industry, and of its mills and factories as a component of a highly organised industry concentrated in Northern Ireland. He concluded that 'to subject the Newry group of mills and factories to the handicaps involved in separation by a [Free State] customs barrier from their centre for organisation and for distribution of their products [Belfast] and to place them in a different customs area to their competitors, in which the system of taxation had a distinctly protective character, exposes them to special risks'.[41]

Feetham's analysis of these economic risks was largely speculative: 'It is impossible in such a case to predict results with certainty, but it is necessary to take account of the *probabilities* . . . A small increase in their [the linen factories of Newry] costs of production, or even the *fear* of such an increase, *may lead* to the partial or complete closing down of the local undertakings . . . such *risks* which affect the employment and livelihood of large numbers of the population, and the prosperity of the town as a trading centre, cannot, in the opinion of the Commission, be disregarded.'[42] As Feetham came to his determination, speculation gave way to certainty: 'The Commission has come to the conclusion that the change which *would* be involved in the separation of Newry and its surrounding area from the rest of Northern Ireland cannot be regarded as a change which is compatible with economic and geographic conditions.'[43] Having satisfied himself that his analysis had shown that the guiding elements which the Commission was directed to take into account, the wishes of inhabitants and economic and geographic considerations, were definitely in

41   Hand, *Report* (1969), p. 137.
42   Ibid. (author's italics)
43   Ibid. (author's italics)

conflict with respect to the Newry area, he concluded that 'under the terms of Article XII economic and geographic conditions *must* prevail'.[44] This conclusion could not be justified by reference to the terms of Article 12, which failed to give any direction as to what should happen when there was conflict between the wishes of inhabitants, on the one hand, and econo-   mic and geographic factors, on the other. Feetham's 'must prevail' adds a dimension to the Article, as if it should have been read as signifying that the Commission was to determine the boundary primarily in accordance with economic and geographic conditions, with the wishes of the inhabitants exercising some vague and indeterminate qualifying influence.

The vote in Upper Silesia was taken in March 1921. Of the 1,220,514 registered voters, 1,190,846 voted, or 97.5 per cent. Of these, 707,605, or 59.6 per cent, voted for Germany, and 479,359, or 40.3 per cent, for Poland. A map based on these results, especially in the industrial area, would have been an intricate mosaic: the majority of communes there had voted for Poland, but the cities had all given German majorities. It was impossible for the Boundary Commission to award each commune innumerable enclaves. After considerable debate, Germany was awarded 75 per cent of the area of the industrial district and 57 per cent of its inhabitants. The 25 per cent of the area allotted to Poland contained by far the greater part of its mining and manufacturing resources. From the point of view of population, the award was an extremely accurate reflection of the voting percentages. B. C. Waller, commentating on the implications of this for the Irish Boundary Commission, pointed out that along the border of the six counties, there was no area of such overwhelming economic importance as the industrial region of Upper Silesia 'where a division might have such evil results'. He drew the sensible conclusion that if the wishes of the inhabitants were held to be the supreme factor in Silesia, a region where economic considerations might have been considered paramount, there was even a stronger case for holding them to be so in Ireland.[45] The Silesian plebiscite showed that the only accurate method of asserting the wishes of inhabitants was to permit them to express these in a free vote, independently supervised. The available census figures showed that only 35 per cent of the population of the area was German, yet despite this, almost 60 per cent voted for Germany. Had the wishes of the inhabitants been decided for them on the evidence of the census, as Feetham was to do, the territorial outcome would have been far different. As was the case in Allenstein, Marienwerder and Klagenfurt, economic advantage influenced a considerable number of voters.[46]

---

44 Ibid. (author's italics)
45 Waller Memorandum, Kennedy Papers, UCDA P4/390/18.
46 Wambaugh, *Plebiscites since the World War*, Vol. i, p. 227.

IV THE IMPORTANCE OF PLEBISCITES

The vital importance of plebiscites when self-determination was in question was nowhere better illustrated than by the case of Upper Silesia. When this region was part of Germany, out of its eight constituencies for the Reichstag in 1918, five were represented by members of the Polish Party. When the question of a plebiscite on the disposal of Upper Silesia between Germany and Poland as part of the peace settlement was under discussion by the Council of Four, Clemenceau, the French Prime Minister, contended unsuccessfully that a plebiscite was unnecessary in these eight constituencies as they had already expressed their wishes. Yet when a plebiscite was held, the 1918 position was almost exactly reversed: Sixty per cent of the votes were cast for Germany and only forty per cent for Poland. The explanation for this appears to have been that a large number of persons of Polish extraction had voted for Polish candidates in an election at a time when secession from Germany was not a practical issue, as they wanted to be represented by men of their own type, but when the possibility of secession loomed, they had no desire to be transferred from Germany to Poland. Those who had first-hand involvement in the work of the various European commissions had come to learn that existing evidence, whether based on religious affiliation, electoral returns or linguistic patterns, had considerable general value in determining what districts must be regarded as doubtful in regard to their national sentiments. However, the value of such evidence as a guide to the exact delimitation of a boundary once partition is decided upon was found to be much smaller, if indeed it had any value at all. The lesson from Europe for the Irish Boundary Commission was clear: the assumption that religious and electoral evidence was an accurate reflection of the wishes of the inhabitants of Northern Ireland on the political question, on which Feetham relied in the absence of a plebiscite, was fundamentally unsound.[47] An authoritative sixteen-page analysis of this issue was submitted to Lionel Curtis at the Colonial Office in 1923 by Francis Bourdillon, who had represented the Foreign Office on the German-Polish frontier campaign. Bourdillon, who was to become Secretary to the Irish Boundary Commission, strongly emphasised the need for a plebiscite in the Irish case.

Some of the new post-war frontiers of Europe were, *faute de mieux*, mainly fixed according to existing statistical evidence: religious affiliation, ethnic background and the most recent parliamentary election results. In such cases, doubts prevailed as to the possibility of obtaining genuine, credible plebiscites. This was the position which confronted Feetham and the Irish Boundary Commission. European experience showed that frontiers drawn on the basis

47   Bourdillon to Curtis, PRO CO 739/25/60802, 7 Dec. 1923.

of existing evidence and in the absence of plebiscites hardly ever corresponded to the wishes of the inhabitants. As a result of the failure to make use of plebiscites, areas were segregated from countries of which they had formed part for centuries. Bourdillon had come across areas transferred on the basis of statistical evidence only, in which 'hardly five per cent of the population had wished to change their nationality'.[48] Frontiers so created are liable to result in a series of irridentas: districts adjacent to frontiers in which the inhabitants feel that they belong to the nation on the other side. Such irridentas were to be found post-Versailles along most of the eastern border of Germany and in the area transferred from Germany to Czechoslovakia, under a settlement based on the evidence of language. This example of boundary drawing was to have disastrous political consequences 16 years later for the Czechoslovak State, as would the Irish experiment at a later stage still, for similar reasons.

Language was not an evidential issue in Ireland, but religion was, to the extent that a person's religious affiliation was generally regarded, as it was by Feetham, as the surest guide, indeed the only one, to political preference. In parts of East Prussia, religious statistics were taken into account where they conflicted with language statistics. The East Prussia plebiscite showed that in the rural district of Allenstein, where over 60 per cent of the population were Polish-speaking Catholics, fewer than 16 per cent wished to be transferred to Poland. In West Prussia, in the rural district of Stuhm, where over 40 per cent of the population were Polish-speaking Catholics, only 20 per cent voted for Poland. In Upper Silesia, in three adjacent districts, where over 80 per cent of the population were Polish-speaking Catholics, the votes for Poland formed only 46, 50 and 25 per cent respectively. These instances are especially striking in view of the clear association, in most parts of the German-Polish borderland, of religious and national sentiment, Catholicism being the national religion of the Poles, and Protestantism that of the Silesian Germans. Bourdillon, who was in an excellent position to know, remarked that Polish peasants in West Prussia believe that the Virgin was Polish, 'while in Upper Silesia Polish priests have been known to declare that prayers offered in any language but Polish would not be understood.'[49] The inescapable conclusion here is that the great divergence in such an area, between the evidence of religious statistics and the voting pattern in the plebiscite, indicates the impossibility of basing a frontier on religious statistics.

The evidence from the proceedings and outcomes of contemporary boundary commissions supports the view that plebiscites were the only desirable or

---

48   Bourdillon submission to Curtis, Section B, p. 3. PRO CO 739/25/60802, 7 Dec. 1923. Henceforth cited as 'Bourdillon article'.

49   Bourdillon article, pp 4–5.

rational and fair means of determining the wishes of inhabitants. In the Irish case, requests for such plebiscites came exclusively from Nationalists. This implied a Nationalist expectation that if Feetham ordered border plebiscites, and even conceded the extreme Nationalist demand that Fermanagh and Tyrone should be single units for voting purposes, the result would support the Nationalist case for large-scale territorial adjustment in favour of the Free State. There are, however, indications that an Irish border plebiscite might well have confounded expectations based on religious affiliation as reported in a 14-year-old census. While Unionists had long been working successfully to raise Protestant numbers in Fermanagh in particular,[50] and demonstrating a purposeful determination to keep their territory intact, Nationalists were unable to agree on a united approach to boundary adjustment: the Boundary Commission clause, like the Treaty itself, was a fruitful source of division among them. The bitter disputes on the issue between the two Nationalist groups, Republicans and Nationalist supporters of the Treaty, reflected in the 1924 Westminster election, would almost certainly surface once more in a border plebiscite, with many border Republicans, committed to Irish unity, likely to abstain or even to vote against incorporation in the Free State. An example from Tyrone provides a good illustration. In July 1924, a Dungannon Nationalist, John Doris, wrote a worried letter to Cosgrave painting a pessimistic picture of the relatively weak exertions of Tyrone Nationalists in the promotion of their own presumed interests. Doris was concerned that if a plebiscite were deemed necessary by the Boundary Commission to ascertain the wishes of inhabitants, it would be based on the parliamentary register, which, in the course of a year, had become far less favourable to the Nationalists of Tyrone and Fermanagh. The explanation for this state of affairs reflects the extent to which Unionists were prepared to go to preserve the 1920 partition settlement, and the negligence, lethargy and divisiveness prevalent among Nationalists. 'At present,' Doris told Cosgrave, 'the register in Tyrone is stuffed with thousands of Craig's Specials, large numbers of them imports from other counties, and owing to the unfortunate differences among ourselves, registration last year was sadly neglected.'[51] Similar evidence was tendered to Eoin MacNeill in January 1925 by a local man in a sensitive border area who advised against a plebiscite there because although there was, on paper, a Catholic majority in the district, it seemed likely that enough

50   See Terence Dooley, 'Protestant migration from the Free State to Northern Ireland, 1920–5: A private census for Co. Fermanagh', *Clogher Record* Vol. xv, No. 3 (1996). Dooley lists the names of just over 2,100 Protestants who migrated to County Fermanagh from the 26 counties in the years from 1920 to 1925.

51   John Doris to W. T. Cosgrave, Boundary Bureau Papers, NAI, Carton 29, 24 July. 1924.

Catholics, particularly Republicans, would abstain, or even vote for inclusion in Northern Ireland as a method of undermining the significance of Article 12.[52] In the Westminster General Election of November 1924 almost 7,000 people in the Fermanagh-Tyrone constituency voted for Republican candidates standing on an anti-partition, and by extension, anti-Boundary Commission, platform.[53] Whatever the result of a plebiscite, it would have been a useful practical expression of public feeling on the partition of 1920, and a means of avoiding the largely barren arguments to which Feetham's procedures inevitably gave rise.

If the primary focus is on the principle of self-determination rather than on the aspirations of rival governments, the work of any boundary commission is to be judged on whether the people of the area received the maximum of satisfaction according to their vote. In the case of the Silesian plebiscite, the final award gave satisfaction to 64.5 per cent of those who voted. Comparison with the Irish Boundary Commission is inhibited by Feetham's decision not to hold a plebiscite, with the result that the wishes of inhabitants can only be guessed at on the basis of religious affiliation recorded in the 1911 Census, an unreliable guide to how people might have voted in a plebiscite, as the European precedents showed. If religious affiliation is used as a guide to the wishes of inhabitants, however, some comparisons can be attempted between the Irish Boundary Commission and others. A claim presented to the Commission by a group of border Nationalists involved the transfer to the Free State of an area with a population of 464,145, of whom 258,617 were Catholics and 205,528 members of other religious denominations.[54] These were the only inhabitants of the six counties whom the Commission might have been expected to transfer, even if Nationalist claims were to be fully met. Meeting the full Unionist claim would have meant transferring none of these inhabitants. Thus, had the full Nationalist claim been conceded 55.7% of those in the area that the Commission could consider would have been satisfied. Feetham's final award transferred 27,843 Catholics to the Free State and 2,764 to the six counties, achieving the net result of satisfying 25,079 Catholics, or 9.6 per cent of those who might, in Feetham's terms, have wanted to join the Free State. The award transferred 4,830 inhabitants of other denominations to the six counties, and 3,476 to the Free State. This meant that since there was no net transfer of Unionists to the Free State, the Unionist satisfaction rate was 100 per cent. Despite this Unionists could argue that these transfers should be considered in an all-Ireland partition context. If this argument were to be

52   See Hand, in Martin and Byrne, *The Scholar Revolutionary*, p. 212.
53   See Brian M. Walker, *Parliamentary Election Results in Ireland 1918–92* (Dublin, 1992), p. 16.
54   Hand, *Report* (1969), pp. 74–5.

accepted, the statistics of satisfaction would be significantly different. If the most effective partition is 'that which creates the smallest minorities on each side of the dividing line',[55] both the 1920 partition and that proposed by Feetham were seriously defective when measured by contemporary standards.

The Schleswig plebiscite of 1920 was held in order to determine the boundary between Germany and Denmark in the northern half of the province of Schleswig. The plebiscite area, comprising all the north and part of Central Schleswig, had 270,000 inhabitants. Both parties to the boundary dispute agreed that whatever frontier emerged should correspond to the principle of nationality and self-determination. In Northern Schleswig, the total vote was 75,431 for Denmark and 25,329 for Germany, giving the Danes 74.2 per cent. In Central Schleswig, Germany won 79 per cent of the vote. The most telling feature of the Schleswig question from an Irish point of view concerned not the destiny of the two plebiscite zones, but that of Southern Schleswig, which was predominantly German in population. The Danish Government disclaimed all desire for Southern Schleswig and even for those parts of Central Schleswig where Danish had never been spoken. This was because to remain a national state was a matter of life and death to Denmark, and because it wanted to protect the homogeneity of the Danish Kingdom and 'to prevent it, a country with only three million inhabitants, from being increased by 300,000 foreigners who would always look on Germany as their fatherland'.[56] The Danes were worried by the possibility that a new boundary arrangement might make 10 per cent of their population look to another state as their homeland, and at some future time try to bring all of Schleswig back to Germany.

In 1920 and again from 1924 to 1925, northern Unionists insisted on incorporating over three times that percentage of irredentist border Nationalists, with consequences that continue to be felt to this day. There was, however, a practical distinction between the Danish and six-county situations. Had the Unionists wished to homogenise their state and shed their alien minority, they would at the same time have lost perhaps one fifth of their own number or else have had to engage in a drastic programme of assimilation, expulsion, transportation or exchange of minorities.[57] The Danes were trying to avoid this predicament. It is worth noting that the Schleswig parallel to the Irish situation cuts both ways, since it could be argued that the Free State claim on the north as a whole, like the Ulster Unionists' claim on the border counties, contrasts with the Danes' view that they did not want Southern Schleswig

55   F. W. Boal, J. Douglas and J. A. E. Orr (eds), *Integration and Division: Geographical Perspectives on the Northern Ireland Problem* (London, 1982), p. 112.

56   Wambaugh, *Plebiscites since the World War*, Vol. 2, p. 58.

57   Arend Lijphart, *Democracy in Plural Societies: A Comparative Exploration* (London, 1971), pp. 44–5.

because it would mean incorporating a turbulent minority whose national allegiance lay elsewhere. Whether the Irish Boundary Commission had yielded to the Free State claim on Tyrone and Fermanagh, or to the Northern Ireland claim to retain the two counties, the inevitable result would have been a large discontented irredentist minority on one side of the border or the other.

My analysis of a variety of European examples of boundary resolution demonstrates that the only reliable way of ascertaining the wishes of inhabitants was the plebiscite. It also demonstrates that the principle of self-determination was uppermost in the minds of those who framed the relevant statutory arrangements, and of those who implemented them.

The Irish boundary Article left it open to Feetham's Commission to adopt a similar approach as that taken in the case of Silesia, Klagenfurt, Allenstein, Marienwerder and Schleswig. Instead, Feetham decided that the territorial shape of the already established six-county State had to be substantially preserved, even if this meant occulting the wishes of considerable border populations. In this way, contrary to European practice which was based on democratic preference as ascertained in carefully supervised plebiscites, the Feetham Commission allowed territorial integrity to prevail over self-determination, and made no attempt to ascertain the current wishes of border inhabitants. Had the Irish border been redrawn in 1925 in accordance with these expressed wishes, making allowance for geographical and economic conditions as subordinate considerations as European Commissions did, there would have been no grounds for the suspicions, recriminations and long-term bitterness that Feetham's proceedings left in their wake in Nationalist minds. The larger theoretical issues arising from the nature of the Irish partition are dealt with in the next chapter.

SEVEN

THE DIVISION OF IRELAND

NORMATIVE ISSUES

––

I SELF-DETERMINATION IN 1920: PROBLEMS OF DEFINITION AND APPLICATION

The debate on the Irish partition settlement has, since the beginning, focused on the related concepts of sovereignty, nationality, self-determination, territorial integrity and minority rights. The debate remains inconclusive because none of its five main elements lends itself to the kind of definition that might compel the reasonable assent of all the participants. The two principal protagonists, Irish Nationalists and Irish Unionists, base their conflicting arguments on what they see as legitimate interpretations of self-determination and nationality in particular. Each side has long felt justified in drawing support from the often contradictory ways in which these two concepts have been interpreted and applied internationally. The ambiguities inherent in state practice, the pronouncements of influential statesmen, and even precepts of international law have facilitated the efforts of both Nationalists and Unionists to make an arguable case based on the right to self-determination. Nationalists assert that the application of the concept can only result in a single Irish state, Unionists that it gives a clear warrant for the continued partition of the island and the provision of a separate northern state.

Before considering the use made by partitionists and anti-partitionists of self-determination as the foundation for their respective claims, it is useful to examine the status and general understanding of the concept in the period when partition was being considered and finally implemented. In 1920, it was still not possible to talk of self-determination as an element of positive international law, but it was, nevertheless, the pre-eminent political ideal animating the post-war world order. It was not mentioned in the Covenant of the League of Nations, and this undoubtedly contributed to the conclusion drawn by the International Commission of Jurists in 1920 that despite its widespread promotion as a political slogan, it had not yet given rise to customary international law and that even the recognition of the principle in a number of international treaties 'was not sufficient to put it on the same footing as a positive rule of the law of nations'.[1]

The promotion of self-determination as a central element of modern political philosophy was largely the work of President Woodrow Wilson, who, between 1916 and 1919, continuously advocated it as the means by which 'a fair and just peace' might be secured. The post-war public enthusiasm of American and British statesmen for self-determination was, however, deceptive, as Irish Nationalist leaders would discover. Initially, the British delegation to the Paris Peace Conference supported a consistent and thorough-going application of the principle, until its members became conscious of its implications for their own large subject Empire. The diplomat and historian Harold Nicolson observed that the most ardent British advocate of self-determination found himself, sooner or later, in a false position. 'However, fervid might be our indignation regarding Italian claims to Dalmatia and the Dodecanese,' he wrote, 'it could be cooled by reference not to Cyprus only, but to Ireland, Egypt and India. We had accepted a system for others which, when it came into practice, we should refuse to apply ourselves.'[2] In general, the victorious Allies decided that it would be impracticable to put the principle into practice in territories they themselves controlled. For example, in pre-Armistice negotiations the Italians made it clear that Italy expected to get the transfers of territory she regarded as necessary for her security, regardless of ethnic considerations or the wishes of the populations concerned.[3] A memorandum of the British Foreign Office of November 1918 explained that it would

> clearly be inadvisable to go even the smallest distance in the direction of admitting the claim of the American Negroes, or the Southern Irish, or the Flemings, or Catalans to appeal to the International State Conference over the head of their own government.

In the same memorandum, it was acknowledged that if a right of appeal were granted to the Macedonians or the German Bohemians, 'it would be difficult to refuse it in the case of other Nationalist movements.'[4] The British argument

---

1 'Report of the International Commission of Jurists entrusted by the Council of the League of Nations with the task of giving an advisory opinion upon the legal aspects of the Aaland Islands question', *League of Nations Official Journal*, Special Supplement 3, Oct. 1920, p. 5.

2 Harold Nicolson, *Peacemaking 1919* (London, 1933), p. 193.

3 Alfred Cobban, *The Nation-State and National Self-Determination* (New York, 1969), p. 69.

4 Ibid., pp. 61–2.

was that self-determination was not intended to apply to Ireland because Ireland had long been a part of the British political system, and that the establishment of Ireland as an independent nation would be an act of secession.

A further British argument was that the Irish question was a domestic one for Britain, and for Britain alone, to settle within an Imperial framework. This was a position accepted by Britain's allies and by governments elsewhere. In 1919, when Seán T. O'Kelly, on behalf of the Dáil Government, went to present the Irish case for self-determination at the Paris Peace Conference, he was told that national questions involving the victors were simply 'domestic issues' in which Britain's allies could not properly interfere.[5] It was a measure of the resolve of the victorious Allies not to permit their own territorial interests to be undermined by the widespread application of national self-determination, particularly in the case of their own possessions, that neither during the internal exile of the Provisional Government of the Irish Republic, from June 1919 to December 1920, nor during de Valera's exile 'with a purpose' in the United States, did the Irish Republic receive any official recognition by other states.[6] The absence of such recognition suggests general international support for the position adopted by Britain, whose leaders indicated that 'they did not consider self-determination an axiom of universal validity',[7] and certainly not one that could apply to the Irish case. Any grant of self-determination to all or part of Ireland would have to be regarded as a concession, not a right, and would not, in any case, involve national self-determination. This was an attitude which informed the British approach to the negotiation of the Anglo-Irish Treaty of 1921, as suggested in the formula devised by Lloyd George, who envisaged a continuing British involvement in Irish affairs.

In taking this approach, the British could invoke significant recent international legal precedent. In July 1920, the Council of the League of Nations appointed a commission of three jurists to examine whether, under international law, the inhabitants of the Aaland Islands in the Baltic Sea, off the coast of Sweden, and which had a Swedish-speaking majority of 97 per cent, were free to secede from Finland and become part of the Kingdom of Sweden. The islands had been Swedish until 1809, were then ceded to Russia, and became part of Finland in 1917 when Finland separated itself from the

5   Earl of Longford and T. P. O'Neill, *Eamon de Valera* (Dublin, 1970), p. 89.

6   Stefan Talmon, *Recognition of Governments in International Law: With Particular Reference to Governments in Exile* (Oxford, 1988) p. 288. The British argument that Ireland was a British domestic issue enjoyed another, more positive, kind of international sanction. Under the terms of Article X, members of the League of Nations undertook to preserve the existing territorial boundaries of member nations.

7   Walker Connor, *Ethnonationalism: The Quest for Understanding* (New Jersey, 1994), p. 38.

collapsing Russian Empire. The Government of Sweden argued that the principle of self-determination gave the Aaland Islanders the right, following a plebiscite, to register their claim to transfer their allegiance to Sweden. The Finnish case was that under international law, the Aaland Islands question was one to be determined solely by the Finnish Government. The International Commission of Jurists, in its report on the legal aspects of the case, decided that although the principle of self-determination had been vigorously promoted during the First World War, it could not be regarded as an international legal norm. This was obviously appropriate to the Irish situation in 1920, when the entire country was still constitutionally part of the United Kingdom. In deciding in favour of Finland, the Commission, although recognising that the great majority of Aaland Islanders would choose union with Sweden over their existing incorporation with Finland, upheld the contention of the Finnish Government that under positive international law 'it pertains exclusively to the sovereignty of any definitely constituted state to grant to, or withhold from, a fraction of its population the right of deciding its own political destiny by means of a plebiscite, or in any other way'.[8]

The Commission was guided by the principle that the preferences of minorities in relation to sovereignty did not constitute a valid reason for altering existing state boundaries. It took the view that to make these boundaries contingent on 'the wish' or 'good pleasure' of minorities, whether of language, ethnicity or religion, and to allow such minorities to withdraw from 'the community to which they belong' would be 'to destroy order and stability within states'. It would also 'inaugurate anarchy in international life', and 'uphold a theory incompatible with the very idea of the state as a territorial and political union'.[9] It is clear from the judgement on the Aaland Islands case that had the Irish Republic, which had been declared the year before, been in a position to make a case to The League of Nations for Irish self-determination, the Council of the League would have rejected the Irish case. The British Government would have been able to argue successfully, and with manifest legality, on the basis of Article 15, Paragraph 8, of the Covenant of the League, that the Irish case fell 'solely within the domestic jurisdiction of Great Britain, and was not a matter for the League'. Had the Provisional or Free State Governments brought a case to the League against the 1920 partition of Ireland, the verdict would have been similar: when it was imposed, the partition was a purely British domestic concern.

---

8 Sarah Wambaugh, *Plebiscites Since the First World War: With a Collection of Official Documents*, Carnegie Endowment for International Peace Vol 2 (Washington, 1933), pp. 489–90. Wambaugh is quoting from the *League of Nations Official Journal*, Special Supplement 3, Oct. 1920, p. 5.
9 Wamaugh *Plebiscites since the First World War*, p. 490.

A second League of Nations report, on the Aaland Islands question, however, this one from the Commission of Rapporteurs, raised issues concerning the relationship between self-determination and the protection of minorities which might have provided the basis for a case on behalf of the northern minority under permanent Unionist rule as a result of partition. The Commission foresaw one set of circumstances in which the separation of a minority from the state of which it formed part and its incorporation in another state could be considered 'as an altogether exceptional solution, a last resort'. This possibility would arise if the state 'lacked either the will or the power to enact and apply just and effective guarantees' to the minority, 'or if the state abused its authority to the detriment of the minority, by oppressing or persecuting its members'. This was precisely the kind of complaint made by and on behalf of the northern minority for over 50 years following the establishment of the six-county state. Since the case considered by the Commission of Jurists was solely that of the Aaland Islands, whose political or civil rights had not been violated under Finnish rule, the verdict inevitably was that 'the Aalanders had no right to secession, for they had not been oppressed'. The clear implication here was that they might have had the right to secession if convincing evidence of oppressive treatment had been placed before the Commission. Given its limited brief, the Commission, while strongly affirming principles, was reluctant to give a definitive judgement as to whether 'a manifest and continued abuse of sovereign power, to the detriment of a section of the population of a state' would have to be considered as not being 'confined to the domestic jurisdiction of the offending state but as coming within the sphere of action of the League of Nations'.[10] In the light of the Commission Report any objective consideration of the situation of the minority in Northern Ireland would suggest that a judicial tribunal, under the auspices of the League of Nations, would be bound to take seriously a case against the northern state based on the violation of fundamental minority rights.

The verdict of the International Commission of Jurists on the rights of the Aalanders may be taken as representing traditional international norms on the relation between existing state boundaries and the claims of minorities in relation to sovereignty. The Anglo-Irish process, however, culminating in the Belfast Agreement of 1998, represented a significant modification of the territorial principle as it had hitherto been understood in international law, confirmed with particularly strong emphasis in the 1921 judgement of the Aaland Islands case. Under the terms of the 1998 Agreement, Northern Ireland was acknowledged by all the parties to be legally part of the territory of the United Kingdom of Great Britain and Northern Ireland. However, the

10   Ibid., pp. 487–90, quoting from the *League of Nations*, Oct. 1920, p. 27.

Agreement, made a substantial contribution to the development of international law on requirements for state composition and reconfiguration. As a result of the Agreement specifically Article 1 (ii), it seems possible to propose a new criterion whereby 'a state can contract out to its own citizens the right to decide their territorial status *vis-a-vis* a neighbouring state'.[11] The Aaland Islands judgement meant that even the overwhelming preference of a minority within a state in relation to sovereignty could not be permitted to override existing state boundaries. The Belfast Agreement, in contrast, meant that two states, the United Kingdom and the Republic of Ireland, had ceded control of their territorial identity to popular electoral mandate: the expressed wish of a majority within part of a territory to change its national and territorial status 'trumps established borders'.[12] Implicit in Article 1 of the Agreement was a suspended recognition of the reconfiguration of two Irish states, subject to the will of a majority of those living in Northern Ireland. To the extent that the Agreement represented a definitive contribution to international law on state boundaries, it could no longer be asserted that territorial cession was 'about the transfer of sovereignty by means of an agreement between a ceding and an acquiring state, but rather the ceding of the decisive power to the citizenry itself, with the prior consent of the implicated states'.[13]

II THE NATIONALIST CASE FOR IRISH SELF-DETERMINATION

The most celebrated formulation of the Irish Nationalist case for external self-determination was that presented by Eamon de Valera to the Government of the United States on 27 October 1920, on behalf of the Government of the Republic of Ireland declared by Dáil Éireann in 1919.[14] Firstly, de Valera asserted, giving no indication of the acute ideological, political and religious divisions in the territory of the secessionist project, that 'the people of Ireland constitute a distinct and separate nation, ethnically, historically as tested by every standard of political science'. Here de Valera was being tactically astute even if his assertion was notoriously contested. He knew that the international

---

11   Colm Campbell, Fionnula Ní Aoláin and Colin Harvey, 'The frontiers of legal analysis: reframing in transition in Northern Ireland', *The Modern Law Review* 66 (May 2003), pp. 317–45, reference to p. 329.

12   Ibid., p. 330.

13   Ibid., p. 329. See paragraph 1 of the section of the Agreement devoted to constitutional issues.

14   The Irish case was outlined in a pamphlet, consisting of 136 pages, entitled 'Ireland's claim for recognition as a sovereign state', Irish Diplomatic Mission (Washington DC, 1920). Henceforth cited as 'Ireland's claim'.

community was more likely to support a secessionist movement in territory whose people were united in their desire to secede than in one in which a significant proportion of the population had resolutely declared its opposition to secession, as was the case in Ireland. Many subsequent commentators have been dismissive of the notion that there is an ethnic foundation for Ireland's claim to be a separate nation. Martin Mansergh points out that even the strongest cultural Nationalists of the early twentieth century were conscious that 'the historic Irish nation', even prior to the Norman Invasion, did not have a homogeneous racial origin.[15] The same, of course, could be said about many other nations, including the historic British one, which is compounded of diverse stocks: Celtic, Danish, Anglo-Saxon and Norman.

Secondly, de Valera claimed,

> the people of Ireland in a general and regular parliamentary election, in effect a national plebiscite, held under British supervision . . . declared unmistakably by an overwhelming majority their desire to be an independent republic.

The reference here was to the Westminster General Election of 1918, in which 70 per cent of all the votes cast were for candidates who campaigned for an independent, united Ireland.[16] The use of 'the people of Ireland' in this context is as problematic as de Valera's earlier reference to the Irish nation, and is scarcely less appropriate than the common Unionist reference to 'the people of Ulster' when only the Protestant inhabitants of six counties of that province are really being referred to. Thirdly, de Valera claimed the British authority in Ireland, operating as a rival to Dáil Éireann, was 'an alien usurpation, commanding neither the respect nor the obedience of the people of Ireland'.[17] Again, the invocation of 'the people of Ireland' is misleading, since on the evidence provided in the 1918 Westminster Election, 30 per cent of these did not regard the British authority as 'an alien usurpation'.

There is a sense in which de Valera's articulation of the Irish Nationalist case for independence is, like Wilson's passionate wartime utterances in favour of self-determination, a series of rhetorical flourishes rather than a commanding and logically coherent argument. De Valera seemed to believe that to invoke Wilson's own words and ideas in a document addressed to the US Government was in itself almost sufficient to make the Irish case. He thus reminded the Americans that Wilson was fond of affirming the rights of

---

15   See Martin Mansergh's chapter, 'Identity, security and self-determination', in Ronnie Hanna (ed.), *The Union: Essays on Ireland and the British Connection* (Newtownards, 2001), p. 113.

16   Brian M. Walker, *Parliamentary Election Results in Ireland 1918–92* (Dublin, 1992), pp. 4–9.

17   'Ireland's claim', p. 4.

smaller nations in the face of dominance by the greater ones. In 1916, de Valera recalled, Wilson had proposed that

> no nation should seek to extend its polity over any other nation or people but that every people should be left free to determine its own polity, its own way of development, unhindered, unthreatened, unafraid, the little along with the great and powerful

and again, that

> every people has the right to choose the sovereignty under which it shall live, that the small states of the world would have the right to enjoy from other nations the same respect for their sovereignty and for their territorial integrity that great and powerful nations expect and insist upon.[18]

Wilson's comments on the rights of people to determine their own polities are not entirely supportive of the case de Valera was making for a unified, independent Ireland: a supporter of Unionism might well assert that Unionists, as a distinct people, should enjoy the freedom to pursue their own political destiny even if this differed from that of the majority of people on the island as a whole.

De Valera, however, dealt effectively with the standard British argument that the political grievances of Irish people were a domestic issue for Britain, and that the principle of self-determination did not apply in the Irish case. He invoked Allied practice elsewhere, pointing out that the principle had already been applied to bring freedom to 'the most oppressed peoples' of Czechoslovakia and Poland, the first of which had long been in the political system of Austria, the second in the political systems of Germany, Austria and Russia. To the argument that national questions involving the victorious Allied powers could not be subject to external scrutiny, de Valera replied that 'every foreign tyrant that has ever sought to be allowed to do as he wills with a subject people has claimed that the determination of his relations with them was purely a domestic question for himself'. There was the further consideration that

> if the argument that Britain seeks to have applied to Ireland were accepted in the case of other countries, then Greece and other nations of the near East would still

18 Ibid., pp. 5–6.

be struggling with the Sultan, and the countries of Latin America would still be struggling with Spain.[19]

In the event, it was futile for representatives of Irish nationalism to expect Wilson to become an advocate for a united Ireland independent of Britain, even if his early advocacy of self-determination seemed to imply his support for such an outcome. Wilson, when he propounded his theory in the international arena, was not conscious of its practical implications for his allies. His Secretary of State, Robert Lancing suggested, on 30 December 1918, that Wilson should never have propounded so ill-defined a concept as self-determination, which could only raise futile aspirations and generate impossible demands among 'the Irish, the Indians, the Egyptians, and the Nationalists among the Boers'.[20] Wilson eventually came to share this point of view. On 19 August 1919 he told the Committee of Foreign Relations of the Senate that when he articulated the principle of self-determination, he did so 'without the knowledge that nationalities existed, which are coming to us day after day', and spoke of the anxieties he had expressed 'as a result of the many millions of people having their hopes raised by what I have said'.[21] Among those who came in response to what Wilson had said were members of an Irish delegation. His treatment of this delegation was hostile, as he himself recalled. When he spoke of the Irish question he said

> that he had been made very angry by a delegation of the Irish who had visited him while in the United States, and requested him to ask the Peace Conference to make Ireland independent. Of course he had refused to promise anything about it. His first impulse had been, from his fighting blood getting up, that he had wanted to tell them [the Irish] to go to hell.[22]

Wilson consistently refused to entertain the many petitions from subject nationalities of the Allies, and did not endorse the right of secession. The furthest he would go in the direction of self-determination was that such national groups who sought it should be given autonomy within the states to which they belonged. In Ireland's case, this meant continuing to be part of the British

19   Ibid., p. 10.
20   Cited in Antonio Cassese, *Self-Determination of Peoples: A Legal Reappraisal* (Cambridge, 1995), p. 22.
21   H. M. V. Temperley, *A History of the Peace Conference of Paris*, Vol. 4 (London and New York, 1969), p. 429.
22   Cobban, *The Nation-State*, p. 66.

imperial system under some form of Dominion home rule.[23] Both houses of the American Congress, however, voted in March and June 1919 in favour of 'the aspiration of the Irish people for a government of their own choice'.

The argument that the political destiny of Ireland was a domestic British concern was in turn partly based on the British equation of legitimate government with existing government, and on the belief that 'prescription', acceptance of a government over even a short term of years, made it irreversibly the legitimate government. This argument, often supported by Catholic moralists, left no room for the consideration that widespread and continued repudiation, as was manifest in Ireland from 1916 onwards, could abolish the title of what might initially have been a legitimate government, however much it owed its title to conquest. It also failed to recognise that unless there is continuous consent of the governed, the rule of the prevailing government is bound to be regarded as alien.[24] The Maynooth theologian, Walter McDonald, gave no comfort to Irish separatists when he asserted in 1919 that

> the whole trend of the tradition of Catholic ethics is in favour of allowing annexa-
> tion of people vanquished in a just war, even though previously independent and
> of different stock from their conquerors. The tradition goes even further, allowing
> such a nation, vanquished in just war, to be reduced to slavery.

McDonald was arguing from the premise that the British wars of conquest 'were declared and conducted in good faith'. He had no doubt that Irish people were bound to obey laws made by the Imperial Parliament.[25]

Those Nationalists who affirmed Ireland's right to external self-determination often overstated their case by resorting to questionable, and often simplistic, historical analysis, particularly when partition was at issue. The idea of Ireland as a natural, historically conditioned political unit is an essential component of Republican tradition. Boyle and Hadden argue that there is little historical foundation for that idea. 'Ireland,' they claim, 'has never been united in a single independent state. The northern part of Ireland was for centuries more closely linked with Scotland, both in its population and in its political structures, than the rest of Ireland. It was British conquest that first united Ireland in any real sense.'[26] A fundamental premise of the Irish

---

23   Wambaugh, *Plebiscites since the World War*, Vol. 1, p. 4. 'Ireland's claim', p. 41.

24   Patrick Corish, 'Political problems 1860–78', in *A History of Irish Catholicism*, Vol. 5 (Dublin, 1978), p. 18.

25   Walter McDonald, *Some Ethical Questions of Peace and War* (Dublin, 1998), pp. 34–5, pp. 129–32.

26   Kevin Boyle and Tom Hadden, *Ireland: A Positive Proposal* (London, 1985), p. 20. For a well-argued contrary view see Brendan Bradshaw, 'Nationalism and historical scholarship in modern Ireland', *IHS* Vol. XXVI, No. 104 (Nov. 1989), pp. 329–51.

Nationalist case for self-determination has long been that 'only the nation, acting as a whole, can decide its own future, and that minorities within its territory are bound by its decisions, even if they form a majority within part of the nation's territory'.[27] Furthermore, it was the Irish Nationalist position that there could be only one territorial unit of self-determination: the island of Ireland as a whole. This position relied on geography and cartographic symmetry rather than on history or ethnography. It was the one favoured by Griffith and de Valera, the former memorably asserting that 'Ireland cannot shift her boundaries. The Almighty traced them beyond the cunning of man to modify'.[28] For de Valera, Bowman observes, 'geography was the final arbiter in determining the Irish nation . . . Fundamental to his anti-partition stance was his belief in natural boundaries.'[29]

This was not an eccentric, novel or uncommon point of view. Bowman quotes a comment made by Mussolini in 1939, of which de Valera approved as being applicable to the Irish case, to the effect that 'frontiers traced by inks or other inks can be modified. It is quite another thing when the frontiers are traced by providence.'[30] Heslinga points out that French revolutionary leaders justified the annexation of the Low Countries and the German provinces on the left bank of the Rhine by explaining that this rounded out the natural frontiers of the nation, from the Alps to the ocean, from the Pyrenees to the Rhine.[31] The geographical argument featured strongly in the propaganda issued by the Irish Boundary Bureau in preparation for the Boundary Commission hearings. Kevin O'Shiel, who directed the work of the Bureau, wrote that Ireland was

> by natural design a complete geographical entity, and there is no better instance in either hemisphere of a country all of whose parts are bound closely together, and which has no area throughout its whole extent separated by natural barriers from the main body of the country.[32]

---

27   Michael Gallagher, 'How many nations are there in Ireland?', *Ethnic and Racial Studies* 18:4 (1990), p. 11.

28   Griffith quote in John Bowman, *De Valera and the Ulster Question 1917–1973* (Oxford, 1982), p. 11.

29   Ibid., p. 301.

30   Ibid.

31   D. M. W. Heslinga, *The Irish Border as a Cultural Divide: A Contribution to the Study of Regionalism in the British Isles* (Assen, The Netherlands, 1979), p. 41.

32   Kevin O'Shiel, *Handbook of the Ulster Question*, published by North-Eastern Boundary Bureau (Dublin, 1923), pp. 5–6.

A recent commentator emphasises the difficulty of overcoming the geographical image as an influence on the political, if not the legal, interpretation of self-determination: general political practice, as Guelke points out, favours the preservation of the territorial integrity of islands, so that divided sovereignties on islands are rare occurrences.[33]

Until the early 1980s, the general Irish Nationalist position on self-determination was the traditional one: that the only appropriate unit for its exercise was the island as a whole.[34] In many Nationalist eyes, the compelling argument for this approach was the geographical one: it appeared contrary to the law of nature that so clear cut a geographical entity should not also be a single political one. There is, however, no objective, incontestable theoretical norm by means of which this position may be deemed preferable to any other. There is nothing intrinsically natural in the notion that a single Irish state should extend over the entire island of Ireland, just as there is nothing intrinsically unnatural in the existence of two nation states, Haiti and The Dominican Republic on one small island.[35] The political map of the world offers examples of natural geographical entities, the Iberian peninsula, for example, which accommodate more than one political unit. The Irish Nationalist position, however, should not be seen as totally aberrant: divided sovereignty on islands is not universally approved; the partition of Cyprus remains unrecognised by any member of the international community except Turkey, which imposed it. The modern Turkish state, conterminous with the 'Anatolian rectangle' is circumscribed by boundaries which make it a 'natural' geographical unit. Its territorial integrity is no less sacred to Turkish Nationalists than that of the island of Ireland has traditionally been to Irish Nationalists, underlying for one Turkish commentator the importance of recognising that 'neither national identity nor territorial nationalism are illegitimate, pathological or outdated concepts'.[36] The Turkish state is home to a large Kurdish minority: the presumptive Kurdish project of carving out a separate state for Kurds is popularly conceived in Turkey as 'threatening the ultimate criterion of Turkey's political being, its territorially circumscribed geography, the Turkish rectangle'.[37]

33 Adrian Guelke, *Northern Ireland: The International Perspective* (Dublin, 1989), p. 100.

34 In varying degrees, however, the political parties in the Republic, notably Fine Gael, were moving towards the acceptance of the Northern Ireland state in the belief that a political settlement of the northern problem would necessitate the kind of recognition formalised in the 1985 Anglo-Irish Agreement.

35 Liam Kennedy, *Two Ulsters: A Case for Repartition* (Belfast, 1986), p. 17.

36 Umit Cizre, 'Turkey's Kurdish problem', in Brendan O'Leary, Ian S. Lustick and Thomas Callaghy (eds), *Rightsizing the State: The Politics of Moving Borders* (Oxford, 2001), p. 245.

37 Ibid.

Cizre's analysis of the treatment by post-imperial Turkish Nationalists of the Kurdish minority in Turkey, for example, suggests significant parallels between the views on territory and national allegiances promoted by Turkish and Irish Nationalists, on the one hand, and Kurds and Ulster Unionists, on the other. Turkish and Irish Republican conceptions of statehood are profoundly territorial: the Anatolian rectangle and the island of Ireland are seen as irreducible national territories, however large the minority of non-Turkish and non-Irish residing within these clearly defined geographical boundaries. Kurdish and Unionist demands for a recognition of separate national identity within internationally recognised borders were thus repugnant to the fundamental principle that both Turkey and Ireland were homogeneous territorial entities based on a common allegiance to being Turkish or Irish. For Turks, as Cizre observes, even to consider new state boundaries to facilitate Kurdish identity would be regarded as an act of 'wrong-sizing', a fatal contradiction, putting the life of Turkey in danger.[38] Griffith appealed to a similar principle in defence of the territorial integrity of Ireland. Nationalists, he argued, could not acquiesce 'in the loss of any portion of her territory without forfeiting all her rights as a nation'.[39] When Griffith was making this claim, the dominant Magyars were making a similar one for Great Hungary, their policy being to create a Magyar state by assimilating other groups. Although Hungarian speakers comprised only about half of the population in the Hungarian part of the Habsburg Empire, the ruling Magyar elites insisted that Hungary was a single nation with which all citizens, whatever their native language or ethnic origins, were expected to identify.[40] But as McGarry remarks, the two national communities in Northern Ireland have consistently refused to accept the other's identity or state. Political accommodation was possible in 1998 only when Republicans dropped their insistence on a united Ireland and Unionists agreed to substantive recognition of the identity of northern Nationalists, while both sides ceased to insist on incorporating the six-county area into their respective nation states.[41]

The Lebanon parallel to Ireland is also instructive, as well as being persuasive. Many of Lebanon's problems spring from the decision to add Muslim-majority territory to the Christian heartland of Mount Lebanon in order to create a state large enough to be viable. The incorporation of Catholic-majority territory in Northern Ireland in order to serve a similar purpose

---

38   Ibid., p. 225.

39   *Sinn Féin*, 18 Apr. 1912.

40   See Hugh Seton-Watson, *Nations and States* (Colorado, 1977), p. 164.

41   John McGarry (ed.), *Northern Ireland and the Divided World: Post-Agreement Northern Ireland in Comparative Perspective* (Oxford, 2001), p. 23.

makes for interesting parallels with Lebanon. At the time when the Irish boundary was still provisional, its limits subject to the deliberations of a boundary commission, French policy in the Middle East dictated the further contraction of what remained of Syria and the resizing of Lebanon. The main objective of this boundary-drawing exercise, with its long-term adverse consequences for the stability of the region, was to weaken Arab nationalism, the growth of which might have had anti-French repercussions among the Arabs of French North Africa. Lebanon, with its Christian majority, was enlarged by the addition of predominantly Muslim districts, including the Bekaa Valley, the Mediterranean ports of Tyre, Sidon, Beirut and Tripoli, and land in the south, north of Palestine. Despite the large accretions of Muslim-occupied lands, transferred without reference to the wishes of their inhabitants, Christians still outnumbered Muslims over 20 years later by a ratio of six to five, when Lebanon gained independence from France.[42] As a means, perhaps the only means, of achieving political stability, the political elites of the four main communities, Maronite and Greek Orthodox Christians, Sunni and Shiite Muslims, established a consociational democracy, in which executive power was shared between them. The resort in each case to a right-shaping consociational remedy for ethnic conflict is one parallel between the Irish and Lebanese situations. In each case, boundaries established in 1920 cut across previous boundaries and were without historical precedent. Both entities might be regarded as artificially contrived states with arbitrary borders, their wrong-peopling based to some extent at least, on the felt need of their creators to ensure economic viability and political credibility.[43] In the Lebanese case, largely Muslim populations, hostile to being incorporated, were used to make up territory and numbers; in the case of Northern Ireland, Unionists, who portrayed the state as their own, as the Christian Maronites tended to do in Lebanon, won more territory than their numbers might have warranted, in the sense that a large proportion of the regions of the six counties where they did not form a majority and some of which were inhabited by populations predominantly anti-partitionist in outlook, south Down and south Armagh, for example, ended up in their state. In each case, too, the ethnic composition of the two entities, directly attributable to the nature of principles guiding boundary drawing, created the conditions for later ethnic conflict, in Northern Ireland since 1969, and in Lebanon in 1975.

Neither in Northern Ireland nor in Lebanon did boundary drawing involve any political arrangements that might have resulted in an inclusive civic identity for the citizens of these states. On the contrary, ethno-religious

42 N. Kliot, 'The collapse of the Lebanese state', *Middle Eastern Studies* Vol. 23, No. 1 (1987), p. 62.
43 Guelke, *Northern Ireland*, pp. 174–80.

allegiance was the basis for boundary determination and state formation in each case. The introduction of right-shaping, consociational arrangements, coinciding with Lebanese independence but only recently implemented in Northern Ireland as part of the Belfast Agreement, merely emphasised the failure to find a basis for civic democracy. The need to resort to the consociational model, with its institutionalisation of ethno-religious divisions and its tendency to solidify vertical cleavages among competing groups, was a consequence of the original preoccupation of those who drew the borders with ethnicity as their primary basis, and of the 'wrong-peopling' and 'wrong-shaping' character of the states these borders enclosed. Further French boundary drawing in Syria was based as much on ethnicity as the Irish partition had been. Syria was divided into four separate administrations following ethno-national lines of segregation. Jebel Druse became one administration, the region of the Alawis, an offshoot of the Shia, another; Alexandretta, because its population contained a large proportion of Turks, a third, while the fourth and principal administration was established in Damascus, with its majority of Sunni Muslims.[44] The result was to intensify the fears and grievances of minority groups inhabiting these administrations, and as in the Irish case, to create the conditions for ethnic conflict.

III COUNTERING THE GEOGRAPHICAL ARGUMENT

Many attempts have been made on the Unionist side to undermine the Nationalist argument that natural, physical frontiers were the preordained confines of political entities, and that Ireland was a pre-eminent example of this. However, two of the most interesting and persuasive attempts came from prominent Nationalists, Father Michael O'Flanagan, who was elected a vice-president of Sinn Féin in 1917, and Arthur Clery, a Professor of Law at University College Dublin. Both were Civil War Republicans. O'Flanagan, writing in 1916, saw no point in basing a claim for self-determination for Ireland as a political unit on the assertion that Ireland is an island with a definite geographical boundary. Such an argument, he suggested, if made to influence continental nations with shifting boundaries, would have no force whatever. He further observed that national and geographical boundaries scarcely ever coincided. 'Geography,' he observed,

---

44 Edward Atiyah, *The Arabs: The Origins, Present Conditions and Prospects of the Arab World* (Middlesex, 1958), p. 121.

would make one nation of Spain and Portugal; history made two of them. Geography did its best to make one nation of Norway and Sweden; history has succeeded in making two of them. Geography has scarcely anything to say to the number of nations upon the North-American Continent; history had done the whole thing.

Applying this line of reasoning to the Irish question, O'Flanagan asserted that geography had worked to make one nation out of Ireland but that history had worked against it. The British plantations since the sixteenth century had ensured that 'the island of Ireland and the national unit of Ireland simply do not coincide'.

O'Flanagan, while he could not recognise the existence of a homogeneous Irish nation, dismissed the 'homogeneous Ulster' of the Unionist publicists as 'a sham and a delusion'. At this point, he turned the common Nationalist argument that there was no homogeneous Ulster against those who argued that there was a homogeneous Irish nation. 'If,' he concluded reasonably enough, 'there be two Ulsters, there must surely be two Irelands.' In response to the argument that Ireland was 'an historic, economic, social and legal entity', O'Flanagan responded by claiming that for centuries the country had been 'an historic and social duality', and was now merely a portion of another economic and legal entity, the United Kingdom. He made the case for the right of northern Unionists to claim self-determination on the same basis that Nationalists claimed it. 'After three hundred years,' he wrote, 'England has begun to despair of compelling us to love her by force. And so we are anxious to start where England left off and are going to compel Antrim and Down to love us by force.'[45] A modern variation of one part of O'Flanagan's thesis is Barritt and Carter's argument that 'there is no reason to think that an island surrounded by water should be under one political rule'.[46]

Clery, writing in 1907, denied, as O'Flanagan did, that there was a homogeneous Irish nation, and dismissed the common Nationalist idea that the Irish nation covered all 32 counties of the island as a defiance of political reality. Clery wanted Irish Nationalists to admit that northern Unionists could not be part of an authentic Irish nation, but were instead an alien immigrant collectivity, not Irish and, more significantly, not wanting to be so. If, he asked rhetorically, 'three quarters of a million Dutchmen or Transvaalers had their residence in the north-east of Ireland, should we consider them Irishmen?'[47]

45 *Freeman's Journal*, 20 June 1916.
46 Denis P. Barritt and Charles F. Carter, *The Northern Ireland Problem: A Study in Group Relations* (Oxford, 1972), p. 36.
47 Arthur Clery, *The Idea of a Nation* (Dublin, 2002), p. 63.

Clery's solution to the problem of Irish self-determination was a scheme of partition based on local option by counties. The two principles he wanted to see adopted in any such division of Ireland were, first, that as many as possible of what he called 'the Protestant immigrants' should be left to govern themselves, or to be governed by Great Britain, according as they desired, or to throw in their lot with Ireland, if they so wished; and secondly, 'that as few real Irish [which in Ulster practically means Catholics] as possible should be left under the sway of the stranger.'[48] Clery's partitionism, as Patrick Maume points out, 'arose from recognition that the same arguments Nationalists employed to defend their own political aspirations obliged them to treat the loyalties of Ulster Unionists seriously.'[49] It also arose from a concept of self-determination involving the reduction to a minimum of the number of people who would be governed against their will: his local option scheme would have left merely a quarter of a million people of each religion under a system of government of which they disapproved.[50]

In its pristine form, as Walker Connor observes, the doctrine of self-determination 'makes ethnicity the ultimate measure of political legitimacy, by holding that any self- differentiating people, simply because it is a people, has the right, should it so desire, to rule itself'.[51] By another token, it is possible to conceive of a self-differentiating people which is not ethnically homogeneous. If this were not possible, the United States could not be descried as a nation. In 1916, Hugh Alexander Law, a Protestant Redmondite from Donegal, who by 1916 had converted to Catholicism, offered a definition of nationhood which might be held to offer support either to the Nationalist case for full Irish self-determination or the Unionist one that an undefined 'Ulster' is a separate nation. Law argued that nationality could be a question of choice rather than ethnicity. 'That people is a nation,' he suggested, 'which feels itself to be a nation, and those rightly belong to a nation who desire to belong to it.' He pointed out that as in the case of the southern Slavs, for example, a common racial origin was the foundation of national sentiment. Quite as often, however, as in Ireland, great national figures have transcended their original racial inheritance. Parnell is Law's best example, 'Irish to his fingertips', but 'no more Celt than were Choctaws'.[52] The problem for 'one-nation' theorists is that few north-eastern Protestants shared Parnell's view of Irish

48   Ibid., p. 65.
49   Patrick Maume, Introduction to Clery, *Idea of a Nation*, p. xv.
50   Clery, *Idea of a Nation*, p. 66.
51   Connor, *Ethnonationalism*, p. 38.
52   Quotation by Hugh Alexander Law in David Fitzpatrick, *The Two Irelands 1912–1939* (Oxford, 1998), p. 34.

nationality at the time when partition was imposed, and that the passage of time has done little if anything to modify this outlook. What Clery asserted, however bluntly, in 1907 still reflects the broad Unionist position: 'The East Ulster Unionists are not Irish, and they don't want to become Irish, nor to suffer for not becoming so.'[53]

IV DEFINING THE NATION

Acceptance or rejection of the full-blooded Nationalist case for Irish political unity depends to a great extent on the meaning given to the concept of 'nation', whether its guiding impulse is civic and territorial or ethnic, whether, in the Irish context the only unit entitled to enjoy self-determination is the island as a whole, and whether the right to national unity is absolute and inalienable, and is 'of a different order from, and transcends, any right claimed by any group which might come into conflict with it'.[54]

The overwhelming obstacle to the creation of an Irish nation state based on this concept is that a significant coherent minority has militantly refused to forgo its sense of being a distinct political entity, and like Clery, has insisted on acting 'in direct contravention of the ideas of Davis and all those who look upon every man born in this island as an actual or potential Irishman'.[55] The success of the Unionist project in keeping the area where Unionists predominate politically separate from the rest of Ireland may suggest that in its present conception the Nationalist vision of a united Irish nation state is capable of realisation only when all citizens are members of the same national collectivity, and when the national territory does not include one or more powerful minority groups unwilling to share the polity with the dominant national grouping.

Only a month after de Valera submitted the Irish case for national self-determination to the American Government, the British Government partitioned the country. The 'people of Ireland' mentioned throughout in the Irish submission could not include those Irish Unionists whose idea of self-determination involved the maintenance of their link with the British Empire and who insisted on enforcing this. The assertion of Irish Republican separation had its price. Alfred Cobban observes that this price was the partition of Ireland. In Ireland in 1920, Cobban suggests,

---

53 Clery, *Idea of a Nation*, p. 72.
54 Gallagher, 'How many nations?', p. 13.
55 Clery, *Idea of a Nation*, p. 70.

the fatal logic of the nation state had triumphed. Except where a community is culturally homogeneous, the principle of the nation state means that the success of a majority in achieving self-determination will involve the assimilation, extinction or exclusion of a minority. The Ulster Orangemen, with Great Britain behind them, were able to insist on the third of these possibilities.[56]

The logic of the Nationalist view of Ireland as one nation was that Unionism could, paradoxically, work out its own political destiny only within the framework of a united Ireland. Given this belief, it would seem inevitable that those who urged the inclusion of Unionists in a single Irish state should do everything possible to facilitate their willing assimilation. This was far from being the case. A significant strand in Nationalist discourse was that the tenure of twentieth-century Unionists in Ireland was less defensible than that of the indigenous or native Irish population: they were the descendants of planters living on confiscated Irish land, on whom even the passage of centuries could confer no prescriptive rights. Horowitz observes that such an attitude is not uniquely Irish, and that it is not unusual for self-defined indigenous groups who have been colonised and 'forced to accept the entry of ethnic strangers for colonial purposes' to regard the presence of these as illegitimate from the beginning, and to derive political and moral gratification from entertaining 'vestigial perceptions of the alienage of another group'.[57] Identification with the descendants of the dispossessed Nationalist population in North-East Ulster has tended to keep the historical grievance of usurped or sequestered territory alive from one generation to the next. How, in practice, Irish Nationalists might remedy the historical wrongs of illegitimate annexation, particularly in the six-county area, in the light of national self-determination, has always remained in dispute. De Valera, the most noted theoretician of the subject, wavered between conflicting positions. However, he considered that geography was the ultimate arbiter in determining the extent of the Irish nation, and from this it followed that all the inhabitants of the island of Ireland had a duty of loyalty to it, which was why he felt obliged to argue that Unionists were 'fundamentally Irish'. The other position he put forth was that if Unionists refused to be members of the Irish nation, he sometimes urged that their preference for British nationality should logically induce them to go and live in Britain.[58] Douglas Hyde, arguing that Ulster Unionists owed their presence to the fact that 'the Gaelic race was expelled and the land planted

56   Cobban, *The Nation-State*, pp. 163–5.
57   Donald Horowitz, *Ethnic Groups in Conflict* (Berkley, 1985), p. 210.
58   See *The Irish Press*, 23 June 1948.

with aliens', still hoped that their future destiny might be with the Irish nation, regretting that Ireland, 'assimilative as she is, has hitherto failed to absorb them.'[59]

Gallagher argues that the persistent Nationalist view of Unionists as non-indigenous inhabitants of Ireland, is 'of central importance in sustaining the conviction that no dissenting minority on the island has the right to stand in the way of a united Ireland'.[60] Leading Nationalist politicians tended to imply that Unionists could compensate for past wrongs done by their ancestors to the native population by abandoning their settler identity and becoming part of an Irish nation. In 1919, Kevin O'Higgins, during his revolutionary phase, gave eloquent expression to this point of view. He characterised the Unionist minority as an alien element forced on the Irish nation by British confiscation and plantation. Their modern descendants represented 'forces of disloyalty in Ireland' with which, O'Higgins argued, no Irish Republican could ever temporise. In his view, the territorial integrity of Ireland took precedence over the wishes of disloyal settler populations in the north-east: Sinn Féin, he declared, would 'never admit the right of any portion of Ireland to secede from the Irish nation' and if those Unionists who now enjoyed possession of the confiscated territory of the native Irish were not prepared 'to live in loyalty and obedience to the Government of Ireland', then they could leave the country and the Irish Government would be prepared 'to acquire their interest not by confiscation but by purchase'.[61] On several later occasions, de Valera articulated the same belief: the right of Unionists to remain in Ireland was not absolute but conditional: their entitlement to do so was derived from their willingness to abandon their Unionism and embrace full citizenship of an Irish state. In 1939, he told the Fianna Fáil Ard Fheis that a remedy for Unionist disloyalty to the Irish nation might be found in the transfer of recalcitrant Unionists to Britain in exchange for Irish emigrants there.[62] Even after 1925, when the southern Government accepted partition both *de facto* and *de jure*, the one-nation theory continued to govern the thinking of Republican Nationalism.

De Valera's radio broadcast to the United States on 12 February 1933 exposed the contradictions inherent in mainstream Nationalist discourse on the subject of partition, and on the appropriate way to deal with this and with the sequestered Unionists of the north east. De Valera was still committed to

59 Horowitz, *Ethnic Groups in Conflict*, p. 238.

60 Gallagher, 'How many nations?', p. 11.

61 Michael Laffan, *The Resurrection of Ireland: The Sinn Féin Party 1916–1923* (Cambridge, 1999), p. 227. Laffan was quoting from the *Nationalist and Leinster Times*, 12 July 1919.

62 Bowman, *De Valera and the Ulster Question*, quoting from *The Irish Press*, 14 Dec. 1939.

a territorially united nation state, but nowhere explains how this could be compatible with the entrenched resistance of almost a million inhabitants of the island to this concept.[63] Not surprisingly, his vision of the nature of his ideal state only further reinforced Unionist determination not to be part of it: 'Ireland not free and Gaelic merely but united also – that is the objective of the Irish people today and it will remain their unshakeable resolve until it has been finally attained.'[64] The reference to the undefined and undifferentiated 'Irish people' was, on the face of it, absurd, given that de Valera's territorially united one-nation state must have contained substantial numbers of Unionists, who could scarcely be imagined to share the view that a united, Gaelic Ireland should be their ideal. It is difficult to conceive the emergence of a 32-county Gaelic Ireland without the elimination or expulsion of the great majority of north-eastern Unionists, which may explain why that solution was sometimes suggested. A further comment by de Valera illustrated the difficulty encountered by even so subtle a mind as his in commenting sensibly on partition and the status of the Unionist minority from the perspective of a one-nation theory. He declared that 'the area that Ireland has lost contains many of her holiest and most famous places', including Belfast, 'the birthplace of the Irish Republican movement.'[65] In this context, 'Ireland' meant the historic 32-county Irish nation. By way of remedy for this loss, 'the efforts of her people will inevitably be bent upon the undoing of partition until all the land within her four seas is once more united.'[66] The 'people' who were to work for territorial unity were not defined, but unless they included a considerable body of Unionists, an outcome becoming increasingly unlikely in 1933, there could have been little sense to the project.

V THE ARGUMENT FROM HISTORIC RIGHTS

The project of credibly asserting, as distinct from enforcing, the Irish will to self- determination in a 32-county state was complicated by a number of

---

63 Those who framed the Belfast Agreement suspended judgement on the long dominant and highly contested issue of whether Ireland was one nation or two, instead emphasising *institutional* reconfiguration and accountability. The Agreement demonstrates 'that making the idea of nation conceptually malleable is a means of circumventing protracted conflict rooted in opposing claims to national identity'. Campbell, Ní Aoláin and Harvey, 'The frontiers of legal analysis', p. 328.

64 Maurice Moyhihan (ed.), *Speeches and Statements of Eamon de Valera 1917–1973* (Dublin, 1980), p. 235.

65 Ibid.

66 Ibid.

factors. Attempts to assert national self-determination by force, undertaken early in 1922 when Michael Collins conspired with competing factions in the IRA to make Northern Ireland ungovernable, quickly proved abortive, and had the effect of enhancing Loyalist determination to remain aloof from a 32-county Irish state. No British government was politically in a position to implement a scheme to facilitate a homogeneous Irish state by transplanting Loyalists who refused to subscribe to it. All that remained in practice for constitutional Nationalists was to recognise, while not openly admitting, that the status quo in the north east was so firmly consolidated that the recalcitrant Unionists were entitled to the defence of adverse possession. The lack of immediacy in the Nationalist historical grievance was another obstacle to any large-scale armed attempt to rectify ancient wrongs, and to undo the effects of over 300 years of history. After early 1922, no such attempt was undertaken by the southern authorities or even seriously proposed. It was left to physical-force irredentists to perpetuate the tradition inaugurated by Collins, while constitutionalists relied on propaganda, and, to some degree, on myth making, mainly centred on the favoured argument of Nationalists justifying their superior right to the whole national territory based on historic entitlement, on its prior occupation by their ancestors, and on its relatively recent settlement by the ancestors of Unionists, introduced by the British authorities as a means of maintaining a colonial foothold in Ireland.[67]

The argument that indigeneity and prior possession confer superior entitlement to territory is not a distinctively Irish Nationalist one. Following the Second World War, the Polish Government claimed entitlement not only to territory colonised by Germany since 1939, but to German provinces east of the Oder-Niesse line, on the ground that prior to the thirteenth century these had been Slav lands; the Polish Communist leader Gomulka explained that they 'must expel all the Germans because countries are built on national lines and not on multinational ones'.[68] Arguments such as these, including the Irish Nationalist one, face the serious problem that it is impossible, as Moore points out, 'to develop an adequate principle or mechanism to adjudicate such rival claims to territory: it depends on where in history one starts, and whose history one accepts.'[69] No definitive answer is possible to the question: how many years does it take to convert settlers into natives? Miller makes an arguable case when he suggests that if one group occupies the territory previously occupied by another, the strength of its claim to exercise authority in that territory will increase with time, and that 'the competing claims of the

67 Gallagher, 'How many nations?', p. 26.
68 Michael Burleigh, *The Third Reich: A New History* (London, 2000), p. 799.
69 Margaret Moore, *National Self-Determination and Secession* (Oxford, 1998), p. 145.

present and original inhabitants increase and diminish respectively with time'.[70] The Nationalist case for an undivided Ireland based on historic settlement deriving from prior occupation must deal with the inconvenient fact of migration across the North Channel in both directions, which as Stewart observes, means that 'some at least of the planters who arrived in Ulster in the early seventeenth century were direct descendants of earlier Ulster invaders of Scotland'.[71] Thus, a significant element in seventeenth-century Scotch immigration to Ulster was merely the return of Irish colonists with Ulster ancestry to their original home.

Stewart's observation, which there is no good reason to dispute, deprives the ethnic argument for Irish partition of some of its force. It also calls into question the ethnic dimension of the two-nation theory, which derives much of its status from constant, often ill-informed repetition. It is impossible to discern the limits of the supposed two nations, and it has long been thus. Racial descent cannot be the criterion since the Irish population is so incorrigibly mixed that few individuals can safely be assigned to one racially based category or another unless they define themselves thus. At the heart of the two-nation theory there is a troublesome paradox. The elements of the Irish population, the northern Protestants of Scottish descent, who appear to exhibit the clearest divergence from the main body, and who assert this divergence most forcibly, are racially much closer to the older native stock than the Norman and English settlers in the south of Ireland, whose assimilation has been much more complete. Many of the ancestors of the Scottish settlers in Ulster and those of the native Irish were Celts who spoke the same language, and shared the same culture, while many of the former were Christianised by Irish missionaries.

The common description of the two Irish nationalities as of Celt and Saxon descent is inadequate. Some leading British advocates of the two-nation theory failed to recognise the complexities involved in Irish ethnic taxonomy. John St Loe Strachey, an opponent of Home Rule and defender of Ulster Unionism, wrote of two Irelands,

> the Ireland of the north and the Ireland of the south, the Ireland of the Celt and of the Teuton, and above all, the Ireland in which Roman Catholics formed a large majority of the population and the Ireland in which the Protestants form the local majority.

Ireland, he declared,

70 David Miller, 'Secession and the principle of nationality', in ibid., p. 77.
71 A. T. Q. Stewart, *The Narrow Ground: Aspects of Ulster, 1609–1969* (London, 1977), p. 34.

was not a homogeneous country . . . the 26 counties of the south and the six counties of the north differed in every respect. Neither could justly be put in control of the other, though both might be united through a Union with England, Scotland and Wales.[72]

A problem with this analysis is the claim that the 26-county unit differed in 'every respect' from the six-county one. In one respect at any rate, the ethnic one which is central to Strachey's objection to Home Rule, his argument is based on the false premise that the Celt and the Teuton are the predominant ethnic groups in the south and north of Ireland respectively. Differentiation of the people of Northern Ireland, or of Ireland as a whole, into Celts and Saxons, or Celts and Teutons, is at odds with the historical record, which indicates a degree of affinity between native Irish and planter inhabitants in Northern Ireland. The seventeenth-century plantation of Ulster was not exclusively a settlement of people of Teutonic or Saxon descent. The Scots were more determined planters than the English. Within a generation, a great part of Antrim and Down 'had been transformed, in population and way of life, into a sort of extension of the Scottish Lowlands'.[73] In the late fifth century, a parallel process was at work in the opposite direction, when Gaelic adventurers from the Kingdom of Dal Riada in the Glens of Antrim began the colonisation of Scotland. The first Irish settlements were made at Argyle, 'the eastern province of the Gael.' For more than a century, territory on both sides of the North Channel formed a single kingdom hose monarch 'raided islands as far apart as the Orkneys and the Isle of Man'.[74]

Miller's argument that competing claims of the present and original inhabitants of territory increase and diminish respectively with time implies that since the sense of historical grievance fades with time, the right of rectifying this can correspondingly abate. In an effort to give practical effect to this abstract principle, Buchanan suggests the addition of what he calls 'the pragmatic premise', based on the consideration that since the pages of world history are so crowded with unjust takings, stretching back so far into the past, we must, if somewhat arbitrarily, close the books at some point, and be guided by 'a moral statute of limitations'. Acknowledgement of this imperative would, Buchanan argues, avoid 'endless recriminations about ancient wrongs vying for priority'. He even visualises the adoption by the International Court of Justice of a convention granting a strong presumption of legitimacy to the claims of existing states to their territory, subject to the proviso that these

72 John St Loe Strachey, *The Adventure of Living: A Subjective Autobiography* (London, n.d.), p. 389.
73 J. C. Beckett, *The Making of Modern Ireland 1603–1923* (London, 1966), p. 47.
74 Jonathan Bardon, *A History of Ulster* (Belfast, 2001), p. 17.

claims can be defended by convincing evidence that unjust acquisition occurred 'within, but not earlier than, say three or four generations'.[75] Such a convention, operating according to the norms suggested by Buchanan, would validate the appeal of some states and secessionist movements to rectificatory justice. Buchanan argues that independence movements in Latvia, Estonia and Lithuania, sovereign states unjustly and forcibly annexed by the USSR in 1940, had a strong and clear justification for secession, since each had 'as clear a title to territorial sovereignty as one is likely to find',[76] none of them having taken their territory 'from an identifiable group that could be said to have an identifiable claim on it', and each of them enjoying the right to secede conferred on all Soviet republics by the Constitution of the USSR. Buchanan's moral statute of limitations would render inadmissible the Indian claim to Goa, a Portuguese territory since 1510, annexed by India in 1962 without consultation with its inhabitants. The Indian claim was based on the assumption that the Portuguese conquest of Goa had been unjust, as well as being a violation of the territorial integrity of the subcontinent. The Zionist assertion of a right to establish a state on Palestinian territory because in biblical times this was a Jewish homeland, although long since the homeland of another people, would be in more serious conflict with Buchanan's moral statute of limitations than would India's claim to Goa, or the claim of Irish Nationalists to Irish territory forcibly acquired more than 300 years ago by British planters at the expense of the indigenous population.

There is also a Unionist version of historic rights to planted Irish territory. In this version, which, like the parallel Zionist one, is nourished by justificatory myth making, mere indigeneity confers no superior entitlement to land, since this entitlement derives from a more than human source. As Terence McCaughey ironically explains, the original Ulster colonists got their land in accordance with a divine plan for a chosen people, the model being the people of Israel under Abraham taking territory from 'the damned, unclean, lazy Canaanites'.[77] Ian Paisley and William McCrea claimed that their forefathers carved civilisation out of the Irish wilderness which was 'all bog land' before their arrival.[78] Such imaginative accounts of British colonial settlement and confiscation have a venerable provenance. Seventeenth-century British historians discovered clear biblical precedents for the conquest of Ireland. The Old Testament God gave the Land of Canaan to Abraham

75 Allen Buchanan, *The Morality of Political Divorce: From Sumter to Lithuania and Quebec* (Boulder, Colarado, 1991), p. 88.

76 Ibid., p. 87, p. 159.

77 Quoted in the *Sunday Tribune*, 26 Mar. 2000.

78 *The Sunday Press*, 23 Jan. 1994.

and his descendants because its inhabitants, particularly those of Sodom, were wicked and sinful. In similar fashion, in Sir John Temple's account of the first conquest of Ireland, King Henry the Second, 'when he entertained the first thoughts of transferring his arms over into Ireland, made suit unto the Pope, that he would give him leave to go and conquer Ireland, and reduce those beastly men unto the way of truth.' When King Henry arrived in Ireland, he found that its inhabitants were indeed 'devoid of all manner of civility, governed by no settled laws, living like beasts, biting and devouring one another'. What God had done for the Israelites, Pope Adrian IV did for the first colonists. King Henry, Temple observes, 'without any manner of scruple, or further inquisition into particular titles, resolving as it seems to make good by the sword the Pope's donation, made a general seizure of all the lands of the whole kingdom.'[79] The dealings of twentieth-century northern Loyalists with the Catholic minority, transformed by the 1920 Partition from being part of a national majority into a subject people, were influenced by the tradition that their ancestors were a chosen people who had taken possession of the promised land from inhabitants who were not part of the elect.[80]

VI UNIONIST CLAIMS TO SELF-DETERMINATION

The Unionist defence of partition and of separate statehood for Ulster Protestants involves the deployment of some of the elements of self-determination theory. Rejecting geographical determinism as a basis for nationhood, Unionists commonly insist that they differ decisively from the other people in Ireland 'in religion, ethnic origin, economic interests and sense of national identity' and that whatever Irish identity they might have, either culturally or ethnically, 'is consistent with their British national or political identity and allegiance.'[81] These fundamental differences between the two Irish groups are considered sufficient warrant by Unionists for the provision of a separate political entity in which they are free to pursue their special interests, preserve their cultural and religious values and their distinctive political allegiance. In

79 *Temple* (1646), p. 5. Quotations from the first edition. The authenticity of the Pope's donation of Ireland to Henry the second had long been a matter of controversy. However, recent scholarship has tended to regard the donation as a matter of historical fact. See F. X. Martin's chapter on 'Diarmait MacMurchada and the coming of the Anglo-Normans', in Art Cosgrove (ed.), *A New History of Ireland*, vol. 2 (Oxford, 2008), pp. 57–8.

80 D. H. Akenson, *God's Peoples: Covenant and Land in South Africa, Israel and Ulster* (Cornell, 1992), p. 120.

81 John McGarry and Brendan O'Leary, *Explaining Northern Ireland: Broken Images* (Oxford, 1995), p. 97.

his exhaustive analysis of the subject, Heslinga concludes that the Unionist two-nation theory is valid on the basis that it satisfies three criteria: separate political affinities, separate religious affinities and separate traditions and symbols. He feels justified in saying that 'Ulstermen do form a separate nation' and that 'Ulsterism is essentially a form of nationalism with too many political implications to be considered mere regionalism'. There is, as Heslinga observes, a vital distinction between what he calls Ulsterism and Irish nationalism: the latter finds its fulfilment in separatism, the former in the maintenance of the constitutional link with the British crown.[82] He quotes the words of a Nationalist leader at a New York rally on St Patrick's Day 1960 in support of the idea that even Nationalists accepted the two-nation theory: 'We can see no point in trying to come to terms with people [Unionists] utterly alien in their outlook and so remote from the traditions of this nation.'[83] However, the Unionist two-nation theory might be plausible but for the political geography of the six-county state. The 1920 Partition was far from marking a division between two distinct nations or two ethnically homogeneous groupings. Even Unionists would be forced to acknowledge that the border marks the political isolation from their fellow Nationalists in the southern jurisdiction of hundreds of thousands of northern Nationalists who profess allegiance to an Irish nation. Kevin O'Shiel puts the point strongly, describing Ulster Unionism as:

> unique in only one respect; it is the only religious minority in the world which has, through the assistance of powerful outside influences, been able to frustrate the organic development of the nation for more than a century, and then to insist on cutting off from the nation not only its own adherents but a large minority whose traditional allegiance was to the nation as a whole.[84]

However, an objection that might be made to O'Shiel's statement of the case is that he assumes that the Ulster Unionists are a religious minority rather than a national minority.

Initially, Unionism was anti-partitionist and operated in an all-Ireland context in its opposition to Home Rule, the fundamental Unionist argument being that since no Irish nation existed, there could be no valid claim to Irish self-determination.[85] The only nation visualised by those who put forward such an argument was a British one, comprising the two islands. This was

82 Heslinga, *The Irish Border*, p. 56.
83 Ibid., p. 64.
84 O'Shiel, *Handbook of the Ulster Question*, p. vi.
85 For useful surveys of Unionist two-nation theories see John Whyte, *Interpreting Northern Ireland* (Oxford, 1991) and McGarry and O'Leary, *Explaining Northern Ireland*.

made clear in an editorial comment in a Unionist newspaper in February 1920, in which the writer explained that Irish Unionists, north and south, objected to partition because they objected 'to being divorced from full representation in the Imperial Parliament, not just for ourselves alone, but for our country'.[86] A parallel strand in Unionist thinking, however, far from being unable to recognise any Irish nation, affirmed, on somewhat dubious historical grounds, that there were two distinct ones, or at least two nationalities, of Celt and Saxon descent respectively, and that any solution to the Irish problem must be founded on a recognition of this. After the Ulster Unionist Council decided in March 1920 not to oppose the new Government of Ireland Bill embodying partition, Unionists became more anxious 'to stress the distinctiveness of the two Irish entities and their peoples than they were to disprove the existence of an Irish nation', and 'self-determination had become as dear to the heart of Belfast as it was to that of Dublin'.[87]

In July 1921, when Craig met de Valera following the Truce, he responded to de Valera's statement that his only demand was for self-determination for the Irish nation by saying that 'that was all he himself wanted for the six counties'. After meeting Lloyd George, Craig used the language of natural and moral right. Since self-determination had been advanced as a principle by southern Nationalists, he would accept this on behalf of 'the people of Northern Ireland, who had already, by an overwhelming majority, determined their own parliament'.[88] At first glance, it might appear that if the principle of ethnic self-determination was a valid one, Craig had the better of the moral argument. Acceptance of de Valera's view that the island as a whole was the appropriate unit of self-determination would deny the right to Ulster Unionists. However, Craig's demand that the six-county entity should enjoy self-determination would prevent the principle from being applied to hundreds of thousands of Catholic Nationalists, an ethnically distinct group in Unionist terms, who were consigned to a state they had not chosen. Craig's terminology illustrates a fundamental feature of Unionist discourse: 'the people of Northern Ireland' is a shorthand phrase for the Loyalist population of the entity and leaves out of account almost 35 per cent of its population.

The principle of local self-determination advocated by Ulster Unionist leaders would, if rigorously applied, leave itself open to an endless series of refinements. Hancock expresses this sentiment well. 'If,' he argues, 'the majority in the six-counties were able to claim self-determination against the majority of Ireland, the majority of Fermanagh and Tyrone might in their turn claim

86 *Belfast News Letter*, 28 Feb. 1920.

87 Denis Kennedy, *The Widening Gulf* (Belfast, 1988), p. 36.

88 Craig's statement in *The Times* (London), 19 July 1921.

self-determination against the majority in the six counties.'[89] Here Hancock isolates one of the most fundamental dilemmas facing those who argue for self-determination: recognising the rights of one self (in this case north-eastern Loyalists) entailed the denial of the rights of two competing selves: the Irish nation as a whole and the Nationalist population of the six counties. The fundamental objection of Unionists to Home Rule, unwillingness to be made part of a political arrangement which seemed inimical to their welfare, was equally valid in the case of the Nationalist minority whom Unionists insisted on incorporating in their state against their will. If anything, the Nationalist case carried more weight, since Nationalists constituted a proportionately larger minority in the six counties (34.4 per cent) than Unionists in Ireland as a whole (approximately 26 per cent). There was the further consideration that if the British Government was justified in applying the principle of self-determination to permit the political exclusion of six-county Unionists who formed 19 per cent of the total Irish population, there could be no good reason for not extending the same treatment to the much more significant minority in the newly excluded area. During the Commons debate on the Irish Boundary Bill in September–October 1925, Captain Wedgwood-Benn, a Liberal MP who joined Labour in 1927, pointed out that the case of the Ulster Unionists used to be 'why should we, who are 26 per cent of the population of Ireland, be put under the domination of the remainder? We claim the right of the minority.' Why should Unionists, Benn asked, 'who are 26 per cent of the population of Ireland, now claim to put 34 per cent of their population under a government they do not desire? There is no defence in equity for such a claim.'[90]

The Unionist insistence on partition as a means of facilitating separate self-determination raises fundamental questions of principle and practice. To judge its validity, it is necessary to adjudicate between this Unionist claim and the claim to territorial integrity or political independence put forward by the national unit of which the secessionist Unionist 'self' is felt to be a part. The difficulty inherent in resolving such conflicting claims to self-determination is underlined in David Miller's analysis of the independence movements in Quebec and Catalonia. In such cases, as Miller observes, the principle of self-determination may point in one of two opposing directions. If the Quebecois or the Catalans come to think of themselves as having identities distinct from those of the Canadians or the Spanish, and seek political independence on that basis, then the principle of self-determination would appear to support

89   W. K. Hancock, *Survey of British Commenwealth Affairs Vol. 1: Problems of Nationality 1918–1936* (Oxford, 1937), p. 132.
90   *Hansard*, House of Commons, Vol. 177, Col. 157, 1 Oct. 1925.

such claims. However, there is another, arguably larger and superior claim: 'The Canadians and the Spaniards have a claim to be self-determining too, and a claim to determine the future of the territory that has historically been identified as Canada or Spain.'[91] As applied to the position of the Catalans, the Quebecois and the Irish Unionists, and to the larger territories of which they are a part, the principle of self-determination is problematic because it does not tell us who the peoples are that are entitled to self-determination or the jurisdictional unit they are entitled to.

Even if democratic criteria are applied, with a view to letting the people involved decide by plebiscite, this idea faces the difficulty that 'the people cannot decide until somebody decides who are the people'.[92] Furthermore, the jurisdictional area in which a plebiscite might be held is likely to be essentially contested in relation to cases like the Irish one. Where the majority of people in an area want the boundaries of that area to be the boundaries of the state, which is the Irish Nationalist position, and a minority do not, the minority here being Unionist, the issue is in effect decided by the area of the plebiscite. The difficulty of determining the appropriate jurisdictional unit has a vital significance in the application of self-determination to Ireland. The indeterminacy of the principle is indicated by the fact that this unit has been variously defined as the United Kingdom as a whole, the island of Ireland, the historic province of Ulster, the six counties, or local government areas within the latter. In the parallel case of Quebec, a referendum based on the principle would yield different results if the unit were taken to be the whole of Canada, the province of Quebec, or part of the province of Quebec.[93]

A common Unionist response to the Nationalist argument that the only valid jurisdictional unit to be considered is the island as a whole, is that Unionists are not an Irish minority but a loyal British population who did not secede from Britain in 1921, and still wish to adhere to their old allegiance. The logic of this position is that the relevant plebiscitary unit should be the British Isles. This position was strongly defended by St Loe Strachey, the pro-Unionist editor of *The Spectator*, who held that British Union with Ireland was as much an incorporating union as the union between the several states the American Republic, and that the will of the majority must prevail within the United Kingdom. The area which he thought was the right one to give a decision was the United Kingdom, since, if any other were adopted, 'You might very soon fritter away the whole United Kingdom.'[94] Many leading British Conservatives

91 Miller, 'Secession', in Moore, *National Self-Determination*, p. 62.
92 Ivor Jennings, *The Approach to Self-Government* (Cambridge, 1956), p. 56.
93 Moore, *National Self-Determination*, p. 135.
94 Strachey, *The Adventure of Living*, p. 389.

shared this approach. Philip Kerr, Marquess of Lothian, Private Secretary to Lloyd George from 1916 to 1921, believed that the destinies of Ireland and Britain were so intertwined that the secession of Nationalist Ireland from the Empire had to be resisted: Britain's case in this respect was exactly the same as that of the north in the American Civil War. The essential aim was to maintain the fundamental political unity of the United Kingdom, and by extension, of the British Empire. The enemy, as Kerr saw it in April 1921, was 'excessive nationalism', the creed of Sinn Féin, which, 'if it had full play, would Balkanise the world.'[95] Throughout the Home Rule era the comparison of Irish Nationalists with American Confederates, and Unionists with the American Federals was widely made by Unionists. The warrant for these comparisons was to be found in Lincoln's position during the Civil War that the Union was fundamental law and not open to debate, which was how many Irish Unionists wished their Union with Great Britain to be treated. From Lincoln's point of view, even to discuss or advocate secession from the Union was illegitimate: in 1864 he was re-elected not as a Republican but as a Union candidate, thus demonstrating that the issue was above party politics. The point was reinforced by the choice of a southern Democrat as Vice President. The fact that German and Italian nationalism involved merging many previously independent states into larger units[96] against significant Catholic opposition led to their example also being cited by Irish Unionists, especially before the First World War.

Bonar Law's vigorous attempt to undermine the whole principle of Irish Home Rule was also founded on the assumption that the unit entitled to self-determination was the British archipelago, not the island of Ireland or part of it: to concede a Nationalist claim to separate political treatment would violate the right of the people of the United Kingdom as a whole to preserve their polity from an undesirable secession with consequences similar to those feared by Kerr. On 26 January 1912, Bonar Law, in his first important announcement as Conservative leader, dismissed the granting of Home Rule on the ground that 'the Nationalists of Ireland as compared with the whole of the United Kingdom are about a fifteenth of the population', and could therefore have no right to dictate to the overwhelming majority of the only unit to which self-determination could apply.[97] Some leaders of modern Unionism have sought to

95   Philip Kerr Memorandum to Lloyd George, 11 Apr. 1921, cited in G. K. Peatling, *British Opinion and Irish Self-Government 1865–1925: From Unionism to Liberal Commonwealth* (Dublin, 2001), p. 154.

96   German unification involved the incorporation of such states as Prussia, Westphalia, Bavaria, Hanover and Saxony. The united Italy came to include, Tuscany, The Kingdom of the Two Sicilies, The Papal States and some smaller entities.

97   Robert Blake, *The Unknown Prime Minister: The Life and Times of Andrew Bonar Law 1858–1923* (London, 1955), p. 127.

defend the legitimacy of the six-county state by arguing that in the period before the Anglo-Irish Treaty of 1921, the whole of Ireland was part of a single state, the United Kingdom, to whose legislative procedures it had been subject, since the Act of Union of 1801, in the same way as was any British region. A further step in this argument is that partition should not be seen as a concession to northern Unionists, but the inevitable outcome of a secession from the United Kingdom by ethnocentric southern Irish Nationalists. Part of the same argument is that even if the 26 counties had a right to secede in accordance with the principle of self-determination, this did not mean that Unionists were obliged to secede along with them. If this position is tenable, then the forcible separation of the Nationalist south from the British State was a violation of the principle of territorial integrity, by then enshrined in Article 10 of the Covenant of the League of Nations, and a violation of the right to self-determination for the United Kingdom as a whole. This insistence on seeing the whole archipelago of the British Isles as the true geographical frame of reference for the Irish question was perhaps the most effective Unionist method of countering the Nationalist emphasis on the overriding importance of the island of Ireland. For Unionists, the British Isles framework had the advantage of not appearing partitionist; instead it could be used to attribute the blame for partition to the Nationalist secession from the United Kingdom rather than to the Unionist insistence on exclusion from the Irish Free State. It was the logic of this position that led John Taylor, Deputy Leader of the Ulster Unionist Party, to defend the territorial integrity of Yugoslavia, to discover a parallel between the fragmentation of that State and the secession of southern Ireland from the United Kingdom, and to deem it wrong for European statesmen to recognise the former states of the Yugoslav Federation. Taylor took the view that Croatia and Bosnia ought not to have been allowed to secede from Yugoslavia. Taylor believed that Bosnia, for example, which he described as 'a failed entity', a term used by Charles Haughey in 1981 to describe Northern Ireland,[98] had little cohesion as a nation state. He believed that if the republics seceded, their Serbian populations should be allowed to partition them (as the British had done with Ireland), and remain attached to Serbia (just as Ulster Unionists availed of partition to remain attached to Britain).[99]

---

98 Comments made by Charles J. Haughey in Wexford during his 1981 General Election Campaign speech. 'Ugly scenes as Taoiseach campaigns in border counties', 1981 General Election, General Elections, RTE Libraries and Archives. Originally broadcast 2 June 1981, reporter Tom MacSweeney. http://www.rte.ie/laweb/ll/ll_to8f.html. Retrieved 15 Dec. 2010.

99 Quotation by John Taylor in Brendan Simms, *Unfinest Hour: Britain and the Destruction of Bosnia* (London, 2001), p. 288.

VII THE LIMITS OF SELF-DETERMINATION

Those who make principled self-determination claims similar to that advanced by Northern Ireland Unionists must confront the fragmentation and even anarchy implicit in the principle. If the six-county claim to self-determination was valid, the principles underlying its validity made a further secession, that of the border Nationalists, equally valid. Here, however, *realpolitik* was allowed to supersede principle, and the will of Loyalism was able to enforce itself within the six-county area. Thus a limit was set to the process of self-determination in Ireland, to the disadvantage of Nationalists. If self-determination were to be the only operative criterion for determining international boundaries without regard to the principle of territorial integrity, there could be no principled objection to the promotion of further secessions within the original seceding entities. Examples might be multiplied from many parts of the world. Even as the 13 New England colonies severed themselves from the British nation, did the American southern states have the right to separate themselves from the north? After Nigeria separated itself from the British Empire, did the ethnically distinct Biafra have the right to be independent of the rest of Nigeria? Should minorities within states, the Kosovar Albanians, for example, or further minorities resulting from the dissolution of states, like the Bosnian Serbs, be granted self-determination? If consultation with the inhabitants of such territories resulted in a majority in favour of secession, how could it be in accord with democratic principles to deny this right? Those who would, and in the case of the United States and Nigeria, did, deny the right of secession to significant separatist groups, contend that the argument of the secessionists is fallacious, since it assumes, without proof, that the individuals to be consulted are the members of the secessionist group, or a majority of these, rather than the population of the territory as a whole. Consultation with the latter might reveal, as it would have in the case of Ireland, that the majority wanted a single state.[100]

It is worthy of note that during the Irish War of Independence, Lloyd George and de Valera each opposed a different group of Irish secessionists, each thinking he was following Lincoln's example in confronting the southern states. For Lloyd George, Sinn Féin were the Confederates, while for de Valera Ulster Unionists were. The use made of the concept of self-determination by both parties to the Irish debate raises issues which have a universal application. Is it, for example, theoretically coherent to attempt to apply the principle of external self-determination to all multinational and multi-ethnic

---

100 See Lea Brilmayer, 'Secession and self-determination: a territorial interpretation', *International Law Anthology* (1994), pp. 197–8.

states, to conclude that if a group believed itself to be a nation it should have its own state if it desired one? There are some sound reasons for contending that the argument for establishing any independent nation state is essentially an *ad hoc* one, and that, as Hobsbawm observes, 'any finite number of sovereign states must exclude some potential candidates from statehood', thus undermining the case for *universal* self-determination by separatism. Hobsbawm points out that the argument for the separation of Scotland from England is exactly analogous with the argument for the separation of the Shetlands from Scotland, 'and so are the arguments against both separations.'[101] The same might be suggested in the case of the separation of Ireland from the British archipelago, of the six-county entity from the rest of Ireland, and of a Nationalist enclave from the rest of the six counties. A major complicating factor is the constant change in the ethnic composition of states, especially in Europe, as a result, for example, of emigration, on the one hand, and of the migration of people from less developed countries, on the other. As Brubaker observes, even if territorial frontiers could be correctly drawn at a given moment, 'the momentary match between the division of territory and the distribution of persons would not endure, since nations are inherently mobile and dynamic.'[102]

The theoretical consequences of extending the principle of external self-determination to its logical limit are potentially catastrophic for a world system based on sovereign states. Gellner illustrates one of these consequences, arguing that although we live in a world which has the space for only two or three hundred national states, there are many thousands of potential nations which could in principle claim statehood in line with a thoroughgoing application of the principle of external self-determination.[103] If such a policy was to be pursued, only Iceland, South Korea, Japan and a few other states, Swaziland, Lesotho, Botswana and Somalia for example,[104] would be politically secure, and some larger states, like India, China and Russia would be victims of an enhanced version of the kind of inter-ethnic chaos which marked the fragmentation of the Soviet Union.[105] The outcome of this process would be a long vista of secessions, secessions from secessions, a massive multiplication of the number of states, and a correlative exponential increase in the number of

---

101 E. J. Hobsbawm, 'Some reflections on the break-up of Britain', *New Left Review* (Sept.–Oct. 1977), p. 13.

102 Roger Brubaker, *Nationalism Reframed: Nationhood and the National Question in the New Europe* (New York, 1996), pp. 39–40.

103 Ernest Gellner, *Nations and Nationalism* (New York, 1983), p. 2.

104 Cassese, *Self-Determination*, p. 317.

105 Gellner, *Nations and Nationalism*, pp. 44–5.

minority groups within states. It is therefore not surprising that state
authorities have been notably reluctant to countenance the disruption of
territorial integrity through secession, since international law is not designed
to force or encourage states to dismember themselves. The Irish partition
settlement and its consequences may be regarded as a mistaken application of
the principle of external self-determination, since this application, particularly
to the six-county state, satisfied the demands of one ethnic group at the
expense of the democratic rights of another. As Gallagher points out, it can
make sense to think in terms of an absolute right to self-determination only
when a 'self' can determine its own destiny 'without thereby trampling on
someone else's'. In Northern Ireland, indeed in Ireland as a whole, 'the
geographical intermingling of the two groups means that neither can exercise
determination only for itself' without the major movements of population that
have characterised inter-ethnic conflicts elsewhere in Europe. Thus, 'the very
idea of an absolute right to self-determination for either Nationalists or
Unionists is a chimera.'[106]

VII REFLECTIONS

Judgement of the merits or defects of the 1920 Partition of Ireland will depend
on whether one starts from one or other of two conflicting sets of premises.
The Irish Nationalist position, shared by Indian, Palestinian and Cypriot
Nationalists, was that any form of partition violated the self-determination
and full independence within clearly defined boundaries, by setting aside the
will of the majority in the national territory demarcated by those boundaries.
From the Irish Nationalist perspective, this territory was the island as a whole.
The Unionist claim, in its most extreme form, was that the Unionist community, specifically in the north east of Ireland, had emerged as a separate
nation, and in its qualified form, that Unionists were part of the British
nation. If those who framed the 1920 Act had followed the logic of the former
position, the predominantly Unionist part of the north east should have been
constituted as a separate state; if north-eastern Unionists were indeed part of
the British nation, the territories in which they predominated should have
been integrated into Great Britain. In the course of the debate on the 1920
measure, Lloyd George implicitly rejected the single-nation theory as
contrary to present facts. It would be better, he claimed, that 'Ireland should
recognise this fact, that Ulster does not want to be governed from Dublin, that
Ulster has got her own ideas, her own thoughts, which are not common with

106 Gallagher, 'How many nations?', p. 28.

those of the rest of Ireland'.[107] Lloyd George was using the term 'Ulster', as Unionists then and since had the habit of doing, as if the excluded counties constituted a totally homogeneous Protestant Unionist territory, or as if the hundreds of thousands of Nationalists who lived there were deemed either invisible or of no account.

A common British and Unionist defence of the 1920 Partition was that it acknowledged the demand of Ulster Unionists for the right to self-determination, a right which could not be withheld from them if it were to be conceded to southern Nationalists. The basis for this analysis was challenged by Nicholas Mansergh, who argued that the provisions of the Act which partitioned Ireland 'might be construed in terms of self-determination if each self-determining population had constituted a long-established political community'.[108] But, as Mansergh observes, this was not so. In the five centuries of British rule preceding the 1920 Act, Ireland had been regarded as an entity, with a parliament of its own in earlier centuries, and since 1800 as one of the kingdoms merged into the United Kingdom of Great Britain and Ireland. Thus, Mansergh asks, if that union were to be undone in 1920, 'then, even having regard to British precedent alone, should not the exercise of self-determination by Ireland be as a unit, since it was as a unit that the Irish Parliament [in 1800] had approved of union?'[109]

There is a further dimension to the question raised by Mansergh. When Ireland was partitioned in 1920, the Act of Union of 1801 was still fully operative, which meant that the entire island of Ireland was fully integrated with the British political system. The British Parliament had the constitutional right to legislate for the island as a whole, a right fully recognised in international law, which gave no credence to the claim of Dáil Éireann to be the parliament of the Irish people. In partitioning Ireland, therefore, the British legislature was establishing a new boundary within part of the United Kingdom over which it exercised the same political control as it did over the other parts. The boundary settlements in Central and Eastern Europe, in contrast, were the result of external interference with the territorial integrity of states which found themselves on the losing side in the First World War.

The two-nation argument, whether in the case of Ireland, India, Palestine or Cyprus did not, as O'Leary points out, automatically make a case for partition. To make this case, additional premises are needed. These include the infeasibility of efforts to establish binominal, federal, consociational or

107 *Hansard*, House of Commons Debates, Vol. 127, Cols 1322–36, 31 Mar. 1920.
108 Nicholas Mansergh, 'Northern Ireland: the past,' in Diana Mansergh (ed.), *Nationalism and Independence: Selected Irish Papers* (Cork, 1997), p. 15.
109 Ibid.

other arrangements with a view to making Ireland as a unit an equal democratic society in which the origins of its Nationalist and Unionist inhabitants were subordinated to their common welfare. In the case of Ulster Unionists, the Muslim League and the Zionists, there appeared to be no willingness to experiment with any such formulae. Their leaders took it for granted that these options were either unrealistic or impossible. Their veto of alternative formulae, as O'Leary observes, 'was rendered effective by the declarations of the imperial powers that they would not coerce the relevant minorities.'[110] A characteristic common to the Irish and continental post-war partitions is described in O'Leary's account of partition in general as 'an externally proposed and imposed *fresh* border cut through at least one community's national homeland, creating at least two separate units under different sovereigns or authorities, and as involving at least one loser who always regards the partition as an imposition, a violation'.[111] What makes partition objectionable as a means of managing ethno-national differences is that it invariably creates a victim group, unless, of course, it conforms to the ideal proposed by Arend Lijphart, who argued that partition can be acceptable where it is not externally imposed, but instead the result of negotiation by all the groups who might be affected by it, when it involves a just division of territory and resources, and where it results in homogeneous, or significantly less plural independent countries.[112] These desiderata, however, were not met either in the case of the Irish partition or the many other contemporary boundary settlements, such as the post-Versailles ones, which created new states or assigned parts of the territory of one state to another. The principle of common consent to partition was almost universally ignored, as was the need to achieve ethnic homogeneity. Instead, the major territorial adjustment decided upon by the British Government in the case of Ireland, as well as many of the boundary adjustments made by the victors after the First World War, were imposed without the involvement of those who were victimised by them but with the connivance of the beneficiaries.

The boundary established by the Government of Ireland Act of 1920, which proved to be the source of so much dissatisfaction to both six-county Nationalists and Unionists in the three remaining counties of Ulster, represented, from the point of view of self-determination, the crudest kind of partition the British Government could have chosen to impose, apart from a nine-county one which would have ignored the wishes of almost 700,000 Nationalists. Other possibilities were available, based on borders already

110 Brendan O'Leary, 'Debating partition: justifications and critiques', *Working Papers in British-Irish Studies* 48, Institute for British-Irish Studies (UCD, 2006), p. 11.
111 O'Leary, Lustick and Callaghy (eds), *Rightsizing the State*, p. 54.
112 Arend Lijphart, *Democracy in Plural Societies: A Comparative Exploration* (London, 1984), p. 10.

existing, constituency or district council ones, for example, or alternatively, the 1920 boundary might have been based on the holding of a plebiscite, a common prelude to the drawing of boundaries in other jurisdictions at that time and later. Some of the post-Versailles settlements provide examples of painstaking efforts to achieve equity in the creation of new boundaries in accordance with the principle of self-determination, and the need to satisfy the wishes of as many inhabitants of disputed areas as possible.

The British preoccupation with county boundaries meant that the possibility of creating a border much more in accord with the wishes of inhabitants than the six-county one, received little or no consideration. The parliamentary constituency boundaries established by the Redistribution of Seats Act (Ireland) 1917, would have provided a much more refined basis upon which to mark out a partition line. Had those who drafted the 1920 Act based a northern state on those constituencies which had returned Unionist members in 1918, its territorial extent would have been considerably less than the six-county unit that emerged. The constituencies of Derry City, south Down, south Armagh, south Fermanagh, north-west and north-east Tyrone would have been assigned to the Free State while the result would still have made geographical sense. This arrangement would still have given the northern state a Catholic population of 28 per cent. Of six-county Catholics 148,239 would have been placed south of the border, along with 96,197 Protestants.[113] Partition based on local government rural district boundaries would also have been more equitable than the six-county one, and given a Catholic population of 26 per cent to the northern state.[114] Had a boundary been based not on the results of the elections in the northern constituencies but on the declared religious affiliations of the populations of these constituencies, as recorded in the most recent Census, that of 1911, even fewer Nationalists would have been assigned to the northern state. Its total population would have been 939,047, consisting of 690,808 Unionists and 248,239 Nationalists. The Nationalist percentage would have been 26.5. Under this arrangement, 185,922 Catholics would have been on the Free State side of the border, and 129,562 Protestants. The six-county partition arrangement had the advantage of geographical tidiness, achieved, however, at the cost of ethnic homogeneity. An arrangement based on the 1918 constituencies would have been less tidy geographically but much more homogeneous. Another model, canvassed by Nationalists, had the advantage of leaving far fewer dissatisfied Nationalists in a more homogeneous state. This would have involved the exclusion of the predominantly

113 These figures based on O'Shiel, *Handbook of the Ulster Question*, p. 48.
114 See F. W. Boal, J. Douglas, H. Neville and J. A. E. Orr (eds), *Integration and Division, Geographical Perspectives on the Northern Ireland Problem* (London, 1982), pp. 110–12.

Nationalist areas of west Ulster, in practice Tyrone and Fermanagh. Its most detailed exposition was Bishop Patrick O'Donnell's memorandum of March 1920, in which he claimed that 'the only form of partition that ever had any semblance of justification was the county option, as proposed under the 1914 amending Bill'.[115] Here, O'Donnell was reflecting the views of the many Nationalists in west Ulster who were willing to accept a partition based on the exclusion of four counties from an all-Ireland state under Home Rule.

A nine-county partition, while it would have denied self-determination to approximately 700,000 Nationalists, would have served the interests of the minority to a much greater extent than the six-county arrangement did. A nine-county Northern Ireland would have commanded greater historical and geographical credibility. More significantly, it would have been a religously balanced polity in which permanent majority domination would have been difficult to sustain, thereby facilitating the operation of normal democratic processes. The 1920 Partition was characterised by many of the faults evident in other exercises in boundary drawing. It left the six-county entity too heterogeneous. Just as Pakistan had too many Hindus, and Sikhs, India too many Muslims, Israel too many Arabs, Northern Ireland had too many Catholics. The fundamental defect of the 1920 Partition was that 'the double standards of British Governments, which, to avoid imposing on Ireland a system of Home Rule rejected by a quarter of its population, created and defended an artificial Northern Ireland rejected by one third of its population'.[116]

---

115   For O'Donnell's Memorandum, see Eamon Phoenix, *Northern Nationalism, Nationalist Politics: Partition and the Catholic Minority in Northern Ireland, 1890–1940* (Belfast, 1994), p. 78, Cardinal O'Donnell Papers AAA.

116   Michael Laffan, *The Partition of Ireland 1911–25* (Dundalk, 1983), p. 123.

EIGHT

CONCLUSION

—

From the mid-nineteenth century until 1920, the main problem in Anglo-Irish relations was whether or how an Irish demand for Home Rule might be reconciled with the interests and aspirations of Great Britain, its Empire and Ulster Unionists. This examination of the course of events between 1886 and 1920 makes one thing abundantly clear. Since Ulster Unionists were numerous enough, and determined enough, and had a sufficiently strong case and an influential support base in Britain to resist Home Rule under a Dublin Parliament, Nationalists could achieve Home Rule only by acquiescing in partition. The 1920 partition, which gave six-county Unionists Home Rule, something they had not asked for, dealt with one aspect of the problem raised by the long Home Rule debate. It also gave rise to a new problem which had to be confronted during the Treaty negotiations in 1921. At the root of the Ulster problem after 1920 was that the new Northern Ireland state was far too heterogeneous. Both parties to the Treaty negotiations recognised that the demographic composition of that state was not defensible, since it was based on the incorporation of a disproportionate number of Catholic Nationalists into a state designed for Protestant Unionists. The British and Irish sides considered a number of ways of overcoming this problem.

The fundamental Irish demand was the essential unity of Ireland, which, in the Nationalist understanding, meant that an Irish administration based in Dublin should exercise legal sovereignty over the entire island, with strong guarantees for Unionists. This was a demand impossible of realisation in the circumstances. To enforce it would have involved the coercion of the six north-eastern counties, with the danger of Unionist military resistance and the consequent need for British military intervention. On the Irish side there was no appetite for trying to coerce Unionists. With their separate parliament and rapidly developing administrative apparatus, six-county Unionists had no intention of relinquishing these hard-won advantages in return for being governed by a Dublin parliament with a Catholic majority which they could only regard as being inimical to their interests. Nor did they feel they should have to submit to this state of affairs since, in 1920, the British Government had given their leaders a pledge that their newly established political entity would not be subject in the future to any but minuscule territorial adjustment, and that the sanctity of its boundaries would be guaranteed. Given these facts, all the southern negotiators could hope for was some form of token unity: a council of Ireland, for example, to discuss problems common to north and south. As a means of getting an overall settlement, Lloyd George, in the face of determined Unionist resistance to any form of national unity acceptable to the Irish side, suggested a rectification of the 1920 border by a boundary commission, in accordance with the wishes of inhabitants. There was a sound reason for appointing such a commission in the wake of the 1920 Partition: the most serious consequence of that settlement was that the new Northern Ireland State had a larger minority than the country as a whole had before 1920. Had Lloyd George's administration set up the proposed commission with clear terms of reference on the ratification of the Treaty or immediately following this, much later confusion, controversy and bitterness might have been avoided.

I BRITISH DUPLICITY AND IRISH BLUNDERS

The evidence outlined in the course of this account of the genesis of the Commission proposal tends to the conclusion that the Irish acceptance of the boundary clause in the Treaty was partly the result of the duplicitous behaviour of Lloyd George and partly the result of the incompetence of Arthur Griffith, the chief Irish negotiator. Lloyd George, acting through the Assistant Cabinet Secretary, Thomas Jones, initially gave Griffith to understand that the Commission he had in mind would make its determination simply in accordance with the wishes of six-county inhabitants. It soon transpired, however, that the proposal he actually had in mind was for a nine-county commission with the power to transfer territory in either direction. More significantly, the clause governing its operation would impose disabling qualifications on the wishes of inhabitants, in practice making these wishes subservient to economic and geographic considerations. Without consulting his colleagues, or the Dáil Cabinet, Griffith subscribed to a memorandum drawn up by Jones agreeing to accept the proposed Commission if Ulster could not be persuaded to settle for an all-Ireland parliament. As a result of what Griffith did, the Irish plenipotentiaries were committed to Lloyd George's solution to the Ulster problem: the establishment of a boundary commission at some time in the future, with extremely vague terms of reference. This very vagueness served Lloyd George's purposes well. It enabled him to give contradictory impressions of the likely effect of a commission to those directly involved. Evidence from both British and Irish sources suggests that he gave Collins and Griffith to understand that the Free State might well be awarded areas in the six counties with Nationalist majorities, including even the counties of Tyrone and Fermanagh. At the same time he was privately telling his Cabinet that only small transfers of territory would be involved, and giving similar assurances to Craig. He was even hinting to British Parliament that such transfers as would be made could favour Northern Ireland rather than the Free State. This process of devaluing the Commission as a vehicle for addressing the Nationalist case was to persist until it had completed its work at the end of 1925. The principal agents of this devaluation included leading members of the Conservative Party, including people who had helped to negotiate the Treaty and who had signed it. The signatories well knew that their Irish counterparts had been persuaded to sign on the understanding that the function of a boundary commission was to adjust large territorial anomalies in favour of the Free State. They also knew that no treaty would have been agreed without such an understanding. Their widely proclaimed revisionist views helped to relaunch their careers in a party whose membership resented their involvement in the negotiation of such an unpopular treaty.

The widespread contention as to the scope of a commission could not have been generated had the Irish plenipotentiaries, particularly Collins and Griffith, behaved more responsibly. Their dealings with the Boundary Commission Article betray a surprising lack of due diligence on behalf of those inhabitants of the six counties whose political destinies would be in the hands of the Commission. Neither Collins nor Griffith insisted that the section of the Article providing for a commission should be more precisely framed. What, for example, was to be understood by economic and geographic conditions? What weight was to be attached to these? How, precisely, were the wishes of the inhabitants to be ascertained? Who were these inhabitants? In ascertaining their wishes, which geographical, demographic or administrative units should be considered? Should whole counties be considered as units? What was to happen if the Northern Ireland Government refused to appoint a commissioner? The Dáil Cabinet as a whole was equally remiss. Its members were given the opportunity to scrutinise the Ulster clauses of the Treaty during the weekend before it was signed, but their preoccupation with such ultimately less important issues as the oath of loyalty to the British monarch rendered them oblivious to the central long-term significance of the Ulster question.

The lack of priority given to the Ulster clause, however, may have been a reflection of a deep-seated indifference to the problems posed by the north east, soon to be displayed in the Treaty debates. It is significant that in the course of these, very little was said about either Ulster or partition. Members of the Dáil seemed happy to defer the Ulster question to some future time, in the interest of progressing towards a settlement of the issues dividing Britain and the 26 counties. After 1920, generations of Irish Nationalist politicians engaged in futile rhetoric about the evils of partition. Rhetoric to the contrary notwithstanding, the southern Nationalist position involved a trade-off between Irish unity and sovereignty for a southern state. Nationalist politicians in the Free State were unwilling to diminish 26-county sovereignty even if this meant entertaining partition. When they spoke of Ireland, they tended to have the 26 counties in mind, with the exception of a few border deputies such as Seán MacEntee and Eoin O'Duffy. It is significant that de Valera successfully resisted proposals to make Fianna Fáil a 32-county party and to permit representatives of six-county Nationalists to sit in the Dáil. In some Nationalist quarters, there lurked an unacknowledged fear that a united Ireland might undermine Gaelic culture and the Catholic ethos. Many Irish Nationalists insisted that Unionists were part of the Irish nation; others saw them as aliens foisted on the country through plantation and dispossession. Again, a not uncommon view was that Unionists were pathetic instruments in the hands of British politicians. Some actions of southern governments were patently partitionist in tendency. The boycott by Dáil Éireann in 1921 of Belfast goods in reaction to attacks on Belfast Catholics inevitably reinforced the dependence of Belfast on British markets, adding an economic partition to the administrative division already being reinforced by Lloyd George's Government. Further evidence of the partitionist mentality in the Free State was the establishment of a customs barrier on 1 April 1923.

During the early months of 1922, Collins and Griffith felt obliged to enlarge on the capacity of the Boundary Commission to effect a major reduction in the territorial extent of Northern Ireland. Privately, however, many southern statesmen, Collins in particular, believed that even if such claims proved valid, the cause of a united Ireland, the cornerstone of Nationalist policy, would be set back for generations to come. As Collins saw it, the Commission might reduce Northern Ireland to such narrow limits that it could not survive without incorporation with the south. He realised that a truncated Ulster forced to join the south would leave discontented, rancorous minorities which it would be probably impossible to govern. This line of thinking induced Collins, prompted by Winston Churchill, to embark on a novel exercise in statesmanship. Early in 1922, within weeks of having subscribed to the Boundary Commission proposal by signing the Treaty, Collins entered into private but abortive negotiations with Craig with the purpose of avoiding recourse to the Commission. Craig was pleased to explain to his followers that by virtue of negotiating with him on vital matters, Collins had afforded formal recognition to the Northern Ireland State. Having failed to settle the boundary issue with Craig, Collins presided over an undertaking scarcely conducive to his project for a form of Irish unity which would leave no legacy of bitterness or discontent. This involved military intervention in Northern Ireland by a combined force consisting of units from both sides of the fractured southern IRA. One purpose of this was to restore unity to the IRA by channelling its energies into a campaign against Northern Ireland, the common enemy. This fruitless and misguided endeavour, later disowned by Cosgrave and his Executive Council, reinforced the determination of Unionists to preserve their territory intact. The attempt to engage with Craig on a scheme to abandon the Boundary Commission suggested to border Nationalists that the southern Government no longer regarded the Commission as the best solution to the Ulster problem. In this, they judged rightly.

II DIVIDED COUNSELS AMONG NATIONALISTS

There is abundant evidence to suggest that a boundary commission had never been regarded in Dublin as the best solution to the deferred Ulster problem. Whatever its outcome, it was likely that a majority of northern Nationalists would be left behind. Kevin O'Higgins, the most astute and realistic of southern statesmen, believed that it would have been better for the northern minority to have sent representatives to the Northern Ireland Parliament after 1920, embraced its administrative institutions, and carved out their own destiny. Even Kevin O'Shiel, who was central to the propaganda campaign of the Irish Boundary Bureau to exact the maximum of northern territory from the Boundary Commission, feared that his efforts might lead in the opposite direction to national unity. Cosgrave thought that the Boundary Commission might be jettisoned in return for the withdrawal by the Northern Government of all hostile acts against the Catholic minority.

The appointment of Eoin MacNeill as Free State Representative on the Boundary Commission appeared to afford further evidence that Cosgrave did not take the Commission seriously or at least that he feared that its operation would be futile. MacNeill, a mild-mannered scholar, already tired of politics, proved a largely indifferent, ineffectual Commissioner. If Cosgrave believed that large-scale changes were possible, he might have chosen a barrister like Kevin O'Shiel, with a northern background, who was well qualified, which MacNeill was not, to debate legal procedures and technicalities. Furthermore, MacNeill could only be a part-time commissioner, since Cosgrave did not relieve him of his duties as Minister for Education. The cause of border Nationalists in relation to the Commission was severely hampered by the intervention of de Valera and his Sinn Féin Party in northern politics. In October 1924, as the Nationalist Party prepared to contest the Northern Ireland seats in the British General Election, de Valera announced that Sinn Féin would contest seven of the thirteen seats. In protest at this attempt to split the Nationalist vote, the Nationalist Party boycotted the election, while Sinn Féin failed to win a seat. Had Sinn Féin remained aloof, Nationalists would have won the two seats in Fermanagh and Tyrone. Their Party had hoped that this would demonstrate to the Boundary Commission that Tyrone and Fermanagh were Nationalist counties. In the event, the result of the election made the two counties appear overwhelmingly Unionist. Part of de Valera's strategy was to sabotage the chances of border Nationalists of making a successful case to the Commission, his argument being that this would amount to deserting their fellow Nationalists in the north east of the six counties and leave them a helpless minority.

III FORCES WORKING AGAINST THE NATIONALIST CASE

By this time it was clear that neither the British nor Irish Governments had much enthusiasm for the Boundary Commission. Kevin O'Higgins circulated a memorandum to his Government colleagues incorporating a possible offer to the Northern Ireland Government before the Bill setting up the Commission became law at the end of September 1924. The British Prime Minister, Ramsay MacDonald, hoped that the Bill to establish the Commission would not be brought into operation. Both he and Stanley Baldwin, his successor, gave private assurances to the Unionist leadership that even if the Commission were established, it would make only modest transfers. How they could have known this in advance is an interesting matter for speculation. There is, however, a plausible answer. In 1924, Baldwin, leader of the Conservative opposition, paid a secret visit to Belfast to assure Craig that he had nothing to fear from the imminent Boundary Commission. If returned to power, Baldwin was prepared to give the Unionists a veto over any Commission award. He was determined that if the Commission gave away counties, Ulstermen could not accept this, and the Conservative Party would back them.

By the time the Commission was ready to do its work under the chairman-ship of the British-born South African Judge Richard Feetham, border Nationalists had good reason to feel that they were at a severe disadvantage in pressing their claims under the boundary clause of the Treaty. Powerful forces and adverse circumstances were united against them. The Civil War in the south, which lasted for the best part of a year from 1922 to 1923 made it impossible for the Free State Government to promote their cause. Both the

British and the Unionists took it for granted that their concerns should take precedence over those of Irish Nationalists, north and south, since the southern Nationalists did not have equal standing. The British authorities made it clear to the Ulster Unionists, in advance of any determination by the Commission, that they would not uphold a decision by Feetham favouring the Free State position if this decision met with Ulster resistance. The British turned down the Nationalist demand for local plebiscites, which were in line with European precedent. Churchill overruled his own treasury officials by insisting on the continued funding of the Ulster Special Constabulary as the time for a boundary commission decision approached. In such ways, the British Government did not meet the Free State expectation that it would be a neutral arbitrator. The same observation might be applied to the appointment of Feetham, whose judgements on all issues before the Commission were decisive, since the other two Commissioners cancelled each other out. Lionel Curtis of the Colonial Office, who was responsible for having Feetham appointed, was able to assure Churchill that the latter was an ideal choice for the post from a British point of view, being a man of conservative temperament. When he told Feetham that 'England expects, [every man to do his duty]', he meant that Feetham was expected to keep British interests in mind in the course of his work. In opposition, Stanley Baldwin, who did not conceal his distaste for Irish Nationalism, was sure that Feetham would do what was 'right', which meant that he would make only minor changes to the border.

Neither the Free State Government, even had it been willing, nor the northern Nationalists, who were deeply divided in their approach to the Commission, could hope to contend with the united resolve of northern Unionists to prevail. Their confidence in their ability to do so was strengthened by their consciousness of a general British unwillingness to override Ulster Unionist opposition backed by armed resistance, and by their assurance that whatever the Commission decided, no British government would permit their interests to be compromised. The British veto on an unsatisfactory decision by the Commission would operate only if this decision was unsatisfactory from the Unionist point of view: Nationalists could hope for no such veto if they found the decision unfair. Feetham's decision made the veto unnecessary, to the relief of the British and Northern Governments.

The Northern Ireland Government refused to appoint a member to the Commission because it would not accept that its present boundaries should be subject to change. Legal difficulties then had to be overcome before the British Government was given authority to appoint a commissioner on behalf of Northern Ireland. The delay thus occasioned held against the Nationalist case, as the administrative apparatus in the north was progressively reinforced, and the viability of the six-county entity was impressively demonstrated. It is not easy to imagine how any findings by the Commission significantly favour-able to Nationalists could have been implemented after almost five years of independent and increasingly stable constitutional government in Northern Ireland. Aside from other considerations he might have entertained, it was most unlikely that a man of Feetham's conservative outlook would have been willing to truncate an entity so firmly established as Northern Ireland was in 1924–5. The inherent, and probably calculated, ambiguity of the boundary Article gave Feetham every opportunity to justify his general acceptance of the Unionist case for the retention of the *status quo*.

It is important to note that the overall Nationalist case for large-scale one-way transfers of territory was not entirely coherent. This applied to the 'maximum demand' formulated by Collins in early 1922 and validated by the North-Eastern Boundary Bureau, involving the transfer of counties Fermanagh and Tyrone, as well as south Armagh, south Down, Derry City and its hinter-land. Demands for the entire County Fermanagh were also presented to the Boundary Commission on behalf of its Nationalist inhabitants. Unionists, however, had good grounds for dismissing the overall 'maximum demand' as inherently contradictory. It was inconsistent to argue, for example, that the fate of Fermanagh should be decided by the majority in the county as a whole, and at the same time to demand the transfer of parts of counties Armagh, Derry and Down even though there were large Unionist majorities in all three counties.

IV THE TREATY AND THE 1920 ACT

A key issue in contention between the Free State and northern Nationalists, on the one hand, and Ulster Unionists and British Governments on the other, was the relation between the Government of Ireland Act of 1920 and the Anglo-Irish Treaty of 1921. One view of this relation was that at the time the Boundary Commission convened, Northern Ireland was a pre-existing entity created by the 1920 Act and hence enjoying prescriptive rights which limited the authority of the Treaty and hence of the Commission, to dispose of its territory. In 1920, Walter Long laid the foundation for this position when he promised Carson on behalf of the British Government that the 1920 boundary would not be changed except perhaps in insignificant details. The contrary view was that the Treaty superseded the 1920 Act, and hence made Northern Ireland subject to large-scale revision under its terms, something which Lloyd George induced Griffith and Collins to believe in 1921. They were all the more ready to accept that the Treaty did envisage the large-scale revision hinted at by Lloyd George because they assumed that its boundary clause had been devised as a means of rectifying the injustice perpetrated in the 1920 Act, of including disproportionate numbers of Catholics in Northern Ireland. The choice made by Feetham between these two fundamentally different interpretations was to be crucial in determining the logic of his adjudication. Setting aside the obvious interpretation of the boundary Article in the Treaty, based on the reasons for its emergence during the negotiations as an instrument for significant territorial transfers to the Free State, and as a deliberate modification of the 1920 Act, he effectively accorded superior standing to the British and Unionist interpretation. He started from the premise that the division of the country implemented in 1920 must remain substantially intact. He thus ignored the strong case for the contrary view, and in so doing, deprived the Free State and Nationalist position of any real substance.

In according to the 1920 Act the significance he did, Feetham was failing to give due weight to the fact that the task he had to perform was to implement an Article of the Treaty which had been specifically framed in order to modify what had been done under the 1920 Act. Had the boundary article not had this modifying effect, it would have made no sense. Had it not been understood by the Irish plenipotentiaries as having had a considerable modifying effect, the Treaty would not have been signed, something acknowledged by both British and Irish statesmen, Birkenhead and Cosgrave among them. Even Craig's Government, which professed to find no significance for Northern Ireland in the boundary Article, or in the Treaty in general, regarding the 1920 Act as their *Magna Carta*, used the Treaty to avail of an option which came into existence only by virtue of the Treaty. In 1924, Birkenhead, the outstanding legal authority among the British signatories of the Treaty, in a letter to his fellow-signatory Austen Chamberlain, acknowledged that the Treaty and its ratifying legislation superseded the 1920 Act, in the same way that the 1920 Act had repealed the 1914 Home Rule Act. This acknowledgement, whose validity there is no reason to question, utterly undermined the foundation of Feetham's approach to the boundary adjustment. Article 12 of the Treaty gave Northern Ireland the right to vote itself out of the single Irish State provided for in the Treaty and was the only means by which it could so do. This being the case, the 1920 Act had ceased to matter, and the boundaries it established had no relevance in the post-Treaty situation. This in turn meant that the Boundary Commission provided for in Article 12 had the power to make extensive changes to the territorial extent of Northern Ireland, contrary to Feetham's view, shared by many British Conservatives and Ulster Unionists, that Article 12 contemplated the maintenance of Northern Ireland as an existing entity with boundaries defined by the 1920 Act. If Birkenhead's interpretation was the correct one, Feetham's interpretation of his brief was fundamentally flawed.

Feetham's role as Chairman of the Commission and ultimate arbiter of the political destinies of large border populations remains contentious for many reasons. There is a frequently rehearsed argument that since Britain was a party to the boundary dispute, international best practice would have suggested that the chairman should be drawn from a country not involved in the dispute. This course, if followed, might have taken much of the force out of the Nationalist response to Feetham's findings that under his chairmanship justice was not seen to be done. In dealing with this argument, it is only fair to take account of the British position: the Irish dispute was between two members of the Empire, whereas other European cases were between sovereign states. Thus, from the British point of view, it was appropriate that the chairman should be drawn from the Empire. Furthermore, the Government which appointed Feetham was not acting as the Government of Britain but as the Imperial Government. However, the fact that the membership of the two Governments was the same makes this position somewhat fanciful.

Nationalist reservations about Feetham's decisions were based on the fact that almost all of those that mattered favoured the Unionist point of view, although in several of the relevant examples Nationalists had as strong, or even a stronger case. This trend was evident in Feetham's approach to the larger, overarching issues. Feetham gave precedence to the territorial integrity of an existing entity over the principle of self-determination, exemplified in the wishes of inhabitants. East European referenda, as Bourdillon, the Secretary to the Commission well knew, showed that large numbers of inhabitants were prepared to choose economic advantage over national identity. Feetham, however, dismissed this possibility when he failed to take practical measures to ascertain the wishes of inhabitants, and instead acquiesced in the crude measuring device of old census returns based on religious affiliation as a test of these wishes. His decision that very small units of population, rather than Poor Law Unions, for example, should be considered for transfer, was inimical to the Nationalist case, as was his arbitrary decision to require an undefined substantial majority, in practice 70 per cent or over, before a given area could be transferred. Even these majorities did not satisfy him in the cases of such Nationalist strongholds as Newry and Derry. In refusing to transfer these to the Free State, he invoked economics and geography to trump the wishes of inhabitants. His treatment of Newry and south Down is particularly open to criticism. In the case of the former, he decided, on highly contestable grounds, that a town, near the border, in which over 70 per cent of the people were Catholic should not be transferred to the Free State because he believed that even if its inhabitants desired this, they should not, in their own economic interest, be allowed to sacrifice what he had decided this interest was. He also decided that Nationalists in the Silent Valley in south Down, who constituted a significant majority there, should remain in Northern Ireland because the security of the Belfast water supply might be compromised by Nationalist terrorists if Nationalist south Down were made part of the Free State.

Feetham spoke about the considerable majority he deemed appropriate if a particular area were to be transferred. He also decided that the presumed wishes (always assumed from religious statistics) of settled populations (predominantly Unionist) should be favoured over supposedly migratory ones (largely Nationalist and Catholic). In respect of the considerable majority requirement, it might be argued that in many states a bare majority is not decisive when a decision is being made on whether a particular district should be transferred from one state to another. The difficulty with this position, the Irish case being in question, was that it would implicitly assume that member-ship of the United Kingdom for the entire area of the six counties was the status quo at the time the Boundary Commission was sitting. To insist on this, as Feetham did, was to introduce an unwarranted bias in favour of Northern Ireland. By doing so, Feetham was refusing to recognise the Nationalist position, based on the *raison d'être* of the boundary clause, that Northern Ireland as a whole could not be part of the United Kingdom, but that it subsisted as a provisional entity until the decision of the Boundary Commission had been made and implemented. Feetham's acceptance of the Unionist position on this issue had the effect of ending Nationalist hopes that large areas would transfer to the Free State and opened the way for the implementation of two-way transfers. The latter, which the Free State Government could not have accepted without causing a major political crisis in the 26 counties probably resulting in its fall from office, helps to explain Cosgrave's hasty move to bury the Commission Report.

VI ARTICLE 12 AND ITS CONSEQUENCES FOR NATIONALISTS

The influence of the boundary clause in the Anglo-Irish Treaty on Nationalist parties and on the fortunes of border Nationalists was overwhelmingly negative. It led to harmful divisions among Catholics, depending on whether these lived close to the 1920 border or were remote from it, between those who believed that they had a chance of being transferred to the Free State and those (in Antrim, east Derry, north Down and north Armagh) who knew they had none, and whose interest lay in losing none of their Catholic fellow country-men to the Free State (those in Derry and its eastern hinterland, Fermanagh, Tyrone, south Down and south Armagh). The acceptance in the Treaty of a boundary commission meant the inevitable exclusion of Catholics east of the Bann: the result was an understandable apathy towards the Boundary Commission in north-east Ulster. Here, the Nationalist inhabitants who desired a united Ireland nurtured the grievance that the Free State negotiators of the Treaty had betrayed the principle of unity in the interest of a qualified form of sovereignty for the 26 counties. Six-county Republicans, whether or not they lived close to the border, being ideologically committed to the achievement of an all-Ireland republic, recognised that the more Catholics the Boundary Commission transferred to the Free State, the less likelihood there would be of a united Ireland, since a truncated northern state would be increasingly dependent on the British connection and more politically homogeneous and stable. Moreover, since the destiny of Nationalists in the north east was now to be under a Belfast parliament, the prudent course for them would be to reach an accommodation with the Northern Ireland political system.

In stark contrast, border Nationalists who believed in the promises of pro-Treaty politicians that their citizenship of Northern Ireland was merely temporary because the Boundary Commission would convert many of them into citizens of the Free State naturally felt that there was little point in playing a part in the northern political system, with the result that many Nationalist local authorities withheld recognition from the Northern Ireland Parliament, and some transferred their allegiance to the Free State. Faith in the optimistic interpretations of what the Boundary Commission held in store for them thus encouraged border Nationalists to cease participation in local politics, leaving Unionists in control of local councils, thereby jeopardising their own interests. This policy proved costly in the long term. It is possible, though by no means certain, that had Nationalists entered wholeheartedly into the northern political system, they might have achieved the continuance of Proportional Representation and the control of many public bodies which gerrymandering ousted them from. Instead, they placed their faith in the ability of the Free State Government to extract a large area of border territory from the Boundary Commission.

The collapse of the Commission at the end of 1925 demonstrated how misplaced this faith had been. In the light of the Boundary Commission debacle, it is easy to characterise border Nationalists and their leaders as the authors of their own misfortune in pursuing futile policies, above all that of non-recognition between 1922 and 1925. In 1922, however, it seemed wise to many Nationalists to refuse recognition to the Belfast Government. This refusal was based on the belief that by accepting the political institutions of Northern Ireland they might compromise their prospects of getting a favourable award from the Boundary Commission, since recognition might suggest that they were content with living under a Belfast parliament. There was an intellectual basis for non-recognition, in view of the fact that the Unionist case rested on the argument that Northern Ireland was a pre-existing entity rather than something that was coming into existence *de novo* and which should be modified, as Nationalists believed, by the wishes of local majorities. The non-recognition policy represented a practical affirmation of the latter, and a refusal to accept the Unionist argument that Northern Ireland was a pre-established, rather than a provisional, entity. However, long-term abstentionism was a mistake from the point of view of political expediency and of making the Nationalist position count.

Government representatives in the Free State found it in their interest to maintain high expectations for the Commission, since they had been intimately associated with its genesis. Ernest Blythe, himself a northerner, encouraged such expectations among his Government colleagues, telling them that the Free State had a clear claim to at least two-and-a half of the six counties. All these expectations were shattered by the outcome of the Commission's lengthy deliberations. The Free State Government, in return for financial benefits for the 26 counties, explicitly accepted Northern Ireland as defined under the 1920 Government of Ireland Act, thus acknowledging a permanent partition. The border Nationalists were deprived of what they thought of as their *Magna Carta* and of any benefit the continuing trusteeship of the Free State might have offered. Cosgrave's Free State Government disowned their cause, advising them to fend for themselves and accept the new arrangements. De Valera told a supporter that he had never placed a particle of faith in the Commission. Blythe came to regard its establishment as an act of folly, feeling ashamed that a government of which he had been a member, had been a party to its proceedings. Blythe's reassessment was based on his conviction that any territorial award made to the south by the Commission was bound to consolidate partition and to perpetrate a further partition by dividing countries. One monument to the Boundary Commission debacle survives. Its collapse, the discredit this reflected on the Free State Government, and the opportunity for political profit thus opened for de Valera, soon led to the creation of Fianna Fáil, the self-professed champion of northern Nationalist interests.

VII SUMMING UP

Criticisms of Feetham's interpretation and implementation of the boundary clause might be multiplied. It is difficult to imagine how even an Ulster Unionist chairman could have delivered a report more favourable to Unionists and more dismissive of almost every Nationalist position than Feetham did. However, a considerable weight of evidence points to the conclusion that had

Feetham shown himself more open to Nationalist arguments and ruled accordingly, his report would have been unacceptable to the British Government, and unenforceable in Ulster in the face of strong armed resistance from angry Unionists. In such an eventuality, the British would have been confronted with three main possibilities. The first would have involved trying to persuade the Free State Government not to press for the implementation of the Commission report, in the interest of peace. The likely consequences of Cosgrave's acquiescence in such a solution are not difficult to visualise: political and civil unrest culminating in the fall of his Government. British refusal to implement a decision made by a chairman appointed by a British government would have left the British open to the charge of having violated a treaty registered with the League of Nations. Enforcing Feetham's judgement against armed resistance by Ulster would have involved the use of considerable military force against British citizens, which no British government would have been likely to contemplate, as the events of 1912 had shown. Ulster acquiescence in an award favourable to Nationalists was not a realistic hope. All of this suggests that the only practicable outcome of the Commission was the actual one, and that Feetham had, unwittingly or otherwise, saved the British Government that had appointed him from having to confront a major crisis. In any event, to dismiss the essentials of the Nationalist case was to follow the line of least resistance. It was evident to all sides that Cosgrave's Government and the northern Nationalists lacked the capacity to resist an unfavourable finding or to enforce a favourable one. The *realpolitik* of the situation was that whatever way the award went, Nationalists must inevitably lose out.

Appendix 1

ARTICLE II

Until the expiration of one month from the passing of the Act of Parliament for the ratification of this instrument, the powers of the Parliament and the Government of the Irish Free State shall not be exercisable as respects Northern Ireland and the provisions of the Government of Ireland Act, 1920, shall so far as they relate to Northern Ireland remain of full force and effect, and no election shall be held for the return of members to serve in the Parliament of the Irish Free State for constituencies in Northern Ireland, unless a resolution is passed by both Houses of the Parliament of Northern Ireland in favour of the holding of such election before the end of the said month.

ARTICLE 12

If before the expiration of the said month, an address is presented to His Majesty by both Houses of the Parliament of Northern Ireland to that effect, the powers of the Parliament and Government of the Irish Free State shall no longer extend to Northern Ireland, and the provisions of the Government of Ireland Act, 1920 (including those relating to the Council of Ireland) shall, so far as they relate to Northern Ireland, continue to be of full force and effect, and this instrument shall have effect subject to the necessary modifications.

Provided that if such an address is so presented, a Commission of three persons, one to be appointed by the Government of the Irish Free State, one to be appointed by the Government of Northern Ireland, and one who shall be Chairman to be appointed by the British Government, shall determine in accordance with the wishes of the inhabitants, so far as may be compatible with economic and geographic conditions, the boundaries between Northern Ireland and the rest of Ireland, and for the purposes of the Government of Ireland Act, 1920, and of this instrument, the boundary of Northern Ireland shall be such as may be determined by such a Commission.

ARTICLE 13

For the purpose of the last forgoing article, the powers of the Parliament of southern Ireland under the Government of Ireland Act, 1920, to elect members of the Council of Ireland shall after the Parliament of the Irish Free State is constituted be exercised by that Parliament.

ARTICLE 14

After the expiration of the said month, if no such address as is mentioned in Article 12 hereof is presented, the Parliament and Government of Northern Ireland shall continue to exercise as respects Northern Ireland the powers conferred on them by the Government of Ireland Act, 1920, but the Parliament and Government of the Irish Free State shall in Northern Ireland have in relation to matters in respect of which the Parliament of Northern Ireland has not power to make laws under that Act (including matters which under the said Act are within the jurisdiction of the Council of Ireland) the same powers as in the rest of Ireland, subject to such other provisions as may be agreed in manner hereinafter appearing.

Appendix II(A)

Awards made by the Boundary Commission, 1925
Summary of transfers to the Irish Free State

Number in Schedule	Acreage	Population	Roman Catholics	Other Denominations
B (ii)	34,228	2,716	2,163	553
C (ii)	51,650	5,428	4,688	740
C (iv)	16,167	2,591	2,222	369
C (v)	18,623	3,808	3,147	661
E (i)	8,928	2,100	1,764	336
E (iii)	53,694	14,676	13,859	817
Total:	183,290	31,319	27,843	3,476

Key: B (ii) =Tyrone; C (ii) + C (iv) = C (v) = Fermanagh; E (i) + E (iii) = Armagh

Appendix II(B)

Awardswards made by the Boundary Commission, 1925
Summary of transfers to Northern Ireland

Number in Schedule	Acreage	Population	Roman Catholics	Other Denominations
A	30,295	5,149	1,919	3,230
B (i)	819	60	....	60
C (i)	11,510	1,339	497	842
C (iii)	3	....	....	....
C (vi)	336	51	13	38
E (ii)	6,279	995	335	660
Total:	49,242	7,594	2,764	4,830

A = Donegal; B (i) + C (i) + C (iii) = Donegal; C (vi) = Monaghan; E (ii) = Monaghan

Bibliography

—

PRIMARY SOURCES

ARCHIVES

NATIONAL ARCHIVES OF IRELAND (NAI)
Dáil Éireann Papers (DE)
Robert Barton Papers
Boundary Bureau Papers

DEPARTMENT OF FOREIGN AFFAIRS
Taoiseach's Files

NATIONAL LIBRARY OF IRELAND (NLI)
John Redmond Papers
Michael Collins Papers
Timothy Healy Papers

UNIVERSITY COLLEGE DUBLIN ARCHIVES (UCDA)
Desmond FitzGerald Papers
Eamon de Valera Papers
Eoin MacNeill Papers
Ernest Blythe Papers
Frank Aiken Papers
Hugh Kennedy Papers
Michael Hayes Papers
Richard Mulcahy Papers
Seán MacEntee Papers

TRINITY COLLEGE DUBLIN ARCHIVES (TCDA)
Erskine Childers Papers
R. M. Stephens Papers

HOME OFFICE PAPERS
Boundary Commission Papers P6532/6534

HOUSE OF LORDS RECORD OFFICE
Lloyd George Papers

THE BODLEIAN LIBRARY OXFORD
Lionel Curtis MS

RHODES HOUSE LIBRARY
Richard Feetham Papers

PUBLIC RECORD OFFICE LONDON
(now THE NATIONAL ARCHIVES)
Cabinet Minutes and Papers
Colonial Office Papers
Dominions Office Papers
Ramsay MacDonald Papers

PUBLIC RECORD OFFICE OF NORTHERN IRELAND (PRONI)
Cabinet Conclusions (CAB)
Cabinet Minutes and Papers
Edward Carson Papers
Cahir Healy Papers

BRITISH PARLIAMENTARY DEBATES

IRISH BOUNDARY
Extracts from Parliamentary Debates, Command Papers, etc., relevant to Questions arising out of Article 12 of the articles of an agreement for a treaty between Great Britain and Ireland, dated 6 December 1921. H. M. Stationery Office, London, 1924.

DAIL DEBATES
Private Sessions of the Second Dáil, Dublin, 1972.
Public Sessions on the Treaty, Dec. 1921–Jan. 1922. Dáil Éireann, 1922.

NEWSPAPERS
Belfast News Letter
Belfast Telegraph
Fermanagh Times
Freeman's Journal
Irish Independent
Irish News
Irish Press
Irish Times
Londonderry Sentinel

Northern Whig
The Times (London)
Ulster Herald

PAMPHLETS
Collected anti-Home Rule Pamphlets. The Irish Loyal and Patriotic Union, Grafton Street,
Dublin and King Street, Westminster, 1886.

SECONDARY SOURCES

(A) BOOKS AND JOURNALS

Abels, Jules, *The Parnell Tragedy* (London, 1966).

Adams, Gerry, *The Politics of Irish Freedom* (Dingle, 1986).

Adamthwaite, Anthony, 'The lost peace: international relations in Europe 1918–1939',
Documents of Modern History (London, 1980).

Akenson, D. H. and J. F. Fallin, 'The Irish Civil War and the drafting of the Free State
Constitution', *Éire-Ireland* Vol. v, No. 11 (Summer 1970) pp. 42–93 and Vol. v, No. iv
(Winter 1970), pp. 28–70.

Akenson, D. H., *God's Peoples: Covenant and Land in South Africa, Israel and Ulster* (Cornell,
1992).

Arthur, Paul, *Special Relationships: Britain, Ireland and the Northern Ireland Problem* (Belfast, 2000).

Atiyah, Edward, *The Arabs: The Origins, Present Conditions and Prospects of the Arab World*
(Middlesex, 1958).

Bardon, Jonathan, *A History of Ulster* (Belfast, 1992).

Bardon, Jonathan, *A Shorter Illustrated History of Ulster* (Belfast, 1996).

Bardon, Jonathon, *History of Ulster* (Belfast, 2001).

Bardon, Jonathan, *History of Ulster* (Belfast, 2005).

Barrington, Donal, in Brian Farrell (ed.), *The North and the Constitution: De Valera's Constitution
and Ours* (Dublin, 1988).

Barton, Brian, *Brookeborough, The Making of a Prime Minister* (Belfast, 1988).

Beaverbrook, Lord, *Decline and Fall of Lloyd George* (London, 1963).

Beckett, J. C., *The Making of Modern Ireland 1603–1923* (London, 1966).

Bell, Christine, *Peace Agreements and Human Rights* (Oxford, 2000).

Bell, P. M. H., *The Origins of The Second World War in Europe* (London, 1986).

Bew, Paul, Henry Patterson and Paul Teague, *Between War and Peace: The Political Future of
Northern Ireland* (London, 1977).

Bew, Paul, Peter Gibbon and Henry Patterson, *Northern Ireland 1921–1994: Political Forces and
Social Classes* (London, 1995).

Bew, Paul, *John Redmond: Life and Times*, Historical Association of Ireland Life and Times
Series, no. 8 (Dundalk, 1996).

Bew, Paul, *Ideology and the Irish Question: Ulster Unionism and Irish Nationalism, 1912–16*
(Oxford, 1994).

Blake, Robert, *The Unknown Prime Minster: The Life and Times of Andrew Bonar Law, 1858–1923* (London, 1955).

Blanke, Richard, *Orphans of Versailles: The Germans in Western Poland 1918–1939* (Lexington, 1993).

Boal, F. W., J. Douglas and J. A. E. Orr (eds), *Integration and Division: Geographical Perspectives on the Northern Ireland Problem* (London, 1982).

Boemeke, Manfred F, Gerald D. Feldman and Elizabeth Glaser, *The Treaty of Versailles: A Reassessment after 75 Years* (Cambridge, 1998).

Boland, Kevin, *The Rise and Decline of Fianna Fáil* (Dublin, 1982).

Bowen, Desmond, *The Protestant Crusade in Ireland* (Dublin, 1978).

Bowen, Desmond, *History and the Shaping of Irish Protestantism* (New York, 1995).

Bowman, John, 'De Valera and Ulster, 1919–1920: what he told America', Paper read to the Royal Irish Academy National Committee for the Study of International Affairs (Dublin, 10 Nov. 1977).

Bowman, John, *De Valera and The Ulster Question 1917–1973* (Oxford, 1982).

Boyce, D. G., 'British conservative opinion, the Ulster question, and the partition of Ireland, 1912–21', *Irish Historical Studies* Vol. XVII, No. 65 (Mar. 1970), pp. 89–112.

Boyce, D. G., *Englishmen and the Irish Troubles:. British Public Opinion and the Making of Irish Policy 1918–22* (London, 1972).

Boyce, D. G., 'British opinion, Ireland and the War, 1916–18', *Historical Journal* (17 Mar. 1974), pp. 575–93.

Boyce, D. G. (ed.), *The Revolution in Ireland 1879–1923* (Dublin, 1988).

Boyce, D. G., *Nationalism in Ireland* (London, 1991).

Boyle, Kevin, and Tom Hadden, *Ireland: A Positive Proposal* (London, 1985).

Bradshaw, Brendan, 'Nationalism and historical scholarship in modern Ireland', *Irish Historical Studies* Vol. XXVI, No. 104 (Nov. 1989), pp. 329–51.

Brett, C. E. B., *Long Shadows Cast Before: Nine Lives in Ulster, 1625–1977* (Edinburgh, 1978).

Brilmayer, Lea, 'Secession and self-determination: a territorial interpretation', *International Law Anthology USA* (1994), pp. 197–8.

Brock, Michael and Eleanor (eds), *H. H. Asquith: Letters to Venetia Stanley* (Oxford, 1982).

Brubaker, Roger, *Nationalism Reframed: Nationhood and the National Question in the New Europe* (New York, 1996).

Buchanan, Allen, *The Morality of Political Divorce: From Fort Sumter to Lithuania and Quebec* (Colorado, 1991).

Buckland, Patrick, 'The southern Irish Unionists, the Irish question, and British politics, 1906–14', *Irish Historical Studies* Vol. XV, No. 59 (Mar.1967), pp. 228–55.

Buckland, Patrick, *Irish Unionism 1885–1923: A Documentary History* (Belfast, 1973).

Buckland, Patrick, *The Factory of Grievances: Devolved Government in Northern Ireland 1921–39* (Dublin, 1979).

Buckland, Patrick, *A History of Northern Ireland* (Dublin, 1981).

Buckland, Patrick, 'Irish Unionism and the new Ireland', in D. G. Boyce (ed.), *The Revolution in Ireland, 1879–1923* (Dublin, 1988).

Buckland, Patrick, 'Carson, Craig and the partition of Ireland', in Peter Collins, *Nationalism and Unionism: Conflict in Ireland 1885–1921* (Belfast, 1994).

Burleigh, M., and W. Wippermann, *The Racial State: Germany 1933–1945* (Cambridge, 1991).

Burleigh, Michael, *The Third Reich: A New History* (London, 2000).

Callanan, Frank, *T. M. Healy* (Cork, 1996).

Campbell, Colm, Fionnula Ní Aoláin and Colin Harvey, 'The frontiers of legal analysis: reframing the transition in Northern Ireland', *The Modern Law Review* Vol. 66 (May 2003), pp. 317–45.

Campbell, John, *F. E. Smith: First Earl of Birkenhead* (London, 1983).

Canning, Paul, *British Policy Towards Ireland 1921–1941* (Oxford, 1985).

Canny, Nicholas, *From Reformation to Restoration: Ireland 1534–1660* (Dublin, 1988).

Carroll, F. M., *American Opinion and the Irish Question, 1910–23* (Dublin, 1978).

Carty, Anthony, *Was Ireland Conquered? International Law and the Irish Question* (London, 1996).

Cassese, Antonio, *Self-Determination of People: A Legal Reappraisal* (Cambridge, 1995).

Churchill, W. S., *Lord Randolph Churchill* (London, 1906).

Cizre, Umit, 'Turkey's Kurdish problem', in Brendan O'Leary, Ian S. Lustick and Thomas Callaghy (eds), *Rightsizing the State: The Politics of Moving Borders* (Oxford, 2001).

Clery, Arthur, *The Idea of a Nation*, Classics of Irish History Series (Dublin, 2002).

Cobban, Alfred, *The Nation-State and National Self-Determination* (New York, 1969).

Cochrane, Fergal, *Unionist Politics and the Politics of Unionism since the Anglo-Irish Agreement* (Cork, 2001).

Cole, John, *Ulster at the Crossroads* (London, 1969).

Collins, Michael, *The Path to Freedom* (Cork, 1996).

Collins, Peter (ed.), *Nationalism and Unionism: Conflict in Ireland* (Belfast, 1994).

Colum, Padraig, *Arthur Griffith* (Dublin, 1959).

Colvin, Ian, and Edward Marjoribanks, *The Life of Lord Carson* (London, 1934).

Connor, Walker, *Ethnonationalism: The Quest for Understanding* (New Jersey, 1994).

Coogan, Tim Pat, *Michael Collins: A Biography* (London, 1990).

Coogan, Tim Pat, *De Valera: Long Fellow, Long Shadow* (London, 1993).

Corish, Patrick (gen. ed.), 'Political problems 1860–78', in *A History of Irish Catholicism* Vol. v (Dublin, 1967).

Cronin, Seán, *The McGarrity Papers* (Kerry, 1972).

Cukwurah, A. Oye, *The Settlement of Boundary Disputes in International Law* (Manchester, 1967).

Curran, J. M., *The Birth of the Irish Free State* (Alabama, 1980).

Curtis, E., and R. B. McDowell (eds), *Irish Historical Documents, 1172–1922* (London, 1943).

Dahl, Robert A., *Democracy and its Critics* (Michigan, 1989).

Curtis, Edmund, and R. M. McDowell (eds), *Irish Historical Documents, 1172–1922* (London, 1943).

Curtis, Lionel, 'The Irish Boundary question', *The Round Table* Vol. 15, No. 57 (Dec. 1924), pp. 24–47.

Curtis Lionel P., *Coercion and Conciliation in Ireland, 1880–1892: A Study in Conservative Unionism* (Princeton, 1963).

Curtin, Liz, *The Cause of Ireland: From the United Irishmen to Partition* (Belfast, 1994).

Dáil Éireann, *Official Correspondence: Peace Negotiations* June–Sept., 1921 (Dublin, 1921).

Daly, T. P., 'James Craig: Chamberlainite imperialist, 1903–14', *Irish Historical Studies* Vol. XXXVI, No. 142 (Nov. 2008), pp. 188–201.

Dangerfield, George, *The Damnable Question* (London, 1977).

De Blaghd, Ernan, *Briseadh na Teorann* (Baile Átha Cliath, 1955).

De Valera, Eamon, *Ireland's Claim for a Sovereign Independent State* (Washington DC, 1920).

Diamond, Larry and Marc F. Plattner (eds), *Nationalism, Ethnic Conflict, and Democracy* (Baltimore and London, 1994).

Dillon, Charles and Henry A. Jefferies (eds), *Tyrone: History and Society* (Dublin, 1999).

Doherty, Gabriel and Dermot Keogh (eds), *Michael Collins and the Making of the Irish State* (Cork, 1998).

Doherty, Gabriel and Dermot Keogh (eds), *1916: The Long Revolution* (Cork, 2007).

Dooley, Terence, 'From the Belfast boycott to the Boundary Commission: fears and hopes in County Monaghan, 1920–26', *Clogher Record* Vol. xv, No. 1 (Enniskillen, 1994), pp. 90–106.

Dooley, Terence, 'Protestant migration from the Free State to Northern Ireland, 1920–25: a private census for Co. Fermanagh', *Clogher Record* Vol. xv, No. 111 (Enniskillen, 1996), pp. 87–132.

Dwyer, Ryle T., 'The Anglo-Irish Treaty and why they signed', *Capuchin Annual* (Dublin, 1971), pp. 333–72.

Dwyer, Ryle T., *De Valera: The Man and the Myths* (Dublin, 1991).

Dyboski, Roman (ed.), *Cambridge History Of Poland 1697–1935, Vol. 2: From Augustus II to Pilsudski* (Cambridge, 1951).

Edwards, Owen Dudley, *The Sins of our Fathers: Roots of Conflict in Northern Ireland* (Dublin, 1970).

Edwards, Ruth Dudley, *Patrick Pearse: The Triumph of Failure* (New York, 1978).

Elliot, Marianne, *Wolfe Tone: Prophet of Irish Independence* (London, 1989).

Elliot, Marianne, *The Catholics of Ulster: A History* (London, 2000).

Ervine, St John, *Craigavon: Ulsterman* (London, 1949).

Fair, John D., 'The king, the constitution and Ulster: interparty negotiations of 1913 and 1914', *Éire-Ireland* Vol. vi, No. 1 (Spring 1971), pp. 35–52.

Fanning, Ronan, 'The Unionist Party and Ireland 1906–10', *Irish Historical Studies* Vol. xv, No. 58 (Sept. 1966), pp. 147–71.

Fanning, Ronan, *Independent Ireland* (Dublin, 1983).

Fanning, Ronan, Michael Kennedy, Dermot Keogh and Eunan O'Halpin (eds), *Documents on Irish Foreign Policy, Vol. 1 1919–1922*, Royal Irish Academy/Department of Foreign Affairs (Dublin, 1998).

Farrell, Michael, *Northern Ireland: The Orange State* (London, 1980).

Farrell, Michael, *Arming the Protestants: The Formation of the Ulster Special Constabulary and the Royal Ulster Constabulary, 1920–27* (London, 1983).

Ferguson, Niall, *Empire: How Britain Made the Modern World* (London, 2003).

FitzGerald, Desmond, 'Mr Pakenham and the Anglo-Irish Treaty', *Studies* Vol. xxiv, No. 95 (Sept. 1935), pp. 406–14.

Fitzpatrick, David, *The Two Irelands, 1912–1939* (Oxford, 1998).

Fitzpatrick, David, 'The Orange Order and the border', *Irish Historical Studies* Vol. xxxiii, No. 129 (May 2002), pp. 52–67.

Follis, Bryan, *A State Under Siege: The Establishment of Northern Ireland, 1920–1925* (Oxford, 1995).

Foster, R. F., *Modern Ireland 1600–1972* (London, 1988).

Foster, R. F., *Lord Randolph Churchill: A Political Life* (Oxford, 1988).

Fraser, T. G., *Partition in Ireland, India and Palestine: Theory and Practice* (London, 1984).

Gailey, Andrew, 'King Carson: an essay on the invention of leadership, *Irish Historical Studies* Vol. xxx, No. 117 (May 1996), pp. 66–87.

Gallagher, Frank, *The Indivisible Island: The History of the Partition of Ireland* (London, 1959).

Gallager, Frank, in Thomas P. O'Neill (ed. and introduction), *The Anglo-Irish Treaty* (London, 1965).

Gallagher, Michael, 'How many nations are there in Ireland?', *Ethnic and Racial Studies* Vol. 18, No. 4 (1995), pp. 715–39.

Gallagher, Tom, *Nationalism in the Nineties* (Edinburgh, 1990).

Gallagher, Tom and James O'Connell (eds), *Contemporary Irish Studies* (1983).

Garvin, Tom, *1922: The Birth of Irish Democracy* (Dublin, 1996).

Gaughan, J. A., *Memoirs of Senator of Senator James G Douglas (1887–1954)* (Dublin, 1998).

Gellner, *Nations and Nationalism* (Ithaca, New York, 1983).

Gibbon, Peter, *The Origins of Ulster Unionism: The Formation of Popular Protestant Politics and Ideology in 19th Century Ireland* (Manchester, 1975).

Gilbert, M. S., *Winston S. Churchill, Vol. 3: The Challenge of War 1914–16* (London, 1976).

Gilbert, M. S., *Winston S. Churchill, Vol. 4: The Stricken World 1917–22* (London, 1975).

Gilbert, M. S., *Winston S. Churchill, Vol. 5: The Wilderness Years 1922–39* (London, 1976).

Guelke, Adrian, *Northern Ireland: The International Perspective* (Dublin, 1989).

Gwynn, Denis, *The Irish Free State 1922–1927* (London, 1928).

Gwynn, Denis, *The Life of John Redmond* (London, 1932).

Gwynn, Denis, *The History of Partition, 1912–1925* (Dublin, 1950).

Hammond, J. L., *Gladstone and the Irish Nation* (London, 1938).

Hancock, W. K., *Survey of British Commonwealth Affairs, Vol. 1: Problems of Nationality, 1918–1936* (Oxford, 1937).

Hand, Geoffrey (ed.), *Report of the Irish Boundary Commission 1925* (Shannon, 1969).

Hand, Geoffrey, 'MacNeill and the Boundary Commission', in F. X. Martin and F. J. Byrne, *The Scholar Revolutionary: Eoin MacNeill: 1867–1945 and the Making of the New Ireland* (Oxford, 1973).

Hanna, Ronnie (ed.), *The Union: Essays On Ireland and the British Connection* (Newntownards, 2001).

Harkness, David, *The Restless Dominion: The Irish Free State in the British Commonwealth of Nations, 1921–31* (London, 1969).

Harkness, David, *Northern Ireland Since 1920* (Dublin, 1983).

Harris, Mary, *The Catholic Church and the foundation of the Northern Irish State* (Cork, 1993).

Harris, R. L., *Prejudice and Tolerance in Ulster* (Manchester, 1972).

Hart, Peter, 'Michael Collins and the assassination of Sir Henry Wilson', *Irish Historical Studies* Vol. xxviii, No. 110 (Nov. 1992), pp. 150–70.

Hart, Peter, *Mick: The Real Michael Collins* (London, 2005).

Hawkins, F. M. A., 'Defence and the role of Erskine Childers in the treaty negotiations of 1921. *Irish Historical Studies* Vol. xxii, No. 87 (Mar. 1981), pp. 251–70.

Heskin, Ken, *Northern Ireland: A Psychological Analysis* (Dublin, 1980).

Heslinga, M. W., *The Irish Border as a Cultural Divide* (Assen, 1979).

Hobsbawm, E. J., 'Some Reflections on the break-up of Britain', *New Left Review* 105 (Sept.–Oct., 1977), pp. 3–23.

Hopkinson, Michael, *Green against Green: The Irish Civil War* (Dublin, 1988).

Hopkinson, Michael, 'The Craig-Collins pacts of 1922: two attempted reforms of the Northern Ireland government', *Irish Historical Studies* Vol. XXVII, No. 106 (Nov. 1990), pp. 145–58.

Horowitz, Donald, *Ethnic Groups in Conflict* (Berkley, 1985).

Hughes, A. J. and William J. Nolan (eds), *Armagh: History and Society* (Dublin, 1999).

Hyde, Hugh Montgomery, *The Life of Sir Edward Carson: Lord Carson of Duncairn* (London, 1953).

Hyde, Hugh Montgomery, *The Londonderrys: A Family Portrait* (London, 1979).

Jackson, Alvin, *Home Rule: An Irish History 1800–2000* (London, 2003).

Jackson, Alvin, 'Irish Unionists and the Empire, 1880–1920: classes and masses', in Keith Jeffery (ed.), *'An Irish Empire?' Aspects of Ireland and the British Empire* (Manchester, 1996).

Jackson Alvin, *The Ulster Party: Irish Unionists in the House of Commons 1884–1911* (Oxford, 1995).

Jalland, Patricia, *The Liberals and Ireland: The Ulster Question in British Politics to 1914* (Brighton, 1980).

Jalland, Patricia and John Stubbs, 'The Irish question after the outbreak of War in 1914: some unfinished party business', *English Historical Review* Vol. XCVI, No. CCCLXXVII (Jan. 1981), pp. 779–807.

Jalland, Patricia, 'Irish home-rule finance: a neglected dimension of the Irish question, 1910–14', *Irish Historical Studies* Vol. XXIII, No. 91 (May 1983), pp. 233–53.

Jalland, Patricia, *The Liberals and Ireland: The Ulster Question in British Politics to 1914*, 2nd edn (Aldershot, 1993).

Jeffery, Keith (ed.), *An Irish Empire? Aspects of Ireland and the British Empire* (Manchester, 1996).

Jenkins, Roy, *Asquith, Portrait of a Man and an Era* (New York, 1964).

Jennings, Ivor, *The Approach to Self-Government* (Cambridge, 1956).

Johnson, Joseph, *Civil War in Ulster: Its Objects and Probable Results* (Dublin, 1999).

Johnson, Paul, *A History of the Modern World: From 1917 to the 1980s* (London, 1983).

Johnson, Paul, *A History of the English People* (London, 1985).

Jones, Thomas, in Keith Middlemas (ed.), *Whitehall Diary* (London, 1971).

Kee, Robert, *The Green Flag, Vol. 3: Ourselves Alone* (London, 1972).

Kendle, John, *The Round Table Movement and Imperial Union* (Dublin, 1975).

Kendle, John, *Ireland and the Federal Solution: The Debate over the United Kingdom Constitution 1870–1921* (Montreal, 1989).

Kendle, John, *Walter Long: Ireland and the Union 1905–20* (Dublin, 1992).

Kennedy, Dennis, 'The first customs barrier', *Irish Times*, 31 Mar. 1983.

Kennedy, Dennis, *The Widening Gulf* (Belfast, 1988).

Kennedy, Liam, *Two Ulsters: A Case for Repartition* (Belfast, 1986).

Kennedy, Michael and J. M. Skelly (eds), *Irish Foreign Policy 1919–66: From Independence to Internationalism* (Dublin, 2000).

Keogh, Dermot, *Ireland and Europe 1919–1939* (Cork/Dublin, 1990).

Kerr, Philip, 'Ireland and the empire', *Round Table* VI (1916), pp. 614–52.

Kettle, Thomas, *The Open Secret of Ireland* (Dublin, 2007).

Kliot, N., 'The collapse of the Lebanese state', *Middle Eastern Studies* Vol. 23, No. 1 (1987), pp. 54–74.

Laffan, Michael, *The Partition of Ireland 1911–25* (Dundalk, 1983).

Laffan, Michael, *The Resurrection of Ireland: The Sinn Féin Party 1916–1923* (Cambridge, 1999).

Lavin, Deborah, *From Empire to International Commonwealth: A Biography of Lionel Curtis* (Oxford, 1995).

Lawlor, S. M., 'Ireland from truce to treaty: war or peace? July to October 1921', *Irish Historical Studies* Vol. XXII, No. 85 (Mar. 1980), pp. 49–64.

Lawlor, Sheila, *Britain and Ireland 1914–23* (Dublin, 1983).

Lawrence, R. J., *The Government of Northern Ireland* (Oxford, 1965).

Lee, J. J., *Ireland 1912–1985: Politics and Society* (Cambridge, 1989).

Lijphart, Arend, *Democracy in Plural Societies: A Comparative Exploration* (London, 1971).

Lijphart, Arend, *Democracy in Plural Societies: A Comparative Exploration* (London, 1984).

Lloyd George, *The Truth about the Peace Treaties*, 2 vols (London, 1938).

Longford, Earl of, *Peace by Ordeal: The Negotiation of the Anglo-Irish Treaty, 1921* (London, 1972).

Longford, Earl of, and T. P. O'Neill, *Eamon de Valera* (Dublin, 1970).

Loughlin, James, 'Joseph Chamberlain, English nationalism and the Ulster question', *History* Vol. 77, No. 250 (June 1992), pp. 202–19.

Lyons, F. S. L., *Parnell* (Dublin, 1963).

Lyons, F. S. L., *John Dillon: A Biography* (London, 1968).

Lyons, F. S. L., *Ireland since the Famine* (London, 1974).

Lyons, F. S. L., *Parnell* (London, 1978).

Macardle, Dorothy, *The Irish Republic* (Dublin, 1951).

Macartney, C. A., *National States and National Minorities* (Oxford, 1934).

MacBride, Ian, *The Siege of Derry in Ulster Protestant Mythology* (Dublin, 1997).

MacDonagh, Oliver, *Ireland: The Union and its Aftermath* (London, 1977).

MacDonagh, Oliver, *States of Mind: A Study of Anglo-Irish Conflict 1780–1980* (London, 1983).

MacDonagh, Oliver, *Ireland: The Union and its Aftermath* (Dublin, 2003).

MacKnight, Thomas, *Ulster As It Is, vols I and II* (London, 1896).

Mansergh, Nicholas, *The Government of Northern Ireland* (London, 1936).

Mansergh, Nicholas, *The Irish Question* (London, 1965).

Mansergh, Nicholas, 'Eoin MacNeill: a re-appraisal', *Studies* Vol. LXIII, No. 250 (Summer 1974), pp. 133–40.

Mansergh, Nicholas, *The Unresolved Question: The Anglo-Irish Settlement and its Undoing 1912–1972* (London, 1991).

Mansergh, Nicholas, *Nationalism and Independence: Selected Irish Papers* (Cork, 1997).

Marjoribanks, Edward and Ian Colvin, *The Life of Lord Carson* (London, 1934).

Martin, F. X., and F. J. Byrne, *Eoin MacNeill: The Scholar Revolutionary 1867–1945* (Shannon, 1973).

Martin, Ged, in Malcolm Anderson and Eberhard Bort (eds), *The Irish Border: History, Politics and Culture* (Liverpool, 1999).

Matthews, Kevin, 'Stanley Baldwin's Irish question', *Historical Journal* Vol. 43, No. 4, (2000), pp. 1,027–49.

Matthews, Kevin, *Fatal Influence: The Impact of Ireland on British Politics 1920–5* (Dublin, 2004).

Maume, Patrick, *The Long Gestation: Irish Nationalist Life 1891–1918* (Dublin, 1999).

Maume, Patrick (ed.), *A Correct Narrative of the Rise and Progress of the Repeal Invasion of Ulster* (Dublin, 2003).

Maye, Brian, *Arthur Griffith* (Dublin, 1997).

McColgan, John, 'Implementing the 1921 Treaty: Lionel Curtis and constitutional procedure', *Irish Historical Studies* Vol. xx, No. 79 (Mar. 1977), pp. 312–33.

McComb, William, *The Repealer Repulsed*, ed. Patrick Maume (Dublin, 2003).

McDonald, Walter, *Some Ethical Questions of Peace and War* (Dublin, 1998).

McDowell, R. B., 'Edward Carson', in Conor Cruise O'Brien (ed.), *The Shaping of Modern Ireland* (London, 1960).

McDowell, R. B., *The Irish Convention 1917–18* (London 1970).

McGarry, John (ed.), *Northern Ireland and the Divided World: Post-Agreement Northern Ireland in Comparative Perspective* (Oxford, 2001).

McGarry, John and Brendan O'Leary, *Explaining Northern Ireland: Broken Images* (Oxford, 1995).

McMahon, Deirdre, *Republicans and Imperialists: Anglo-Irish Relations in the 1930s* (New Haven, 1984).

Meleday, Dermot, *Redmond: The Parnellite* (Cork, 2008).

Middlemas, Keith (ed.), *Whitehall Diary, Vol. 3: Ireland 1918–1925* (Oxford, 1971).

Miller, D. W., *Church, State and Nation in Ireland, 1898–1921* (Dublin, 1973).

Miller, David, *On Nationality* (Oxford, 1995).

Miller, David W., *Queens Rebels: Ulster Loyalists in Historical Perspective* (Dublin, 2007).

Moore, Margaret (ed.), *National Self-Determination and Secession* (Oxford, 1998).

Moynihan, Maurice (ed.), *Speeches and Statements of Eamon de Valera 1917–1973* (Dublin 1980).

Murphy Brian P., *John Chartres: Mystery Man of the Treaty* (Dublin, 1995).

Murphy, Eileen, and William J. Roulston (eds), *Fermanagh: History and Society* (Dublin, 1999).

Murphy, Richard, 'Walter Long and the making of the Government of Ireland Act 1919–20', *Irish Historical Studies* Vol. xxv, No. 97 (May 1986), pp. 82–96.

Murray, Patrick, 'Obsessive historian: Eamon de Valera and the policing of his own reputation', *Royal Irish Academy* Vol. 101c., No. 11 (2001), pp. 37–65.

Murray, Paul, 'Partition and the Irish Boundary Commission', *Clogher Record* Vol. xviii, No. 2, Clogher Historical Society (2004), pp. 181–217.

Nicolson, Harold, *Peacemaking 1919* (London, 1933).

O'Brien, Conor Cruise, *States of Ireland* (London 1994).

O'Brien, Conor Cruise, *Essays on Nationalism, Terrorism and Revolution* (New York, 1988).

O'Brien, Gerard (ed.), *Derry and Londonderry: History and Society* (Dublin, 1999).

O'Broin, Leon, *Michael Collins* (Dublin, 1980).

O'Callaghan, Margaret, 'Old parchment and water: the Boundary Commission of 1925 and the copperfastening of the Irish border', *Bullán: An Irish Studies Journal* Vol. iv, No. 11, Winter 1999/Spring 2000 (Notre Dame, 1999), pp. 27–55.

Ó Corráin, Daithaí, '"Ireland in his heart north and south": the contribution of Ernest Blythe to the partition question', *Irish Historical Studies* Vol. xxxv, No. 137 (May 2006), pp. 61–80.

Ó Cúiv, B (ed.), *Eigse* xi (n.d.), pp. 57–62.

O'Day, Alan, *Irish Home Rule 1867–1921* (Manchester, 1998).

O'Dochartaigh, Niall, *From Civil Rights to Armalites: Derry and the Birth of the Irish Troubles* (Cork University Press, 1997 reprint).

O'Donnell, F. H., *A History of the Irish Parliamentary Party, Vol. II* (London, 1910).

O'Farrell, Patrick, *England's Irish Question: Anglo-Irish Relations 1534–1970* (London, 1971).

O'Halloran, Claire, *Partition and the Limits of Irish Nationalism: An Ideology under Stress* (Dublin, 1987).

O'Halpin, Eunan, *Defending Ireland: The Free State and its Enemies Since 1922* (Oxford, 1999).

O'Hearn, Denis, 'Catholic grievances, Catholic nationalism: a comment', *British Journal of Sociology* Vol. XXXIV, No. 3 (1983), pp. 438–45.

O'Hearn, Denis, 'Again on discrimination in the north of Ireland: a reply to the rejoinder', *British Journal of Sociology* Vol. XXXVI, No. 1 (1985), pp. 94–101.

O'Hegarty, P. S., *A History of Ireland under the Union 1801–1922* (London, 1952).

O'Kelly, J. J., *Dáil Éireann Comes of Age* (Dublin, 1940).

O'Leary, Brendan, Ian Lustick and Thomas Callaghy, *Rightsizing the State: The Politics of Moving Borders* (Oxford, 2001).

O'Leary, Brendan, 'Debating partition: justifications and critiques', *Working Papers in British-Irish Studies*, Institute for British-Irish Studies, UCD no. 78 (2006), pp. 1–29.

O'Leary, John, *Recollections of Fenians and Fenianism* (London, 1896).

O'Neill, David, *The Partition of Ireland: How and Why it was Accomplished*, 3rd edn (Dublin, 1949).

Ó Néill, T. P., agus P. O'Fiannachta, *De Valera*, 2 vols (Dublin, 1970).

O'Shiel, Kevin, *Handbook of the Ulster Question*, North Eastern Boundary Bureau (Dublin 1923).

O'Shiel, Kevin, 'The problem of partitioned Ireland', *Studies* Vol. XII, No. 48 (Dublin, 1923), pp. 625–38.

O'Sullivan, Donal, *The Irish Free State and its Senate: A Study in Contemporary Politics* (London, 1940).

Pakenham, Frank (Lord Longford), *Peace by Ordeal* (London, 1972 edn).

Peatling, G. K., *British Opinion and Irish Self-Government, 1865–1925: From Unionism to Liberal Commonwealth* (Dublin, 2001).

Petrie, Sir Charles, *The Life and Letters of the Right Hon. Sir Austen Chamberlain*, 2 vols (London, 1939–40).

Phillips, W. Allison, *The Revolution in Ireland 1906–1923* (London, 1923).

Phoenix, Eamon, *Northern Nationalism, Nationalist Politics, Partition and the Catholic Minority in Northern Ireland 1890–1940* (Belfast, 1994).

Privilege, John, *Michael Logue and the Catholic Church in Ireland, 1879–1925* (Manchester, 2009).

Proudfoot, Lindsay (ed.), *Down: History and Society* (Dublin, 1999).

Quekett, Sir Arthur, *The Constitution of Northern Ireland*, compiled for the Government of Northern Ireland (Belfast, 1928).

Rafferty, Oliver P., *Catholicism in Ulster 1603–1983* (Dublin, 1983).

Rankin, K. J., 'County Armagh and the Boundary Commission', *Armagh History and Society* (Dublin, 2001), pp. 947–90.

Rankin, K. J., 'The creation and consolidation of the Irish border', *Working Papers in British-Irish Studies* 48, Institute for British-Irish Studies, UCD (2005), pp. 1–29.

Rankin, K. J., 'The search for statutory Ulster', *History Ireland* May/June (Dublin, 2009), pp. 28–32.

Read, Donald, 'History: political and diplomatic', in C. B. Cox and A. E. Dyson (eds), *The Twentieth-Century Mind, 1900–1918* (London, 1972).

Regan, John M., *The Irish Counter-Revolution 1921–1936* (Dublin, 1999).

Ryan, John, 'Eoin MacNeill, 1867–1945', *Studies* Vol. 34, No. 136 (Dec. 1945), pp. 433–48.

Savage, D. C., 'The origins of the Ulster Unionist Party, 1885–6', *Irish Historical Studies* Vol. XII (Mar. 1961), pp. 185–208.

Savage, David W., 'The attempted Home Rule settlement of 1916', *Éire-Ireland* Vol. III, No. 11 (Autumn 1967), pp. 132–45.

Seton-Weston, Hugh, *Nations and States* (Colorado, 1977).

Shakespeare, Geoffrey, *Let Candles Be Brought In* (London, 1949).

Shannon, Catherine, *Arthur J. Balfour in Ireland, 1874–1922* (Washington, 1988).

Simms, Brendan, *Unfinest Hour: Britain and the Destruction of Bosnia* (London, 2001).

Sinclair, I. M., *The Vienna Convention on the Law of Treaties* (Manchester, 1973).

Smith Jeremy, 'Bluff, bluster and brinkmanship: Andrew Bonar Law and the Third Home Rule Bill', *Historical Journal* Vol. 36, No. 1 (1993), pp. 161–78.

Smith, Jeremy, 'Federalism, devolution and partition: Sir Edward Carson and the search for a compromise on the Third Home Rule Bill, 1913–1914', *Irish Historical Studies* Vol. XXXV, No. 140 (Nov. 2007), pp. 496–518.

Staunton, Enda, *The Nationalists of Northern Ireland 1918–1973* (Dublin, 2001).

Steel, D. C., 'Gladstone and Ireland', *Irish Historical Studies* Vol. XVII, No. 65 (Mar. 1970), pp. 58–88.

Stewart, A. T. Q., *The Ulster Crisis* (London, 1967).

Stewart, A. T. Q., *The Narrow Ground: Aspects of Ulster, 1609–1969* (London, 1977).

Stewart, A. T. Q., *Edward Carson* (Dublin, 1981).

Stewart, A. T. Q., *The Ulster Crisis: Resistance to Home Rule 1912–14* (Belfast, 1997).

Stewart, A. T. Q., *The Shape of Irish History* (Belfast, 2001).

Strachey, St. John Loe, *The Adventure of Living: A Subjective Autobiography* (London, n.d.)

Stubbs, John O., 'The Unionists and Ireland, 1914–18', *Historical Journal* Vol. 33, No. 4 (1990), pp. 867–93.

Talmon, Stefan, *Recognition of Governments in International Law: With Particular Reference to Governments in Exile* (Oxford, 1998).

Tansill, Charles Callan, *America and the Fight for Irish Freedom 1866–1922* (New York, 1957).

Taylor, A. J. P., *English History, 1914–1945* (Oxford, 1965).

Taylor, A. J. P., *The First World War: An Illustrated History* (London, 1981 edn).

Taylor, Telford, *Munich: The Price of Peace* (London, 1979).

Temperley, H. M. V., *A History of the Peace Conference of Paris, Vol. IV* (London and New York, 1969).

Temple, Sir John, *The Irish Rebellion: or A History of the Beginnings and First Progress of the General Rebellion Raised Within the Kingdom of Ireland, Upon the Three and Twentieth Day of October in the Year 1641* (London, 1646).

Tierney, Michael, in F. X. Martin (ed.), *Eoin MacNeill: Scholar and Man of Action 1867–1945* (Oxford, 1980).

Towey, Thomas, 'The reaction of the British Government to the 1922 Collins–de Valera Pact', *Irish Historical Studies* Vol. XXII, No. 85 (Mar. 1980), pp. 65–76.

Townshend, Charles, *Ireland in the 20th Century* (London, 1998).

Townshend, Charles, *Easter 1916: The Irish Rebellion* (London, 2006).

Travers, Pauric, *Settlements and Divisions: Ireland 1870–1922* (Dublin, 1988).

Trimble, David, *The Foundation of Northern Ireland* (London, 1991).

Walker, Brian M., *Parliamentary Election Results in Ireland 1918–92* (Dublin, 1992).

Wall, Maureen, 'Partition: The Ulster question (1916–1926)', in T. D. Williams (ed.), *The Irish Struggle, 1916–1926* (London, 1966).

Waller, Bolton, *Hibernia, or the Future of Ireland* (London, 1928).

Wambaugh, Sarah, *Plebiscites since the World War: With a Collection of Official Documents*, Carnegie Endowment for International Peace (Washington, 1933).

Wheatley, Michael, 'John Redmond and federalism in 1910', *Irish Historical Studies* Vol. XXXII, No. 127 (May 2001), pp. 343–64.

Whyte, John, *Interpreting Northern Ireland* (Oxford, 1991).

Wichert, Sabine, *From the United Irishmen to Twentieth Century Unionism* (Dublin, 2004).

Williams, T. D., *The Irish Struggle 1916–26* (London, 1966).

Wilson, Tom (ed.), *Ulster under Home Rule: A Study of the Political and Economic Problems of Northern Ireland* (Oxford, 1955).

Wilson, Tom, *Ulster Conflict and Consent* (Oxford, 1989).

Younger, Calton, *Ireland's Civil War* (Glasgow, 1979).

(B) THESES

Dooher, J. B., 'Tyrone nationalism and the question of partition, 1910–25', MPhil Thesis (University of Ulster, 1986).

Elliot, Sydney, 'The electoral system in Northern Ireland since 1920', PhD Thesis (Queens University Belfast, 1971).

Index

—